MAN, I NEED A JOB!

Finding Employment with a Criminal History

3rd Edition

Ned Rollo
Executive Director
OPEN, INC.

OPEN, INC. Information Series
Series Editor
Katherine S. Greene

OPEN INC.

Dedicated To

John M. Stemmons, Sr.

For His Consistent Encouragement,

Kindness, and Support

Of an Ex-Convict's Dream

Foreword

Each year, more than half a million people are released into the community after serving time in state or federal prison. Those who reenter society after incarceration come in all shapes, sizes, and colors, but they have one thing in common: most are looking for a job. The job market is normally tough enough, even under ideal circumstances. Finding a job can be an even bigger challenge when you have spent time behind bars.

Employment is one of the most vital factors in the successful transition of ex-offenders, allowing them to become productive members of the community. This important step is not easy, but it can be made, and we want ex-offenders to know that there is help. *Man, I Need a Job!* explains the process of finding employment while considering the unique needs of individuals with a criminal history. The book offers solid advice on the nuts and bolts of job hunting, such as finding job leads, preparing a resume, and interviewing. It also addresses concerns specific to ex-offenders, such as disclosing a criminal history.

The author, Ned Rollo, is an ex-offender and correctional counselor. He is the founder and executive director of OPEN, Inc., a non-profit organization devoted to helping offenders improve their lives. He understands the challenges facing newly released offenders because he has faced those challenges. His book is an invaluable resource to help ex-offenders start off their new lives in the right direction with confidence.

The vast majority of incarcerated offenders will be released at some time. It is in everyone's best interest to do everything reasonable to help these individuals reintegrate into society. This means taking action before their release as well as after. Programs that include job training, prerelease counseling, substance abuse treatment, and life skills training should be among the standard services that corrections provides to those in their care. This book should be available to all offenders while they are inside, and they should keep it with them when they get out.

JAMES A. GONDLES, JR., CAE
Executive Director
American Correctional Association

Official Notice

Special Thanks

We at OPEN, INC. extend our sincere thanks to Cherie Hohertz, MLS, Head of Access Services at the William A. Blakley Library of the University of Dallas, for her assistance in preparing the Reading List at the end of this book.

We also thank Ron and Caryl Krannich of Impact Publications for their review and comment and for providing information about One-Stop Career Centers and additions to the Reading List, which added greatly to the quality and usefulness of this book.

Author's Background

Ned Rollo was kicked out of prison for the second time in August 1977 with something he didn't have the first time he was released in 1969: an absolute determination to reconstruct his life and to help others do the same.

His goal is not unique – many former prisoners return to the free world wanting to help other people as a way to feel good about themselves and make positive use of their painful experiences. What makes the author unusual is that he has stuck with his goal for 30 years, refusing to give up in spite of all obstacles. This handbook is the result of an unbending commitment made in a solitary cell in a north Louisiana jail in 1974. Since that time, Ned has paid a lot of dues to build the knowledge, opportunity, and support needed to turn the dream of being a true helper into reality.

What Ned writes about, he has lived. His writing offers practical insights gained from 38 years of active involvement on both sides of the criminal justice system: first as a habitual criminal with four felony convictions, and later as a correctional counselor and criminal justice planner. This book provides practical insights gained from working with thousands of people as they have struggled with employment, social rejection, and personal renewal.

As you read this material, listen closely and you will hear Ned speaking directly to you about what it takes for a former felon to survive and make steady progress toward "the good life." *Anyone*, with a criminal history or not, who puts as much love and determination into their quest for a job as Ned Rollo did in pursuing *his* goal MUST succeed!

Contents

Introduction

This book has three important goals. First, to help people labeled as offenders or criminals find and keep a job. No matter what level you're in – jail, probation, prison, parole, or after completing supervision – *if you have been convicted of a crime*, this book applies to *you*. The second goal is to help correctional personnel and counselors provide more meaningful employment training and support. And the third is to show the families of offenders how to help their loved ones and share in the joy of their successes.

Finding a job is a tough experience for anyone. Sometimes it turns into a nightmare of rejection and frustration. This is especially true for those of us seen as outcasts, outside the circle of social acceptance. One way to become an outsider is to be convicted of a crime. From the day the gavel falls, those branded as criminals or outlaws live under the shadow of their pasts. This burden often follows us as we search for a job and strive to put our lives together.

Being viewed as an outcast has a severe impact on how we relate to ourselves, loved ones, and the community. It may also affect our family and friends, bringing them emotional, financial, and social hardships. While society often rejects the crimi-

nal, those we love also pay a heavy price of guilt by association.

For many who get caught in the criminal justice process, the effects are minor and will pass with time. But for others, the weight of a criminal label follows them to the grave. Anyone who carries that label throughout life will face serious obstacles in job hunting, restricted housing opportunities, and in many other areas as well. However, it is NEVER the end of the world – you *can* grow beyond it! To better prepare yourself for success in the community, be sure to read the other books in the *OPEN Information Series* (see rear of book).

Life after involvement in the criminal justice process is truly a rebirth, just as a town reconstructs after a devastating flood. After confronting the shock and dismay, we face years of hard work and determination in order to build a new and better life. While this is a constant, unending struggle, there are times of great achievement and satisfaction! This small book offers practical ideas and support for people determined to turn their hardship into a positive future. Not just a collection of empty words, *Man I Need a Job!* is a rich source of useful direction in the quest for a rewarding future.

As with every heavy experience in

1

life, you stand at a crossroads: *give up or get up!* A criminal conviction seriously changes the lives of all involved, but it seldom ends our lives unless we let it. This crisis can be turned into a spring board to new opportunities – but *only* if it is viewed as a challenge and confronted with a strong heart.

For the ex-offender and his or her loved ones, employment is a critical part of the path back to self-respect and social acceptance. It is not the only requirement, but it plays a major role in rebuilding our pride, independence, and quality of life. Above all, this effort takes courage and determination. Never give up, because employment is an essential key to your future. Success IS possible – and YOU can achieve it!

Why Work?

Before you can succeed in finding a job, there's an essential question you have to answer: *why even bother?* When you're in a state of rage and depression, the answer to this question doesn't just appear by magic. You have to go within yourself, seeking ways to keep yourself going even when you're tempted to give up.

In fact there are some good reasons for working: survival, freedom, security, meeting supervision requirements, recreation, satisfaction, and outgrowing the past. In this section we'll look at why it's in your better interest to work. When you're facing problems and disappointment, looking back at these reasons will help you find the strength and motivation to keep trying.

Survival

The first concern for all humans is simply to survive. In our society, we use money as a key way to meet our survival needs. But the punishment experience drains the accused and his or her family – mentally, emotionally, and financially. Their money has been spent on bonds, lawyers, fees, restitution, drug tests, prison visits, and so on. At some point, everything is GONE.

When you're on the streets with a criminal history and few resources, you have two choices: work for a living or take someone else's resources. A job is a slow path to personal growth, while dishonesty and criminal behavior are a surefire ticket back to a cell block. Once you snap to this fact, you realize that taking the easy way isn't worth it if it means growing old in a cage.

The sooner you really understand this, the better your chances to succeed. So like it or not, *real* survival does require a job. Sorry if you don't want to hear that, but you have to deal with reality as it stands. As a bonus, a job offers rewards that go WAY beyond a safe way to survive.

Freedom

Nothing can replace freedom: being able to make decisions, control the direction of our lives, oversee our own growth, and experience pride and dignity. But being free requires work, on a variety of levels. This means more than just holding down a job to stay out of prison. If you don't *earn* what you need, you will be a slave, always dependent on someone or something else. This is true whether you are a prisoner, a welfare recipient, or a hustler spong-

3

ing off people who *do* work for a living. Other books in the *OPEN Information Series* (see rear of book) also deal with the issue of true freedom and ways to obtain it.

Security

When you have a job, you can begin to stand up and take care of yourself. After years of feeling powerless, a job offers a much needed path to self-reliance. It helps you build a sense of security, independence, and increasing faith in your ability to take care of business. This is a great feeling for those who are lost and overwhelmed after their criminal justice involvement.

With a steady job, you can also offer support to the loved ones who helped you survive the correctional experience. After many months or years of worry, loved ones look forward to and deserve some relief from their financial burdens. Also, a lot of personal satisfaction comes from helping the people we care about, and a job can make that possible.

Supervision Requirements

Many folks are under the eye of the system, as in some form of probation or parole supervision. They are required to pay for monthly fees, past fines, restitution, counseling or treatment, drug tests, child support, etc. With all the expenses you've already faced, this may seem like too much punishment. Still, it's far better than watching your kids grow up in a visiting room.

Clearly you must have a job to handle the wealth of supervision requirements. In fact, it's not unusual for a person to hold a part-time job as well as a full-time one just to pay court-ordered fees. If you get stressed out, you may think it would be better to just go crazy on the world and get it over with. Think again! You won't find anything back in the joint but funny business, fools, and fear. And when you get out, you'll still have to make it on the streets. You'll never get any younger, so you may as well deal with it NOW.

Be sure you *never* let supervision hassles, fees, or fines drive you into desperate or illegal activity. Never break the law to feed the law! Better to admit you can't pay and take the heat than risk everything for nothing. Even if you get a technical revocation, it's not as deadly as picking up a whole new conviction. No matter how tough it gets, you cannot let anyone or anything drive you over the edge.

A Chance to Have Fun

In order to survive and meet your responsibilities, you must keep your mental and emotional balance. If daily stress gets too heavy, it helps to focus on the positive results of working and the joys of being free. In other words, trace your progress, acknowledge your achievements, and count your blessings.

Isn't it worth a lot of hard work to be in the free world instead of racked down in a cage? Even more, a steady income, no matter how modest, lets you do a lot of neat things. The community is full of unexplored places and events that are as close as the weekend section of the local newspaper. Just being able to take a walk on a beautiful spring day is a real treasure. With time, patience, and financial stability, you can regain a sense of enjoyment and the ability to relax and have a good time.

Sometimes we see our lives as so serious and heavy that we feel fun is simply beyond our grasp. It's too easy to get lost and overwhelmed. The fact is, having a good time is a logical reward for hard work, and it is essential for our health and the quality of our lives. We must give ourselves the time and opportunity to learn to enjoy life again – or, perhaps, for the first time. Income from employment, no matter how small at first, helps make that possible.

Personal Satisfaction

Working for a living is not the end of the world – not at all. In fact, work is a normal part of life and can bring a great degree of satisfaction. A job is an ideal opportunity to apply your time, knowledge, energy, and skill in productive ways. If you don't use your talents, it is a tragic waste. But as you become increasingly better at what you do, you are rewarded by a sense of competence, pride, and self-confidence. Even if you didn't need the money, you have an even greater need to feel the satisfaction of constructive activity – of a job well done!

Growing Beyond the Past

It's absurd for the most memorable thing in a person's life to be the length of their rap sheet! One great thing about a job is that by working, you are creating a new future for yourself. A good job, no matter how long it takes to achieve, is a real blessing. It is a way to move beyond mere existence into a stage of life that brings comfort and fulfillment – a higher quality of life.

The sense of accomplishment we get from holding a job and doing it well is one of the best ways to grow beyond the agony of the past. It helps us put our mistakes behind us and step into a future of progress and achievement. This is where pride and dignity come from.

By holding a job and paying your own way, you become a valid member of your family and the world. As a productive worker, you are participating in the process that makes our society function. Over time, this role will earn greater respect – from yourself and from others – and give you a stronger sense of belonging to the world around you.

Facing Our Ex-Offender Status

A main goal of this book is to help people with a criminal history get and keep a job. One big step toward this is learning how to cope with the negative image of an outlaw past – both your reputation and how you feel about yourself after an arrest and conviction.

If you just roll over and play dead, you won't survive on the streets. You must learn to get control over yourself and the future. And that means learning how to deal with your criminal history and the impact it will have on your life. It takes some unique attitudes and skills to find a job when you have a record. This section looks at some of the special concerns ex-offenders must face and overcome.

Dealing With Special Problems

■ Bad Reputation

"No employer wants to hire Public Enemy Number One."

First, many people see a criminal history as a warning not to trust you. Having been convicted of a crime labels you as bad or a high risk in their eyes. This makes it hard to find a job because it undercuts the first thing an employer looks for: someone they can trust. Based on their policy or just personal attitudes, they may automatically reject you or review your background more critically than normal.

If you are rejected because of your past, don't let it break your heart or make you go crazy! *Expect it and be prepared.* Above all, remember that *you* define your worth, not the people around you. We will discuss ways to handle this in the section on **Overcoming Rejection** later in this book.

In the long run you will be accepted only when you can get a person to look past the negative label of criminal and trust you as *an individual.* That person has to make a favorable judgment about your current values, intentions, honesty, and competence. One way to show you can be trusted is to develop a network of supporters, as described in the section **Support from Others**. You should also work on your interview skills to make sure you come across as an honest, sincere person who has come to grips with past mistakes.

Improving your credibility and trustworthiness is a long-term process. The efforts you make right now will continue to reward you for many years to come. As your support network grows, your relationships lengthen, and you can show positive work history over a period of years, it will be much easier for potential employers to trust you. Positive activity in the community, such as volunteer work, educational growth, and church participation, may also help.

■ *Nature of Convictions*

"After robbing sixteen liquor stores, I'd make a first-rate security guard!"

Your success at finding a job will be strongly influenced by the seriousness of your charge(s), how much time has passed, and the relationship of the offenses to the job you're looking for.

It's frustrating when you are highly qualified for a specific job but can't get it because it is too closely linked to your crime(s). You don't have much chance for a job where you could commit the same type of offense again. An example would be seeking a job as a child care worker if you have a sexual abuse history, or as a bank teller with a bank fraud conviction. No matter what your training or qualifications, you should avoid jobs that carry a high risk of rejection. Since you can't change the nature of your past convictions or when they occurred, it is logical to avoid jobs that are closely related to the offense(s) you've been convicted of.

Go after jobs that offer the greatest chance for acceptance. The best situation is where you already are known, trusted, or have a standing offer. Those situations are rare, however. Most people have to start from scratch. If you want to use your prior

training and skills, try to think of jobs that will let you apply your experience but don't offer the same direct barriers. Books such as the *Occupational Outlook Handbook* and *O*Net Dictionary of Occupational Titles* published by the U.S. Department of Labor (see the **Reading List** at the end of this book) may give you some ideas.

■ *False Expectations*

"All I want is EVERYTHING ... right NOW!"

When you base your plans on what you want things to be rather than what they actually are, you are setting yourself up to fail. The first rule of survival is to be honest with yourself. This means being realistic – making choices and decisions based on fact rather than on pride, illusion, or a desire to somehow beat the game.

People who have just been released from jail or prison need to be especially careful. The longer you've been locked up and away from the free world, the more out of touch you will be with the job market and the realities of everyday life. Special programs to help ex-offenders do exist, but they are still rare in smaller communities. To make things worse, much of the information you hear on the prison grapevine about special loans, grants, social security, etc., for ex-prisoners is totally false.

Offenders and their loved ones often get lost in the trap of wanting "everything right now." For example, it's not real to expect Bob will get out of jail or prison and within six weeks become the main source of support for his wife and kids. It is also not real to expect to come home from prison, start your own plumbing business, and be an independent businessman six months after your release. *Investing your hope and effort in something that cannot be achieved is a trap!* It creates great stress and can tear you and your relationships apart. Offenders and loved ones need to test their hopes and expectations against what is really do-able.

Remember that looking for a job is always difficult and time-consuming. A high-paying job with easy hours is hard to find – even for well-established citizens. So be patient, steady, and realistic in your search. Be prepared to take a lot of little steps. Counting on overnight success will just bring you stress and frustration.

In fact, most people need work immediately, so they end up taking the first job they can find. This often means an entry-level or high turnover job like fast food or day labor. These jobs usually don't ask a lot of questions or put you through an in-depth background check and waiting period. Unfortunately, they are often low wage and hard to get by on. In this case, you should just look at them as a short-term preparation for something better. If you get frustrated, remember that it is five times easier to find a job when you already have one than when you're out of work and desperate. And every job, no matter how humble, can be a stepping stone to a better, more rewarding future.

■ *Addictive History*

"Junkies are poor job risks; their lives are totally messed up!"

Let's be up front: most of us with a criminal past also have a history of addictive behavior. I don't mean just dependency on drugs or alcohol. We live in an addicted society which teaches us to get along by using something outside of us to change how we feel: using people (in our relationships), objects (chemicals, money, TV), or feelings (power, sex, love, anger) to alter our moods. Yet we lie to ourselves and others, denying that we are strung out and out of control.

Until we stop it, addiction keeps growing stronger, pulling us in deeper and deeper until our compulsive behavior tears our lives apart … again. Maybe we get busted, get fired, lose our family, overdose, or just don't care about anything anymore.

No matter what, addictions absorb our time, energy, concentration, and resources, and fool us into thinking we are satisfied. By offering short-term relief, they trap us, consuming the very strength we need to overcome them.

If you have a history of addiction, you will always have a *serious* problem when trying to get and keep a job. A job demands that you get involved, be responsible and alert, make a reliable contribution – or you're out the door. If you're addicted, you are constantly distracted. It probably takes all of your attention and resources just to feed your addiction. As a result, you don't have enough left over to meet the responsibilities of your job. This results in flaky behavior – and no one wants or can afford to have such people on the payroll.

Because an addiction develops by repeating a behavior over a long period of time, just wanting or wishing won't make it go away. It will *never* go away by itself. If you're strung out on any level, chemical or emotional, GET HELP NOW! OPEN's handbook *Life Without a Crutch* (see rear of book) can help you face your dependency and find assistance in overcoming it. Also review **Community Resources** later in this book for ideas on how to find help.

■ *Poor Work Skills and Record*

"Ten years of ripping and running doesn't qualify you even to throw a paper route."

One area an employer always looks at carefully is what skills you have and how you have performed in the past. Obviously your chances are much better when you have a skill the employer needs and a track record as a reliable, productive worker.

Unfortunately, people with a criminal history often have very few **job skills**. This is especially true for those who are young or have been in and out of trouble for a long time. Stealing and pushing dope are not the kind of experience employers are looking for. Therefore, you have to be prepared to learn new skills that will improve your chances for a good job.

When a person is locked up, it is all too easy to develop an isolated or hostile attitude. Some folks refuse to do anything but sleep, write home,

and watch TV. No good!! To be successful in the free world, you must be ready to take advantage of *any and all* chances to improve your skills. Both in the system and in the community, personal growth is the key to realizing your dreams!

Whether you are in prison preparing for exit or in the community on probation or parole, you can do some very practical things to improve your job skills. Look at the gap between where your education left off and where you want to go in life. Then plan to take the next step. If this means working for your GED, do it. If you can become a better bricklayer by learning to read blueprints, *do it*. If you are on the street and want to learn a new trade, go find a school and *do it*. If you already have a trade or profession, continue to improve by reading and learning the most up-to-date methods.

In the free world you won't have the luxury of postponing job hunting while you improve your education and job skills. You may need to work and take classes at the same time. This can be a real drag at the time, but *do* it! It is an investment in a better future. It will also show a prospective employer that you are motivated and willing to work hard.

Another concern is your **work history**. It may show that you went for long periods without a job, had a lot of jobs in a short time, or that you were fired from a job. Also, you may not have any personal or job references. If you disclose your criminal record, you can explain some of these problems. If you *don't* tell the truth, it will be hard to account for the gaps and you may get caught or rejected anyway.

To overcome a poor work history or a criminal record, it helps to develop a list of three to five people who trust you and are willing to say you are OK. These people are your personal references. They can also be helpful when you're trying to get an apartment, credit, training, etc. They are allowing you to use their good reputation to help support yours, which is currently in the dumpster. For more information, read the section **Using People as References** later in this book.

As you re-enter the work force, keep in mind that you need to develop a good work history. And whatever you do now becomes a part of your job history in the future. It's smart to hold onto your first job until you can move on to something better. Don't quit without a good reason, but if you find yourself out of work, jump up and find another one as quickly as you can so you won't have a long gap between jobs. Although you may not have a good work record in the past, you can change that through consistent, dependable effort.

■ Limited Resources

"You start with less than nothing and slowly but surely rebuild."

Most people involved in the criminal justice process have lost much or all of their money and material possessions. In the beginning they may not have what they need to find and hold a job: transportation, tools, proper clothing, or child care, for example. This burden may force them to seek temporary help from friends, family, or the community.

To seek and receive help is OK if done in the right ways. This is discussed in the section **Support from Others** later on.

When the need for money and a job reaches a crisis point, stress levels shoot way up and people tend to do something that puts themselves and others at risk. To make matters worse, many people exit the criminal justice system with an intense desire and impatience to put their lives together overnight. This is understandable, but it cannot be done. Such efforts simply increase their stress and break down their ability to cope. They become even more confused and desperate. This cycle must be controlled!

Give yourself a break. It takes *time* and *persistence* to dig out from under your present situation. Do the best you can and don't hesitate to ask for help. Lots of people will try to assist you when they see you're serious about getting yourself together. There are also many churches, agencies, and government programs which offer short-term aid. Also ask your probation or parole officer for suggestions.

There is one sure rule: no matter how crazy things may get, don't do anything stupid that would place you in danger of losing your freedom or chances for a rewarding future. And above all, don't give up!

■ Occupational Restrictions

"They won't let me do what I'm good at – I get the feeling they want me to fail."

There are many occupations with restrictions that bar ex-offenders from working in that field. These restrictions are set by the state or local government or by an oversight agency. They can vary depending on your location, but some common examples are driving a cab or limo, being a barber, or working as a licensed nurse or health care aide. This can seem totally unfair and make you really frustrated, but it does no good to get lost in anger and resentment. You need your energy for more productive things.

When preparing for a job search, going to school, or starting vocational training, you should check first to see if there are any restrictions which would keep you from getting certain jobs. DO THIS! You may ask your local city attorney, branches of county and state government, or organizations that issue certifications in your area of interest. The public library can help you identify these certifying agencies and boards. You can also look in the help pages and government section of your local telephone book. Often people who work in the field you're interested in, or who hire others into it, know of any restrictions against persons with a criminal history. Don't be afraid to ask them.

Recently, a national organization has collected and published information about legal barriers facing people with a criminal record. You may be able to find some information about barriers that exist for your state and job interest, as well as other useful information, from their web site www.lac.org (Legal Action Center) and an affiliated group, the National H.I.R.E. Network (www.hirenetwork.org).

The fact is, barriers exist even when there is no official policy against hiring ex-offenders. For example, if you graduate from truck driving school but have a DWI or DUI history, no one is going to hire you. And if you're on probation or parole, you may have to get special permission to drive out of your local area or out of state. Therefore, it's better to ask a lot of questions *before* you invest your time, money, and hopes. If you're going to get hit with bad news, it is far better to learn the truth up front. At least you will have a chance to find a way to overcome the restrictions and move forward.

Some occupations have time limits (such as three to five years after you get off supervision), after which you can apply to work in that field. If there are, you may wish to work toward certification, but in the meantime don't sit around and wait ... just keep cooking.

■ *Emotional Hang-ups*

"Nobody in their right mind will hire Mr. Bad Attitude!"

Having been branded an outcast creates some unique social and emotional hang-ups. To become balanced, successful people, we have to learn to handle these mental traps. Just because the law says you've been bad doesn't make you bad; only you can choose. But many of us carry around negative feelings, especially hostility and bitterness, due to our criminal history. This affects our attitudes toward ourselves, our loved ones, and the community.

Often a person leaves the criminal justice system with a poor self-image, insecure and fearful of rejection. Being defined as a criminal can make you feel extremely isolated and apart from everything around you. This can produce a lot of anxiety, anger, depression, and even violence. You may develop a bad attitude as a defense against feeling cut off and rejected. Eventually your negative attitude will show itself in everything you say and do. And when you are rejected because of your attitude, you will just feel more isolated and angry.

This is a deadly cycle because *no one* wants to hire or be around a person who is angry or hostile. To hold onto a job, you have to be flexible, get along with others, be ready to follow instructions, and learn to do things the way your employer requires. Being respectful and following instructions are not signs of weakness. In fact, they are signs of a mature, responsible person.

Whenever you allow your negative feelings to run your life, you must wake up and see that you are still under the control of the Man. Whenever you're being driven or controlled by the past, you are not yet truly free!! The key to success is to live in the present, motivated by your faith in what the future holds.

If you find your anger or any emotions growing out of control, seek professional help. Pain and rage are like deadly poisons that can rot everything away, including your personal life, employment, and freedom. Too often we try to control these painful feelings with drugs, alcohol, or some other escape, but in the long run it only makes the problem worse.

Unfortunately, many ex-cons and people who have spent a lot of time on the streets think that counseling is for wimps or squares. This is not true. If you believe it, you are setting yourself up to fail. Be real and adult: reach out for someone to help you get control and cope with your feelings. See **Community Resources** later in this book for ideas on how to find help.

■ *Under Supervision*

"As long as you're on paper, you've got to dance for the Man."

Many job seekers with a criminal history are under the supervision of a probation or parole officer (P.O.). If so, you have the added concern that your officer may communicate with the employer, show up at the work place, or cause other problems for your employment.

Therefore, do everything you can to establish a positive, honest relationship with your P.O. In your first interview with your officer, find out where you stand concerning disclosure of your record and discuss it again if your officer changes. In many cases you have NO CHOICE but to tell the employer about your record. Even if it's not officially required, officers prefer that you disclose your history. But if you have a choice and decide not to tell your employer, your officer needs to know so he or she will not accidentally put your job in danger.

The goal of your P.O. is for you to successfully complete your supervision. Therefore, it is usually a good idea to ask your officer's advice, especially if you are new to the community or not sure if your actions are acceptable under the terms of your supervision. Discuss your plans in advance in order to avoid future problems.

The Big Question

Being aware of their negative image, ex-offenders often wonder whether they should risk telling about their past or not. Many times they take what they believe is the easy way out and try to hide their record because they're afraid nobody will hire them. This approach may or may not get them what they want at the moment, but it often causes problems down the road.

"Do I Disclose My Criminal History or NOT?"

The first question is: Do you have any choice at all? People on probation or parole are often required to disclose their pasts. Also, correctional personnel and halfway houses are often required by law to inform a potential employer of your background. Plus, many employers will run a background check. So, in the end, the only safe course is to prepare yourself to reveal your criminal past – and learn to do it in a way that will give you the best shot at getting hired.

If you're *not* required to disclose, you have a choice to make. The decision whether or not to reveal your criminal conviction(s) is a very difficult and sensitive issue. It should not be taken lightly or done in haste;

there are some serious concerns and risks to be considered.

In the beginning most ex-offenders admit their pasts, even if it's not required. But after a half dozen rejections they decide that if they keep on they are going to starve to death! Also, being rejected brings a lot of anger and hurt, so they begin to lie and cover up, just to meet the needs of sheer survival.

No path you take in this situation will be easy or free of risks. If you lie in order to get the job and later your boss finds out, you can be fired just because you lied. It's a classic "damned if you do and damned if you don't" situation. As you consider this issue, ask yourself the following questions:

"What type of job am I seeking and how does it relate to my past arrests and convictions?"

Give this question a lot of thought, especially if you plan to disclose your past. Your chance of acceptance is lowest when your criminal history directly relates to the job you are seeking (like a cashier who stole money or a driver who drank and killed someone in a company truck). This can be a real bummer if your skills or training come into conflict with the nature of your conviction(s).

This doesn't mean you have to turn your back on what you do best or enjoy the most. But be prepared to put some serious time and effort between your crime and the same kind of job. Often you will have to spend a few years working your way back. If so, use that period to study and sharpen your mind and skills. Above all, don't give up!

"How much responsibility and trust are involved?"

Take a look at the job to see if it would involve handling money or goods, as a salesperson or cashier for example. Or would you have the authority to make a commitment on behalf of the business? And would you have to be bonded? Generally the greater the connection with money, trust, or the welfare of others, the greater the chance of a background check. Not just a criminal history check, but *everything* you put on your application.

Entry-level and low-wage positions are easiest to get and ask the fewest questions. On the other hand, it is usually impossible to hide your past when going after a job that involves major responsibility. It will take time and persistence to repair your reputation so that you can be honest about your past and still get these more demanding and more rewarding positions.

"Would I be responsible for the safety or welfare of others?"

Examples of such jobs are a bus driver, a child care worker, or a nurse's aide. These types of jobs carry a greater burden of concern for other people. They also may lead to more extensive background checks. If you apply for such a job, you must plan to be up front about your criminal record.

The issue of responsibility has legal, practical, and moral sides. This is doubly true if your offense is directly related to the job, for example if you are applying as a bus driver with a DWI record, or as a human service provider with a history of client abuse.

Since background checks on safety-related jobs are all but automatic now, you will not have much chance to get a job where your conduct could endanger others. And even if you could hide your past, the question is: should you? If you know you wouldn't get the job if the employer knew your history, it's better to look elsewhere.

Above all, if you *know* that your behavior might endanger someone, it is not right for you to take that job. Be honest with yourself about your reasons for wanting the job. You must be able to trust yourself before you take on responsibility for other people.

"What's the chance of a background check and how extensive would it be?"

Some places don't run a check, but most DO. As a rule the greater the

MAN, I NEED A JOB!

degree of responsibility and pay, the greater the likelihood of an extensive check which would uncover your criminal history. If you apply to some branch of government, no matter what the job, the chances are that nine out of ten will check you out.

In the past, background checks were conducted by a law firm, private investigator, or specialized company. Now employers are turning to Internet services that charge a fee to provide a report on your past. Small companies may choose to avoid the costs of background checks, but major companies require them as a matter of policy. Frankly, unless you know for a FACT that an employer doesn't run checks, *you should assume it will be done!*

A background check may cover the total picture we present to an employer as to who and what we are. This includes past education, jobs, length of employment, references, credit history, and so forth. One of the big problems with not disclosing a criminal history is that we have to try to fill in all the holes in our lives to make things look normal. For most of us, there is just no way!

Keep in mind that any false information you give, no matter what, is dangerous, even if it doesn't relate to your criminal history. When it is discovered, it will cause the employer to assume that you are dishonest.

"Does the job look like something I'd want to keep for just a few months or would I like to stick with it for a long time?"

If it's a day labor or temporary job, then your past may not be important to anybody but you. But if there is hope for promotion and growth in a job you could really enjoy, that's a different issue. This is important because if you get a good job without telling the truth, you will live in constant fear of being found out.

Picture this: after three years of excellent service they call you in and give you a promotion. The boss tells you what a great future you have with the company. You feel great! Then, a week later, they call you in again and fire you because a background check uncovered your record or some false claim about your work history or qualifications. Your world explodes!! This is another reason for being up front and disclosing your record and overall past. I'm not suggesting it's easy or without risk – only that it's better in the long run to be honest.

"What's the chance that my criminal history would be revealed by my probation or parole supervision or through another employee?"

Even if there is no law or policy requiring you to disclose your record, your probation or parole officer may check up on you and unintentionally expose your status. Each department and program deals with things in a different way. In your first interview, be sure to ask how your officer intends to handle the issue of disclosure. It's too important to your survival and future just to ignore. If he or she says you do not have to disclose, ask that that fact be noted in your file.

If you already have a job and didn't reveal your past, you can have a serious problem if you suddenly get a new officer (as often happens). This is another risk you run when you don't inform the employer, so it's important to get your business straight with your new P.O.

One cold fact: if *anyone* finds out, the chances are high that the news will eventually get around to the boss. So if you decide not to disclose, don't blow your cover. No war stories, no barroom slips. Keep your mouth SHUT to everyone on and off the job. Even then some old buddy may pop up out of your past and give you away.

The need for secrecy can become a problem in itself, since it will tend to make you feel more isolated and cut off from everyday life. It's hard to make friends if you have to guard every word you say.

"Can I pass a drug test?"

More and more jobs require drug testing, both before you're hired and randomly on the job. And if you fail the test before you're hired, they don't tell you the real reason you're not hired. They "just can't use you," and you never hear from them again.

Even if you don't test positive at the time of hire, if you are using it will eventually catch up with you. Things didn't used to be this way. A person could smoke a joint during lunch and still slide by. But THC stays in your system 30 to 60 days or more, and can be quickly detected with modern drug tests by your employer or your P.O. Even alcohol can be detected a day or two after you drink it. So if you're still using, no matter what your drug of choice, it's time to clean up if you intend to get and keep a meaningful job. If you need help in facing an addiction, review the section on **Community Resources** and study the handbook *Life Without a Crutch* (see rear of book) to get started on the road to recovery.

"So, if I do disclose my past, what are some of the possible effects?"

You may get the job! If so, this is ideal because the best foundation for employment is built on truth and trust. Dishonesty is not a good way to begin a new relationship that is important to your survival and future welfare. If you are hired after disclosing your past, you want to be extra careful to avoid any hint that you are doing anything that could be taken as illegal, dishonest, or morally questionable. Not only do you have to avoid such actions, you have to be very careful not to give even the *appearance* of doing something wrong.

On the other hand, if you disclose your past you run the risk of rejection right on the spot. But you run that risk even if you don't tell! Rejection is a fact of life that you would have to face even if you were an average citizen who had never been in trouble and had an ideal past.

But let's be real. When you are turned down because of your criminal history, it really hurts! You still don't have a job, *and* you have to cope with the disappointment and depression of being turned away.

This is no easy matter when you're trying to pull your life together. That is why you have to be well prepared on all levels and pick your shot *very* carefully.

And if I don't tell, what can happen?"

Again, you might get the job ... but it would be based on falsehood. You will always worry if they are going to find out and what will come down if they do. Be aware that if you're finally discovered, it will result in a lot of embarrassment and you will probably be fired. From your boss' point of view, you are deceptive and untrustworthy. That will hurt his or her faith in you and probably break company rules. So you are likely to get flushed just because you lied on your job application, no matter how good a worker you are or how long you've been there.

If this happens, you will lose both your income and personal stability. Your opportunity for long-term employment or a chance of promotion is dead and stinking, and you can kiss goodbye any hope for a positive job reference. Such situations lead to a lot of anxiety, stress, and confusion for both you and your loved ones. One fact to remember: if you get the job without telling the employer, be careful not to tell anyone *ever*. A company's employees will always be more loyal to their jobs than to you.

So You Must Decide ...

Once again, you may not have a choice. But even if you do, ideally it's best to be honest about your record. This way you can pick your shot and do it in a way and at a time that gives you the best chance of success. The **Job Interview Hints** later in this book will make it a lot safer to be up front about your past. One thing for sure: don't let rejection break you down!

Don't be surprised if your efforts to get a government job (city, county, or Federal) are not effective. No one is more cold blooded about hiring an ex-con than the government. So it's not unusual to be denied a government job while you're still under supervision or for a fixed period after you get off. Even though there may be an official policy against discrimination based on criminal history, that doesn't mean the government agency will be receptive. You may still be rejected due to an unwritten policy or a personnel decision that someone else is better for the job. As with all job efforts, hope for the best but don't sit and wait for the phone to ring ... get up and move forward!

As I've suggested, you can sometimes get hired without disclosing your past when it's a low-pay, short-term, minimum responsibility job with little chance of a background check. Employers usually spend more effort to find the right person for higher level jobs and thus check a lot closer. On the other hand, many companies now check everybody. There is no hard and fast rule and no guarantee.

Usually your best shot at being accepted is with an individual who has the authority to make a decision based on his or her judgment of your character and skills. Your goal is to do a good job of selling yourself and hope that you will get a chance to prove yourself in daily performance. *That* is what you're looking for!

The decision to tell or not often hinges on how much risk you can afford to take – or think you have to take. Whenever possible, it is best to think on a long-term basis rather than be ruled by impulse or short-term survival. But IT'S YOUR LIFE and only YOU can decide. A lot depends on your legal status, plus how strong your finances and your emotional health are.

Do what you have to do. One way or the other, it is always a risky choice, but try not to make your decision out of panic or fear because you've been rejected for other jobs. Above all, if you choose to or are required to disclose, it is absolutely critical to be well-prepared.

Commitment

"Success in job hunting requires commitment and faith – total dedication to the effort and an unbending belief in your ultimate victory!"

I have watched the attitude and actions of many thousands of ex-cons. Most fall into one of two categories: those who are ready to take control of their lives and those who are not. Having personally done time in both frames of mind, I promise you that being out of control is never rewarding.

So make a commitment to yourself right now to take charge of your life. No matter how modest your advances, your intent and effort will start a process of positive growth and self-discovery.

And employment is an essential step on this path. To succeed, you must have a burning desire to find a job and be ready to do whatever it takes. If it means getting up early every day, going on even when you are turned down, taking the janitor's job when you wanted to be manager – do whatever it takes. If you're not ready to pay the price, you aren't really committed.

As with anything else, actions speak louder than words. You must be prepared to *focus* your energy totally on the job hunt and then *follow through* until you complete your efforts. If you only go halfway to the finish line, you will never finish the race – much less come in a winner.

Motivation

"Nothing is more critical to success, in employment and in everyday life, than the will to win!"

The first step to achieving our goal is to want it bad enough. And the more we want it, the harder we try and the longer we stay at it. Motivation is essential to survive and to win. It's been called heart, drive, dedication, and strength of purpose. But whatever it is, every general, coach, and teacher throughout history has sought to bring it forth.

It is a powerful drive that comes from the very center of our selves. Therefore, we must each look within ourselves to find that special power that will move us toward our goal no matter what the odds or opposition we have to face.

19

Focusing on the Job Search

"If you want a job, you have to get out there and pursue it, because the job isn't going to come get you!"

We must focus our energy and pursue the job consistently. Not every other day but every day. Not every other hour but every hour. This is not the time to kick back!

Finding a job is serious business. The more hooks you drop in the water and the better you bait them, the better your chances of a strike. Put your faith in the law of averages: try enough times and you've *got* to score. This means making your job search a *full-time activity,* both mentally and physically. For now, getting a job *is* your job. We are talking about reasonable efforts here, not becoming obsessed or lost in a mission impossible (like, "Baby, go get me a job, I'll be out sometime next spring").

Follow Through

"The best intentions in the world don't mean zip unless we get up and make things happen one step at a time."

Why do we so often make plans and get all excited but never quite get around to carrying them out? Why?? One powerful reason for many people with a criminal history is just plain old *fear.* Fear of failure, of being rejected, looked down on, or treated like they're a second-class person because they've made mistakes.

It is extremely hard to tell people about your past. If someone denies this they are usually not being honest with themselves or others. When you ask for a job, you are giving someone a chance to say "take a walk" (no matter what the reason), and that's an uncomfortable thing to do. But the rewards are worth the risk. You have to be mentally ready to let rejection roll over you like water off a duck's back. In truth, your worth as a person is not based on someone else's acceptance or rejection. If you take rejection personally, it will hurt your motivation and cost you your ability to win.

Be careful! Give a lot of thought to the section on **Overcoming Rejection**. If you *are* rejected, analyze the experience to learn what works and what does not. Then improve your technique and keep trying till you reach your goal!

After you have worked to get this far, you owe it to yourself to finish what you started. Put that last push into your effort and see it through to the end. Whether you get the job or not, you will have the satisfaction of knowing you did your best and completed the effort.

In the end, alibis and excuses count for nothing. You don't exist to lose – you are here to win! Never forget that your goal of employment isn't just to get by or to get a probation or parole officer off your back. A job helps you be self-sufficient and that gives you a sense of pride and self-respect. *That* is why it's worth going after.

MAN, I NEED A JOB!

Preparing for the Job Search

Now that we know what a person with a criminal history has to face, let's get down to business.

Realities of the Job Market

The job market consists of two basic elements – jobs that are advertised or known outside the company and those which outsiders don't know about. Most people only see the visible jobs, which means that 98% of job seekers are looking in classified ads and Internet job listings to find a job. This results in tremendous competition and reduces your chance of getting one of those jobs.

Although they contain many job listings, job ads in newspapers and on the Internet are not necessarily the best place to look for a job. They are, however, a good indicator of what the job market is like in your community. If there are 20 ads for mechanics and only two for carpenters, you know it will be easier to find a job as a mechanic than as a carpenter.

The other segment of the so-called visible job market consists of jobs that are given to private employment agencies, recruiters, or headhunters to fill. As we will dis-

cuss later in **Finding Job Leads**, those companies are not usually an economical or effective way to hunt a job. More jobs are filled through published job listings than are filled by these firms.

So where are the rest of the jobs? We know they're out there, we just don't know exactly where. They can be located by using the resources described in the sections on **Finding Job Leads** and **Networking**. Networking means telling others you are looking for a job and asking them to let you know if they hear of an opening.

Networking is a lot of work, but it can be the most effective method of job search. It requires a lot of effort, personal involvement, and some luck, but it offers an advantage because there isn't so much competition for any one job. It gives you access to insider knowledge about job openings that exist or will be available soon. And it may give you an inside track if you are recommended by a current employee or someone the employer already knows.

Be aware that the job market is always changing based on how the economy is doing, which businesses and industries are growing, and what kinds of skills they need. On any day you may have a great chance of getting some types of jobs while others are almost impossible to get. For example, construction jobs are seasonal and closely tied to the local economy and weather, whereas service jobs such as warehouse work are usually more stable but less rewarding.

We cannot change or control the job market. What we can do is get an accurate picture of what's happening and then work to fit ourselves to it.

Let's review what it takes to prepare for the job search. Then we will discuss how to hunt for a job and handle job interviews.

Preparation

Preparation is the process of thinking through the realities, focusing your energy and attention, and developing a plan to make everything work. You will need motivation, skills, opportunity, and the discipline to apply yourself if you're going to make it in the job market.

Be aware that many jobs now require you to use a computer in some way. This is true even if the job isn't high tech and doesn't seem to have anything to do with computers, for instance a car repair job. Also, some companies now expect you to complete their job applications on a computer; this process is similar to filling in forms on the Internet. So take any chance you get to learn about computers. At the minimum, you should try to learn to type, at least a little.

If you are currently a prisoner within six months of release, be sure to obtain and study the book *99 Days & A Get Up* (see rear of book)

to help you organize your passage out of the joint into community life. Good preparation is *absolutely essential* to your survival and success!

■ *Attitude*

Mental and emotional preparation is the foundation for everything that will occur during your job search. The more focused, stable, realistic, determined, and motivated you are, the more successful you will be.

The single most important factor is your attitude. What you tell yourself –about yourself and about others – determines what your attitude will be. And your attitude is reflected in everything you say and do. If you believe you will be successful in finding a job, the chances are very good that you *will* be successful.

Certainly if you tell yourself you won't find a job, you probably won't. And if you walk in angry and hostile, rejection is assured. It's easy to set yourself up to fail. All you have to do is tell yourself all the reasons why nobody would hire you or that the prospective employer is your enemy. On the other hand, you can prepare yourself to succeed by reminding yourself of the reasons you would be a good employee.

So before you begin your job search, be sure to have the right attitude about yourself and your ability to find a job. The need for a positive attitude includes your approach to an employer and fellow employees. If you act negative, talk trash, or are just plain rude or hostile, why in the world would anybody pay you to be a jerk?

Personal Evaluation

Job hunting does not begin with resumes, want ads, contacts, or interviews. It begins with *you* ... inside your head. If you don't know what you have to offer an employer, you won't know who to offer it to or how to sell yourself.

Success depends on making a good match between four factors: what you can do, what you want to do, what's out there to be done, and what it takes to get the job. So instead of writing up a resume, you should start by reviewing your strengths, weaknesses, and your values and ambitions. This is hard, but the following suggestions should help.

IDENTIFY YOUR ASSETS

First, look at your assets – your strengths and skills. Everyone has skills, most of which can be applied in many different types of jobs. You have both general skills and skills that are related to a specific job.

Examples of general skills are: adaptable, efficient, well-organized, cooperative, motivated, dependable, thorough. Other examples would be: mechanical ability, a problem solver, able to handle multiple tasks, a good speaker, good writing skills, work well under pressure, detail-oriented, a self starter, or good with people.

Job-related skills apply to a specific type of job. They would only be useful when you are applying for that job or one in the same field. Examples of job-related skills include: accounts payable, machinist, computer networking, retail sales, house painting, truck driving, waiting tables, carpentry, data entry, electrician, short-order cooking, operating a forklift.

Your criminal record doesn't wipe out all the good things you have done. Although you may not feel like it right now, you have made some positive accomplishments during your life. Begin to develop a list of your own assets, including both general and job-related skills. Take your time to do this right. People often take their strengths for granted, so do yourself justice and make your list as complete and realistic as possible.

These may be job-related achievements or things you've done in your personal life, for instance in hobbies or volunteer work. Don't forget that some of the skills you developed on the streets and in the joint can be very valuable, although you probably should not emphasize *how* you developed them. For example, you've had to get good at evaluating people and operating under pressure. The point is, you have a number of strengths that are valuable to an employer.

Remember that a good attitude is always your best asset. If you have a positive attitude and a lot of determination, it will not only help you find a job – it will make you a valuable employee after you are hired.

IDENTIFY YOUR PERSONAL WEAKNESSES

Now list your liabilities – things that would make you unqualified for a particular job or less desirable to a prospective employer.

Everyone has liabilities. There is no perfect person in the job market even though employers always wish for one. Many liabilities are just an employer's *opinion* about how that characteristic would affect your job performance. For instance, some employers see workers over 50 years old as inflexible and unproductive; other employers want to hire older workers because they are reliable and have valuable experience.

Obviously a criminal or drug related history is a major burden that most people in the job market don't have. We discussed such problems in the section **Facing Our Ex-Offender Status**. But you may have other more common barriers to employment. For instance, some employers are still reluctant to hire women, young people, minorities, or handicapped persons. Or you may not have the tools, clothing, or transportation you need to qualify for some jobs.

As you list your liabilities, be honest with yourself. By knowing your weaknesses, you can best prepare to handle them. Often times you can reduce their impact or find a way to overcome them. Despite other people's opinions or your own self-doubt, you have the ability to overcome many barriers that might otherwise make you a poor employee.

WHAT DO YOU WANT TO DO?

Now decide what kinds of jobs you are interested in. Start by making a list of the things you like to do. Also look at your list of strengths; people usually like to do the things they are good at. From these ideas, you can begin to develop a list of jobs that interest you. Remember any jobs you've had in the past that you enjoyed.

If you have trouble thinking of specific jobs, look at the classified ads in the newspaper. Libraries in the free world will have the local newspaper, as well as books that describe jobs in different fields. The *O*Net Dictionary of Occupational Titles* and *Occupational Outlook Handbook* (see the **Reading List**) contain descriptions for several hundred jobs.

■ *Goal Setting*

A ship with no destination has ZERO chance of getting to port. People are no different. We must set a goal before we can achieve it.

For those who have been involved in the criminal justice process for a long time, especially in prison, setting positive, achievable goals is no easy matter. Often we forget the difference between a dream and an illusion. The dream can be achieved; the illusion cannot. Make sure you base your goals on your dreams, not your illusions.

After you have identified your strengths and weaknesses and things you like doing, it is time to set your goals. To be effective your goals need to pass these tests. They need to be:

Conceivable - You should be able to see the goal in your mind so that you can identify what the first few steps would be to achieve it.

Believable - You must truly believe you can reach the goal.

Achievable - Your goal must be something you can actually do with your personal strengths, or with new

abilities you are willing to develop.

Measurable - A goal must be something you can measure so you can tell if you've made it or not. If you say you want to be a better person, you must define specific steps toward that goal so you can see your progress. The more concrete the better. For example, if you say you want to run a mile a day, you can tell when you have reached your goal.

Growth-Producing - Your goal should be positive and constructive – never harmful to you, others, or your community.

Your **short-term goal** must be to find a job that will let you survive and meet your responsibilities. You should aim for jobs you can realistically hope to get right now: the ones that match your strengths and that you are qualified for despite your weaknesses. The clearer your goal, the better off you are. What job are you after? What skills are required? What part of town? What minimum pay do you need to survive? How would you get to the work site?

If you're under a lot of pressure, you may not have much choice about your first job. In short, you may have to take one you don't really want. But you should still keep looking for something you like and are well-suited for. Otherwise you may find that you can't or won't stick with it very long. Be careful: if you lose or leave your first job too quickly, it may be even harder to find the next one.

Your **long-term goal** should be to find a job you enjoy, can do well, and earn a good living at. Such jobs would be more rewarding for you,

but you will need more training, experience, job references, tools, contacts, and so on before you have a good chance at them. When you have the time, find out what you would need to do to be qualified for these jobs. Whatever this means – going to school, serving as an apprentice, or buying tools – learn what the cost will be and how long it will take to become qualified. With all of this information, you can decide whether you're willing to work that hard and pay the price to get that job. Keep in mind that upgrading your education or skills will improve your chances for promotions and advancement.

Make sure your goals are realistic, based on what you have decided you can and will do, now and later. You probably won't be able to land a management position or a big salary just yet, no matter how much experience or education you have. But if you are successful in your short-term goals, you will have a better chance of reaching the long-term ones.

Do not devote yourself to a goal until you know what it will take to get there and decide that you are willing to spend the time and effort it requires. And don't plan for a job that is closed to you because you're an ex-offender or have some other barrier that you can not or have chosen not to overcome. Last, don't plan on reaching a goal through short cuts or lucky breaks; there is no substitute for the real thing!

■ *Develop an Action Plan*

With your goals in mind, write out a plan for how you are going to accomplish them. Your plan would start with the things you need to do to prepare – working on your attitude, your resume, and so on – and go on to include the actual job search methods described in **Conducting the Job Search**. You may also make plans for getting help in the community, getting more education and training, or finding a better job later on. If you have several practical goals, you can make a plan for each one.

Whatever it will take to reach your goal, it belongs in your plan. Be specific about what you need to do and when, as discussed in the sections on **Strategy** and **Managing Your Plan**. Be sure to break your overall plan into small steps you can manage. As you do this, you will get a clearer picture of what you need to do to reach your goal.

Your plan doesn't have to be complicated or take up a lot of your time if you are desperate for a job right now. A simple, direct approach will make you more effective and actually save you time and effort.

Be smart. For every plan, you should have a back up. Realistically, you cannot expect to find what you're looking for immediately. So your plan needs to be flexible, with alternatives in case your original goals aren't practical right now. As things change and you learn more, be ready to revise and update your efforts as often as needed to keep moving forward.

▪ *Establish a Survival Plan*

One essential part of a job search is a survival plan. Job hunting is demanding and stressful by itself. If you must also struggle to survive, you will have to include your survival needs in your plan.

The first step is to figure out how much cash you have now and how much, if any, you can count on during your job search. Next, determine your weekly expenses. This includes basic living expenses such as food and shelter, and also the expenses you will have due to job hunting. Job search expenses might include a uniform or work clothes, transportation, phone calls, stationery, postage, photocopies, child care, and so on.

Now figure out how long you can survive on the cash you have available. If you're getting help with some survival needs – for example, living with family or in a halfway house – decide how long you can count on that help. This will tell you how long you have to find a job before you go completely broke.

People who have plenty of resources and can afford to be choosy often take several months to find the job they want. You may not be able to go that long without work. In fact, you may not have any cash at all. In that case, cut any expenses you can and seek help from loved ones and community agencies.

Find ways to survive – working day labor jobs, staying in overnight shelters, staying longer in the halfway house, taking an extra part-time job – and fit these into your survival and job search plans. Be creative, be ready for hardship. This is what it takes to get up after a hard fall.

▪ *Necessary Documents*

While making your plans, be aware

of any documents you will need in order to get the kind of job you want. Above all, you must be able to supply your Social Security card or number. If your job will require you to drive, make sure you have the right kind of operator's license and that your driving record is good enough to satisfy your employer's insurance company. If your proposed job requires a special license, certificate, or union card, decide how you are going to get the needed documents as quickly as possible.

Since 1986, every new employee is required to show documents proving he or she has the legal right to work in the United States. A U.S. passport, green card, or employment authorization document will satisfy this requirement. Other documents or combinations of documents that identify you and prove you have a right to work in the U.S. will also meet the requirement. An example is a drivers license (or state-issued identification card) with your photograph, along with a Social Security card that is valid for employment.

You must fill out a form and show your employer these documents within three days after you start to work. If you don't have the documents, you must show proof that you have applied for them. Then you have 21 days to provide them to the employer. It will be much easier for you (and your employer) if you collect all needed documents before you start job hunting.

You will be asked to supply identification over and over again, so expect it and be prepared. You can find out about the documents you need from the U.S. Citizenship and Immigration Service, the Social Security Administration, and drivers license offices for your state, or ask at a library or workforce development agency for information.

■ *Strategy*

Along with the plan you develop for your job search, you need a strategy that will let you use your time to your best advantage. You must decide how to find job leads, how to approach employers, and how much time to devote to each task.

Job search is basically a numbers game. The more people you can contact the better your chances of getting a job and getting it quickly. Consider every possible method of job search and allocate your time to each according to how successful you think it will be.

Your strategy should also allocate your time based on how much ground you have already covered using a given method. If you plan to devote most of your time to networking, then once you have contacted most of the people in your network and gotten it established, you can shift some of that time to another area.

For most people with a criminal record, the following is the best strategy for finding a job.

1. Answer every newspaper ad that fits into your plan. Usually there are not many ads that a person can respond to in any given week. Since most responses will be by letter, fax, e-mail, or phone call, this will not take much of your time.
2. If you have access to a computer and the Internet, identify some

web sites that have listings in your geographic area for the type of job you are seeking. Check these web sites and respond to any ads that fit into your plan. Again, this should not take a lot of your time.

3. Use the services of the state and local government (for example, workforce development offices) and private social service agencies. They can help you make contact with employers and sometimes even set up interviews for you. Although they may not get you a job, they are available and often are free. Except for the initial contact, they usually don't take much time.

   In addition, the agency people you meet are sometimes willing to become a part of your network or may take a special interest in you. Your parole officer or probation officer may also provide you with job leads.

4. Invest a lot of your time and effort in building a strong and extensive network. This will take a lot of planning, contacting, and follow up. This should be where you allocate most of your time.

5. Locate and contact employers yourself as often as you can. This takes research and planning, as described in **Conducting the Job Search**.

6. Follow up with employers, agencies, and people in your network.

Note that the use of recruiters or private employment agencies is not a recommended strategy. The reasons for this are discussed in the section on **Finding Job Leads**.

■ *Managing Your Plan*

No matter how good your plan, if you don't make it happen you won't see any results! Managing your plan requires more than just carrying out each step. You must also evaluate your progress and make decisions about how much time to spend on different approaches. If you aren't getting the results you expected, you may need to adjust your plan.

After you've outlined your plan, you should break it down into *action steps* – the specific things you must do to make the plan work. Your plan should provide a schedule for each week and contain some goals for what you expect to accomplish in that week. At the end of the week, you should review your progress and then prepare action steps for the next week.

When you do something which will require follow up later, go ahead and schedule it. That way you won't forget. Your weekly schedule should include time for networking, research, contacting employers, and interviews, or whatever you have decided on as your strategy. You should schedule a full work-week for yourself, eight hours a day, five days a week. This will increase your self-confidence and make you more business-like in your approach to potential employers.

You can keep your schedule in a notebook, in a scheduling book or planner available at office supply stores, on a computer, on a calendar, or you can use 3 by 5 cards and arrange them by date in a file box. The cards or notebook will let you keep more information, but a calendar or planner will give you a clearer picture of your responsibilities for the week and will let you balance your workload.

Be sure you keep good records of what you have done: who you have contacted, how and why you contacted them, what you told them or gave them, copies of letters you sent, what is to happen next and when. This way you can keep track of what you've already done and what is left to do. It makes a bad impression if you can't remember what you told someone or what information you have already given them.

Set realistic goals for yourself each week: number of calls to make, number of letters to send out, number of applications to make, hours you will spend doing research, people you will ask to join your network, etc. At the end of the week, you can review your success in meeting your own goals, even if you don't have a job in your pocket yet.

There's a lot to do in job hunting. To have only one goal – to get a job – can leave you with a sense of failure if you don't find one soon. But as long as you are out there looking, you are not failing. When you feel depressed or confused, look back at your schedule and realize how much you have really learned and accomplished. The secret is to just stick with it!

Conducting the Job Search

What's Out There

Once you have defined what you're looking for and figured out how to survive during the job search, it's time to really get serious! Now you are ready to comb the community for leads and all-important interviews.

■ *Networking*

Networking is the skill of using your personal contacts to learn about job openings and other useful information. This makes it possible for you to reach many more people than you could as an individual person.

To do a good job of finding a job, you need to be in twenty-five places at once. *You* can't be, but your network can. So get to know more people; use every contact you have. Everyone you know needs to be aware that you're looking for work. The number-one mistake of job hunters is they don't tell other people that they are looking for a job.

Sit down and make a list of all the people you know: family, friends, neighbors, former employers and co-workers, former classmates and teachers, clergy, church members, members of clubs, social or recreational groups and support groups you know of or belong to, business people, criminal justice personnel, anyone you can think of.

Networking is a simple step-by-step process.

1. List the name and contact information (address, phone number, e-mail address, etc.) of everyone you can think of; don't leave anyone out.
2. Contact each person on your list and explain what you're looking for.
3. Give each person a copy of your resume or qualifications and ask for advice and help.
4. Express your interest and appreciation, but remember to be a good listener.
5. Follow up on any suggestions the person makes.
6. Contact each person in your network regularly to let them know your progress.
7. Let everyone know when you get a job, and remember to show your gratitude for their willingness to help.

Along with this informal networking, you may want to use the techniques described later in **Mentors and Professional Relationships**.

30

■ Finding Job Leads

In addition to networking, there are a number of ways to find job openings. Let's look at the most common ones.

1. Your state employment agency or workforce development office is the obvious place to begin. It will not offer any magical remedy, but it would be silly not to register and take advantage of any help you can get. Learn about job listings, which are posted daily, and how to follow up. And be sure to get information on the Work Opportunity Tax Credit and Federal job bonding program. These programs are some of the few benefits to help you as an ex-offender.

Most state employment services offer One-Stop Career Centers (web site www.careeronestop.org), which include a variety of useful employment services. Many of these centers provide computer access to America's Job Bank (www.ajb.org), offer testing and counseling services, and assist job seekers in writing resumes. For more information on these services, and to locate the center nearest you, check out these useful U.S. Department of Labor web sites: America's Career InfoNet (www .acinet.org) and America's Learning Exchange (www.servicelocator .org).

2. Some special programs work specifically with ex-offenders. These programs are run by the government or by private community service or faith-based agencies. They may offer services that aren't available through the state employment agency, such as special counseling or pre-employment workshops. Take advantage of

anything that's available in your location, but remember to think of any program as a resource, *not* a solution!

3. Company and employment web sites include a wealth of information on jobs, from resume advice and salary information to job postings. In fact, millions of job openings are listed on the Internet each day. Many employers list job vacancies on their own web sites. Others use public employment web sites such as America's Job Bank (www.ajb.org), or commercial employment web sites, such as www.monster.com, www.hotjobs. com, www.careerbuilder.com, or www.flipdog.com.

These job sites cover the entire country, but they generally give you a way to focus on jobs in your local area. You may also find web sites, for instance the local newspaper's, that list local job openings. Web sites change often, so if any of these links don't work, you can find other sites by using a search engine and searching for words like "job hunting" or "job search."

If you're new to using the Internet, it may help to review a book on how to search for a job online. Two good examples are *America's Top Internet Job Sites* and *Guide to Internet Job Searching* (see the **Reading List**). As you will discover, the Internet is a wonderful tool for researching jobs. Many web sites will also allow you to apply for jobs or post your resume online. If you don't have Internet access, you can use the free Internet connections available to the public through a local library or One-Stop Career Center.

4. Classified ads in your local

newspaper are the way most people look for job openings. However, this can be a hard way to actually get a job, because everybody else is looking there, too.

5. The Yellow Pages of your local telephone book will help you identify the businesses that offer the kind of job you are looking for. You can then call to ask if they have any job openings and how to apply. This is a simple, inexpensive way to research a community. However, don't ever try to sell yourself by phone. Use the call to get as much information as possible and find out how to apply.

6. Temporary services can be a good way to get a new start. They let you earn some money while looking for a permanent position. This gives you a chance to find out what kind of work you want to do and what kind of company might hire you. You are also building a work history instead of another gap in your resume.

Sometimes a temporary job may give you a head start if there is an opening for a permanent job with that company. This can be a real advantage for an ex-offender. It gives you a personal track record with the company to help offset any prejudice you face due to your criminal record.

In the past most temporary jobs seemed to be for clerical workers, but today temporary services offer many different kinds of jobs and represent a significant part of the work force. They are listed in the Yellow Pages under "Employment Agencies" or "Employment Contractors – Temporary Help," or you can search on the Internet for "temporary jobs."

7. Bulletin boards in offices, companies, and schools are a good place to check. Sometimes job openings are posted there and nowhere else.

8. Company personnel offices are an obvious source of leads. It's always smart to call, write, or drop in to ask what's available. You should also ask what other jobs may be opening up in the future and when. Just be courteous and brief.

9. Help Wanted signs are an invitation to apply. They are used most often for low-pay, high-turnover types of jobs. Although those jobs don't seem attractive, they may offer you a chance to get on the payroll quickly. If you see a Help Wanted sign at a business you are interested in, respond as quickly as you can. If you can't apply right then, try to get a phone number to call, check availability, make an appointment, or take an application form you can fill out and return later.

10. News items and stories, especially in the Business Section of the local newspaper, often carry valuable information about businesses that are starting up, doing well, expanding, or hiring.

11. Libraries have a lot of information about the job market, including directories of local businesses and companies across the country. The directories will help you identify potential employers and get the name and number of a contact person. They also contain information you should know about the company before you go for a job interview. If you don't have access to the Yellow Pages, a newspaper, or a computer, you can find them at the library. The librarian on duty will help you find the information you need.

12. A walk-in approach works with some businesses. If prepared, you may want to walk into the business without an appointment and ask to speak with the owner or personnel director in person. Ask the receptionist or other employee if someone will meet with you. Be ready to fill out an application or to be interviewed on the spot.

13. A private employment agency is a resource that most job hunters think of. We hope they can find the jobs we have missed. Employment agencies charge a fee for placing people in jobs. Usually the employer pays the fee, but for some hourly and low-salary jobs, it is the employee who pays.

In order to get paid, the service has to "sell" a job seeker to a business that is looking for an employee. Most agencies won't present a person with a criminal record to a client, even when this person is very skilled and experienced. Therefore, it's usually a waste of your time to contact an employment agency.

If you do go to a placement service, *remember that its application can be a binding contract*. If you get a job with a company they didn't refer you to, you could still be required to pay their fee even though you believe you got the job on your own.

Anytime you go out into the community, be dressed and prepared as if for an interview. The first impression you make will have a big impact on how much help you get or your chances for an interview.

Contacting Employers

"Your goal at this point is very simple: to get an interview! That's the point when you know you have a chance of getting hired."

You have a number of reasons for approaching an employer. Your first goal is to get information about the business and its needs; the second, to make contact and introduce yourself; and finally, to get an interview, which is your opportunity to sell yourself. As you identify possible job leads, put the openings on your weekly schedule of things to do and make contact with the employer as soon as possible. It's not complicated: do they need a good, productive employee?? If so, there is a good reason to sit down and visit because you are committed to being just THAT!

For those still in jail or prison when you read this, be realistic about your current limitations. Sending a sad plea for a job – when you don't know the employer, don't know if there is a job opening, and don't know when you will be available – is a waste of your time and postage. Better at this point to do your homework. Complete your self-evaluation. Find out what the company does and what type of workers it needs, how to apply, etc., so you will be ready to approach them when you get out. *Preparation is the key!*

■ *First Contact*

You can make your initial contact with an employer by phone, by sending a letter or e-mail, or in person. Your purpose is to find out about their operations, needs, job openings, application procedures, the qualifications they are looking for in job applicants, their location, hours, etc. If possible, you should get the name of the person to see or write to when you apply for a job.

BY PHONE

The phone is a great way to answer an ad in the newspaper or to contact businesses listed in the Yellow Pages. Unless you already have the name of someone to talk to, you should ask to speak to the person in charge of Personnel or Human Resources. Then introduce yourself, explain that you are looking for a job, and ask what openings they have available. Be prepared to describe the type of job you want and your qualifications. For any openings that interest you, ask about the job duties, required qualifications, and how to apply. Keep it brief and straightforward. If they don't need anyone, ask if they know anyone who does.

A telephone is an impersonal tool, best used for obtaining general information, *not* for building a relationship or getting a decision. Anything personal or in-depth needs to be done face to face, not by phone. If you can schedule an interview in a phone call, that's great. But leave any detailed discussion for the interview.

How people respond to you over the phone is largely dependent on your attitude as it comes across in your tone of voice, choice of words, and courtesy. We all respond best to a telephone request when the caller shows respect for us and asks for our help. The Golden Rule is a perfect guide for telephone communication: treat others as you want to be treated.

BY LETTER OR E-MAIL

You can also send a short letter to get basic information about an employer. This is a discovery process. You should briefly explain that you're looking for a job and ask what openings they have available in your areas of interest, what qualifications are required, and how to apply. Inquiring by letter is the ideal approach for someone still locked up, although it is likely that your status as an inmate will be noted on the envelope. Once on the streets, contact by phone or e-mail is quicker and generally preferred.

A letter of inquiry should be brief, neat, and business-like. Don't waste your time or theirs, especially not with details of your status in the criminal justice system. At this point, you're not selling anything. You just want to know what they are looking for in an employee.

When you get their answer, you can decide which job, if any, you will apply for. The information about type of job and necessary qualifications will help you decide how to present yourself, whether to send a resume, which strengths to emphasize in your application, and so on. Don't be surprised if they refer you to their web site for a list of openings and procedures instead of sending you printed information.

If you have access to a computer, be sure to check a company's web site to learn about the organization and its employment needs and procedures. Though this may be impossible from inside a facility, it is a useful way to gather needed information in the free world. Based on what you learn from the web site, you may decide to send your letter of inquiry by e-mail. In fact, many business people today prefer to communicate by e-mail, since it is quicker and gives them an immediate record of their correspondence.

IN PERSON

In some cases, you may decide to approach the employer in person. This was described as a "walk-in" in the **Finding Job Leads** section. This would be most appropriate for a small business where the owner or manager is available to greet the public, or in a business that hires a lot of people for non-professional positions and has a hiring or personnel department for this purpose. Examples would be construction jobs, mechanic work, fast food or retail stores, some government jobs, or businesses that have posted Help Wanted signs. If you're not sure whether to inquire in person, ask a receptionist or other employee if it's OK.

If you decide to make contact in person, you should prepare as if you were going to a job interview. In some cases, that may be what you will get. Study the sections on **The Job Application**, **The Resume**, and **The Interview** to get ready. You may just ask for background information such as you would ask for by phone or by letter. But you may have a chance to fill out an application or even talk to the owner or manager

about a specific job opening. So be prepared!

▊ *To Apply*

After gathering information about a job opening, you need to actually apply for the job. The information you have collected will help you decide what method to use and what kinds of information you should provide when you apply. You may apply by letter or e-mail, in person, or by filling out an application on a computer – depending on what the employer prefers and what is possible in your circumstances.

Inmates often apply for jobs while still incarcerated, in the hope of being hired and thus improving their chances of release. This is unrealistic in most cases, because the employer will want an interview first. No one is going to hire a convict on the blind. The best you can hope for is a formal confirmation that they will be willing to interview you after release. A firm job offer only comes after the employer has looked you in the eye.

BY LETTER OR E-MAIL

You can prepare a short letter stating what job you are applying for and enclosing your resume. Or instead of sending the resume, you may write a longer letter where you describe your qualifications and work history. Such letters should still be brief, just one to two pages.

Address your letter to a specific individual whenever possible. Your application is more likely to get personal attention that way. Be *sure* to spell the name and mailing address correctly. If you don't have the name of a specific person, start your letter "Dear Sir or Madam:".

In your letter, state which job you are applying for, mention how you learned of the job opening or employer, and explain why you are qualified for the position. If you aren't using a resume, you should describe your qualifications and experience in the letter. If you are enclosing your resume, mention your qualifications and refer the employer to the resume for more details. You may also want to explain why that particular company or position interests you.

Close the letter by asking for a response or interview. Be sure to put your address in your letter, not just on the envelope, and include a phone number where you can be reached. Obviously this is not the right approach from inside a cell ... another reason you have to be in the free world to make these kinds of moves.

The finished letter should be informal but business-like, and not too familiar or over-confident. It should be neatly typed (or handwritten) on quality paper, and it *must* be correct in grammar, spelling, and punctuation. Never send a form letter, but develop a basic letter that you can easily change to fit different employers and jobs. Proof read the finished letter several times for even the slightest error and ask other people to review it, also. Remember to sign the letter, and be sure to keep copies of anything you send out.

If you have access to a computer and e-mail, and if the company accepts applications by e-mail, you can send this letter by e-mail instead of typing and mailing it. Be sure to include your complete contact information – your address and phone number as well as your e-mail address. Avoid using fancy fonts or backgrounds in your e-mails. These may not look the same on the recipient's computer and may make your information harder to read. If you are sending your resume, you may include it in the body of your e-mail or send it as attachment.

IN PERSON

If it suits the employer, you may want to apply in person. This procedure will usually include filling out an application form and perhaps some tests (for example, a drug test, skills test, or sometimes a personality inventory). You may also get an interview on the spot, so again, be prepared.

BY COMPUTER

Some companies are now asking job seekers to fill out their job application on a computer. The computer may be at the company's office or retail location, or you may be able to complete the application on the Internet. The questions and the information you need to provide are the same as for a paper form. However, the procedure might seem hard if you're not used to working with a computer, so try to get some practice ahead of time.

Follow Up

Whenever you make contact with an employer, you should keep a record of what you did and note it on your weekly schedule. Also make a note on your future schedule that you are expecting a response from the employer. If the employer doesn't tell you when to expect a reply, allow about 10 days. If you don't get the response by the scheduled date, it is time to follow up.

This follow up can be done by letter, phone call, or e-mail, depending on the company's preference and how you contacted them originally. If you made the original contact in person, you may want to follow up in person as well.

You should **never** complain about the delay but simply state that you had written or made application on such-and-such a date and were wondering if the company would be able to respond to your inquiry or application. You may want to add a brief statement about your interest in the job or your qualifications – something that would reinforce or add to the information in your original contact.

The Job Application

"An application is the first screening tool an employer uses to collect information on a potential employee."

The way you present yourself on the job application has a major impact on whether or not you get an interview and a chance at the job. Even if you provide a resume, many employers also ask you to fill out an application form.

Before we get into the technical points of filling out an application, let's deal with the pressing issue of your background as an ex-offender.

■ *Overcoming Your Criminal Record*

"The dreaded question: Have you ever been convicted of a crime?"

Always assume that you will be asked, in some way or other, if you've been arrested or convicted of a crime. How you deal with this is, naturally, very important. If the law requires you to disclose, there is no choice to be made. If not, you've got to decide what you are going to do. This decision should be made *before* you walk in the door. Frankly, it's always best to prepare to be honest and direct about your history, as we discussed in **The Big Question**.

Remember that you will be held accountable for the information you put on a signed application. If you lie and the employer finds out, you can be fired just for lying. Therefore, you must admit your criminal past on the application before you discuss your record in an interview or bring it up later, after you've been hired. The best approach is simply to admit that you've been in trouble ("Yes, I have been arrested/convicted and will discuss the details at the interview"). It is not advisable to go into your history in depth on the application; that can be done in the interview if necessary.

So, what are your options when the application asks about your criminal history?

1. *You can lie and say "no."* This happens all the time and it may help you get the job, if the company doesn't check your background very carefully. But you will always live with the danger of being found out and

fired for lying on your job application. This can make you very uncomfortable and even hurt your performance on the job.

2. *Or you can just say "yes" and/or offer to "discuss in detail at the interview."* By this means you postpone telling the facts until you are face-to-face with the interviewer. This has been a popular response for many years and is recommended by most experts. On the bad side, this answer indicates you do in fact have a criminal history, which may keep you from getting an interview. Your record will surely have to be dealt with in the interview. On the good side, you bit the bullet and told the truth, and your answer does not actually give any heavy details.

   Although the application may ask for details, it's best NOT to give them. However, if you must provide details in order to be considered, keep your explanation simple and brief. You should state your offense, when it occurred, the sentence, and your current criminal justice status (such as, on parole or probation until 20__, or parole completed 20__).

3. *Last, you may choose to leave the question blank.* Although the best advice is to fill in all the blanks, this strategy may work some of the time. If the job is not highly paid, doesn't carry a lot of responsibility, and there are a lot of applicants, a blank may be overlooked or may not seem important to the person screening the application forms. Often, however, a blank space, especially this one, draws attention, causing the interviewer to ask you why you didn't reply. If you're applying by computer, you may not be able to complete the application and submit it until you have completed all the blanks.

Above all, your goal is to get an interview where you can sell yourself in person as a valuable worker. To make best use of such an opportunity, you must be well-prepared. Study **The Interview** section to start getting yourself ready.

■ *Hints for Filling out the Application*

The following suggestions relate to filling out a job application on paper. Much of the advice is also appropriate for applications on a computer, since the information requested is generally the same.

Before you put pen to paper, check it out. Read the application all the way through before you begin filling it out. (For a computer form, this means scroll down to the bottom of the page, which may not be visible on the computer screen when you first look at it.) Some applications have instructions or comments you should be aware of on the last page or section. It is important to follow directions carefully because it shows the employer that you can read and follow instructions and that you are alert and careful.

Beware the fine print. In many cases, especially on forms used by large companies, there are directions in fine print under some of the headings, for example, "complete in your own handwriting," "please print," or "put last name first."

Be prepared with your identification. Have your Social Security number, your drivers license, and the names, addresses, and phone numbers of people who have *agreed* to give you a reference. You may also take copies of reference letters in case you are asked to submit them with the application. Review the suggestions for using people as references in the section **Support from Others**.

Verify your employment history in advance. Many people don't remember the exact dates when they started or quit their previous jobs, or their job title, salary, or supervisor, especially if it's been a long time. To refresh your memory, you can write to your former employers and ask them to verify this information. Enclose a stamped post card addressed to you with these items written on the card and spaces for their answers. This way you can be sure the information on your resume and application form agrees with their records.

Say "salary negotiable" if the application form asks what salary you want and you aren't sure what to ask for. This way you can find out how much they will offer before you price yourself too high or too low.

Make sure you give a phone number, along with any other way you can be reached, such as an e-mail address or fax number. If you don't have a phone, arrange with someone you know to take messages for you. Be sure the person knows that you may be getting calls on their phone.

When you put this phone number on the application, write "message" beside it.

Create a master application form. Get an extra application form and fill it out completely and perfectly. Double check it for accuracy, spelling, correct names, addresses, and starting and ending dates of your previous jobs, names and titles of supervisors, and reason for leaving each job. Keep this master form and take it with you when you fill out any job application. It is much easier to complete a well-written application if you don't have to recreate the information each time.

Fill out the form carefully. Copy your information from the master form, but don't copy blindly. Make sure to give just the information requested on the form, and in the order requested. Take the time to make your application look neat and well-organized. Remember, all that is left of you when you leave is that piece of paper. How it looks represents you! Fill out all the blanks. If they do not apply to you, put in a dash mark or N/A (for Not Applicable) to show that you didn't just overlook the question.

Don't get frustrated by writing the same information time after time. This can get boring, but a different person reads each form and any application you fill out could lead to a job. So complete each form carefully and neatly.

■ *Common Mistakes*

1. Applications often ask what school you graduated from. Many people write just the name or even the initials of the

school. Unless you graduated from Harvard, be sure to give the full name of the school and the city and state where it is located. Not many interviewers know where Mt. Sterling High School is located.

2. Some people forget to sign the application when it is finished.

3. Women often ignore any questions about military service. Everyone should enter N/A (Not Applicable) if he or she was not in the military.

4. Some applicants use a pencil. The pencil tends to fade or smear very quickly, which makes the application messy and hard to read. If you aren't comfortable writing with a pen, get an erasable pen.

5. Applicants forget to re-read the form, carefully and word-for-word, after they have finished. Thus they don't correct any careless mistakes they might have made.

6. If the application form has a section for comments, most applicants write a simple statement like "I would really like to have this job." Instead you should explain why you want to work for that company instead of someplace else or what you have to offer that would make you a valuable employee. This is a great way to get into conversation later during an interview.

7. Fuzzy information in the job history section. For instance, listing "machinist" but not listing the exact machines you have worked with or "data processing" and not listing the equipment and software you are familiar with.

Fill out the application form as though your future depended on it. IT JUST MIGHT!

The Resume

■ *What Is It, What's It For?*

A resume is a written "sales tool" you create to present yourself as valuable to an employer. The purpose of giving a resume is to focus positive attention on yourself by briefly explaining your employment goals, job history, education, experience (paid and unpaid), and accomplishments.

If you are looking for more than one type of job, you should develop a different resume for each type. The resume should emphasize the education, skills, and experience that fit the type of job you are applying for. Don't waste time describing your ability to repair a car if you are looking for a job servicing air conditioners.

Depending on the type of job you are seeking, a resume may or may not be needed. Jobs that don't require writing skills, such as mechanic, construction, janitorial, or restaurant work, are less likely to ask for a resume. However, having a resume will help you organize your information, identify your strong points, and present yourself in a positive light. It may also help you appear more stable and reliable.

If you are in prison or trying to establish yourself in another city or state, it's *very* smart to create a simple resume to represent yourself. This way you can be in a lot of places at once, making maximum use of your time, energy, and contacts.

■ *The Parts of a Resume*

Most resumes include the following parts.

■ *Personal Information* - This includes your name, local address, and phone number (day and evening), and e-mail address if you have one. Some people also include information such as age, sex, height, weight, health and marital status, but this is not recommended. If it might point up a potential weakness as a job candidate, you should definitely not mention it. And it's better not to include hobbies and personal interests unless they relate to the job you are applying for.

■ *Job Objective* - This is a brief statement that describes the type of job you are looking for or the title of a position you know is open. It isn't necessary when applying for jobs without much responsibility, but it is useful because it gives focus to your resume. It can include the skill level of the job you are seeking (for example, "entry level" or "responsible position"), the type of industry or business you want to work in, and the skills and strengths you will apply in this job. The information in the rest of the resume should be chosen to reinforce your qualifications for this objective. You should not include your salary history or expectations on your resume unless a company specifically asks for that information.

■ *Work Experience* - You can list your work history either by date (a

chronological resume) or by type of work (a functional resume). If you organize by *date*, you will list the jobs you have held in order of the dates you held them, beginning with your most recent job and working backwards. Near the left margin, you would put the starting and ending dates of each job. This may be the month and year for recent or short-term positions, or just the year for older, long-term jobs. After the dates, you list your job title, the name of the company, and a brief description of your job responsibilities. The job description should emphasize the types of experience that would make you qualified for the job you are seeking.

If you organize by *type of work*, you would list the functions or job positions you have held. For instance, you might list Advertising, Auto Mechanic, Waitress, or Bricklayer. Following the function, you would describe your experience, skills, and accomplishments in that area. This type of resume can be useful for people who have worked in a lot of different fields, as it helps them focus on the areas that relate to the job they are applying for. It is also useful for people who have had a lot of jobs, have changed jobs often, or who have gaps in their work history. An interviewer will realize that you could be hiding something, so expect to be asked for details of where you worked and when. You can include a separate section that lists your previous jobs and the dates you worked there.

■ *Education and Training* – Here you list the schools or training programs you have graduated from. For academic education, you should list the highest degree you have achieved first, the date received, the school and its location, and the area you specialized in. For vocational training, you should name the type of training or the certification achieved, the date received, the school and its location. You may also include short workshops or continuing education classes if they are appropriate for the job opening. If you have training in a lot of different areas, list only those that relate to the job you are applying for.

■ *Skills* – List any specific skills that relate directly to the job opening. These might be general skills such as "good communications skills," "work well with people," or they might be job-related skills such as "experienced in Microsoft Excel and QuickBooks" or "experienced forklift operator."

At the end of the resume, you may state, "References available upon request." If you're short of space, you can omit this statement. The employer will assume this is the case, since it is the accepted way to handle references. On a separate sheet of paper, list three to five people who have agreed to serve as a personal or work-related reference for you (see **Using People as References** later in this book). Give each person's name, title if appropriate, address, and phone number; you may also give the person's e-mail address if he or she has agreed. You will only give this paper to employers who are interested in hiring you and want to verify your references. This way you are protecting the privacy of the people who have agreed to help you until their help is really called for.

■ *Tips for Writing a Resume*

Compose a general resume that you can change to suit the different jobs you apply for. When you apply for a particular job, find out the duties and requirements for that job. You can then revise your resume to show that you have the skills and experience required for the job.

Use short sentences beginning with action words to describe your job duties, experience, and skills. Stress your accomplishments. Ideas for your accomplishments may have come out during your self-evaluation.

Be specific; don't use vague terms or information that doesn't relate to the job. Don't say, "Increased production." Instead say, "Increased production by 25%," "Supervised staff of five," "Overhauled transmissions for General Motors and Ford F250 pickups," or whatever is appropriate. Include specialized terms that are common in the business or industry you want to work in. These will catch the attention of an interviewer and may also help you stand out if you post your resume on an employment web site.

Write a first draft of your resume, improve on it, then write a second draft before you do a final copy. Ask someone to proof read the final version for content, typing, spelling, and grammatical errors. Ask for ideas on how to improve it.

A resume should be brief, neat, and to the point. One page is recommended, two pages should be plenty if you have a lot of information to cover. It should be typed or printed from a computer in a font that is clear and large enough to be easy to read. If you don't have access to this equipment, you may be able to use it at a public library or employment service center. If you can afford it, you may find a secretarial service or a quick print shop that will produce your resume for you.

You should keep the format of your resume as simple as possible so it will be clear and easy to follow. Some people have tried to make their resumes look sophisticated or unusual in order to stand out from the crowd, but this can backfire if the resume is hard to read when copied. And if you plan to send your resume by e-mail or post it online, find out what format is preferred.

When in doubt, send it in plain text format; this is most likely to be readable on any computer.

There are many excellent books that describe how to write resumes and some that go into more detail about using resumes on the Internet. Some of these resources are included in the **Reading List** at the end of this book.

Just remember, if you are going to write a resume, take the time to do it right. A job interviewer may see the resume before he or she sees you. So make sure your resume makes a good impression. Have someone else check your work before you send it out.

The Interview

"An interview is simply a special kind of meeting where people exchange information."

During the 30 minutes or so that you are in an interview, you will answer questions about your background, goals, job skills, and experience. At the same time, you will have a chance to ask questions about the company and the job for which you are applying. The purpose of an interview is to let you and the employer find out about each other. The employer's goal is to locate a good employee. Your goal is to get a job offer.

Be Prepared

"Good preparation is critical – it increases your confidence and odds for success!"

When job seekers don't get job offers, often the reason is because they don't prepare thoroughly for each interview. Therefore, try to find out as much information as possible about the potential employer. Company brochures, reference books, present and past employees, the Chamber of Commerce, the Better Business Bureau, and the Internet are all useful sources. Learn about the requirements of the job and

determine how your background and experience qualify *you* for the position.

Next, anticipate potential questions and have your answers ready! Practice your responses to important questions such as, "Why do you want this job?", "Tell me about yourself," or, "Describe your qualifications for this job." Make it a point to be enthusiastic without memorizing your answers.

You should also prepare a list of questions you want to ask toward the end of the interview. This would include information about working conditions, job duties, pay, and benefits. But it should also include questions about how you would fit into the company, how your skills and motivation can contribute, and what opportunities you will have to grow and develop as an employee and a person. These types of questions will help you decide if the job will be good for you. They will also show the interviewer that you can see beyond the next paycheck and have long-range goals and ambitions. See **Sample Interview Questions** for more ideas of questions you may be asked.

For some jobs, you may be tested or go through a screening process before a decision is made about hiring you. This could happen before the interview or could be scheduled during the interview. You might be asked to take a drug test, physical exam, a skills test such as for typing or mechanical knowledge, or a test to identify your personality traits. Although tests can be stressful, you will perform better if you're expecting them.

Control Your Fears

A major step needed for preparation is to take control of your emotions. An interview creates a lot of stress and fear of rejection, so spend at least two hours before the meeting relaxing and collecting yourself. You must know before you walk in exactly how you are going to deal with your ex-offender past. (See **Criminal History** a little later.) Remember that YOU have to be able to deal with it before anyone else can or will.

Cool Your Jets!

Calm down. Everything's going to be all right. Just dedicate yourself to doing the best you can and have faith in your success. Your fate does not rest on the outcome of just one interview; even if you don't get a job offer, you will be much better prepared for the next opportunity. You can help keep your stress down by taking good care of yourself and especially being well-rested. Take a short walk or read something funny to take the edge off before you leave for the interview.

Basic Grooming Tips

Dress for the job. Your grooming has a lot to do with the impression you make on an employer. Cleanliness and neatness are absolutely essential. No one wants to hire a slob.

It's not necessary to spend a lot of money on your clothing, but it should fit well, be clean, neat, and coordinated. The key is to pick your clothes to suit the type of business and the job you are seeking. With money usually tight for former offenders, it's smart to shop at used clothing stores and then have items altered so they fit you well. Just *one* nice outfit (including shoes in good condition and polished) is enough to make the positive impression you desire. You don't have to be on top of this season's fashions. Just choose solid, business-like colors and traditional styles. A white or pastel shirt or blouse with one colorful accent (tie or scarf) will complete the outfit. For a job doing physical labor, work clothes that are clean and neat are acceptable.

Don't smell – either good or bad. Body odor is a poor calling card, but many people are also allergic to some perfumes. So it is safer to avoid cologne or a strong aftershave. Also avoid smoking before the interview, as the odor may be noticeable to the interviewer. Smoking is not allowed at many workplaces today. It is viewed as a health risk that increases a company's insurance costs and as a time waster, since employees may take extra breaks to smoke.

Obviously, the neater and "more together" you are, the better the overall impression you will make. Pay special attention to the condition of your hair, teeth, and nails. Employers will tend to evaluate your attitude and performance by how well you take care of yourself.

"This is your chance to sell yourself to the employer!"

During the interview, the interviewer will be sizing you up in terms of appearance, self-confidence, communication skills, and level of enthusiasm. Before all else, be straight and rested. Arrive early and alone. Be courteous to everyone you meet, not just the interviewer. Some businesses ask other employees for their opinions of job applicants. Also, come organized and prepared: take a note pad and pen, copies of your resume, a list of your references, and your questions about the job and the company.

An interview can be divided into three phases:

■ *Introduction*

The introduction phase may last only a few seconds, but it can play a critical role in your success. This is the time when the interviewer first meets you, sees how you are dressed, shakes your hand, and hears you speak for the first time. This first impression of you will last through the entire interview and afterward.

Greet the interviewer by name and use a firm handshake. Remain standing until invited to take a seat.

Be courteous and patient. Always maintain eye contact by looking the interviewer in the eye while either of you is speaking. Stay alert and let your interest show.

Watch your posture. Sit up straight and keep both feet on the floor; never tilt your chair backward or lean forward and put your hands or elbows on the interviewer's desk.

Often when under pressure we fidget or talk too much. Avoid nervous actions such as playing with objects, cracking your knuckles, etc. Fold your hands in your lap most of the time and try to relax. Be aware of your breathing. If you breathe deeply, it will help relieve your stress.

Hold your head up and speak clearly. Don't use slang or profanity and don't chew gum or smoke (even if offered the opportunity).

■ *Information Exchange*

This phase is the real meat of the interview and takes up the greatest amount of time. This is where you and the interviewer exchange information about the job and the company, and about you and your ability to do the job.

Often the interviewer will begin by telling you about the company and the job. He or she will then ask questions to find out how well-qualified you are and how you can contribute to the company. Besides your job skills, the interviewer will be interested in you as a person. Your personal characteristics – your honesty, dependability, and attitude – have a lot to do with your value as an employee.

In your answers, you want to show that you have the skills and experience to do the job, that you are motivated to succeed, and that you are prepared to fit into the company and work cooperatively with your boss and co-workers.

Stick to the point; don't tell stories or talk about personal, domestic, or financial problems. The interviewer is interested in the company's needs, not in yours. You want to show that you're a good listener, so don't dominate the discussion or interrupt the interviewer. When you have finished answering a question, stop talking.

This is also the time for you to ask questions about the company. Ask about the company's goals, what it is looking for in an employee, and how you can contribute. Show interest. Let your motivation show. Don't limit your questions to the hours, benefits, and salary you would have if you got the job. You might also ask about the opportunity for advancement with the company and whether you would have a chance to improve yourself by learning new skills or getting special training.

BE POSITIVE

What you say during the interview is important. *How* you say it is just as critical! When you respond to questions, the interviewer is observing your ability to communicate well, along with your self-confidence. By all means be direct and honest; don't act slick, evasive, or cute.

Keep your cool at all costs. Never show anger or argue, and be careful not to volunteer controversial opinions, for example about religion, politics, drug usage, or criminal justice. If asked a controversial question, give a mature, balanced response by examining both sides of the question.

Be careful not to criticize former employers when discussing your work history or reasons for leaving prior jobs. If you criticize former employers, you will give the interviewer the idea that you might also become dissatisfied with his or her business.

If you had problems or were fired from a previous job, practice in advance so that you can explain the situation in a neutral way, without putting you in a bad light *or* criticizing your employer. If there is a lot of negative information in your work history, you may explain that you made mistakes in the past but you now know better and are motivated to become a valuable employee.

It is a good idea to avoid *any* negative statements. Strange but true: negative remarks about someone or something else will also rub off on you and leave a negative impression with the person you are talking to. If you want to make a positive impression, *be positive*.

Closing

At some point during the discussion the interviewer will begin to close the interview. He or she will probably thank you for your time and give you a date when the company will let you know if you got the job.

When you can feel that the interviewer is losing interest or wants to end the interview, take the hint. He or she may check the time, shuffle through paperwork, or ask if you have any more questions. At this point, you should help bring the conversation to a close and prepare to leave.

If the interviewer hasn't mentioned a time when you can expect to hear about the job, you should ask what the timetable will be. You could say something like, "Can you give me an idea of when I'll be hearing from you about this job?"

When you exit the interview, you should have one of the following:

1. A job offer,
2. An appointment for a second interview or other screening,
3. The date when you can expect to learn the decision,
4. A clear understanding of where you stand with the company, or
5. A specific time for you to call to learn your status.

Don't leave your future to chance. Make sure – before you leave the interview – that you know what your next step is. Then put that step on your weekly schedule so you will remember to do the appropriate follow up.

How you end an interview is as important as how it began. Be positive, polite, and express appreciation for the chance to interview for the job. Be sure to thank the interviewer for his or her time and the opportunity to be considered for the job. You should close by expressing your interest in the company and the job. This can be done by making a direct statement, for example: "I would really like an opportunity to work for ____ Company; I hope you will give me a chance to show what I can do."

Criminal History

"You want to show the interviewer that you will be valuable as a person and employee *because* of your criminal justice experience, not despite it!"

In the section on **Facing Our Ex-Offender Status**, we reviewed the problems that come with a criminal history. In **The Big Question**, we discussed the pros and cons of disclosing our past. In **The Job Application**, we looked at the best way to disclose our past on paper. Now we will talk about how to reveal our history during the job interview.

As hard as the job search is, *nothing* is more difficult than dealing with your criminal history on a face-to-face basis. Admitting your past on paper is one thing, but explaining it to an interviewer is a lot harder. How well you handle it depends on how much thought, time, and practice you put into it.

Unless we're interviewing for the Mafia, having a criminal history is *never* well-received. So the challenge is to learn how to take this negative and ***turn it into a positive:*** to demonstrate that the experience actually resulted in growth and maturity, and that we are now better, more valuable people because of it.

■ *Howdy - I'm Bob, a Habitual Criminal.*

First, consider what happens in the minds of interviewers when you unfold your past. Usually you can see a red neon "Tilt!" flashing across their foreheads and little puffs of smoke coming out of their ears.

If an interviewer isn't prepared to take your situation in stride, it can disrupt the pace of the interview. Suddenly *you* are in control of what happens next, at a very awkward moment. It becomes your job to help the interviewer cope with this uncomfortable business in a positive way and get everything back on track.

How and When to Discuss Your Past

Once you've made the decision to disclose your past, it's a question of how and when to do it in the best possible way. If you admitted your past on your application, it's sure to come up in the interview. It's only a question of who will bring it up first and how you will deal with it.

Your success will largely depend on your level of honesty, how well you present yourself, and the way you deal with your past. If you make *too little* of your criminal history, it suggests you don't view yourself as responsible for your actions. If you make *too much* of it, your criminal record will overshadow all of your good points. It's a fine line to walk.

Don't forget: people can deal with your past only as well as you have! If you've come to grips with it, have turned it into a painful but useful experience, there is a much better chance that they, too, can mentally put it to rest. Your goal is to show that you have learned from your past and grown beyond it. Courage and practice are essential.

As you prepare mentally and emotionally, remember that *everyone* has a history of past mistakes which has or could have resulted in serious trouble. Your job here is to help the interviewer understand what you did and why without seeming to make excuses. You should make it clear that you accept responsibility for your actions and are sorry for the damage you caused. Also stress that your past mistake has made you highly motivated to improve your

life, and you have learned to be a better person because of it – that you have what it takes to make a good employee if you are hired.

When possible, it's in YOUR better interest to bring it up first because it shows your willingness to look the problem right in the eye. It also takes the burden off the interviewer. Try to slide into it in the discussion phase of the interview with something like this: "On the application I stated that I've had some problems with the law which I would explain in the interview. I'd like to do that now ...."

Or the interviewer may beat you to it and ask you to explain the details of your past. No matter how it comes up, once the door has been opened, go right into the three-minute drill!

THE THREE-MINUTE DRILL

The following steps are a drill that you can use in any interview. You should compose the drill in your head and on paper in your own words, based on your unique situation. Then rehearse to the point that you can calmly, smoothly, and honestly explain your history. This drill should take THREE MINUTES ONLY! When you know exactly how you are going to get through this part of the interview, you will be able to concentrate on the *real* goal of getting the job.

1. Begin by holding your head up and putting your cards on the table: "Out of respect to you and my possible employment here, I should share an unpleasant part of my past," or, "As I pointed out on my application form, I have been convicted of a crime and I'd like to discuss it." Then give the basic background information about your situation.

How this is done is CRITICAL. Maintain eye contact! Be direct, sincere, and as calm as a clam. Be like the weatherman and report. For example, "In 19__ I was arrested and convicted of ____. As a result I was sentenced to ___ years in prison/on probation/parole. I served ___ years and am currently on probation/parole or have completed supervision." Keep it simple and direct: just the facts.

Caution: do **NOT** make excuses or re-try your case!! You cannot undo the past. You want a chance to prove yourself and build a better future!

2. At this moment the interviewer will be very curious about what you did, why you did it, your reaction to your punishment, and the chance you'll do something illegal again. *Remember*, he or she isn't trying to make a judgment about your worth as person, but about your value as a potential employee.

Your purpose is to help the interviewer overcome his or her bias against a criminal. He or she must be able to identify with you and, if possible, understand why you did what you did. Only in this way can he or she see you as a real person rather than a social label.

In truth, the nature of your convictions will play a role in this. Crimes involving sexual misconduct, for example, present special problems because the interviewer is not going to be able to understand or identify with the motivation behind the act. In such cases, as with a history of violence or addiction, it is essen-

tial that you be able to support the fact that you know it was wrong and now have it under control! This typically means that you are active in current, ongoing counseling or a recovery program. In short, you are serious about taking control of your behavior and will do whatever it takes to make that happen.

Make no excuses as you explain, briefly, what you did and why. Present the facts in such a way that the interviewer can grasp what was in your mind or happening in your life that motivated you to make the choice you did. This doesn't mean he or she has to approve of what you did or why, only to UNDERSTAND.

For example, "At the time I committed my crime my judgment was clouded by (drugs, friends, immaturity, financial stress, poor values, etc.), and I made a bad choice as to how to deal with my problems." Or, "At that time, I thought that I could cope with my problems and my personal pain by doing drugs."

3. Next, admit you made a serious error in judgment or surrendered to impulses that were inappropriate, such as rage or greed. Say very directly and sincerely, and in your own words, "I can see that my actions caused a lot of grief for a lot of people. I'm sorry it happened, but it did and I have to deal with that." If there was a victim of your offense, express your concern for them and explain any restitution you have made.

4. You can then distance yourself from that former way of thinking and acting by explaining how your values and decision-making have changed since then ("Looking back, I can see how harmful my actions were").

Your goal at this point is to turn the negative into a positive. Do this by explaining how the experience has forced you to take a hard look at yourself and your values. Show what you have learned and gained from your mistake. "The situation caused me to examine my life and I found a lot that I needed to change. As a result, I am highly motivated to do whatever it takes to grow beyond my past mistakes. This is one important reason I'm so interested in this job."

Remember that people accept a situation better when they understand it. Therefore, your claim to change is best believed when you explain what influenced the change, how you are applying your new insight, and some of the results of that change. You should point out what you've done to grow and improve yourself since your conviction, for example: "I have attended and completed training in _____, completed my GED, joined AA, I've been clean for three years," etc.

Also point out changes in your personal life which make you more stable and a better risk: "I'm now married and have a new son, am an usher at my church, am enrolled in a local trade school, continue to see a counselor once a week," etc. Last, be sure to mention your future goals and plans: "My goal is to advance myself professionally as a _____ and in my spare time to work as a volunteer counselor with the local YMCA," etc.

5. Now be ready to answer some very direct and difficult questions. This is the moment of truth when the interviewer tries to better understand your situation and to test your sincerity and current state of mind. The essential factor here, as with all aspects of this process, is sincerity and honesty ... not just a mask that you wear for the moment, but in FACT!

Tell the interviewer: "I'm aware that my past actions would cause you to question my judgment and character, but I'm willing to do whatever is necessary to prove myself." And if the job requires a high level of trust or responsibility, you may wish to state directly, "I am willing to be watched closely, serve a long probation period, or do whatever it reasonably takes to prove myself to you." Also, if you have had substance abuse problems, offer to take periodic drug tests and to continue with counseling or treatment.

Remember that you don't want the interview to get lost in the issue of your criminal history. Once you have put your past on the table, don't dwell on it unless the interviewer asks for more information. Your goal is to deal with this matter openly and honestly and then *move on*. As soon as comfortable, ask the interviewer if he or she has any more questions and then *change the subject* by asking a question related to the job you are seeking. For example, "If I am hired, what job duties will I have?" This gets the interview back on schedule with the interviewer in charge again.

What Is the Interviewer Looking For?

"The interviewer's job is to hire the right person to help the business be successful."

From beginning to end, the interviewer is trying to determine if you have the qualities the company thinks are valuable to help it make a profit.

To be profitable, a business needs to offer a desirable product or service of good quality at a reasonable price, while operating efficiently and satisfying its customers. To keep its costs low, the business wants to hire the fewest number of employees who can get the job done. If employees are unproductive, unreliable, make a lot of mistakes, cause problems, lie, cheat, or are rude to customers, it costs the business money and eats up the profits.

For the business, this part of hiring is something like guesswork. The company invests time and money when it hires a new worker. If that person doesn't work out, it is expensive to get rid of him or her and to advertise, interview, hire, and train a replacement. If this happens very often, it creates a lot of confusion and the business becomes disorganized and unproductive.

■ *Good Risk or Bad Risk?*

In order to make the right hiring decision, the interviewer is looking for signs of whether the applicant would be a good risk or a bad risk. When he or she interviews someone with no work history or references, or with lots of short-term jobs or

long gaps between jobs, this is a danger sign. It may mean that the applicant is not reliable or doesn't have the skills to keep a job.

A criminal conviction is a *big* danger sign. The interviewer will worry that the person might be dishonest on the job, unwilling to follow company rules, or might get in trouble again and have to be replaced. There is a lot of plain old prejudice in this attitude, but we all know it exists. Also, if the company hires an ex-offender who later causes problems, such as stealing or harming someone, the company may get a lot of bad publicity or even be sued for making a bad hiring decision. So the interviewer will be especially cautious when considering someone with a criminal history.

At the same time, the interviewer will be looking for characteristics that show the applicant has a good chance to become a valuable employee. In addition to good job skills, training, and experience, he or she will look for an applicant who is honest, dependable, hard-working; who has self-discipline and high standards of workmanship; and who will be cooperative, able to get along with others, willing to follow instructions, ready to take initiative, and loyal to the company.

The interviewer also wants an applicant who is stable, both on and off the job. Although your time off is your own, problems in your personal life may have an impact on your job performance. Obviously, someone who has a hangover or uses drugs during lunch break will not perform as well as a more stable, responsible employee. An employee who got arrested last night won't be there to open the store today. And though it is not deliberate, someone who doesn't have reliable transportation or child care may also miss work due to these problems. So personal stability is an important trait in an employee.

The interviewer will be looking for these characteristics on your job application, your resume, and in your interview. It is your task to present yourself so that your positive traits stand out and overshadow your weaknesses.

Sample Interview Questions

Here are some commonly asked interview questions. They fall into five basic categories: personal information about you, information about your criminal history, what you have to offer the company, what you know about the company, and general questions.

1. Tell me about yourself.
2. What are your major strengths?
3. Why should we hire you for this job?
4. What are your major weaknesses?
5. What do you know about our company?
6. Why do you want to work for us?
7. Why were you arrested/convicted?
8. How do we know you won't do it again?
9. What kind of work do you like doing?
10. Where do you see yourself in five years?
11. What motivates you more than anything else?

12. How do you think you could contribute to our company?
13. Why have you had so many jobs?
14. What have you learned from your mistakes?
15. Tell me about your time in prison.
16. What kinds of equipment or machines can you operate?
17. What salary do you want?
18. Are you willing to take periodic drug tests?
19. Describe a situation in a past job where your supervisor insisted that you do something you believed was wrong. How did you handle it?
20. Are you in any form of counseling? Why or why not?
21. Can you get recommendations from former employers?
22. Describe your prior work experience and responsibilities.

In some interviews, you may be asked to describe how you would handle a hypothetical situation or problem that might come up on the job. For example, you might be asked how you would handle an angry customer who wants service while you are busy with other customers.

Follow Up

The interview is over, your work has ended – right? WRONG. Make some written notes about the interview. Write down the name and job title of everyone you met, or keep track of their business cards. Think back over the interview and decide what you could do to improve the next one.

The day after the interview sit down and write a short note thanking the interviewer and expressing your interest in the job. If you believe a note is too formal, you can do this follow up by phone or e-mail.

Look back and recall two or three key points you and the interviewer discussed or that you want to stress. This is a perfect time to re-sell yourself in a subtle way. Be sure to thank the interviewer for taking the time to discuss the job opening with you. You may close by saying that you look forward to hearing from him or her, or that you will get in touch, at the time which was agreed on at the closing of the interview.

If the decision-making date has passed and you haven't heard from the interviewer as promised, you should also call or send another follow-up letter or e-mail. Stay on top of your weekly schedule so these dates don't slip by.

The importance of these contacts and calls is in the interest, enthusiasm, and persistence they demonstrate to an employer. If you don't care enough about the job (or you don't have the self-discipline) to follow up, it will be obvious to the employer that you won't be a valuable employee.

Your calls or letters should always be positive in tone. They should remind the employer of your good qualities so that you will stand out in his or her mind at decision-making time.

Overcoming Rejection

"We cannot control what other people do – but we CAN control how we react to it!"

For better or worse, the experience of being branded a criminal has some unique effects on how we see ourselves and on our relationships with the world around us. This includes our self-image, feelings of belonging, our attitudes, and how we respond when things don't go our way.

Some things are within our power to change and others are not. It is critical to learn the difference! We can never change what has already happened. And in many cases, our criminal record will remain forever. However, we *can* change the reactions of ourselves and others to our past, although it takes time and hard work.

Of those things we can hope to change, very few are immediate. Most will require a lot of time and consistent action on our part. We know our past will create major barriers between us and potential employers, our family, and the general community for some time to come.

Clearly some folks will reject us because of our past behavior and the pain and disappointments we have caused them directly. This is reasonable. We shouldn't get hostile or expect their fears and anger to turn around overnight just because we want it to happen. First we have to give them something to believe in!

On the other hand, you often face blind rejection from people you have never met. Many people already have bad feelings toward *anyone* labeled as a criminal. The way they react to your past often has nothing to do with your actual worth as a person. They are reacting to the picture they have in their heads of what criminals are and do.

Whether you are actually St. Peter or Freddie Kruger is not the point: their attitudes are controlled by blind beliefs, and sometimes fear. What's going on in *their* minds determines how they respond. Their attitudes toward you will *usually* begin to shift when they actually get to know and trust you as an individual. But this requires lots of time, hard work, and patience.

Keep in mind also that some people may find it very hard to give trust because of their *own* problems or past experiences. So don't take blind rejection personally. Although it may keep you from getting what you want, the reasons may not have anything to do with you. Remind yourself that your value is based on *your* attitudes and actions, not on how others react to you.

Since we cannot instantly change the attitudes of others, how do we cope with their suspicion, fear, and rejection? Rather than go crazy, we learn instead to control the way *we react* to them and their attitudes. Learning to control our reactions is the real key to our survival and success.

Avoid a Broken Heart

"Rejection is a normal part of living – never let it break your heart – NEVER!"

Most people are sensitive to rejection and avoid situations that might hurt their pride or self-worth. This is especially true for those who have been labeled criminals and often feel like outcasts from society. For them, the normal risk of rejection while job hunting can do even greater damage to their self-worth. In fact, after ten employers refuse to even interview you, it's easy to get your feelings hurt, go into a deep depression, and become hopeless.

When things get real tough, some ex-offenders throw up their hands and use rejection as an excuse to return to illegal or self-destructive ways. In such a depressed state, it's all too easy to fall back into use of alcohol or drugs just because you're so sad and miserable.

Some people react to the anxiety and stress by getting hostile and defensive ... just plain mean! But this just makes the problem worse: angry people scare employers, and employers don't hire people who scare them! When you walk into a personnel office, you must have your mind in a peaceful place. Gorillas don't get jobs, even in the zoo. Also, if you lose control and begin to have outbursts of anger and violence at home, at work, or on the streets, you will just end up back in jail screaming at the bars.

Keep in mind that when you lose control, you become a victim of *yourself*, of fear, grief, and disappointment. You cannot let your own emotions rob you of the will and courage to keep trying. This is the only true solution: refuse to give up, try again and again until finally you succeed. Remember: *you must not, under any circumstances, let anyone or anything break your heart*. This is the time for true courage and strength. As an ex-con working to reconstruct your life, you need every bit of energy and will power you can muster. So pull yourself right back up and try again, except do it even better.

■ *Some Basic Rules*

■ Be cool at all costs. Remember that you can only lose by going crazy and letting your emotions sweep you away.

■ Look for *positive* ways to release your stress. Seek help from a therapist or talk to a friend so you can stay stable and in control.

■ Stay drug- and alcohol-free. You need all your energy, attention, money, and control at this critical time.

■ Beware of desperation; refuse to be drawn in by false promises of quick-fix solutions that just make things worse.

■ Keep the faith! You *will* score if you stick with it and refuse to let anything break you down.

Use Support System

"Reach out for the encouragement of those close to you."

To overcome rejection, it is important to make creative use of any support you can find. Take a special look at the section **Support from Others** and don't hesitate to reach out for help at this critical time.

It is also wise to sit down with your family and friends. Explain the stress you're under and ask for their emotional support and understanding. Let them know that it's your job to cope and maintain control but you want them to understand why you are sometimes sad, moody, angry, or depressed.

If you find that your emotional state is simply too much to deal with right now, get guidance and support from people trained to provide the special help you need. If your car is broken, you naturally go to a mechanic. The same is true if your way of thinking and acting is on the blink. Be practical and adult about this. Don't let pride or fear stand in the way of a healthy life and the maintenance of your freedom.

Learn From Experience

"Every effort brings you closer to success – never give up!"

Keep trying! Every time you fill out an application or interview for a job, you learn how to do it better. One powerful tool you have is the law of averages. This guarantees that every time you fail you move one step closer to success – just as long as you try again. Most salesmen depend on one out of every ten efforts turning into success. Sometimes we have to extend ourselves and do something 20 times in order to finally get over, but each time the odds get better and better. In the end, we succeed – because now we know enough and have stuck with it!!

▪ *Practice*

Practice does make perfect. The more you rehearse your pitch – in your head and out loud – the smoother and more confident you'll become. Review **The Interview** section, giving special attention to the best ways for disclosing your past. The more comfortable you get with your interview skills, the higher your motivation, confidence, and determination will be.

Why Are You Still Unemployed?

"Continue to study and improve what you do and how you do it."

To get ahead of the game, you have to figure out what you're doing wrong and how to do it better. If you keep trying but nothing works, keep asking yourself "WHY?" If you get off into a self-pity bag, you can tell yourself it's because you're ugly or stupid, or the world is against you. But in reality, you are probably making a few critical mistakes over and over again.

When asked why they reject certain job seekers, many employers list the following reasons: applicants who are poorly prepared, have low motivation (uninterested, unenthusiastic, or don't follow up, for example), a bad appearance, and inadequate work skills.

Therefore, as you evaluate yourself, check to see how you can avoid setting yourself up to fail. You will improve your chances of being hired if you have addressed these problems *before* you walk in the door.

If you have a problem with attitude, preparation, or appearance, it is something you can change right away. It just takes effort and a strong desire to succeed. This whole book is designed to help you overcome those problems. To improve poor work skills will take long-term planning and effort on your part, so start doing something about it as soon as you can. In the meantime, you will have to adjust your goals and approach to fit your limited job skills.

It Only Takes One Good Offer

"Keep the faith! It *will* happen!"

As hard as a job search is, it only takes one good offer to turn it into a success. Sometimes it may feel as though the effort is more than you can handle, but it's all worthwhile when you finally get a job. All the time you're looking, keep focused on your burning desire for achievement and faith in a better future.

Accepting and Keeping a Job

"View this new job as a stepping stone to future growth."

After all your hard work, it finally happens: you get a job offer! Be proud of the fact that your efforts have paid off and you can now take the next step toward your long-term goals. The job opportunity may not be exactly what you would like, but it is still a positive step into the future.

No matter what the nature or conditions of the job, it will offer new opportunities that you don't presently have. It is especially important to have a current job reference when you seek a better position. Employers tend to judge your potential as an employee by what you have done in the past.

Job Selection

"No job is perfect – each has good and bad points. Take a close look and decide what offers the best overall chance to grow and enjoy life."

Sometimes after weeks or months of job hunting, you will suddenly get more than one job offer. If you are lucky enough to have a choice of jobs, be very careful as to which you choose. Think about your goals and which situation offers the best over-all chance to advance yourself. Some things you should consider are the opportunities for training, your chances of advancement, how well the job matches your strengths and interests, and the stability of the company, as well as practical concerns like salary, benefits, hours, and location.

Obviously no job will offer everything you need and want. Each job will have its own drawbacks, such as the distance you have to travel or a shifting work schedule. You have to balance the good with the bad to make the best decision.

As you consider your choices, ask yourself which job offers the best mix of salary, opportunity, and personal satisfaction. If you are on probation or parole, it might be wise to check with your officer to be sure the job you're considering is OK under their rules. Sometimes, as you are working to reconstruct your life, the best job is the one that offers the greatest chance to improve your skills and get a start in a field you really want a future in. And it's real important to be in a situation where you feel comfortable and wanted!

Commitment

"No matter what you elect to do, do it to the very best of your ability!"

Whatever selection you make, once you accept a job, commit yourself to doing the very best you can to make the opportunity a real success! Now is the time to dedicate yourself on three critical levels. First to yourself – to make every effort to develop into the very best person you can be. Second to your employer, who will soon entrust you with new responsibility and opportunity. And equally, to any family and loved ones who have stood by you and supported your efforts.

Job Adjustments

"Every new job brings necessary changes. Give yourself time to get into the flow of things."

Every new job requires some important adjustments, such as changes in our daily schedules and how we take care of personal business. A new job always brings shifts in our home life which may seem to disrupt the ways we are used to doing things. There are also adjustments to be made on the job to cope with demands on our energy and the personalities of the people around us. At first these changes can be very stressful, but after awhile we get into a new routine and things begin to fit into a groove.

Keep in mind that what you're going through is normal; everyone has to deal with these changes when they start a new job. You may feel under a lot of pressure, especially if

you haven't held a real-world job for a while. Just remember to be patient, keep your cool, and pay attention to the new rules of the game.

Job Performance

"Your attitude toward yourself, your job, and other people will have the greatest impact on your success."

In order to be successful and find satisfaction in your new job, you will also have to display the following characteristics:

- *Work Quality* – How well you perform and follow your employer's instructions is the first critical concern. It's the quality of your work which has the most impact on the profit of the company.

- *Dependability* – What every employer looks for are dependable people who take their commitments seriously and do their very best to follow through. Flaky folks just don't last! The best rule is to try to be the kind of employee *you* would want to hire and pay.

- *Be Productive* – Work hard, work fast; doing more with less is the watchword for business today. Finish the task you're working on before you leave for the day. Don't take long lunches or extra breaks. The employer is paying you and wants the full value for this investment.

- *Good People Skills* – A job involves dealing with supervisors, co-workers, and customers. Being friendly and cooperative is very important. A person who gets along well with others is valued a lot more than one who doesn't.

■ *Discipline* – Being a good employee isn't easy; it requires that we learn to discipline ourselves by doing what needs to be done now and not getting side-tracked. This means that when you have a task to do, do it! Be on time, be ready to work, do what is required of you, and meet deadlines. Refuse to be distracted from your goals.

■ *Respect for Property* – The equipment you use or work on is valuable and needs to be treated with respect. This is just as important to you as to your boss. By doing your best to keep others' property in order, you are training yourself to take better care of your own.

■ *Be Thorough* – Don't stop in the middle; finish what you start! No matter how much effort you put into a task, if you don't finish, it doesn't satisfy your job requirements or give you the personal satisfaction of a job well-done.

■ *Handle the Pressure* – Keep a good sense of humor to help you cope with the stress that always comes with deadlines and dealing with other people. Learn to laugh at things which drive others into a state of anxiety and anger. The best way to do this is to keep yourself emotionally and physically healthy. If the pressure gets too heavy, seek professional help outside the job or begin to look for a new job.

■ *Make Good Decisions* – Always stop and think before you act. Actions based on impulse usually don't work well on a job. Before you

do something, consider what effects it might have and ask yourself if those effects are in keeping with the welfare of your employer and yourself. If the answer is "no," then don't do it!

■ *Avoid Improper Behavior*, on and off the job – Too often we do things which are illegal or improper and lead to danger or embarrassment for ourselves and others. It's a mistake to think we can be saints on the job and little devils on the streets; the two will always conflict. You will have the most success on and off the job if you keep your act together all the time. Don't let anyone or anything drive you over the edge – even if it sounds like fun at the time.

Relationships at Work

"How well you relate to others is an absolute KEY to your success!"

Often we carry our anger and pain along with us, like a black cloud full of lightning just looking for someone to strike! This may be a natural result of our past experiences, but it is more deadly to us than to anyone else. Don't let the criminal justice system continue to run your life! Get a handle on your emotions and make your future better than your past.

Remember to do your best to get along with everyone. Join in company activities like baseball or bowling teams, parties and picnics. This will help you come out of your shell and find some folks who are pleasant to be with.

No matter how good a worker you

are, personal conflicts that get out of hand make you impossible to be around and can get you fired overnight! It's hard to hide bad feelings; even if you do, they tend to seep out and affect everybody around. If this begins to happen, sit down and have an honest, adult talk with yourself. Do all you can to understand the *real* basis of your feelings. Don't let your stress and anger spill over where they don't belong.

If you find that you just cannot pinpoint the cause or control the results of your emotions, some part of you **needs help NOW**. Refusing to face it and take responsible action will only poison your heart and your relationship with *everyone* around you.

Usually if we try to be positive and cheerful, most folks will respect that effort and treat us the same way. However there are times when others just insist on playing the fool. No matter how petty or difficult someone else might be, don't let them drag you down to their level!

If you do the very best you can and it doesn't work, seek the private advice of the most mature and experienced person you can find. If you still cannot smooth things out, discuss the problem with your supervisor in private and ask if he/she can suggest some constructive way to handle the situation. Sometimes a transfer or a change in shifts can fix things. Whatever happens, don't get so upset that you do something to hurt yourself. If it comes to a physical conflict, you are probably the one who will get fired or arrested – even if you are in the right.

Dealing with Stress

"The more we keep our personal lives calm and stable, the better we can cope with any jive that goes on at work."

There is no such thing as a stress-free job! Every situation has its unique hassles, so accept them as a part of the situation and learn to roll with the punches. Your ability to cope with job stress is linked with many other factors in your daily life, such as your physical and emotional health. Therefore, it is critical to take good care of yourself, allow time to relax and have fun, and make room for quality time with family and friends.

As with anger, if you find that your stress is simply too much to handle and it's affecting you on the job or at home, don't hesitate to seek help from a counselor or minister.

Tips for Keeping Your Job

"Why go through all the effort of getting a job if you aren't going to keep it?"

Just as you have to work hard to get a job, you must work equally hard to keep it. The best way to keep and advance in your job is to have a good work *attitude*. On the job you are part of a team; what you do is important to the welfare of everyone you work with. You cannot expect fellow workers to adjust to you; it's up to you to become one of them. How well you get along with your boss, co-workers, and customers will have a major impact on your job performance and progress.

Several things will help you adjust to your new job. First, carefully listen to and carry out instructions and take pride in the quality of your work. Second, learn and follow company rules, especially concerning working hours, time off, etc. Next, be honest, sincere, and make an extra effort to get along with your boss and co-workers.

It is especially important to develop a good working relationship with your supervisor. From the first day on the job, work hard to learn and meet your new responsibilities. Be cooperative and show respect for your supervisor's experience and position. Nobody likes a smart aleck – they usually don't last very long.

Don't let your leisure-time activities affect your work performance. If you choose to stay out and party late before a work day, you still have to show up on time and carry out your duties. This doesn't mean you have to quit having fun, but your job MUST be your first priority! A little common sense goes a long way.

The most common reasons for getting fired are: not following orders, poor performance, drinking/drug problems, being absent or late, bad attitude or fighting, personal conflict with the employer, stealing from the company, and misuse of equipment. So keep your work habits in order, and stay away from behavior that causes problems.

Problem Solving

"The best survivors are the best problem solvers!"

Problems are bound to come up for which you have no instant solution. In fact, problems are natural. Some of our best growth occurs when we learn to use our creative abilities to solve problems. When you run into a problem, take your time to think things through. Don't act on impulse or let your emotions push you into anything you'll regret. Look at the problem from all angles; try to see it as it appears to others. It may help to talk it over with a friend outside of your work.

Then think about simple new ways to approach the situation. Discuss your concerns and your ideas for a solution directly and calmly with your supervisor or co-workers. Make suggestions for ways to make the situation better for everyone involved. When a decision is made, work to support it, no matter what it is.

Another trap to watch for is that we often bring our deepest frustrations to work with us, especially when we're having personal problems with loved ones, neighbors, or our P.O. If we are absent-minded or take out our anxieties on customers and co-workers, it can quickly get us in hot water. It's critical to control our emotions both on and off the job. Problems do not solve themselves. They never go away just because we want them to. Whenever we find things about to overwhelm us, it's time to seek professional help to settle and redirect our emotions. Take positive action!

Off-Duty Activities

"Working and playing should be two sides of the same coin: one should not rule out the other."

Life is more than mere survival; just making it day to day gets real old. In fact, one of the important reasons we work is to have the means to have fun! But people don't always realize how their off-duty activities affect their jobs. What we do in our free time greatly influences our health and ability to function while at work. The real question is what types of fun are positive and useful in terms of work and life in general.

Obviously if we're spending our weekends drinking ourselves blind, doing drugs, and running the streets all night, we will likely be absent or late for work, hung-over, and unable to perform well. It's important to learn that having fun doesn't mean abandoning ourselves to the point we cannot function when work time rolls around.

On the other hand, you will be more rested, alert, and in better shape Monday morning if the weekend was spent at the lake with friends, sharing laughs and going fishing, rather than falling out of topless bars at 2 a.m. To be compatible with your work, your fun needs to *give* you energy, strength, and stability, rather than leaving you broke, blind, and beaten half to death!

Use your off-job time to explore social, cultural, or sporting events, meet new people, get involved in positive activities, and fill your life with fresh energy and experiences. The secret here is to find a balance point that offers a chance for *quality* rather than mere quantity.

Support from Others

Importance of Support

"Life is built on sharing. Much of our sense of contentment is built on knowing when and what to give and when and what to take."

To turn our goals into reality often requires help from others. That doesn't mean we're weak or inadequate. It's all right to get help – as long as we don't abuse it or forget that it's our final responsibility to take care of ourselves. It is just as irresponsible *not* to get help when we need it as it is to depend on others to fix our lives.

Does seeking help make you a bum or some type of charity case? No way! Just hold your head up and go look for what you need. The time will come when you will be able to help someone else and that will balance the scale.

Before anything else, a person who has been involved with the criminal justice system will probably need help meeting their basic survival needs: food, shelter, clothing, transportation, health care, and so on. Equally important is emotional support and understanding from someone who cares. Without this, an ex-offender may lose heart and give up trying to overcome the obstacles ahead. Finally, for a person trying to get established in the community, the most valuable aid is trust and support from people who have influence or can give good advice.

All of this help is probably available in your community, if you know where and how to find it. The community can be an enemy camp OR a treasure chest, depending on how you approach it. Your attitude and actions are really the keys.

If you treat the community as an enemy, you will have to fight to survive there. If you approach the community as a friend, you can draw from it the resources you need to grow and improve your life. The better you manage yourself and your ties with the community, the better you will feel about life itself.

Establishing a Support System

"Of all community resources, none is more powerful or important than people."

Depending on the kind of support you need, you may seek help on a personal or professional level, or you may look for assistance from agencies in the community.

◼ Personal Relationships

Your personal support system starts with your family, loved ones, and friends – people who know you personally and care about what happens to you, the people you can go to in a crisis. Other people that you meet in your daily life, such as church members, fellow students, or members of an AA group, may also be willing to offer you some kinds of support, if they believe you are sincere and you approach them the right way.

The foundation of these relationships is honesty, sincerity, and commitment. It is essential that we truly care for and about others, not just about our own well-being or goals. If we want people to care about us, we must also care about them. If we want to be well-treated, we must treat other people well.

Maybe you have been flaky, let your loved ones down, or acted angry and hostile toward them. Then don't be shocked if they don't come across when you need them. Also, after involvement with the criminal justice scene, many families are already bone-dry and don't have much left to offer. So don't demand what doesn't exist.

How we treat those close to us says a lot about our character and who we really are. If we treat the people we care about badly, it is usually a reflection of how we feel about ourselves. Sometimes, when we have met a lot of failure or rejection, we may get so depressed and angry that we lose control of ourselves. Sometimes we just want to hurt ourselves or others and don't know exactly why.

When we are filled with rage or sadness it affects everything we do. Often we carry these feelings out of jail or prison with us. This is not strange, considering how much stress an ex-offender has to face. But it can't be ignored or accepted. Now is the time to deal with negative feelings before they do more damage to us and our relationships.

Most communities have a variety of capable counselors, and many charge on a sliding scale of fees based on your ability to pay. When you find yourself doing things which are simply beyond your control, hurtful to yourself or others, or leading you into addictive behavior, get professional help immediately.

Seeing a professional counselor can do more than just help us deal with crisis. By looking for the *causes* of our feelings, we have a far better chance of improving the quality of our future.

◼ Mentors and Professional Relationships

As you work toward your goals, you can benefit greatly from the advice of those who have years of experience and insight into how things work. A few hours with the right person may save years of struggle and grief down the road. This guidance and support can be an extremely valuable resource, but it takes time and work to establish it. If you start developing these relationships now, they will be there later when you're ready to look for a better job or go after your long-term ambitions.

To begin, you must identify the people who can provide the type of help and guidance you need. If you are preparing for an interview or applying to a training program, you may want to talk to someone who works there or has gone through the program. Or you may want to find three to five people who are prominent in the community or in the field where you want to work and who are willing to offer you advice on decisions and problems you will face. To find the right people, you need to be alert, talk to lots of folks, ask questions. Your network will be helpful with this.

You can approach these people using a gradual method to gain their trust and assistance. Building such relationships always takes time and work.

1. *Call or write to each person.* If someone in your network knows the person, ask if the individual you know will introduce you or let you use their name when you approach the potential advisor. In your letter or call, be brief and concise. Explain that you are trying to get established in the community or in a particular line of work. State that you are aware of their achievements and would appreciate a brief meeting to seek their insight and ask their advice. Very few people will say no.

2. *Show up on time for your appointment.* Look them in the eye, be concise and to the point, explain your ambition to get ahead. Never make excuses or blame anyone else for your past! Just let them know you are highly motivated, then ask their guidance, listen, take notes. You may also ask if they can suggest other people you should talk

to. Then thank them and leave. Don't stay long, and don't hit on them for anything.

3. *Follow up with a call or note of thanks.* Then use their advice, as much as you can or wish to. If they refer you to other people, use the same approach with them.

4. *Stay in touch with these advisors.* Call or send them a note to let them know your progress, what you have learned, and how their advice has helped. Then ask for their suggestions as to your next step. If you make contact with them every few months, you will gradually build a relationship based on credibility and trust.

5. *If you've been consistent in the early steps,* no one will be shocked if you call sometime later to ask for a letter of recommendation, a personal reference, or even a better job. People like to help one another because it makes them feel good about themselves – just as long as they feel the cause is reasonable and their efforts will be put to a positive use.

As with most people you encounter, such advisors tend to come and go, but a few remain a part of your life for years to come. Such people are rare and valuable. Over time there is a bond of trust and respect; these are individuals you can depend on to steer you in the right direction. If a relationship reaches this level, it is fair to say that this person has become your mentor, a guide to your well-being.

One thing for sure: if you intend to run a game, you won't last long. The word will get out that you just talk jive and work a cheap con. No one is going to let you get really close to them until you've paid your dues and they feel confident that you are sincere and solid. Then, slowly, as they grow comfortable that you're for real, more support will be available when you need it. The rules are simple: be honest, sincere, and appreciative at all times.

Using People as References

On applications and during job interviews, you will be asked to give the names of people who will vouch for your work abilities and good character. Since your family may be biased in your favor, you will need to request these personal and business references from past supervisors, the people in your network, or in the professional relationships you are developing. Before you use a person's name in this way, you *must* contact them and ask if they are willing to give you a character reference.

Never use their name without their consent, and be careful not to abuse this kindness. If you do, it will destroy not just one job opportunity, but your entire relationship with that former well-wisher. Don't give out the names of your references too easily. Save your reference list for employers who seem serious about hiring you. This will cut down on the number of calls your references will receive and will let them be more enthusiastic in their response to the calls they do get.

Even after someone has agreed to give you a reference, you should let them know every time you give out their name, to whom, and for what purpose. This way they will be ready to respond if they get a call. You should also call or send them a note afterward to thank them for their support and to let them know the results of your efforts.

Say Thanks

Anytime someone does something kind or helpful for you, it's a good habit to drop them a quick note to say thank you. This doesn't require a long, typewritten letter. Most thank-you notes are very brief and handwritten to make them more personal. In this age of computers, a brief e-mail may be sufficient. In any case it really is the thought that counts. Someone who has helped you get an interview or given you a reference will appreciate your thought-fulness in sending a note of thanks.

Community Resources

You don't have to go through such a personal process with agencies and programs in the community. You can use the following approach to find out what is available in your community and get help to meet your particular needs.

GET YOUR ATTITUDE RIGHT

We have to clean up our emotions and get a grip on ourselves before we pick up the phone, write a letter, send an e-mail, or walk into someone's office. Nobody will tolerate a person with a nasty, rude, or hostile attitude.

We need to keep ourselves humble by remembering that no one

owes us any favors. Looking for a special break because we've been in trouble is usually a waste of time. Everyone has a special problem of one type or another. It's better to ask for help for a positive reason – to improve your life and your ability to contribute to the world around you – *not* because you're down and out.

IDENTIFY NEEDS

Make sure you have a clear picture of what you need to survive and meet your goals. This is a part of the process described in the sections on goal setting and developing an action plan and survival plan. How can you decide where to look for help until you know what you need?

KEEP YOUR BALANCE

Many people who have been in trouble with the law fall into the trap of hiding – becoming isolated in the desire to be safe and secure. Although this may be a good policy at times, it can lead to a slow death when you need to be in touch with other people and locate important resources and opportunities.

So watch yourself closely to be sure you don't become an emotional or social hermit. Pull yourself up out of any depression or self-pity and start to look around! Work to build a useful bridge between yourself and the world.

One essential in dealing with agencies, public or private, is extreme patience. Your best tools are *courtesy* and *persistence*. If you're in a hurry or a crisis, you are in trouble. The wheels turn very slowly. So

don't put everything on hold while you wait for some program to save or fix you. Just keep working and be happy when something finally comes through.

UNDERSTAND SERVICE PROVIDERS

All agencies are limited in what and how much they can do for a client. No agency has the resources to do everything for everybody. Each focuses on particular types of clients with particular types of problems. Be prepared to be turned down several times before you get help. Also don't be surprised if you need help from several different programs. One agency may help with food, another with transportation, and so on.

You are just creating frustrations for yourself if you have false expectations of what an agency can or will do for you. No matter how angry you get or how hard you hope, you can't force an agency to fix all your problems.

It is usually a waste of time to lay a long, sad story on anyone. Keep your focus: discuss only the issues that the agency can help with. Social service staff are often overworked and may resent you for taking up so much of their time.

Sometimes we are so wound up that we've *got* to tell our story – just to get it off our chests. When this happens, be sure to find someone who can and will listen and who can help you deal with it (for instance a counselor or minister). Don't dump it on the director of a social service agency who has three phones ringing at once.

LOCATE RESOURCES

Start identifying the programs that might help you. Your first concern is to learn what's happening in the area where you are living or intend to live.

Start with the Yellow Pages; look for local information and referral (I & R) services, crisis intervention services, vocational training and job placement programs, and social services. Be alert for any services which focus on the needs of ex-offenders, such as the American Friends Service Committee, Salvation Army, or local agencies. If on probation or parole, ask your officer for suggestions. Also check with local churches to see what help they offer or can refer you to. Ask the staff at the library to help you identify the services available in your community. Study recent newspapers and magazines in your area to find out what services and opportunities are available. Also search on the Internet; many agencies have web sites and referral services may offer an online directory of local resources.

Much of what you learn about the community is by word of mouth – people sharing information. So listen carefully to the radio and TV news and talk shows. Also take any chance to talk to family, friends, your network, or other job seekers about programs that might help you. However, don't just believe something because it sounds good: check it out!

This process is easier when you're free on the streets, but many of us had to begin the quest from a cell. Maybe your family and loved ones can be your eyes and ears for awhile. Give them a clear idea of what you need (job placement or housing, for example). But don't run them around as if they have nothing else to do but wait on you. Respect their needs and responsibilities, and be careful not to burn them out.

If you are a prisoner and don't have anyone on the outside to help, check your unit library for information and referral directories, phone books, or newspapers from the area where you will be living. Or write to the library or government offices in that community to find out where to start looking. Then send letters to these potential resources asking if they can help. If you are on good terms with a prison counselor or teacher, he or she may be willing to help you get some information.

GET INFORMATION

It is absolutely essential to do your homework. You have to find out who does what and what it takes to be eligible. When contacting an agency or service, be concise and ask:

- What problems does the agency deal with?

- What services do they provide?

- What does it take to qualify?

- Is there any cost?

- If so, how much? Do they have a sliding fee scale based on your ability to pay?

- What are their hours?

- Do you need an appointment?

- Do you need to bring any documents? What kind?

- Who is the right person to see?

- What is the name of the person you are talking to?

Pay careful attention to what the agency does and does not do. Concentrate on how they can help – even in small ways – not on your disappointment if they can't help. Sometimes it pays to cross-check information by asking different people the same questions. Lots of folks don't explain fully or are not familiar with some of the agency's services.

A phone call or checking out an agency's web site is a good way to get this background information. If necessary send a letter, although agency staff may not respond as quickly since a letter takes more work. In either case, keep your letter or call brief and to the point. A one-page letter or five-minute call is best.

Don't try to apply for services during your first contact. Get information first; then plan how to approach the agency. Whenever possible, you should get an appointment and go in person to apply for their assistance. It is harder to say no when face-to-face. If the agency can't help you, keep your cool, thank them for their time, and ask who might be able to help.

APPLY AS THE IDEAL CLIENT

Your goal is to be screened IN (accepted), not OUT (rejected), with minimum hassles and frustration. You want to make it easy for them to help you.

The secret is to fit yourself to their guidelines. Never expect them to fit what they do to suit you. This doesn't mean you should lie, but you may be able to describe yourself in a different way depending on what you need. Instead of an ex-offender, you may be seen as "someone handicapped by an institutional experience," or as "someone needing vocational training or treatment for a substance abuse problem," or perhaps as "a single parent needing child care."

This is a time when you need to be honest and up front. Forget the "poor me" approach; *nobody has time to listen*. It is your sincerity that sells, not the details of your past, so keep your story short and to the point. If they want to know something that you haven't covered, they will ask. Above all, try to make a friend who will take an interest in you. People help other people best when they care about them.

BE PERSISTENT

Things can get tough while you are trying to fit your needs to the agency's guidelines. It's easy to get upset when you hit problems and delays. Remember, there are no instant solutions; patience is required. When you keep cool and try a different approach, it often works.

You must stand up for yourself if you believe you are being treated rudely or unfairly. But remember that the goal is to score, not to vent your anger. In short, be firm but stay in control of your emotions. It may be wise to deal with another staff person or speak with the supervisor.

Getting help from social service agencies takes a lot of energy and self-control. Don't just lay back and wait for miracles to happen. You need to do as much as possible on your own while looking for help. Keep pushing on all fronts and *never give up*.

FOLLOW THROUGH

Why go through all of the above if you aren't going to finish it? If you need to fill out more forms, do it. Another appointment to make – do it. Yet another person to see, another phone call to make? *Do it!* And do it *now* so things will keep happening.

After all the time and sweat put into getting help in the community, you've *got* to make positive use of what you've learned. Progress is a wonderful rush.

REMEMBER TO SAY THANKS

When someone helps you, they need and deserve to know the results and that you appreciate their efforts. Even if you don't get exactly what you hoped for, it's special when someone cares enough to try or treats you with respect. Therefore, you should always remember to say "thank you," both after the event and later on when you've prospered from their efforts and good intentions.

Duty to Those Who Support Us

"When we accept someone's trust and love, we take upon ourselves a debt of honor."

There ain't no free lunch! Good relationships are two-way streets: if we take, we must be prepared to give. Often what we must give is our willingness to be honest, keep our word, and do our best.

In short, we are honor-bound to meet our promises and commitments in order to do right by the people who have helped us. If we view someone who trusts us as a chump or sucker – just another mark – then we destroy any hope of a meaningful relationship, of shared respect or *self*-respect. The pride and self-worth we all hunger for doesn't come from being a vulture!

As people become more stable and secure in their daily lives, they find less and less need to be takers and users. Instead, they begin to look for ways to help others; to give back some of the kindness and support that has come their way. Many find volunteer or community service work amazingly rewarding. It's a wonderful feeling to pass on to others the trust and help that was granted to us. There is no better way to say, "Thanks!"

Strive for Independence

"The better we can control our own fate, the better we feel about everything, especially ourselves and the world around us."

While it's totally OK to seek help

to survive and grow, the last thing we want to do is become dependent on someone else. Looking to someone else to save us or fix us is a dead end. No one can live our lives for us. No matter what our current status, *our final goal is true freedom and independence.*

Many of us come from backgrounds where other people and things had more control over us than we did over ourselves. Existing under such conditions, at home or in a cell, can be hell on earth. It may have led to some form of self-destructive or addictive behavior, or just a lack of caring and sense of hopelessness.

However, there are ways to recover from slavery, to be truly free. But there is no magic button that can be pushed ... it takes faith and work! Always remember that *YOU* are the foundation of your life and future. As such, your first goal is to stand up, to do what is decent and good to the best of your ability.

Such an approach to daily life is the only true path to increased dignity and self-respect. But good intentions are not enough; our ability to function and contribute to others is built on our state of health – physical, mental, and ethical. We must match positive values with positive actions, within ourselves first of all. This requires that our overall health and emotional balance be a top priority. We must strive constantly to maintain this perspective!

For the Family and Loved Ones

As a family member or loved one of a public offender, you can play a very important role in his or her quest for employment. Too often a loved one is asked to do the impossible: to find a job for someone still in jail or prison. However, it is often possible to help with financial and/or moral support, transportation, food, or lodging while a person tries to find a job and become self-sufficient. This section will help you better understand what can be done, should be done, and what should not be done.

Before all else, you and your loved one need to come to agreement on how you will handle your relationship. This requires honest and open communication.

both for the offender and for themselves.

Usually the biggest problems are not knowing what to expect or how to avoid future disappointments. For this reason, it is best to define a new relationship between you and the offender based on the fundamental rules of true friendship.

This requires a mutual commitment to honesty and respectful concern for one another. Everyone needs to accept responsibility for their own behavior, then set aside the pain of the past and focus on the promise of the future. It is essential to have realistic expectations, as well as an understanding of how to help and what kinds of help are beyond your limits and responsibilities.

Your New Relationship

Having a loved one involved in the criminal justice process, at *any* level, often changes their relationship with you and with other people in the community. When the crime has been very serious or the effects intense and long-term, there may be a wide array of negative results. Many family members and loved ones feel anger and frustration over the situation. They question and often fear what the future holds

Realistic Expectations

Job hunting, even at best, is time and energy consuming and can be very difficult, especially with a criminal history. Many family members are so anxious to see their loved ones reconstruct their lives that they expect overnight results. This just isn't realistic. Both the offender and the family must remember to be patient and have faith that their persistent efforts will eventually result in a job offer. This patience is essential to overcome the stress that is a natural part of life after prison.

One major error is thinking that some government or community program is going to fix things by having a job all ready and waiting. With very few exceptions, this is false. No one is standing by to give an ex-offender a job just because it's the right thing to do.

Face the fact that there will be resistance to a person's criminal history; all the good intentions in the world will not alter this reality. Time and hard work are needed to overcome this barrier. The longer a person has been out of work, the more difficult the search will be. However, the love and support of family and friends go a long way to helping an ex-offender keep his or her balance and motivation in the face of rejection and hardship.

How You Should Help

First, study this book in detail so that you understand what is involved. Next, discuss the situation with your loved one and encourage him or her to think realistically about future plans. Without being pushy, you can help your loved one test the practical aspects of his or her dreams and plans. People who have been in trouble may be so anxious to reconstruct their lives that they don't stop to find out the requirements for the type of job they want.

On a practical level, a person seeking employment after involvement in the criminal justice system has some serious survival needs: food, shelter, clothing, transportation while they look for work, and so on.

Until a person has the income to secure their basic needs, you may be able to help them get what they need to stay alive and hunt a job.

You are also the central element in your loved one's job-hunting network. Through your friends, neighbors, work, church, social groups, and so on, you have contact with literally hundreds of people. You can ask everyone you know to keep your loved one in mind when they hear of any job openings.

Remember that your love and support are invaluable! After being in trouble with the law, most people lack faith in themselves and their ability to function in the community. Therefore, more than anything else, your encouragement and positive attitude can serve as the foundation of your loved one's confidence and morale.

How You Shouldn't Help

While it is good to help in ways that are practical, clearly it is not your job to live another person's life for him or her. It doesn't help a person in the long run to provide for their needs while they lose their pride and self-confidence.

It's good to encourage your loved one to accept responsibility for his or her welfare. Even if you could take care of things for them, you will do them the best service in the end by helping them to help themselves.

Next, don't be a sucker for some dead beat who thinks the world owes him or her a living. It's not your duty to support someone who runs the streets all night and sleeps all day. No one has the right to take advantage of you, so be very clear in your mind as to the limits of your energy and resources. You have the right to decide what to do with your home, your time, and your resources. Don't feel guilty about protecting yourself and insisting on your rights.

If you feel you are being taken advantage of, be honest and discuss it with your loved one. Don't wait until you are ready to explode and throw them out on the street before you express your feelings!

Be fair and reasonable, but once you have laid down the law, stick to it. You can do a great service for your loved one by insisting that he or she respect other people's rights and accept responsibility for his or her own future.

Continued Growth

Personal Growth

"We exist to grow and prosper. And above all, to contribute to the world around us. There is no greater source of satisfaction or self-worth."

If life is a mere search for survival, it is like a rosebud which never opens. Most of us grew up thinking that life is limited to a constant quest for security, good feelings, and power. In fact, our whole society supports this belief. But such thinking makes us prisoners of a limited way of seeing life and our role in it. In fact, there is much more to live for: love, happiness, inner peace, expanded awareness, and rewarding relations with ourselves and others.

We cannot change the past and the future has yet to come. But we *can* influence the here and now. By actively reaching out for growth, we can learn to let go of the old baggage we've collected and replace it with fresh, positive thoughts, feelings, and experiences.

In order to be effective at managing our criminal history, we must first understand the effects it will have on us. Next, we must strive to grow beyond the past by living a positive, constructive life. This needs to take place on many levels: mental, emotional, physical, and spiritu-al. None of these can be neglected if we want healthy, balanced growth. Clearly such growth does not come to us by sitting under a tree and waiting. *We must pursue it with a deep-seated passion!*

Recovery – The First Priority

"For anyone who has lived through 20 carloads of pain, whether it came from others or ourselves, the goal is to heal, to be whole – to find our place in the Universe."

Past mistakes and misfortunes may be a chapter in our lives, but they were never intended to become the whole book. In fact, much of our development and character come from facing our problems. Trouble occurs if we get stuck in the passion and madness of the past and lose sight of hope and the beauty and wonder of life. *Nothing* is more important than our recovery and the growth that follows healing. This includes recovery from addictions, depression, anger, fear, bad relationships, isolation, and false expectations of ourselves and the world.

Never forget that your recovery is the key to a positive future. And if you wonder what recovery is, think of it as achieving balance and harmony in the way you think, act, and relate to the world around you. By working to manage or balance all the different parts of yourself and your life, you will find everything is richer and far more meaningful. Obviously your life is always a work in progress; the nature and quality of your efforts are, in the end, far more important than the final results!

Remember: no one was born knowing how to balance his or her life. If we want our lives to have more purpose and meaning, we have to get off our butts and reach for the help, insight, and support to make it happen. It *is* possible. With determination, persistence, patience, and courage, we'll succeed! For more guidance on how to get started on the road to recovery, read OPEN's book *Life Without a Crutch* (see rear of book).

Vocational Growth

"Growth requires the faith, courage, and force of your will to step forward into the future. You can do it!"

Because our work is such a big part of what we do, it makes sense to seek advancement. By growing on the job, we achieve a lot of goals, such as increased income, greater personal satisfaction, and a higher standard of living.

One way to do this is by seeking promotions. This usually requires learning what your employer considers important and going that extra mile to get it done. Promotions are generally based on high performance or on a formal system of meeting certain requirements (like passing a test or meeting a production quota). In either case, they

come because you earn them.

A number of issues influence our growth on the job. When we have good physical health and emotional stability, we are more capable of dealing with ourselves and those around us. Our health also influences our productivity and dependability, which are usually most important to an employer.

We can become more competent and valuable to our employer by expanding our education. When we go back to school at night or take special classes to improve our skills, it shows a high motivation. It also improves our confidence and self-worth, both on and off the job. Many employers will help motivated workers develop themselves by offering educational benefits, time off, or a flexible schedule.

Growth also produces new opportunities. As you learn and grow, always be alert for job openings that may lead toward your long-term goals. As you become more skilled, there will be a greater demand for your talents. Be ready to move into a more challenging and rewarding situation, whether with a new company or in a new position with your current employer.

The keys to growth on the job and getting a good job reference are largely based on a good attitude, consistency, competence, and dedicated performance. This means doing your job in a cooperative manner, to the best of your ability, and being steady and reliable.

What If I Mess Up?

"It's natural to stumble, but we cannot permit ourselves to fall!"

Will you make mistakes? Of course. Will you have serious disappointments? Naturally. After all, we're human, which means we're less than perfect and so we make mistakes. Reconstruction and growth are often like riding a roller coaster, up and down, fast and slow, but NEVER level and smooth. When you goof, accept responsibility, take your lumps, and jump right back up! Just be sure to use your mistakes as lessons to better prepare for the future: *never give up!!*

Moving into the Future

"Let go of the pain and anguish of the past so that you can embrace a better day. Exist in the NOW! It is all we have ... use it well."

There *is* a path to a rich, meaningful life beyond the madness and frustration of the criminal justice process. With a positive attitude and determined effort, we can all find it. If you have read this entire book, it is a clear signal that you are sincere and deeply determined to achieve a quality future.

Many resources exist to help a motivated person move forward: educational opportunities, apprenticeships, on the job experience. And above all, learning by observing others who have skill, good work habits, and honorable intent. Whatever you need to know, you can learn!

Don't try to make huge steps forward or expect immediate results – these are just traps. As you continue to grow, each positive step, no matter how humble, supports and reinforces every other positive step you take. Like a snowball rolling down hill, this powerful collective force will make your hopes and dreams real and bring quality and meaning into your life.

One goal we all share is to succeed in life. Although success is different things to different people, there are some common aspects we can all agree on. First, each of us wants to feel secure, free from crisis, danger, and unreasonable limits. We need to feel safe before we can attend to our personal growth and the welfare of the world around us.

Second, we all want to feel valuable both within ourselves and in the opinion of our society. Thus we feel most successful when we feel a growing sense of worth and respect for ourselves and in the eyes of others. The true measure of success may not be in physical property or power, but in learning to be happy and at peace.

The wonder of having a job is that it opens up so many positive opportunities. Working is not just something you have to do. It is a bridge to success – to greater comfort, security, and feelings of accomplishment. The better you get at your work, the better your life will get.

I hope this book will help renew your sense of hope and faith in yourself and what the future holds. *The best way to deal with your criminal history is to outgrow it* – like an old shirt that doesn't fit anymore. By growing beyond past mistakes and narrow limits, we replace pain with joy, hate with love, tears with laughter. And as this slowly occurs, those increasing moments of peace and pride make the past worthwhile. So get up and make it happen! I wish you the very best of luck!!

Reading List

There are hundreds of books about job hunting. The ones listed below have useful information, but there are many other good books available. If you can't find these particular books, look for others written on the same subject.

Career Exploration

U.S. Department of Labor. *Occupational Outlook Handbook 2004-2005.* 2004.
  Published bi-annually. Available through several publishers as well as online at www.bls.gov.oco.

U.S. Department of Labor. *O*NET Dictionary of Occupational Titles.* 2004.
  Available through several publishers as well as online at http://online .onetcenter.org.

Complete Guides to Finding a Job

Todd Bermont. *10 Insider Secrets to a Winning Job Search: Everything You Need to Get the Job You Want in 24 Hours – or Less!* 2004.
Richard Nelson Bolles. *What Color Is Your Parachute?* 2004.
Richard Fein. *95 Mistakes Job Seekers Make and How to Avoid Them.* 2003.
Janet Garber. *I Need a Job, Now What?!* 2001.

Roger Jones. *Getting a Job in America: A Step-by-Step Guide to Finding Work in the USA.* 2003.
Ron Krannich. *Change Your Job, Change Your Life.* 2004.
Ron and Caryl Krannich. *No One Will Hire Me! Avoid 15 Mistakes and Win the Job.* 2004.
Lorelei Lanum. *The Procrastinator's Guide to the Job Hunt.* 2004.
Max Messmer. *Job Hunting for Dummies.* 2001.
Susan Morem. *How to Get a Job and Keep It.* 2002.
Chandra Prasad. *Outwitting the Job Market: Everything You Need to Locate and Land a Great Position.* 2004.
Richard W. Swanson. *The Smart People's Guide to Job Hunting.* 2002
Anna Graf Williams. *The Immigrant's Guide to the American Workplace: Making It in America.* 2003.

Inspiration and Empowerment

Stephen R. Covey. *Seven Habits of Highly Effective People.* 1990.
Phillip C. McGraw. *Life Strategies: Doing What Works, Doing What Matters.* 2000.

Networking

Katharine Hansen. *A Foot in the Door: Networking Your Way into the Hidden Job Market.* 2000.

Susan RoAne. *How to Work a Room: The Ultimate Guide to Savvy Socializing in Person and Online.* 2000.

Resumes and Letters

Gene Corwin, Gary Joseph Grappo, Adele Lewis, Gary Grappo. *How to Write Better Resumes.* 2004.

Wendy S. Enelow. *Best Resumes for People without a Four-Year Degree.* 2004.

Wendy S. Enelow and Louise M. Kursmark. *Expert Resumes for People Returning to Work.* 2003.

Tom Jackson. *The Perfect Resume: Today's Ultimate Job Search Tool.* 2004.

Joyce Lain Kennedy. *Cover Letters for Dummies.* 2002.

Joyce Lain Kennedy. *Resumes for Dummies.* 2002.

Ronald L. Krannich and William J. Banis. *High Impact Resumes and Letters.* 2002.

Arthur Rosenberg, David V. Hizer, David Hizer. *The Resume Handbook: How to Write Outstanding Resumes and Cover Letters for Every Situation.* 2003.

Interviewing

Matthew J. DeLuca, Nanette F. DeLuca. *24 Hours to the Perfect Interview: Quick Steps for Planning, Organizing, and Preparing for the Interview That Gets the Job.* 2004.

Cynthia Ingols. *Your Job Interview.* 2003.

Joyce Lain Kennedy. *Job Interviews for Dummies.* 2000.

Caryl and Ron Krannich. *Job Interview Tips for People with Not-So-Hot Backgrounds.* 2004.

Caryl and Ron Krannich. *Nail the Job Interview!* 2003.

Marky Stein. *Fearless Interviewing: How to Win the Job by Communicating with Confidence.* 2003.

Martin Yate. *Knock 'Em Dead 2005: Great Answers to Over 200 Tough Inter-view Questions – Plus the Latest Job Search Strategies.* 2004.

Job Hunting on the Internet

Margaret F. Dikel, Frances E. Roehm. *Guide to Internet Job Searching 2004-2005.* 2004.

Fred Edmund Jandt, Mary B. Nemich. *Using the Internet in Your Job Search: An Easy Guide to Online Job Seeking and Career Information.* 2003.

Ron Krannich, Caryl Krannich, Ronald L. Krannich. *America's Top Internet Job Sites: The Click and Easy Guide to Finding a Job Online.* 2003.

Internet Sites for Job Hunters

The following are some of the most widely used job search sites. Internet sites change often, so if some of these links don't work, you can find similar ones by using a search engine and searching for words like "job hunting" or "job search."

www.ajb.org (America's Job Bank – a public employment web site)
www.careerbuilder.com
www.flipdog.com
www.hotjobs.com
www.jobgusher.com
www.jobs.com
www.monster.com

The following government agencies have authority over who is allowed to work in the United States and what documents are needed to qualify for employment.

www.uscis.gov U.S. Citizenship and Immigration Service
1-800-375-5283 or 1-800-767-1883 for TTY

www.ssa.gov U.S. Social Security
Administration
1-800-772-1213 or 1-800-325-0778 for
TTY

The web sites of many businesses and
government agencies list job vacancies
or ways to apply. Be sure to look for the
state employment service or workforce
commission web site and other commercial employment sites that focus on
your area.

A national organization has recently
collected and published information
about legal barriers facing people with a
criminal record. You may view this and
other information at its web sites:

www.lac.org (Legal Action Center)
www.hirenetwork.org (National
H.I.R.E. Network)

GYNAECOLOGY
Changing Services for Changing Needs

Edited by
SUE JOLLEY

John Wiley & Sons, Ltd

MT

Other Wiley Editorial Offices

John Wiley & Sons Inc., 111 River Street, Hoboken, NJ 07030, USA

Jossey-Bass, 989 Market Street, San Francisco, CA 94103-1741, USA

Wiley-VCH Verlag GmbH, Boschstr. 12, D-69469 Weinheim, Germany

John Wiley & Sons Australia Ltd, 42 McDougall Street, Milton, Queensland 4064, Australia

John Wiley & Sons (Asia) Pte Ltd, 2 Clementi Loop #02-01, Jin Xing Distripark, Singapore
129809

John Wiley & Sons Canada Ltd, 6045 Freemont Blvd, Mississauga, ONT L5R 4J3

Wiley also publishes its books in a variety of electronic formats. Some content that appears in
print may not be available in electronic books.

Library of Congress Cataloging-in-Publication Data

Gynaecology : changing services for changing needs / Susan Jolley, editor.
       p.   ;   cm.
    Includes bibliographical references and index.
    ISBN-13: 978-0-470-02538-3 (pbk. : alk. paper)
    ISBN-10: 0-470-02538-7 (pbk. : alk. paper)
    1. Gynecology.
    [DNLM: 1.   Genital Diseases, Female–nursing–Great Britain.   2.   Nursing Care–Great
Britain.   3.   Nurse's Role–Great Britain.   4.   Nursing Assessment–Great Britain.   5.   Risk
Management–Great Britain. WY 156.7 G9967 2006] I. Jolley, Susan.
    RG101.G962 2006
    618.1 – dc22

                                                                                    2006004515

A catalogue record for this book is available from the British Library

ISBN -13 978-0-470-02538-3
ISBN -10 0-470-02538-7

Typeset by SNP Best-set Typesetter Ltd., Hong Kong
Printed and bound in Great Britain by TJ International Ltd, Padstow, Cornwall
This book is printed on acid-free paper responsibly manufactured from sustainable forestry
in which at least two trees are planted for each one used for paper production.

3/26/07

Contents

List of Contributors

Julie Golding
Julie Golding has worked in the Gynaecology Department at Queen's Medical Centre, Nottingham, for the whole of her career. She was a ward sister from 1986 until 2002 when she became an Oncology Nurse Specialist within the same unit. In 2003 she took on the additional role of Risk Management Coordinator for the Gynaecology Unit. She is also currently acting Head Nurse/Matron for Gynaecology on a job-share basis.

Sue Griffiths
Sue Griffiths's basic nursing skills were gained in Renal Medicine before she moved to Gynaecology in 1987. After many years working as a senior gynaecology staff nurse, she was appointed as a Nurse Adviser in the Gynaecology Outpatients Department at City Hospital, Nottingham. In 2002 she moved to Primary Care, working alongside the Community Gynaecologist in Contraception and Sexual Health to set up a Medical Termination Service. She now works 'cross-boundary' in both primary and secondary care.

Sue Jolley
Sue Jolley was a mature entrant into nursing, previously working as a primary school teacher. She has been a Gynaecology Nurse for 15 years and has developed a special interest in teenage sexual health. She currently has dual responsibility for promoting research and managing the Gynaecology Pre-operative Assessment Unit. She has had several articles published on issues relating to women's health.

Sarah Kordula
With dual qualifications in both general nursing and midwifery, Sarah Kordula has worked in women's health since 1989. She has undertaken specialist training in continence, family planning, menopause and bone densitometry (operation and safety). She is currently studying for the postgraduate certificate in Osteoporosis and Falls Management at Derby University. She provides probably the only DXA service within a gynaecology/menopause clinic in the UK.

Judith Lee
Judith began her working career as a physiotherapist at the Radcliffe Infirmary, Oxford. After moving to Nottinghamshire, she became interested in the

management of incontinence in the elderly and also began conducting antenatal parentcraft classes at a local Health Centre. Since then she has worked
in the specialty of obstetrics and gynaecology. For the past 16 years she has
held senior positions at King's Mill Hospital, Mansfield, and Queen's Medical
Centre, Nottingham, where she is now the Clinical Specialist Women's Health
Physiotherapist. She is an active member of the Association of Chartered
Physiotherapists in Women's Health and has a specialist interest in the promotion of continence.

Joan Meyerowitz
Joan Meyerowitz has been a qualified nurse for 30 years, spending the last 15
years in women's health both in Oxford and Nottingham. She has specialised
in colposcopy, family planning and the menopause. Her interest in the
menopause started 10 years ago and in 1999 she initiated a nurse-led implant
service in Nottingham. Since then she has provided this service along with
menopause advice in the gynaecology menopause clinic. She is an active
member of the British Menopause Society and responsible for teaching about
the menopause on local gynaecology and sexual health study courses and
practice nurse study days.

Sian Schmidt
Sian Schmidt qualified as a Radiographer in 1994 and subsequently qualified
in Medical Ultrasound from St Martins University College, Lancaster. She has
worked in several ultrasound departments throughout the UK and her positions have included a superintendent post. She currently works at Queen's
Medical Centre, Nottingham, and specialises in obstetrics, gynaecology, and
abdominal and vascular ultrasound.

Liz Towell
Liz Towell started her career as a gynaecology nurse at the City Hospital in
Nottingham. She subsequently trained as a midwife but later returned to
gynaecology nursing, eventually working at Queen's Medical Centre, where
she became a ward manager. After transferring to the Gynaecology Outpatients Department, she was involved in setting up the Gynaecology Urodynamics Service in the early 1980s. Initially a research venture, this later became
part of the gynaecology service. Liz widened her scope of practice by undertaking courses in both urodynamics and continence. She regularly teaches
different groups of staff about urodynamics and female continence, and is
particularly involved in teaching medical staff who are attached to the gynaecology unit. She is now Divisional Nurse for Gynaecology.

Anne Walton
Anne Walton works as a Gynaecology Nurse Practitioner at Queen's Medical
Centre, Nottingham. She set up and manages the Early Pregnancy Assessment

Centre. Anne qualified as a state registered nurse and then as a midwife in Birmingham and has worked as a ward manager on gynaecology wards. She has qualifications in Family Planning and Clinical Developments in Nursing Care. Anne has recently been appointed as a Trustee for the Miscarriage Association.

Helen White
Helen White chose to work in gynaecology when she qualified in 1987. She has worked on three different gynaecology wards and became a ward manager in 1993 at Queen's Medical Centre, Nottingham. After 10 years in the post, she looked for a new challenge in women's health, which involved more individual patient contact. She was subsequently appointed to a Specialist Nurse role in the Medical Termination of pregnancy. This involves work in gynaecology outpatient clinics, community clinics and also inpatient care.

Cindy Wilson
Cindy Wilson trained at University College Hospital, London, and moved to take up a post on a gynaecology ward at Queen's Medical Centre, Nottingham, in 1985. She has worked in women's health since then, gaining a Diploma in Professional Studies. Her current role is as a Gynaecology Liaison Nurse in the Early Pregnancy Assessment Centre, where she has worked for five years and developed her expertise in supporting women with problems in early pregnancy.

Sally Wright
Starting her career as a gynaecology staff nurse, Sally Wright went on to train and work as a midwife. She later returned to gynaecology and became a ward sister in 1990. As a ward sister she became very interested in oncology and was subsequently seconded to do a specialist Oncology Course (ENB 237). Following this Sally was appointed as Oncology Nurse Specialist and has developed the Gynaecology Oncology Service at the Queen's Medical Centre, Nottingham. This also involves working with the oncologists at Nottingham City Hospital. She has since trained as a Nurse Colposcopist and is currently acting Head Nurse/Matron for Gynaecology on a job-share basis.

Jill Yates
Jill Yates has had a very varied career. After training at Gloucester Royal Hospital, she worked as a staff nurse in medicine, surgery and research in Southport. She became a sister in the Endoscopy Unit in Greenock, Scotland, before moving to Nottingham and a post in Endoscopy at Queen's Medical Centre. She worked as a Fertility Sister for 10 years and obtained a Diploma in Sexual Health. She currently works as a Practice Development Nurse in Gynaecology.

Preface

Gynaecology in the twenty-first century is much more than just a surgical speciality. The range of services and associated care has expanded rapidly in recent years, reflecting the changing health needs of women. Many exciting developments have been initiated by nurses and professionals allied to medicine (PAMs).

The chapters in this book each focus on a main area of gynaecological care, providing a general overview of the issues involved as well as specific examples of how nurses and PAMs are making a difference. All of the contributors have used their interest and expertise in a specific field to develop a gynaecology service for women. They are all keen to promote gynaecology by sharing best practice.

The book will have a special appeal for all nurses and PAMs already working in gynaecology. Hopefully it will motivate and encourage them to look at new ways of delivering care. However, anyone interested in women's health in general would gain a useful overview of gynaecological problems and modern service provision.

Sue Jolley

Introduction

This book discusses a wide range of topical gynaecological issues. The areas chosen reflect the changes that are taking place in gynaecology services, with an emphasis on how nurses and PAMs can make a difference to the delivery of care, either through nurse-led clinics or the development of roles within the multidisciplinary team. This exemplifies the action advocated in recent government reports (*Making a Difference*, Department of Health 1999 and *The NHS Plan*, Department of Health 2000).

The book may be read as a whole in order to gain an overview of recent developments in gynaecology, but as each chapter stands on its own it would be useful for those professionals, or students, with an interest in one particular field. The first chapter gives an overview of nurse-led assessment in gynaecology and is a natural introduction to the work covered by the following chapters. Topics are arranged roughly in the order they may be experienced as a woman matures, starting with sexual health problems, frequently associated with teenagers, and ending with the menopause and gynaecological oncology. However, there is considerable overlap with, for example, more mature women now contracting sexually transmitted infections and an increase in gynaecological cancers among younger women.

Common to each of the chapters is an outline of the challenges resulting from the needs of women with particular gynaecological problems and how services are developing to meet those challenges. A helpful summary of this is included in box form at the start of each chapter. Otherwise the chapters are all written differently, reflecting the style and interests of each of the contributors. They all deliver gynaecology services at Queen's Medical Centre, Nottingham, so many examples of good practice are drawn from that hospital. However, these examples are chosen not only to demonstrate what is possible but also to illustrate similar changes that are taking place at many different centres across the UK.

Each chapter is evidence-based and fully referenced. Useful help lines and websites are included. At the back of the book is a glossary, which explains the different gynaecology terms used in the book.

1 Nurse-led Assessment in Gynaecology

SUE JOLLEY

Assessment refers to a continuous process of collecting and organising both subjective and objective data about a patient's health status. This is an implicit part of all ongoing nursing work as nurses continually assess the patients in their care in order to offer the appropriate interventions. Indeed, for many years student nurses have learned about assessment as an integral part of the nursing process, included in most nursing models (Aggleton & Chalmers 2000; Pearson *et al.* 1996; Roper *et al.* 2001). *Nurse-led assessment* is a much more specific and directed activity, carried out to help with either diagnosis or treatment. It has become important as new nursing roles have developed. This chapter discusses the implications of nurse-led assessment and describes how it is used within gynaecology.

Challenges	Service developments
• The need to improve waiting list management in response to government targets • The reduction in junior doctors' hours • Improving patient access and optimising flow • Constant pressure on hospital beds • Inappropriate emergency admissions to gynaecology wards	• Nurse-led clinics to fast-track admissions for suitable cases, e.g. sterilisation service • Nurse-led Pre-operative Assessment Units • Guidelines and protocols to support extended roles • Nurse-led Gynaecology GP Emergency Admission Units

WHY ARE NEW NURSING ROLES DEVELOPING?

The expansion of nursing roles and development of nurse-led clinics has undoubtedly been driven by the need to reduce doctors' hours, reduce costs and improve waiting list and bed management. The *New Deal* for junior

Gynaecology: Changing Services for Changing Needs. Edited by Sue Jolley doctors, introduced in 1991, limits the working week to 56 hours on average (NHS Management Executive 1991). The *European Working Time Directive* (93/104/EC) should reduce doctors' working hours even further, to 48 hours a week by 2009 (British Medical Association 2004; Department of Health 2005). Progress towards meeting these targets has been very slow and figures suggest that almost half of junior doctors in the UK work more than 56 hours a week (British Medical Association 2004). *The NHS Plan* (Department of Health 2000a) promised patients a modern, flexible service with reduced waiting times. The target waiting times were three months for an outpatient appointment and six months for inpatients. These have been superseded by even more optimistic promises, culminating in the government pledge that 'no patient will wait more than eighteen weeks for hospital treatment from GP referral to admission' (*The Times* 2005).

This has created both a challenge and an opportunity for the NHS to modernise its services and look at different ways of working. There has been pressure for nurses to improve their professional status (Department of Health 1999) and the nature of nursing has changed in response to demands for more flexible and relevant healthcare services (Department of Health 2000b). One of the central features of health policy is to introduce innovative services that use the specialist skills of nurses (Knape 1999). Nurses now share a wide range of clinical work with medical colleagues in primary care, accident and emergency departments, specialist clinics and maternity services (Savage *et al.* 2000). This has also led to an increase in nurses' autonomy as they run clinics, perform minor surgery, admit and discharge patients and request tests and investigations (Collins 1999; Magennis *et al.* 1999; Royal College of Nursing 1997).

ISSUES AROUND NEW NURSING ROLES

The emergence of new roles such as nurse consultant, liaison nurse, specialist nurse and nurse practitioner has sometimes been controversial. Partly this is because nurses and midwives are adopting a variety of titles without any clear consensus as to what they all mean and what qualifications are required. There is no agreed definition for a nurse practitioner in the UK (Hicks & Hennessy 1999; Wadsworth *et al.* 2002). There is some degree of uniformity in the work of nursing and midwifery consultants but, as yet, no regulation of their training. All the new titles sound important and imply that the bearer possesses some higher knowledge that will lead to better care for patients. However, without appropriate regulation patients could be put at risk (Carroll 2002). Trusts use a wide range of methods to decide which staff should be given advanced positions. Sometimes prior experience is enough, but sometimes extra training is also required. This can vary from a few days on a course to a doctorate requiring several years' study. There are now moves by the Nursing and Midwifery Council (NMC) to address this problem. Hopefully new standards and competencies will make the situation clearer, and setting up a part of the register specifically for nurses and midwives in advanced practice could protect certain titles.

There is also concern about the over-medicalisation of nursing. If nurses are asked to expand their roles for reasons other than their own professional development, there is a danger that they may be exploited (Magennis *et al.* 1999). There is sometimes resentment when expanded roles do not necessarily attract appropriate remuneration (Collins 1999; Rose *et al.* 1998). Being expected to perform mundane medical tasks may compromise the quality of nursing (Edwards 1995), and Cahill (1998) argued that many nurse practitioners are pretending to be doctors. The legal position for nurses in expanded roles may also be unclear and nurses do have some concerns about their perceived increased vulnerability to litigation (Magennis *et al.* 1999). Under *The Scope of Professional Practice* (United Kingdom Central Council 1992) nurses are accountable for their own practice, but how practitioners determine their own competence is sometimes unclear. This is important because vicarious liability refers to the employer being responsible for their employees' actions providing they are working within their remit and agreed protocols.

There are fears that the continued pressure for nurses to expand their roles will be done at the expense of essential nursing care and that nursing should be valued in its own right (Kitson 1999). However, this argument forgets that nurses have always informally guided junior doctors and some nurses want to expand their role (Collins 1999; Magennis *et al.* 1999). If the development of new specialist roles are led by nurses for the benefit of the patients and not dictated by the needs of trusts, there are considerable advantages. Castledine (1995) argued that advancing the boundaries of nursing practice could be used to the profession's advantage, and Rounds (1997) highlighted the benefits of nursing input because nurses can 'offer a unique blend and broader scope of healthcare but physicians can offer only medicine'.

Clearly without appropriate education and training to support new roles, health workers may be placed under stress and the quality of patient care could be compromised. However, evidence suggests that many nurses lack the appropriate skills and preparation for such roles. Read *et al.* (1999) found that 93 % of 618 practitioners in innovative roles felt that they needed further education and training. Educational requirements should be formalised by professional bodies and the Nursing and Midwifery Council (Carroll 2002) and there have been calls for major investment in educational programmes, both at pre- and post-registration levels, to give nurses the skills they need (Hicks & Hennessy 1999; Magennis *et al.* 1999).

A key component of any nurse-led service is the ability to carry out a thorough, accurate and relevant assessment. For this there are both general and specific training requirements. General issues include different interview techniques and communication strategies (Shaw 1997) and the ability to conduct sensitive patient interviews using high-level consultation skills (Price 2004; Redsell *et al.* 2004). More specific training depends on the area of practice and, in gynaecology, would include learning how to take a sexual history. Unfortunately, the evidence suggests that most gynaecology nurses do not receive specific training in this area (Jolley 2002). Assessment does not involve asking questions about everything – this would be both intrusive and irrelevant. Selectivity should be based on a sound knowledge of the problem being assessed.

Relevant guidelines and protocols are also needed. Protocols offer an explicit framework for healthcare professionals 'to guide their clinical activities and promote quality patient care' (Handy 2002). Local protocols also usually include guidelines to assist the practitioner in making decisions about appropriate care. Some consider that these may restrict nursing practice rather than develop it because protocols should not be used as rigid tools of assessment, but nurses may be unwilling to compromise because of fears of litigation (Garrett 1999; Handy 2002). However, they are needed to set standards and support practice. This in turn protects both the practitioner and the patient.

ASSESSMENT IN GYNAECOLOGY

The female genito-urinary system includes the urinary tract and the reproductive organs and structures. Disorders of this system can have wide-ranging effects on general health. For example, ovarian dysfunction can alter the endocrine balance, and menstrual disorders can cause problems with bladder and bowel function and cause anaemia and pain. More women seek healthcare for reproductive disorders than anything else (Shaw 1997). Assessing problems in this area can be difficult because not only is the reproductive system very complex but its functions also have far-reaching psychosocial implications. It is sometimes difficult to differentiate signs and symptoms because the urinary and reproductive organs are so close to each other.

There are many areas within gynaecology where nurses are not only performing work traditionally undertaken by doctors but also setting up new and innovative services. These are listed in Table 1.1. Some are described more generally in other chapters but three contrasting areas have been chosen for discussion in this chapter because they illustrate the importance of nursing assessment and how it can be implemented in practice.

1. GP EMERGENCY ADMISSION UNITS FOR GYNAECOLOGY

Gynaecology departments have to deal with women who present as 'emergencies' with acute gynaecological symptoms. There are five main categories of symptoms:

- vaginal bleeding
- pelvic pain
- pelvic mass
- vulvovaginal symptoms
- problems in early pregnancy (not related to bleeding or pain).

Table 1.1. Specialist nursing roles in gynaecology

Services	Related skills

Early pregnancy assessment	Ordering investigations
	    ultrasound scans
	    recurrent miscarriage investigations
	Bereavement counselling

Fertility clinics	Ordering investigations Speculum examinations
Unwanted pregnancies	Promotion of sexual health Medical termination of pregnancy nurse prescribing

Family planning	Speculum examinations
	    taking smears
	Contraceptive implants (etonogestrel)
	    nurse prescribing

Advisory clinic for women undergoing pelvic radiotherapy (White 2004)	Counselling
Menopause advice	Hormone replacement therapy (HRT) implants
Postmenopausal bleed clinics	Hysteroscopy
Sterilisation clinics	Sexual history taking Counselling
Menstrual disorder clinics	Hysteroscopy Insertion of mirena coils

Oncology nursing service for
    gynaecology
	Colposcopy
	    taking a biopsy
	    carrying out treatments
	Palliative care and support

Nurse-led diagnosis and advice in
    Genitourinary Medicine (GUM)
    Clinics
	Collecting and examining swabs
	Treatments in GUM Clinics
	    cryocautery to genital warts

Osteoporosis advice	Bone densitometry
Continence advice	Bladder pressure cystometry
Urodynamics	
Emergency Admission Units	Triage Ordering investigations ultrasound scans Referrals
Pre-operative assessment	Medical and sexual history taking Auscultation of chests Counselling
Post-operative hysterectomy follow-up (Walsgrove 1999)	Speculum examinations (to check vault) Health promotion

Table 1.2. Causes of vaginal bleeding

Pregnancy	Miscarriage
	threatened
	incomplete
	inevitable
	missed
	Ectopic pregnancy

Atrophic vaginitis
Coital trauma

Cervicitis
Cervical polyp
Cervical ectropian
Cervical cancer

Endometrial polyp
Endometrial cancer
Fibroids
Intrauterine contraceptive device
Dysfunctional uterine bleeding
Hormone therapy

Post-surgery	Secondary infection
	Vault haematoma
	Bleeding from vaginal granulation tissue
	Retained products (following evacuation of retained products of conception (ERPOC) or termination)

Postpartum haemorrhage

Abnormal vaginal bleeding is the most common symptom, and women usually seek help if the bleeding requires immediate investigation or is heavy, prolonged or unusually painful. Bleeding during pregnancy, following a recent delivery or after surgery gives rise to concern and needs immediate investigation. Unexpected bleeding can also be intermenstrual, postcoital or postmenopausal, but usually these would not necessitate an emergency admission unless the bleeding was particularly heavy. Acute menorrhagia, or heavy vaginal bleeding, can be very severe, distressing for the patient and requires prompt emergency management. The causes of abnormal vaginal bleeding in women are listed in Table 1.2.

Acute pelvic pain can also be associated with problems during pregnancy, such as miscarriage or an ectopic pregnancy, which may be about to rupture. Other causes may be related to the menstrual cycle such as the passage of blood clots or a ruptured corpus luteum cyst. Pain can also be caused by ovarian problems such as cysts, which can be severely painful if they tort or twist, and ovarian hyperstimulation syndrome. Sometimes post-surgical complications can be painful. Pelvic inflammatory disease, usually associated with pelvic infections, can cause severe pain. Pain is often an exacerbation of symptoms associated with cancer or may not actually be related to the reproductive system but caused by urinary retention, constipation or acute bowel disease.

Women may present with a sudden swelling or mass. Unusually this may be an unsuspected pregnancy, sometimes seen in teenage girls or women approaching the menopause. More common reasons include fibroids, ovarian tumour, hydrosalpinx and urinary retention. Occasionally young girls present with a non-tender mass in the pelvis and are diagnosed with haematocolpos arising from an intact vaginal membrane. After surgery patients sometimes develop a haematoma or an abscess. Acute vulvovaginal symptoms are usually associated with trauma (accident, self-mutilation, assault), inflammation or discharge (bacterial vaginosis, ectropian, vulvitis, sexually transmitted infections) or swelling (Bartholin's abscess, polyp, prolapse). Some women have problems during an ongoing pregnancy, which are not related to bleeding or pain. The most obvious example is hyperemesis, when a woman can become extremely dehydrated.

Gynaecological emergency admissions usually arrive at hospitals in two ways. Either the patient is referred to hospital having seen her GP or she goes straight to a general emergency department. The important difference is that the GP referrals forewarn the hospital that the patient's problem is likely to be gynaecological. Although these patients are still sometimes sent to a general accident and emergency (A and E) department, increasingly they are being sent directly to a gynaecology unit in order to relieve some of the pressure on A and E.

The majority (approximately 75 %) of gynaecological emergencies involve women who have pregnancy-related bleeding or pain (MacKenzie 2005). During the past 10 years the management of these problems has changed dramatically with the introduction of Early Pregnancy Assessment Units or Centres (EPAU or EPAC), led either by a gynaecologist or specialist nurse. This work mainly relates to threatened or actual miscarriages and is described in Chapter 4. However, similar and often more urgent attention is needed for other gynaecological emergencies. Traditionally these patients have been admitted to a gynaecology ward for assessment. Some of these patients stay in hospital for medical management or observation and some need surgery, which is usually performed on an emergency list, often out of hours when an operating theatre is available. However, following assessment, some patients do not need to stay in at all. In effect the admission is unnecessary. Clearly this is neither cost-effective nor desirable for the patient. In order to improve management of this situation, many hospitals are now setting up outpatient GP emergency admission units in gynaecology departments. Frequently these are led by suitably qualified and experienced nurses.

When a patient arrives at the emergency admission unit, the nurse's role is to carry out an initial quick assessment to see if the patient is in any immediate danger. This would include a set of observations (blood pressure, pulse and temperature) and assessment of any blood loss. A pregnancy test is always carried out on any woman who could possibly be pregnant, because the result significantly influences the management of any presenting symptoms. Clearly conditions such as severe haemorrhaging causing shock or a likely ectopic pregnancy would require prompt action, intravenous access and medical assistance.

Fortunately most patients are fairly stable and the nurse can then proceed to carry out a more thorough assessment and order relevant clinical investigations (blood tests, urinalysis, ultrasound scan). This follows an agreed protocol with supporting guidelines. Following this the nurse can contact a doctor with details of the case history, arrange for abdominal and vaginal examination if necessary and then a decision can be made about whether the patient should be admitted. A negative result to a pregnancy test often avoids the need for admission. Sometimes patients are admitted to a different department, e.g. a general surgical ward or an obstetric ward if the patient is more than 16–20 weeks pregnant (depending on local practice). Patients who are discharged may need an appropriate follow-up appointment in a gynaecology clinic or EPAU. Some may need a prescription, usually for antibiotics and analgesia.

Nurses working in emergency admission units need to use assessment skills at different levels including basic observations, understanding non-verbal signs and taking and interpreting a logical patient history. Since the patient is likely to be very anxious, good communication skills and a calm reassuring manner are clearly important. Table 1.3 is a breakdown of emergencies seen during

Table 1.3. Referrals to a gynaecology emergency admission unit over 12 months

Indications for referral	Number
Bleeding and/or pain during pregnancy	216
Pain (not associated with pregnancy)	164
Vaginal bleeding (not associated with pregnancy)	77
Possible ectopic pregnancy	62
Post-operative problems, including haematomas, wound problems, vaginal bleeding, retained products	60
Bartholin's abscess	30
Hyperemesis	30
Postpartum problems	6
Miscellaneous general gynaecological problems, including lost coils, vaginal laceration, vulval swelling, sexually transmitted infections, procidentia, hyperstimulation of ovaries, dysfunctional bleeding	169
Not recorded	20
Other symptoms, not gynaecological, including appendicitis, constipation	12
Total	846

Local figures supplied by Libby Millett, Lead Sister for the Gynaecology Emergency Admissions Unit at Queen's Medical Centre, Nottingham.

the first 12 months on a newly established gynaecology emergency unit at Queen's Medical Centre (QMC), Nottingham. The range of problems demonstrates why a broad experience of gynaecology nursing and a thorough understanding of acute gynaecological problems are essential. Since this work is usually supported by clear protocols and the availability of a designated doctor for advice, extra training requirements are minimal and most senior gynaecology nurses could easily cope. However, maintaining relevant emergency care skills via courses such as *ALERT* (Smith 2003) is highly recommended.

The main advantage of a nurse-led service for patients is that it is more efficient and consistent. Patients can be seen promptly, especially those who are deemed less urgent and might therefore wait a long time to see a doctor busy with other priorities. Most importantly there are less unnecessary admissions. Figures collected on the emergency gynaecology unit at QMC, Nottingham, show that out of 846 patients seen in a year, only 431 were admitted. This represents a huge saving and more than justifies the new service. Owing to staffing problems, the unit is only open from Monday to Friday, during the daytime, but the figures support the need for a continuous service. It is important to point out that the number of women being seen with problems during pregnancy is only a fraction of the total because the vast majority go directly to the EPAU. During the same period of time 2931 women were referred to EPAU and together this represents 79 % of the overall emergency admission work, a similar proportion to that reported by MacKenzie (2005) for another large teaching hospital. In fact some hospitals, like St Thomas's, London, now have the GP emergency admission unit and EPAU in one department. It is also interesting to note that out of the 62 women sent in to the emergency unit with a possible ectopic pregnancy, over half ($n = 35$) did not have an ectopic pregnancy and 21 of these were not even pregnant.

2. NURSE-LED STERILISATION CLINICS

Sterilisation has become the most popular method of contraception worldwide. Approximately 190 million women and 50 million men have chosen to be sterilised (Glasier & Scott 2005; Royal College of Obstetricians and Gynaecologists 2003). In 2001, 10 % of women aged 16–49 in Great Britain had been sterilised (Royal College of Obstetricians and Gynaecologists 2003).

Female sterilisation involves blocking or excising both fallopian tubes. This prevents the ovum from being fertilised by sperm in the fallopian tube. The procedure is usually performed under a general anaesthesia by laparoscopic techniques, but sometimes a mini laparotomy is required. The most common method of occluding the fallopian tube is by applying a Filshie clip (see Figure 1.1). Less common methods include a Falope ring, which is applied around a loop of tube; diathermy, which makes reversal impossible and carries risks of causing damage to other organs; and salpingectomy, which involves cutting and removing the tubes.

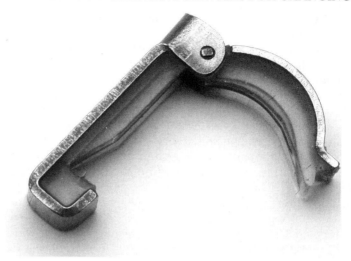

Figure 1.1. Filshie clip (actual size = 14 mm length)

The main advantages of female sterilisation are that it is the only permanent method of female contraception and has a good success rate. The general failure rate is 1 in 200 (Glasier & Scott 2005), but the effectiveness varies depending on which method is used. Filshie clips are considered the most effective, with a failure rate of between 2 and 3 per 1000 sterilisation operations (Kovacs & Krins 2002). The main disadvantages are that it is a surgical procedure involving an anaesthetic and that it is not easily reversed. Therefore correct and adequate counselling is essential before any female sterilisation. Despite counselling, up to 10 % of couples regret sterilisation and 1 % will request a reversal (Filshie *et al.* 1998; Glasier & Scott 2005). Factors influencing this are age (under 25 years), sterilisation immediately following a pregnancy, psychiatric illness and couples without children.

Women requesting a sterilisation usually wait in the normal way for a hospital appointment with a gynaecologist. Counselling forms the main part of this appointment and can be quite time-consuming. Another important decision is whether the woman is suitable for day surgery. If there are no problems, sterilisation may be carried out laparoscopically as a day case and the woman usually goes home the same day. Any problems such as obesity or a history of previous gynaecological surgery may require the patient to be admitted as an inpatient.

It is possible for this whole process to be carried out by a suitably qualified nurse. The nurse can carry out a thorough assessment, counsel the woman and her partner, decide whether the procedure should be done as a day case or inpatient case and arrange a date. Clearly this fast-track service could reduce waiting list times and speed up the whole process. A proposal supporting this

Table 1.4. Sterilisation pathway – criteria for consultant review

---

Potential gynaecological problems
Menstrual cycle lasting more than 35 days
Heavy menstrual bleeding
Intermenstrual bleeding and postcoital bleeding
Moderate or severe menstrual pain
Pelvic pain
Last smear taken over three years ago

Potential uncertainty
No use of contraception at present
No children
Under 25 years of age
Partner less than 25 years of age
New relationship or recent relationship

Potential health problems
Blood pressure more than 140 systolic and more than 85 diastolic
Major surgery or long-standing history
Medical history of asthma, hypertension, heart problems or diabetes
Body mass index (BMI) less than 20 or more than 35
Drugs

---

argument persuaded the Gynaecology Department at QMC, Nottingham, to pilot a nurse-led sterilisation service.

Before the service was started a proforma was designed to guide the nursing assessment. In addition a set of criteria determined those problems that would require a review by the consultant (see Table 1.4). Local GPs were contacted to inform them of the new service and encourage them to provide more details in their referral letters. Women requesting a sterilisation who did not seem to have any obvious problems were sent directly to the nurse-led sterilisation clinic.

The advantages of this service quickly became apparent. The women are seen and given a date for the sterilisation procedure far more quickly than if they go on the routine waiting list. This has reduced the overall waiting lists for gynaecology. Although some patients need a review by the consultant, most are dealt with completely by the nurse. As nursing confidence and experience has increased there are even less consultant referrals. There is more time for a thorough assessment and counselling session. Often the doctors in a busy clinic can only manage 10–15 minutes, but the nurse allocates at least 45 minutes, allowing for time to talk things through properly. The consultants are happy with the process and, above all, the patients are satisfied. A patient satisfaction audit covering the 6-month pilot scheme highlighted the efficiency and effectiveness of the service (Jager 2002):

- 71 % were seen within 5 minutes of their appointment time.
- 98 % felt that the information given was easy to understand.
- 60 % stated that there were more options than they had realised.
- 81 % felt that they were given adequate time to decide whether or not to have a sterilisation.
- 87 % went ahead with the sterilisation.
- 98 % felt that they received a good or excellent service.

Following the successful pilot, the nurse-led sterilisation clinic at QMC has now expanded. One nurse started the service but there are now two nurses seeing approximately 40 patients each month. In 2004, 69 % of the patients seen by the nurses were booked for a sterilisation (38 % on a day case list and 31 % as inpatients). Only 2 % were referred on to the consultant. The rest either went away to consider the alternatives (16 %) or were discharged (13 %), sometimes because they had changed their minds but often because they had decided to have a mirena coil fitted.

The nurses have had a long experience in gynaecology, which is essential, as the patients often want to discuss other related problems. Many women also suffer with menorrhagia and are often happy to be given information about the mirena coil, which is not only an effective method of birth control but can also help control excessive bleeding. Clearly the nurses need to have a good understanding of the sterilisation procedure itself and general surgical risks. The nurses have been trained in family planning so that they can discuss different methods of birth control. Study sessions and a new protocol on how to take a sexual history have also helped (Jolley 2002). Above all, the importance of communication and counselling skills is paramount in order to assess each woman's suitability for a sterilisation.

3. GYNAECOLOGY PRE-OPERATIVE ASSESSMENT

Patients who are booked for elective surgery usually attend hospital on an out-patient basis prior to their admission for a pre-operative assessment. Although the benefits of pre-admission assessment of patients was recommended as far back as 1972 (Crosby *et al.* 1972), it was not until the 1990s that this was introduced within dedicated clinics throughout the UK. The increasing waiting times for elective surgery highlighted the need for the most efficient use of resources. This included the need to minimise any last-minute cancellations caused by patients being unfit for surgery. Pre-admission assessment of patients means that problems can usually be identified and addressed before admission, and the government is now committed to improving pre-operative assessment at local, regional and national levels (Department of Health 2003).

Although the development of pre-operative assessment was initially driven by the need for greater efficiency, the general advantages for patients soon became apparent. 'The purpose of pre-operative assessment is not solely to determine the medical fitness of patients' (Wadsworth *et al.* 2002). In addition to a physical assessment, psychological and social factors are also important. The opportunity to give patients information and address their concerns is especially important. Research into the benefits of information-giving and patient education pre-operatively has demonstrated that this leads to a lower intake of analgesics, less anxiety, a shorter recovery time and increased coping in general (Caress 2003; Hughes 2002; Royal College of Nursing 1999). This is particularly important for women undergoing gynaecological surgery, because of the sensitive and emotive nature of the treatments. The many advantages of a pre-operative assessment are now recognised and summarised in Table 1.5.

Medical staff, usually house officers, initially carried out pre-operative assessment work, but the organisation of pre-assessment clinics is now very varied, including multidisciplinary staff at different levels. Sometimes anaesthetists lead pre-operative assessment, but increasingly it may be nurse-led. There is some level of nurse involvement in most pre-assessment clinics. If the

Table 1.5. Advantages of pre-operative assessment

A safe admission
    Up-to-date evaluation of whether proposed operation is still appropriate
    Opportunity to identify and resolve medical and anaesthetic problems
    Health promotion, e.g. cessation of smoking, weight reduction
    Patients are 'fit for surgery'
    Time to plan admission and discharge, e.g. social problems
    Reduced risk of infection

Patient-centred care
    Patients understand the need for surgery and are willing to undergo the operation
    Patients are well informed about the surgical procedure
    Patients understand the risks and benefits for informed consent
    Patients have time to reflect on information before admission
    Reduction in patient anxiety

Efficient use of resources
    Streamlining admission process
    Reduced length of hospital stay because patients can be admitted on the day of surgery and discharged earlier due to forward planning
    Reduction in the number of cancelled operations
    Appropriate use of personnel
    Efficient bed management
    Better utilisation of theatre time
    Specialist equipment available

References: Janke *et al.* (2002); Pearce (2004); Reed *et al.* (1997); Royal College of Nursing (1999); Wadsworth *et al.* (2002).

nurse is part of a multidisciplinary team, this may involve only a nursing assessment, but often the nurse carries out a much fuller assessment to include the physical assessment traditionally undertaken by doctors. The development of nurse-led pre-assessment clinics at hospitals throughout the UK (Neasham 1996; Reed *et al.* 1997; Wadsworth *et al.* 2002; Walsgrove 2004) has raised the profile of this area of work, and there are now three nurse consultants (in Birmingham, Chelsea and Westminster) who lead pre-operative services in England (Pearce 2004).

Research supports the role of nurses in pre-operative assessment (Clinch 1997; Newbold 1996) and demonstrates that it is acceptable to patients (Ong 1997; Walsgrove 2004). A study by Jones *et al.* (2000) reported fewer complications among patients pre-assessed by nurses than those by medical staff and concluded that pre-admission clerking by a nurse specialist rather than a doctor is as effective in preventing the cancellation of elective surgery. Kinley *et al.* (2001) found that pre-operative assessments carried out by nurses were equivalent to those performed by doctors, that house officers order more unnecessary tests than nurses and that pre-operative assessment by nurses was acceptable to patients. Further work by Kinley *et al.* (2002) found no reason to inhibit the development of nurse-led pre-operative assessment provided that nurses received adequate training. Rushforth *et al.* (2000) concluded that transferring assessment from senior house officers (SHOs) to nurses maintained and enhanced the quality of patient care.

One concern is that nurses could miss a potential medical or anaesthetic risk. However, this can be covered by:

- a thorough training package approved by the relevant departments and backed by a scheme under *The Scope of Professional Practice* (United Kingdom Central Council 1992)
- strict protocols and guidelines for all investigations and information
- a clearly designated 'advice line' in the event of any problems.

At QMC, Nottingham, the Gynaecology Pre-operative Assessment Unit has always been nurse-led, but patients are seen by a multidisciplinary team including a junior doctor, nurse, physiotherapist, phlebotomist and sometimes a consultant or registrar. Over the last 5 years an average of 1700 patients have been seen annually. Although patients have been generally satisfied with the service, there have been some problems. The process is quite lengthy and there is inevitably some overlap in both the information collected and given. Sometimes doctors have been delayed due to more urgent work and this has resulted in longer waiting times for the patients. The logical response to this problem was to train nurses to carry out more of the pre-operative assessment work. They would then be able to undertake some of the work covered by the junior doctors. This would not only save on the duplication of information collected but also release junior doctors for other duties and learning experiences within the Gynaecology Department.

The Scope of Professional Practice was written on 'patient history taking and physical assessment' specifically for nurse practitioners working in the Gynaecology Pre-admission Unit. The aim of this is to enable the nurse practitioner to obtain an accurate patient history, carry out a safe physical assessment, organise relevant specialist tests, identify patients who are at risk in relation to general anaesthesia and give comprehensive information about the patient's operative procedure based on individual needs (Jolley 2003). The package outlines the knowledge, skills and competence required to carry out this work.

The nurse needs a sound knowledge of:

- the processes involved in taking a patient's history
- the salient anatomy and physiology involved in physical assessment for a general anaesthetic
- the significance of specialist tests
- gynaecological problems and operative procedures
- the protocols that have been developed to underpin practice

and needs to be competent in:

- venepuncture and taking blood
- performing ECGs
- ordering investigations
- auscultating chests.

Training includes a mixture of theory, covered by packages such as *Pre-operative Assessment: Setting a Standard through Learning* (Janke *et al.* 2002) or *Physical Assessment for Nurses* (Cox 2004) and practical experience in performing ECGs and listening to heart and lung sounds. After relevant training, the gynaecology nurse practitioner needs to be observed undertaking a minimum of five full patient assessments to include history-taking, physical assessment, gynaecology assessment and ordering and/or completion of investigations for each of four groups of gynaecological surgical procedures:

- laparotomies (e.g. hysterectomy, oophorectomy, myomectomy, colposuspension)
- major vaginal surgery (e.g. hysterectomy, pelvic floor repairs)
- laparoscopies (e.g. diagnostic work, sterilisation, adhesiolysis, cystectomy)
- minor surgery (e.g. tension-free vaginal tape procedure, hysteroscopy, biopsy)

To help in this process they need to go to theatre to observe a cross-section of gynaecological surgery, attend the gynaecology clinic to appreciate how problems present and decisions about surgery are made and observe how different doctors take histories. The National Institute for Clinical Excellence has issued guidance on the use of pre-operative tests in elective surgery (National Institute for Clinical Excellence 2003). This is very useful in providing a consistent approach while avoiding unnecessary tests. Several new local protocols were also written to support practice, including bowel preparation and pregnancy testing before surgery.

Three different types of assessment are needed pre-operatively: physical, social and psychological (Royal College of Nursing 1999). Related to gynaecology this involves:

Physical assessment includes:

- assessing the patient's cardiovascular and respiratory systems to determine any problems that may adversely affect the patient during surgery and anaesthesia. It includes observations of pulse and blood pressure, blood tests, ECG and X-ray (if appropriate).
- assessing any other physical factors that may have a bearing on the proposed surgery (e.g. previous laparotomy, pregnancy status, anaemia due to menorrhagia, adhesions, diabetes, long-term steroids, warfarin treatment).
- ensuring the operation is still appropriate for the gynaecological condition. This involves assessing whether the symptoms are the same, better or worse. An ultrasound scan may be needed (e.g. of a cyst or to determine the size of the endometrium).
- excluding local and systemic infection. The patient should have no infection at the proposed operation site (e.g. chlamydia prior to hysteroscopy) or other infections that may affect surgery (e.g. urinary tract infection).
- ensuring the patient is neither grossly under- nor overweight.
- considering special anatomical or physical conditions (e.g. a bicornate uterus or recent hip replacement or arthritis, which is important when positioning the patient for general anaesthesia).

Social assessment includes:

- assessment of the patient's social support network (e.g. the number of carers, friends and/or relatives available and willing to help the patient on discharge), which is especially important after major surgery like a hysterectomy and for elderly patients, who may live alone.
- anticipation of specific social needs of the patient on discharge (e.g. help with maintaining nutritional or hygiene needs).

Psychological assessment includes:

- assessing the patient's prior knowledge of the proposed operation and its potential effects on her life.
- assessing her learning needs and how these might best be met before admission.
- ensuring the patient has realistic expectations about the forthcoming surgery (e.g. diathermy to endometriosis is not necessarily a permanent solution, possible outcomes of surgery for different gynaecological cancers,

chances of conceiving after some procedures for women undergoing fertility treatment).

- ascertaining whether the patient has any worries or concerns that need to be addressed, especially relating to body image, misconceptions about gynaecological surgery, loss of fertility, sexuality and sexual functioning.

The nurse practitioner needs to use the information gathered through the assessment process in a variety of ways. Results of any tests need to be coordinated and recorded. Abnormal test results may require deferment or cancellation of surgery and possibly further investigation or treatment. It may be necessary to liaise with the patient over any problems relating to the proposed surgery. Liaison with the admission ward is also important as the patient may have some special problems or need special preparation, such as bowel preparation before some oncology operations. It is also important to communicate with all members of the multidisciplinary team. This may involve contacting the anaesthetist or discussing any potential problems with the physiotherapist, such as the importance of pelvic floor exercises or the risk of lymphoedema after a radical hysterectomy or vulvectomy. Finally, the nurse needs to use the assessment to decide on the most appropriate patient information and education (Caress 2003).

Patient education can cover three separate areas: the proposed operation, the hospital stay and the post-discharge recovery. The amount of information given depends not only on the patient's existing knowledge and understanding but also on her anxiety level. For most patients information helps to alleviate anxiety, but a few patients are too anxious to actually concentrate on what is being said, especially if they are upset about their diagnosis (Caress 2003). Sometimes patients are given too much information and can become confused. Other patients may come armed with information from the Internet, ready to cross-examine staff on the latest available treatments, and patients are often reported to want more information than they actually receive (Jenkins *et al.* 2001). Some patients may have one overriding concern, such as pain control, alternatives to surgery, sexual functioning or the chances of conceiving, and are unable to concentrate on other issues. This is why written information is useful for the patients to take away and read when, or if, they need to. It is also useful for patients with limited recall, but should not be used as a replacement for verbal education.

During the assessment the nurse also needs to be able to handle the more unusual and unexpected questions. Some of those the writer has experienced include:

'What happens to the eggs?' *(often asked relating to a hysterectomy with conservation of ovaries or sterilisation)*
'How come I've got cancer, when my smears have been all right?' *(patients with endometrial or ovarian cancer)*
'Can I see my cyst afterwards?' *(after an ovarian cystectomy)*

'When can I go deep-sea diving?' *(after a hysteroscopy)*
'When can I have oral sex?' *(after a vaginal hysterectomy)*
'Will my partner notice my cervix has gone?' *(after a total abdominal hysterectomy)*
'What will happen to the space in my stomach?' *(after a hysterectomy)*

The overall benefits to patients of pre-operative assessment by nurses include a reduction in waiting times because patients are examined and assessed by one member of staff providing continuity and a patient-centred approach. Agreed protocols mean that the approach to assessment, investigations and patient education is consistent. Research evidence supports the need for a particularly sensitive pre-operative assessment service for gynaecology patients, run by health professionals with relevant expertise (Walsgrove 1997). Patients with gynaecological problems are often more comfortable talking to an experienced nurse than a young, and sometimes male, doctor. They are often embarrassed to talk to a doctor about their sex life or particular symptoms, such as passing urine during sexual intercourse, and may feel silly if they admit that they are scared of needles or do not understand their own anatomy. Patient satisfaction surveys demonstrated that the role is valued and, in general, patients feel reassured by the pre-operative assessment process.

CONCLUSION

Although the development of nurse-led assessment appears to have been driven by the need to reduce doctors' hours and improve waiting list management, it is clear that it is not only safe and effective but also well accepted by patients. The nurse-led approach is more holistic than the traditional medical model and is characterised by a much wider social and emotional assessment. This is especially relevant in gynaecology because of the nature of gynaecological problems and the huge impact they have on women's lives. The three areas described in this chapter reflect practice in one particular hospital, but similar work is developing in Gynaecology Departments throughout the UK (Walsgrove 2004). This is undoubtedly improving the health services available for women.

REFERENCES

Aggleton P and Chalmers H (2000) *Nursing Models and Nursing Practice*, 2nd edition, Macmillan Press Ltd, London.
British Medical Association (2004) *Hospital Doctors – Junior Doctors' Hours*, http://www.bma.org.uk/ap.nsf/content/HospitalDoctorsJunHrs (accessed March 2005).

Cahill H (1998) It isn't what you do, but the way you do it: nurse practitioners in day surgery. *Journal of One-Day Surgery*, Winter, 11–14.

Caress A L (2003) Giving information to patients. *Nursing Standard*, **17**(43), 47–54.

Carroll M (2002) Advanced nursing practice. *Nursing Standard*, **16**(29), 33–5.

Castledine G (1995) Will the nurse practitioner be a mini doctor or maxi nurse? *British Journal of Nursing*, **4**(16), 938–9.

Clinch C (1997) Nurses achieve quality with pre-assessment clinics. *Journal of Clinical Nursing*, **6**(2), 147–51.

Collins K (1999) Nurses and PAMs in innovative roles: job satisfaction and its contributory factors. *Nursing Standard*, **13**(47), 31.

Cox C (2004) *Physical Assessment for Nurses*, Blackwell Publishing, London.

Crosby D L *et al.* (1972) General surgical pre-admission clinics. *British Medical Journal* **3**(819), 157–59.

Department of Health (1999) *Making a Difference: Strengthening Nursing*, HMSO, London.

Department of Health (2000a) *The NHS Plan*, HMSO, London.

Department of Health (2000b) *A Health Service for All Talents: Developing the NHS Workforce*. HMSO, London.

Department of Health (2003) *NHS Modernisation Agency: Operating Theatre and Pre-operative Assessment Programme*, DoH, London.

Department of Health (2005) *European Working Time Directive FAQ*, http://www.dh.gov.uk/PolicyAndGuidance/HumanResourcesAndTraining (accessed March 2005).

Edwards K (1995) What are nurses' views on expanding practice? *Nursing Standard*, **9**(41), 38–40.

Filshie G M *et al.* (1998) Day case sterilisation with the Filshie clip in Nottingham – Ten-year follow-up study: the first 200 cases. In Kruger T *et al.* (Eds), *7th Annual Meeting of the International Society for Gynaecological Endoscopy: Bologna*, Monduzz Editore International Proceedings Divisions, pp. 145–58.

Garrett A (1999) Is the scope of practice endangered by lack of vision?, *Nursing Standard*, **13**(28), 40–2.

Glasier A, Scott A (2005) Control of fertility. In Rees M, Hope S (Eds) *Gynaecology*, Elsevier Mosby, Oxford.

Handy P (2002) Nurse-directed services in genitourinary medicine. *Nursing Standard*, **17**(11), 33–8.

Hicks C, Hennessy D (1999) A task-based approach to defining the role of the nurse practitioner: the views of UK acute and primary sector nurses. *Journal of Advanced Nursing*, **29**(1), 666–73.

Hughes S (2002) The effects of giving patients pre-operative information. *Nursing Standard*, **16**(28), 33–7.

Jager S (2002) *The Sterilisation Pathway and Its Progress. Gynaecology developments – changing with the times*. Internal report to Gynaecology Department at Queen's Medical Centre, Nottingham (unpublished).

Janke E *et al.* (2002) *Preoperative Assessment: Setting a Standard through Learning*. University of Southampton, Southampton.

Jenkins V *et al.* (2001) Information needs of patients with cancer: results from a large study in UK cancer centres. *British Journal of Cancer*, **84**(1), 48–51.

Jolley S (2002) Taking a sexual history: the role of the nurse. *Nursing Standard*, **98**(18), 39–41.

Jolley S (2003) *Expanding Nursing Practice through Scope of Professional Practice – Patient History Taking and Physical Assessment*. In-house document produced for University Hospital, Queen's Medical Centre, Nottingham (unpublished).

Jones A *et al.* (2000) Preadmission clerking of urology nurses. *Professional Nurse*, **15**(4), 261–6.

Kinley H *et al.* (2001) Extended scope of nursing practice: a multicentre randomised controlled trial of appropriately trained nurses and pre-registration house officers in pre-operative assessment in elective general surgery. *Health Technology Assessment*, **5**, 20.

Kinley H *et al.* (2002) Effectiveness of appropriately trained nurses in preoperative assessment: randomised controlled equivalence/non-inferiority trial. *British Medical Journal*, **325**(7376), 1323–6.

Kitson A (1999) The essence of nursing. *Nursing Standard*, **13**(23), 42–6.

Knape J (1999) Nurse accountability in relation to nurse-led services. *British Journal of Nursing*, **8**(22), 1514.

Kovacs G T, Krins A J (2002) Female sterilization with Filshie clips: what is the risk failure? A retrospective survey of 30,000 applications. *The Journal of Family Planning and Reproductive Health Care*, **28**(1), 34–5.

MacKenzie I (2005) Gynaecological emergencies. In Rees M, Hope S (Eds), *Gynaecology*, Elsevier Mosby, Oxford.

Magennis C *et al.* (1999) Nurses' attitudes to the extension and expansion of their clinical roles. *Nursing Standard*, **13**(51), 32–6.

National Institute for Clinical Excellence (2003) *Clinical Guideline 3. Preoperative tests – The Use of Routine Preoperative Tests for Elective Surgery*, NICE, London.

Neasham J (1996) Nurse-led pre-assessment clinics. *British Journal of Theatre Nursing*, **6**(8), 5–10.

Newbold D (1996) An evaluation of the role of the nurse practitioner. *Nursing Times*, **92**(22), 45–6.

NHS Management Executive (1991) *Junior Doctors: The New Deal*, NHSME, London.

Ong B N (1997) Patients approve of pre-operative assessments. *Nursing Times*, **93**(40), 57–9.

Pearce L (2004) Safe admission. *Nursing Standard*, **19**(8), 14.

Pearson A *et al.* (1996) *Nursing Models for Practice*, 2nd edition, Butterworth-Heinemann, Oxford.

Price (2004) Conducting sensitive patient interviews. *Nursing Standard*, **18**(38), 45–52.

Read S *et al.* (1999) *Exploring New Roles in Practice: Implications of Developments within the Clinical Team (ENRiP)*, Report to Department of Health, ScHARR, Sheffield.

Redsell S A *et al.* (2004) Devising and establishing the face and content validity of explicit criteria of consultation competence for UK secondary care nurses. *Nurse Education Today*, **24**(3), 180–7.

Reed M *et al.* (1997) Nurse-led general surgical pre-operative assessment clinic. *Journal of Colorectal Surgery*, **42**(5), 310–13.

Roper N *et al.* (2001) *The Roper–Logan–Tierney Model of Nursing*, Churchill Livingstone, London.

Rose K *et al.* (1998) The extended role of the nurse: reviewing the implications for practice. *Clinical Effectiveness in Nursing*, **1**(1), 31–7.

Rounds L (1997) The nurse practitioner: a healing role for the nurse. In Kritek P (Ed), *Reflections on Healing: A Central Nursing Construct*, NLN Press, New York.

Royal College of Nursing (1997) *Nurse Practitioners: Your Questions Answered*, RCN, London.

Royal College of Nursing (1999) *Orthopaedic Pre-admission Assessment Clinics*, RCN, London.

Royal College of Obstetricians and Gynaecologists (2003) *Male and Female Sterilisation. Evidence-based Clinical Guideline Number 4*, RCOG Press, London.

Rushforth H *et al.* (2000) A pilot randomised trial of medical versus nurse clerking for minor surgery. *Archives of Disease in Childhood*, **83**(3)223–6.

Savage M *et al.* (2000) Inter-professional education and team working. *British Medical Journal*, **320**, 1019–20.

Shaw M (Ed) (1997) *Assessment made Incredibly Easy*, Springhouse, Pennsylvania.

Smith G (2003) *ALERT – Acute Life-threatening Events Recognition and Treatment*, University of Portsmouth.

The Times (2005) Six promises, 12 February, p. 32.

United Kingdom Central Council for Nursing, Midwifery and Health Visiting (1992) *The Scope of Professional Practice*, UKCC, London.

Wadsworth L *et al.* (2002) The nurse practitioner's role in day case pre-operative assessment. *Nursing Standard*, **16**(47), 41–4.

Walsgrove H (1997) Anticipating anxiety. *Nursing Standard*, **12**(1), 2.

Walsgrove H (1999) A sanctuary from anxiety. *Nursing Standard*, **14**(8), 61.

Walsgrove H (2004) Piloting a nurse-led gynaecology preoperative-assessment clinic. *Nursing Times*, **100**(3), 38–41.

White E (2004) Where medicine left off. *Nursing Standard*, **18**(37), 20.

USEFUL WEBSITES

www.pre-op.org
www.fpa.org.uk
www.nhsdirect.nhs.uk
www.femalelife.co.uk

2 Promoting Sexual Health

SUE JOLLEY, SUE GRIFFITHS and HELEN WHITE

'Sex' is a short but powerful word, which instantly attracts attention. Sex can mean different things to different people. It can amuse or shock, satisfy or frustrate and bring happiness or misery. Sex also creates a variety of employment; consider midwives, therapists, prostitutes, designers, filmmakers, counsellors and advertisers to name just a few. Undoubtedly gynaecology staff should be included in this list. Fortunately the focus of each group of workers is different! Gynaecology nurses are involved in promoting sexual health, which presents a number of challenges. This chapter describes how the service is meeting those challenges.

Challenges	Service developments
• Increasing numbers of teenage pregnancies and record levels of chlamydia in the UK • Government targets for improving sexual health • Low profile given to sexual health aspect of gynaecology work • Lack of appropriate training for nurses • Fragmented and inadequate service for women with unwanted pregnancies	• Chlamydia screening programme • Cooperation between local sexual health services • New sexual health training programmes • Sexual health competencies and standards • Nurse-led delivery of medical terminations of pregnancy

WHAT IS SEXUAL HEALTH?

The majority of sexual health textbooks and education programmes start with a consideration of the nature of sexuality. This used to be associated very narrowly with reproduction, but it is now seen as an important part of general health and personal fulfilment. Definitions are therefore very broad. Roper

Gynaecology: Changing Services for Changing Needs. Edited by Sue Jolley
© 2006 by John Wiley & Sons, Ltd

et al. (1996) describe the expression of sexuality in terms of gender, appearance, behaviour, personality, sexual intercourse and reproduction. The Royal College of Nursing (2000) describes it as 'an individual's self-concept, shaped by their personality and expressed as sexual feelings, attitudes, beliefs and behaviours through a heterosexual, homosexual, bisexual and transsexual orientation'.

There is general agreement that biological, psychological, emotional, cultural and sociological elements are involved in expressing sexuality, and health workers cannot ignore this if they want to provide holistic care (Royal College of Nursing 2001). Support for patients' sexual health needs is a recognised part of nursing practice (Royal College of Nursing 2000). However, nurses should be realistic about what can be achieved, so it is helpful to distinguish between sexuality, sexual functioning and sexual health (Gregory 2000). While sexuality refers to issues of gender, identity, self-esteem and self-expression, sexual functioning relates to whether the body is working normally or whether it is (or will) be impaired. Sexual health is an essential component of general health, refers to the capacity and freedom to enjoy and express sexuality, and includes the prevention of unplanned pregnancies and sexually transmitted diseases.

These areas are clearly mutually dependent, but nurses are usually most directly concerned with sexual functioning and sexual health. They do not always have enough time or the appropriate training to deal with gender issues or psychological and relationship difficulties and so should refer the patient to other professionals.

Sexual functioning relates directly to the ability to recover from, or adapt to, medical conditions. The physical causes of sexual problems need not be gynaecological and include cancer, vascular or heart disease, neurological impairment, and rheumatoid and arthritic conditions. Of more direct concern to gynaecology nurses are hormonal dysfunctions, continence problems, difficulties with fertility and the consequences of problems in early pregnancy. These are discussed in later chapters.

Treatments such as medication, surgery, radiation and chemotherapy can also affect sexual functioning. Both general surgery such as mastectomy, amputation or stoma creation and gynaecological surgery such as hysterectomy can result in sexual problems. This is illustrated by a study of sexual activity after radical vulvectomy or hysterectomy, which found that 75% of women had sexual difficulties for more than six months post-operatively and 15% never resumed sexual intercourse (Marquiegui & Huish 1999).

TARGET GROUPS

In practice a large part of sexual health work inevitably relates to issues around both promoting 'safe sex' and dealing with problems arising when it is not practised effectively. There is no doubt that the high rates of teenage pregnancies and sexually transmitted infections (STIs) continue to concern health agencies and have put sexual health on the political agenda (Social Exclusion Unit 1999). Teenagers are becoming sexually active at an earlier age and surveys suggest that a third of 15- to 16-year-olds have experienced sexual intercourse (Botting 1995). Young people under the age of 16 remain the group most likely to have unprotected sex (Thistle 2003).

The UK has the highest rate of teenage pregnancies in Western Europe (Brennan 2002; Nicoll *et al.* 1999; Swann *et al.* 2003). Each year 70 out of 1000 girls aged 15–17 become pregnant (Social Exclusion Unit 1999) and 56000 babies are born to teenage mothers in the UK, with nearly 8000 conceived by girls under the age of 16 and 2200 by those under 14 (Brennan 2002). Much of the research on this topic suggests that child-bearing adolescents are susceptible to both physical and psychological health-related problems (Leishman 2004).

Teenage pregnancy is not the only consequence of unprotected sex for young people. A survey by Weston (1998) reported that only 3 % of young people expressed concern about STIs. Not surprisingly the number of STIs is increasing (Health Protection Agency 2004). Johnson *et al.* (2002) noted that diagnoses of chlamydia, gonorrhoea and syphilis had doubled collectively in the previous five years. Chlamydia is the most commonly diagnosed STI in the UK, with men and women under 25 at the highest risk of acquiring it (Health Protection Agency 2004; Royal College of Nursing 2005). Unfortunately it is difficult to determine the exact size of the problem because chlamydia often has no obvious symptoms and so frequently remains undiagnosed. It is symptomless in up to 80 % of infected females and 50 % of males (Royal College of Nursing 2005). Although easily cured with antibiotics, untreated chlamydia can lead to serious problems, including pelvic inflammatory disease (PID), ectopic pregnancies or infertility.

There has been an alarming rise in syphilis cases, which rose by 28 % in men and 32 % in women during 2003 (Health Protection Agency 2004). The rising incidence of HIV infection is also of great concern. Around half of new HIV infections are occurring in 15- to 24-year-olds and in 1999, for the first time, there were more diagnoses of new HIV infections through heterosexual sex than through sex between men (Thistle 2003). By the end of 2003 approximately 53000 adults in the UK were living with HIV, of whom 27 % were unaware of their infection (Health Protection Agency 2004).

The government is committed to tackling these problems. In 1999 the Social Exclusion Unit published its ten-year plan to reduce teenage pregnancy (Social Exclusion Unit 1999). The goal under *The NHS Plan* is to halve the rate of conception among those aged less than 18 by 2010 and to reduce the risk of long-term social exclusion for teenage parents (Department of Health 2000). To drive through the campaign and implement local teenage pregnancy strategies 150 teenage pregnancy coordinators were appointed. Since then the UK has devolved into four separate administrations, each developing their own policies. In England, the Teenage Pregnancy Strategy and the Sexual Health and HIV Strategy (Department of Health 2001a) provide the framework for developing sexual services and recommend that nurses should expand their role as specialists. Unfortunately, the impact of the steadily increasing rate of STIs on sexual health services has been huge. There has been a 57 % increase in the total number of STIs diagnosed over the past decade 'giving rise to concerns of the ability of the services to cope' (Health Protection Agency 2004). Tackling these problems requires sustained initiatives and investment. The recent government White Paper *Choosing Health* (Department of Health 2004a) includes sexual health as a serious health challenge, and a £300 million programme to modernise sexual health services has been launched.

Although government funding is targeting teenage sexual health, which also receives high media coverage, sexual activity is, of course, not confined to the young. Sexual health problems can affect people of all ages. Women who lived through the 'swinging sixties', liberated by the availability of the oral contraceptive pill, are now middle-aged. The impact of the sexual revolution may have sometimes been exaggerated but there has undoubtedly been a huge change in sexual behaviour. It has become acceptable for mature women to expect active and satisfying sexual relationships. Large numbers of women now wait until they are over 30, or even 40, to start a family, increasing the likelihood that they have more than one sexual relationship. The high divorce rate and larger numbers of single women also mean that women are tending to have more sexual partners. The British Menopause Society (BMS) argues that more mature women 'have largely been ignored within the field of sexual health' (British Menopause Society 2005).

Women of any age can, and do, have unwanted pregnancies. Inevitably more mature women are also catching sexually transmitted infections, especially as they do not consider themselves to be in the same risk category as teenagers. There are those who have been sterilised (men or women) after completing their family and therefore believe that they do not need any sexual protection. Although there has been an increase in cases of chlamydia, herpes, genital warts and gonorrhoea in women aged 45 to 64, they are always forgotten in any prevention programmes (British Menopause Society 2005). However, older women may be at a higher risk of infection because of physiological changes such as the gradual decline in immune function and the presence of other diseases, which may increase infection risks. It is therefore important to remember to promote sexual health to mature women.

THE ROLE OF GYNAECOLOGY NURSES

Many different healthcare departments are addressing the issue of sexual health including public health, family planning and community nurses, school nurses and general practitioners. Gynaecology departments also have an important role to play. Gynaecology is commonly described as a surgical speciality. The gynaecology nurses therefore care for women before and after a range of surgical procedures carried out for both diagnostic and treatment purposes. The sexual health implications are clearly important for all those patients who are, or intend to be, sexually active. However, women also visit gynaecology outpatient clinics or are admitted to gynaecology wards for a variety of other problems: with unwanted pregnancies, problems during ongoing pregnancies, functional problems with sexual intercourse or with pain and symptoms associated with PID. The majority (75 %) of cases of PID are caused by STIs, especially chlamydia and gonorrhoea (Moss 2001). There is clear evidence that the long-term complications of PID such as infertility, ectopic pregnancies and chronic pain are both serious and common (Andrews 1997; Stirrat 1997).

Gynaecology nurses are involved in helping and supporting women receiving treatment for these problems so the promotion of sexual health should be a central part of their work. It is relevant to consider whether this is true in practice. Most of the literature on sexual health promotion refers to staff in the community sector. For example, the *Teenage Pregnancy* report (Social Exclusion Unit 1999) emphasises the role of the school nurse and *Choosing Health* (Department of Health 2004a) refers to multidisciplinary primary healthcare teams. This is not surprising given the importance of primary prevention. However, secondary prevention is also important, and there has been little literature published specifically on the role of gynaecology nurses (Jolley 2001). There are some references supporting a role for gynaecology nurses in sexual health promotion (Weyman 2003), but the role seems to be poorly defined. The low profile given to this aspect of gynaecology nursing work may reflect the fact that the Royal College of Obstetricians and Gynaecologists (RCOG) has traditionally been slow to recognise the speciality of reproductive health or to take much interest in non-reproductive health or the prevention of STIs. It is therefore difficult to tell whether the promotion of sexual health by gynaecology nurses is taken for granted or is not considered very relevant.

In order to investigate this role in more depth, a research study was designed to investigate the knowledge, activities and perceptions of gynaecology nurses in relation to teenage sexual health (Jolley 2001). This was carried out at Queen's Medical Centre (QMC), Nottingham. This is particularly relevant because Nottingham has one of the highest teenage pregnancy rates in the UK (Office for National Statistics 1999), and chlamydia and gonorrhoea rates are particularly high in the Trent region, where Nottingham is situated (Hughes *et al.* 1998; Scott 1999). A cross-sectional survey of all (46) gynaecology nurses at the hospital was carried out, followed by semi-structured interviews with a small random subsample. Results demonstrated poor nursing knowledge about sexual health problems and local sexual health services, a lack of consistency in the approach to sexual health issues and negative perceptions of the service. Both the questionnaire and the interview data revealed a fairly limited nursing role in promoting teenage sexual health. A majority of the nurses (87%) had not received any specific training in sexual health promotion.

Generalisations cannot be made from a study in one hospital. However, this was followed by a wider investigation. One of the problems was that QMC had no policy or guidelines for taking a sexual history. Evidence suggests that nurses do not feel comfortable in addressing sexual health issues (Irwin 1997; Metcalf 2004; Warner *et al.* 1999; Waterhouse 1996). This led to a telephone survey to determine nursing practice in other gynaecology departments (Jolley 2002). The survey included all hospitals in the UK with more than 500 patients. The results confirm that the lack of consistency and guidance at QMC is not an isolated problem. Gynaecology nurses in most hospitals had not had any training in how to take a sexual history (109 out of 129 hospitals, or 84%) and none of the hospitals had any guidelines for taking a sexual history or any specific documentation for recording this information. There was general agreement that effective sexual history taking would improve patient care, and this is supported by research work in other areas (Handy 2002).

IMPROVING SEXUAL HEALTH PROMOTION

These two investigations, and another recent study (Norwich Union Healthcare 2002), demonstrate the need for better organisation and the development of clear policies supported by staff training and education. Gynaecology nurses need to look more closely at how they assess patients' sexual health needs before they can promote sexual health effectively. Several changes have now been made at QMC. A new protocol was written to help gynaecology nurses take sexual histories. Study days have been organised, including a mixture of group work and presentations from different experts in sexual health assessment and gynaecology. Designated nurses with an interest in sexual health have developed support roles, helping to raise awareness and keep staff informed. They have also established links with primary care workers in the field of sexual health. All nurses are encouraged to enrol on different sexual health courses and study programmes.

Effective sexual health promotion is dependent on appropriate communication and counselling skills (Irwin 1997) but gynaecology nurses also need to have an adequate knowledge of STIs in order to offer patients effective advice (Weston 1998). Education and training for all those who provide sexual health services is therefore an important element of the government's sexual health strategy (Department of Health 2001a; Royal College of Obstetricians and Gynaecologists 2003), and the best way to determine exact educational needs is by talking to individual members of staff (Jolley 2001). There are now a number of new training initiatives, and it is imperative that gynaecology nurses take advantage of these. One notable example is the new Sexual Health Skills course by distance learning, launched by the Royal College of Nursing (RCN) in 2004. The aim of the course is to improve the levels of sexual health knowledge and skills of registered nurses, enabling them to contribute towards the action plans of the national strategies on sexual health and HIV. As a foundation programme in sexual health, it is an excellent first step for all gynaecology nurses. It is also possible to complete a degree course in either women's health or sexual health. As well as general training programmes, nurses working with teenagers would also benefit from training specifically related to adolescents (Metcalf 2004; Society of Sexual Health Advisers 2004). The RCN has published competency levels in family planning and sexual health. These provide a comprehensive guide to the skills needed so that nurses can provide safe and effective care (Royal College of Nursing 2004).

The RCOG now recognises the importance of fully integrated sexual health services (Royal College of Obstetricians and Gynaecologists 2003). Successful sexual health promotion depends on cooperation between health workers representing different services and this should include gynaecology. A good example of this is the current initiative to detect, treat and prevent chlamydia. A screening programme was funded as a pilot project in Wirral and Portsmouth between 1990 and 2000 (Department of Health 2001a). This was a success for both patients and healthcare professionals. A large proportion (75 %) of those offered screening accepted and approximately 1 in 10 were found to be infected. Of those diagnosed with chlamydia 95 % returned for treatment (Department of Health 2002a). A national chlamydia screening programme is now being implemented to cover the whole of England by March 2007 (Department of Health 2004a). Although this is a community project, its success depends on good liaison between all the health services.

There are also specific recommendations about screening women before certain gynaecological procedures. These include dilatation and curettage, hysteroscopy, colposcopy and some procedures in the termination of pregnancy (Department of Health 1998). The RCOG also recommends that women under 35 years should be screened prior to interuterine device (IUD) insertion (Templeton 1996).

Women visiting the gynaecology department are often investigated for chlamydia either as a direct result of their admission (for pain or an unwanted pregnancy) or incidentally on the basis of their sexual history. Unfortunately, the results are not immediately available. Sometimes a diagnosis of PID is made without appropriate results, when other causes for pain have been excluded, because it is felt that antibiotic treatment should be started. For these reasons it is often assumed that someone else will take responsibility for giving appropriate advice when, and if, the samples test positive for chlamy-dia. However, if a patient's sexual behaviour indicates that they are even at risk of becoming infected with chlamydia, it is irresponsible for gynaecology nurses not to carry out appropriate health promotion about reducing risks and the importance of early detection through testing for chlamydia. 'The testing and diagnosis of genital chlamydial infection should be discussed with the client and be reinforced by providing clear written information' (Royal College of Nursing 2005). This should include information about the chlamy-dia screening programme and the availability of tests for chlamydia in high street chemists.

Although the number of clinics promoting teenage sexual health is increas-ing, it is difficult to persuade teenagers to use the services (Smith 1997; Wright 1999). Up to a third of young people are sexually active but only one in ten visits clinics for advice (Department of Health 1997). Older people are often reluctant to use the appropriate services precisely because they are often tar-geted at teenagers. Existing research has indicated that sexual health services are often not used owing to a lack of information (Jones *et al.* 1997). There-fore a good knowledge of other services together with methods of publicising them and the competency to make appropriate referrals are essential for gynaecology nurses. At the local level a flowchart of overall service provision can help by making the patient referral pathways clear. This would be an asset in all gynaecology departments.

UNWANTED PREGNANCIES

Cooperation between local health agencies is also a hallmark of the current improvements in service provision for women with unwanted pregnancies. However, in this field gynaecology nurses play a more central role. An unplanned pregnancy may not be an unwanted one, and at least 33 % of continuing pregnancies are unplanned (Paterson 1998). However, 'unplanned *and* unwanted pregnancies are common occurrences in all societies, regardless of the level of medical, economic, educational or religious development present within them' (Murray & Muse 1996). Induced abortion is one of the most commonly performed gynaecological procedures in Great Britain, with around 181 600 being performed in England and Wales in 2003 compared with 175 900 in 2002, a rise of 3.2 % (Department of Health 2004b). At least one-third of women in Great Britain will have an abortion by the time they reach the age of 45 years (Mawer & McGovern 2003; Royal College of Obstetricians and Gynaecologists 2004). Therefore the Family Planning Association (FPA) describes abortion as 'a crucial aspect of the sexual health of many women' (Family Planning Association 2004). The abortion rate is highest for women between the ages of 20 and 24 years. This may come as a surprise, given the recent publicity around teenage unplanned pregnancy and abortion.

Abortion is less traumatic if it can be performed in the first trimester (Royal College of Obstetricians and Gynaecologists 2004) and 89 % are carried out during this period (Paterson 1998). Traditionally all abortions have been carried out by surgical means under general anaesthetic, either as a day case or inpatient stay, if medically indicated. This requires medical input, operating theatre time, anaesthetists, operating department assistants and equipment costs, giving rise to huge funding issues. It has therefore become increasingly difficult to make adequate provision for the increasing abortion demand, which can no longer be sustained by a surgical service alone.

In addition, fewer gynaecological surgeons are willing to perform the operation, so many trusts are providing abortions in private care settings. This is not only very costly but frequently involves women having to travel great distances. Mullens (1998) feels that gynaecologists may be deterred from providing abortions not only on moral grounds but also from fear of repercussions from anti-abortionists. Many younger doctors may declare a conscientious objection to abortion based on a lack of training (Association for the Legal Right to Abortion 1999). Younger doctors are also less aware of the extraordinary lengths women were prepared to go to end a pregnancy prior to legal abortion (Mullens 1998). It is a very emotive subject and, while anti-abortion violence is rare in Britain, there are nevertheless strong views on this issue. Nurses and doctors have no obligation to actively participate in abortion, but they do have a duty of care. When healthcare professionals exercise their right not to be involved, this places a heavier burden on those who continue to provide this service.

The introduction of a medical method of termination has made a huge impact on this situation because the resource requirements are very different. Medical abortion costs less and is less invasive (Family Planning Association 2004). This method, using the abortifacient drug mifepristone (Mifegyne, RU486), was developed in France in the 1980s and Roussel were granted a licence for its use in this country in July 1991. This antiprogestogen when followed by a prostaglandin is a safe and effective method of abortion. Mifepristone can only be purchased and administered in state-approved hospitals and clinics by appropriately trained staff. There are clear guidelines for the use and storage of mifepristone, where every client needs to be entered into a register to enable an accurate record of usage to be made. Early medical termination of pregnancy can be performed safely and effectively up until 63 days from the last menstrual period (Gouk et al. 1999; Urquhart et al. 1997). The use of mifepristone is steadily increasing and the proportion of medical terminations accounted for 17 % of the total in 2003 compared with 14 % in 2002 (Department of Health 2004b). Medical terminations of pregnancy are available through NHS hospitals and approved non-NHS clinics under the terms of the 1967 Abortion Act.

ABORTION LAW

1803 'Lord Ellenborough's Act' made abortion a statutory felony both before and after the 'quickening', punishable by death.

1837 (re-enacted **1861**)   The Offences Against the Person Act made it illegal to 'procure an miscarriage', punishable by life imprisonment.

1929 The Infant Life Preservation Act created the 'fetal viability clause', which was set at a gestational age of 28 weeks, making it a crime to terminate a viable pregnancy unless it was done in 'good faith to preserve the life of the mother'.

1939 The case of Dr Alec Bourne introduced the concept that pregnancy could have detrimental effects on the woman's mental health such as to pose a significant risk to her 'life'. He had in 1938 performed an abortion on a 14-year-old girl who had been raped by a group of guardsmen at the barracks in west London and she became pregnant as a result. Dr Bourne informed the police of his intentions prior to the termination and was subsequently charged with a criminal offence.

1967 The Abortion Act was passed in 1967 and came into force in 1968. This Act made abortion legal when the conditions of the Act were adhered to. The Infant Life Preservation Act still stood, keeping the upper limit at 28 weeks.

1990 The Human Fertilisation and Embryology Act (HFEA) amended the 1967 Act to the lower limit of 24 weeks. The amendments also overrule the fetal viability clause and permit abortion for fetal handicap up until birth. The Infant Life Preservation Act is now irrelevant in English law.

Before an abortion can take place the Act states that two medical practitioners need to sign a certificate authorising the abortion and certifying that the pregnant woman's request for an abortion meets with one of the criteria stated below, which are statutory grounds for termination of pregnancy. Ideally the referring doctor should be the first signatory.

A. 'The continuance of the pregnancy would involve risk to the life of the pregnant woman greater than if the pregnancy were terminated.'
B. 'The termination is necessary to prevent grave permanent injury to the physical or mental health of the pregnant woman.'
C. 'The pregnancy has *not* exceeded its 24th week and that the continuance of the pregnancy would involve risk greater than if the pregnancy were terminated, of injury to the physical or mental health of the pregnant woman.'

D. 'The pregnancy has *not* exceeded its 24th week and that the continuance of the pregnancy would involve risk greater than if the pregnancy were terminated, of injury to the physical or mental health of any existing children of the family of the pregnant woman.'

E. 'There is substantial risk that if the child were born it would suffer from such physical or mental abnormalities as to be seriously handicapped.'

(Abortion Act 1967 as amended by the HFEA 1990)

Most abortions are performed on the grounds of C or D. Termination of pregnancy must be carried out in places approved by the Secretary of State for Health. Following the abortion the 'operating' practitioner must complete a notification form, HSA 4, which is then sent to the Chief Medical Officer within seven days of the procedure being performed. This is not only a legal record but also provides essential national data. With a medical termination of pregnancy the seven days are waived until the abortion is complete. This law applies to England, Scotland and Wales, but not Northern Ireland. Other countries have their own laws governing abortion, some more liberal than others.

SETTING UP A MEDICAL TERMINATION SERVICE

The advent of a medical method of terminating a pregnancy created an opportunity to rethink the provision of abortion within the NHS (Family Planning Association 2004). A new service is emerging that is not dependent on theatre time and doctor availability. Women have more choice and can access a more specialised service provided by committed staff and frequently led by nurses.

The development of a nurse-led service links in with *The NHS Plan* (Department of Health 2000) and incorporates many of the Chief Nursing Officer's 10 key roles for nurses (Department of Health 2002b), as well as strengthening patient choice and nurse autonomy. *The NHS Plan* signalled the government's determination to tackle inequalities in access to healthcare provision. In 2001 the Department of Health published *The National Strategy for Sexual Health and HIV* (Department of Health 2001a), which is more specific to abortion care and the availability of medical abortion. It suggests that commissioners should ensure that women seeking abortion are seen within three weeks of the first appointment with the referring doctor. A more recent report calls for a target waiting time of only 72 hours (Mawer & McGovern 2003). The RCOG makes recommendations for women's access to abortion services (Royal College of Obstetricians and Gynaecologists 2004) and states that the earlier in pregnancy an abortion is performed the lower the risk of complications. This needs a fast and efficient referral service to be in place (Heard & Guillebaud 1992).

The provision of medical terminations is still patchy in the UK (Government Statistical Service 2003), but there are many examples of good practice that are influencing change. The Early Medical Termination Service in Nottingham illustrates this. The number of referrals had gradually increased in Nottingham, so the new service was implemented by the community gynaecologist to counsel, pre-assess and manage the total care of women choosing medical termination. The introduction of this new service presented several immediate questions: Who would provide the service?, How would it be provided?, Where would it be provided?, Who would access it?

Access was an important consideration in being able to offer choice. Women can access the service via their GP or one of the many Contraception and Sexual Health (CASH) Clinics (formerly known as Family Planning Clinics). To enable women to have a choice in the method of termination, the referral process needed to be quicker. To this end a dedicated telephone referral line was set up. Out-of-hours referrals can be taken by fax on a separate, secure, dedicated line. This in itself created the need for a huge amount of administration input to support and coordinate the referral process and allocate subsequent scan and pre-assessment appointments. Cooperation from GPs played a key part in speeding up the referral process. Information and training were provided for GPs.

Pre-assessment and scanning appointments have always been held within the hospital environment. Women often had lengthy waits in a Gynaecology Clinic to see a doctor prepared to discuss abortion with them. In a busy clinic, there was insufficient time allocated for adequate counselling and explanations. Many women were scanned in the antenatal clinic, which was not always appropriate for women who had made a difficult decision and were feeling vulnerable. At the end of this process women were sometimes asked to travel a great distance from their home for their procedure. This was very distressing for both the patients and the staff who were providing this inadequate service.

The Royal College of Obstetricians and Gynaecologists (2004) recommends that an ultrasound scan be performed in a setting and manner sensitive to the woman's situation. The CASH Clinic is more accessible for many women and so scans and pre-assessment clinics were set up in the community, supported by the community gynaecologist. This enabled direct access to day surgery operating lists and dedicated beds, provided by a hospital gynaecology department, for women requesting a medical procedure. This needed the support and backing from the gynaecology department and lead nurse.

Nursing care for women having the medical procedure is an example of collaborative working practice and is a joint venture between primary and secondary care. A community nurse with previous experience of early medical termination was employed to set up the service and was joined by an experienced gynaecology nurse. Staff performing medical abortion should have adequate knowledge of reproductive anatomy, the pharmacology of mifepristone and misoprostol, evidence-based drug regimes and the prevention and management of adverse effects and complications (Family Planning Association 2004; Fielding *et al.* 2001; Royal College of Obstetricians and Gynaecologists

2004). Both nurses felt able to deliver the treatment and care without direct supervision, but with the support of the community consultant. This meant that the service could be provided from start to finish by nurses, providing a more private and seamless service designed to meet women's needs and reducing delays as described by Weyman (2002).

As demand has increased, from 25 cases a month in 2003 to over 40 cases a month in 2005 (White 2005), three extra nurses have joined the team and received training and support. The small team of dedicated nurse specialists have between them expert knowledge in the fields of gynaecology, sexual health and contraception. Weyman (2003) supports the role of gynaecology nurses in sexual health promotion and this is an ideal opportunity. Linking the termination of pregnancy service with the contraception and sexual health service is recommended by the Royal College of Obstetricians and Gynaecologists (2003) and enables clients to discuss their future contraception in order to reduce further unplanned pregnancies and repeat abortions. 'Contraception counselling is an essential element of induced abortion services' (Kumar *et al.* 2004). Unfortunately, this has not always been effective due to lack of time and expertise, so it is more appropriate to use specialist nurses (Kumar *et al.* 2004).

THE PATIENT PATHWAY FOR TERMINATION OF EARLY PREGNANCY

Following referral by a GP or CASH Clinic and a scan to determine gestation, women requesting a termination should have a pre-assessment appointment. Nurse-led pre-assessment has improved the service because women are offered a choice of treatment and time to talk. This is an opportunity to discuss the woman's feelings about the pregnancy, her life, how she feels about what has happened to her and any factors influencing her decision making. All of this should help the woman to feel respected and empowered. Gilchrist (1995) observes that 'ambivalence about abortion is one recognised risk factor' for psychological problems afterwards, highlighting the importance of pre-abortion counselling. A woman should feel that the decision is hers. In Nottingham there is a counsellor attached to the service who often sees women who are having problems making a decision.

A detailed medical and sexual history is needed to assess general health and identify any contraindications to treatment. Women requesting surgical treatment may have anaesthetic risks or not be suitable for day case surgery. Women are not suitable for a medical termination if they suffer from high blood pressure, diabetes or severe asthma, and they should not be on either anti-coagulation therapy or steroids. Treatment options depend to some extent on the pregnancy gestation, with medical termination usually offered up to 9 weeks gestation and surgical termination from 8 to 12 weeks. Medical termination may be offered after 9 weeks, but efficacy is reduced and it is less suitable for day care. Women need a detailed verbal explanation of each treatment, including information about risks and benefits, and written information, describing their chosen treatment, to take away. Not only is this an essential part of the consent process but participants in a study by Zapka *et al.* (2001) rated information and counselling as the most important factor influencing their satisfaction.

Practical organisation includes arranging appointment dates for the chosen abortion method. Blood samples are required (for a full blood count and group and save with Kleihauer) and also endocervical swabs or urine to exclude chlamydial infection, in line with good practice and the chlamydia screening programme. The certificate authorising the abortion (HSA 1) needs to be signed by two doctors. Although there is much speculation on the possibility of reducing this requirement to one signature (Mawer & McGovern 2003), allowing nurses to sign, or even the woman herself, there are currently no planned changes in the law. It is important to discuss suitable post-abortion contraception, and the prescriptions for both the treatment and contraception can be written.

ISSUES RELATING TO CONSENT AND CONFIDENTIALITY

The legal age of consent for medical and surgical treatment in the United Kingdom is 16 years. This is also the age of consent for sexual intercourse, making the management of younger girls very complex. However, young girls do sometimes seek help and are entitled to the same level of confidentiality as everyone else. Usually sexual activity has been consensual, but the possibility of child sexual abuse needs to be considered and the young person should always be carefully and sensitively questioned (Royal College of Nursing 2005). Young people are always encouraged to talk to their parents, but the *Fraser Guidelines* do allow girls less than 16 years of age to consent to medical treatment when they clearly understand the advice and it is considered that the treatment is in their best interest (Medical Protection Society 2005).

Adults are presumed to have the capacity to consent, but where there is doubt, the health professional should assess the capacity of the client to make the decision. A client's capacity to consent may be affected by factors such as confusion, fear, shock and panic. Many of these feelings and emotions are present with a request for a termination of pregnancy. If these factors are present, it should not be assumed that the client is unable to give consent.

Consent should also be given voluntarily and freely without pressure (Cable *et al.* 2003). In the context of abortion, pressure can come from partners and/or family members. Any coercion invalidates consent and makes the decision to terminate much more difficult, which can lead to long-term psychological and sexual problems. Seeking consent when a client is particularly vulnerable could lead to doubt as to its validity. Therefore this should be part of a process, rather than simply signing a form (Cable *et al.* 2003). Suitably qualified nurses are allowed to seek consent with the permission of their employer or the NMC. In the context of a nurse-led termination service, the situation is improved because the nurse provides holistic, non-judgemental care and support in a safe and secure environment.

Consent should always been informed (Aveyard 2002) and nurses have a professional responsibility to ensure that patients in their care are given information about their conditions and understand the risks and implications of any interventions required (Nursing and Midwifery Council 2002). Continuity of care in both primary and secondary care settings allows the client to make an informed choice about her treatment (Walker 2000). Having been given clear and relevant written and verbal information at the initial consultation, there is time then to respond to the client's questions. To be able to impart this information the nurse specialist needs to be 'suitably trained and qualified and must have sufficient knowledge of the proposed treatment and understand the risks involved' (Department of Health 2001b).

Confidentiality is a major concern for many women seeking an abortion. Clause 5 of the *Code of Professional Conduct* (Nursing and Midwifery Council 2002) states that information given by the client should be treated as confidential and only used for the purpose that it was given. Much of the information in relation to termination and sexual history is private and of a personal nature and therefore is privileged. Continuity of care creates trust, which is an essential element in the nurse–client relationship (Rumbold 1999). If any information needs to be shared then the client's consent should be sought.

THE PROCEDURE FOR A MEDICAL TERMINATION

The safest way for managing the medical procedure, from beginning to end, is with an Integrated Care Pathway based on RCOG guidelines (Royal College of Obstetricians and Gynaecologists 2004). The advantages are that all care is laid out clearly and progress can be clearly documented with minimum paperwork. This protects both the patient and the nurse. A record should be kept of all responses to direct questions, information and advice, blood results, observations and nursing actions.

The procedure involves two visits to a designated unit. The first appointment is to administer mifepristone. Before this happens it is important to ensure that the woman is certain and comfortable with her decision. She should be reminded that once the mifepristone is taken the procedure has started and it is then too late to change her mind. It is important to understand how the medication works and that, if taken alone, it does not normally end the pregnancy. There have been a few documented cases where women have gone on to deliver without the second stages but the numbers are very small (Urquhart *et al.* 1997). It is sensible to inform any woman who may consider changing her mind that the medication could harm the fetus. Additionally miscarriage could occur at a later date, either coincidentally or as a direct result of the medication. The likely side effects should be explained, including nausea and vomiting, lower abdominal pain and vaginal bleeding. Consent is needed before the medication is given.

The woman can go home 20 minutes after taking mifepristone provided there have been no ill effects. Before she leaves she needs very specific advice. It is important to refrain from drinking alcohol and keep smoking to an absolute minimum. If analgesia is required, aspirin and brufen should be avoided and paracetamol encouraged. It is recommended that a further tablet be given if there is vomiting within 2 hours of taking the medication. The woman needs reminding about the follow-up appointment with advice to wear comfortable clothes. Finally, contact numbers are essential in the event of any problems or concerns.

The second visit for misoprostol usually takes place after 48 hours, but research shows only small differences in efficacy with 24- and 72-hour intervals (Shaff *et al.* 2000). The woman is shown to a private room and asked about any side effects she may have experienced at home. Anti-emetics are often required on admission. Time is needed to explain what will happen and to familiarise her with the surroundings. Basic admission details and baseline observations are recorded. Misoprostol tablets are inserted into the vagina, where the active ingredient is absorbed by the vaginal mucosa. Although misoprostol is licensed for oral use, research suggests that it is more effective given vaginally and is associated with fewer side effects (El-Rafaey *et al.* 1995; Gouk *et al.* 1999). It is appropriate to allow the woman to self-administer if she wishes, but very few do.

Misoprostol can cause cramping pain, nausea, vomiting, diarrhoea and changes in body temperature. Prophylactic analgesia may be offered, although the Royal College of Obstetricians and Gynaecologists (2004) questions the value of this. The nurse call buzzer should be available to summon help and the woman is advised to remain on her bed for 30 minutes, to allow the active ingredient to be absorbed. After this she may mobilise, but caution is advised as sometimes a drop in blood pressure can cause dizziness. Blood pressure is checked after 2 hours or if clinically indicated.

Bleeding accompanied by cramping pain usually starts approximately 2 to 3 hours after administration of misoprostol. A few women require opiate analgesia but the vast majority describe the discomfort as similar to period pains and only require simple analgesia. Women are advised to use a bedpan when going to the toilet so that blood loss may be monitored and any products of conception verified. It is important to be honest about the appearance of the products of conception as many women choose to imagine that the pregnancy resembles little more than a clot, when in fact there is usually a recognisable fetus. It is easy to assume that all women would be upset at possibly viewing the aborted fetus, but some women feel that personally verifying the result is a positive aspect of the treatment (Murray & Muse 1996). Afterwards the woman should be given written information about the sensitive disposal of pregnancy tissue.

The nurse can discharge the woman once any pain, dizziness and bleeding have settled, her observations are within normal limits and she has passed urine. Bleeding and mild pain can be expected for up to 2 weeks. It is advisable not to have sexual intercourse or use tampons during this time, owing to the risk of infection. The signs and symptoms of infection should be explained so that the woman can seek medical attention if required. Contact numbers are also given. A check-up after 2 weeks is recommended, and sometimes an appointment for a scan is needed if incomplete products have been noted. An appointment to see a counsellor should also be offered. Most importantly, contraception should be arranged with advice on when to start the contraceptive pill or have a coil fitted.

If there is any uncertainty about the success of the procedure, the women are followed up very closely. Often only partial products have been passed but 2 weeks later a scan often demonstrates an empty uterus or evidence of blood. The nurse specialist can review these women according to clear scan guidelines. If there is evidence of retained products, this is discussed with the woman and she is offered the choice of conservative management with a repeat scan or surgical intervention, depending on the amount of retained products and the severity of any symptoms. This also offers a further opportunity to check on how the woman is coping with the whole experience.

THE ACCEPTABILITY OF MEDICAL TERMINATION OF PREGNANCY

Several studies have investigated the acceptability of medical termination, including women's reasons for choosing it (Poenariu 2003), and many report acceptance as high (Beckman & Harvey 1997; Hollander 2000; Winikoff 1995). Gibb et al. (1998) assessed preference for medical abortion using the concept of 'willingness to pay' and found that 64 % preferred to have the medical method. Tang et al. (1993) found that 85 % of those having a medical termination would choose the method again. It is worth noting that many of the acceptability trials in America allowed the woman to self-administer misoprostol at home, which would affect the results. Medical termination is more acceptable the earlier in pregnancy it takes place (Henshaw et al. 1993; Zapka et al. 2001). Holmgren (1992) observes that overall a short waiting time to access an abortion service appeared to be a more important consideration in determining patient satisfaction than the actual method.

Medical abortion requires active patient participation, takes longer to complete than the surgical method and the women are more aware of bleeding and pain. On the other hand, medical abortion offers several advantages including success without surgery or anaesthesia, the similarity to a 'natural miscarriage' and a more private and proactive experience (Henshaw *et al.* 1993; Winikoff *et al.* 1998). Medical termination is associated for many women with the expression of autonomy and the ability to control one's body and privacy. Any unpleasant side effects do not have a major impact on acceptability, provided adequate information and medication is given (Poenariu 2003).

Murray and Muse (1996) feel that the actual setting of a medical termination unit is important in determining women's acceptance. They found that the majority of women prefer treatment in a sitting room atmosphere, although a third of them wanted to lie down. They also describe the importance of having access to comfortable chairs and beds and facilities to accommodate friends or relatives. This influenced the design of the unit in Nottingham, which has en suite bedrooms, a consulting room and sitting room, all located in a quiet and private area within a gynaecology unit.

Women are often surprised by the variety of emotions they experience afterwards, and this also influences acceptability. As well as feeling relieved, many women also feel a sense of loss and grief, or even extreme distress, and they may find it difficult to share these feelings (Gilchrist *et al.* 1995; Hughes 2003). 'General psychological principles suggest we should encourage women to allow mixed feelings of loss and relief, seek support and be aware that they made the best decision for them in a situation where any decision involved loss of some kind' (Gilchrist 1995). When women see the same nurse several times, it does seem to provide an atmosphere of trust where women are comfortable to talk. Partners are frequently overlooked during the whole process and this can cause problems within a relationship, especially if the partner is less sure about the decision. This needs addressing in order to prevent problems within the relationship, including future sexual difficulties.

CONCLUSION

Gynaecology nurses are much more aware of their responsibility for sexual health promotion, and this is evident in the way gynaecology care is developing. As well as using the opportunity to discuss sexual health in gynaecology clinics and wards, gynaecology nurses are becoming involved in collaborative projects such as chlamydia screening and the delivery of medical terminations.

The introduction of medical terminations has improved services for women requesting an abortion by introducing a choice of methods and reducing waiting times. More women can be seen at their local hospital instead of undergoing their terminations elsewhere and there are fewer late terminations.

Nurses delivering the service can offer continuity of care, support through a distressing experience and time to discuss sexual health and contraception.

Despite huge changes, there is room for improvement. Nurses are allowed to prescribe both analgesia and contraception, but they are restricted from prescribing mifepristone and misoprostol. A change in this regulation would allow nurses in this situation to work more autonomously. The development of a self-referral system for women requesting a termination of pregnancy would speed up the process. The FPA also believes that parts of the Abortion Act (1967) are out of date and should be amended (Family Planning Association 2004).

The NHS provision of services for women with unwanted pregnancies is still fragmented (Mawer & McGovern 2003) and accounts for only 71 % of total demand (Paterson 1998; Royal College of Obstetricians and Gynaecologists 2004), making some women disadvantaged compared with others. This is not only unfair but means that the opportunity to offer relevant sexual health promotion may be lost. The abortion service would be improved by reorganising it 'as just one of a range of fertility control services and integrating 'it into mainstream sexual health provision' (Mawer & McGovern 2003).

REFERENCES

Andrews G (Ed.) (1997) *Women's Sexual Health*, Bailliere Tindall, London.

Association for the Legal Right to Abortion (1999) *Education on Termination of Pregnancy – Doctors' Attitudes and Experiences of Abortion*, ALRA, Western Australia.

Aveyard H (2002) The requirement for informed consent prior to nursing care procedures. *Journal of Advanced Nursing*, **37**(3), 243–9.

Beckman L J, Harvey S M (1997) Experience and acceptability of medical abortion with mefepristone and misoprostol among US women. *Women's Health Issues.* July–August, **7**(4), 253–62.

Botting B (Ed.) (1995) *The Health of Our Children. Office of Population Censuses and Surveys*, Series DS:11, HMSO, London.

Brennan K (2002) *Britain is Worst in Europe for Teenage Pregnancy Rates*, www.studentbmj.com/extra/02/september (accessed January 2005).

British Menopause Society (2005) *Sexual Health and the Menopause*, Royal Society of Medicine Press, London.

Cable S *et al.* (2003) Informed consent. *Nursing Standard*, **18**(12), 47–53.

Department of Health (1997) *Family Planning Clinic Services: Summary information for 1996–1997*, The Stationery Office, London.

Department of Health (1998) *Summary and Conclusions of CMO's Expert Advisory Group Report on Chlamydia trachomatis*, The Stationery Office, London.

Department of Health (2000) *The NHS Plan: A Plan for Investment, a Plan for Reform*, The Stationery Office, London.

Department of Health (2001a) *The National Strategy for Sexual Health and HIV. Better Prevention, Better Services, Better Sexual Health*, The Stationery Office, London.

Department of Health (2001b) *Reference Guide to Consent for Examination to Treatment*, HMSO, London.

Department of Health (2002a) *First Phase of Chlamydia Screening Programme Announced*, www.dh.gov.uk/PublicationsAndStatistics/PressReleases (accessed December 2004).

Department of Health (2002b) *Developing Key Roles for Nurses and Midwives: A Guide for Managers*, The Stationery Office, London.

Department of Health (2004a) *Choosing Health: Making Healthier Choices Easier*, The Stationery Office, London.

Department of Health (2004b) *Summary of Abortion Statistics for England and Wales*, The Stationery Office, London.

El-Rafaey H *et al.* (1995) Introduction of abortion with mifepristone and oral or vaginal misoprostol. *New England Medical Journal*, **332**(15), 983–7.

Family Planning Association (2004) *Abortion – Policy Statement*, FPA, London.

Fielding S L *et al.* (2001) Professional considerations for providing mifepristone-induced abortion. *Nurse Practitioner*, **26**(11), 44–8, 51–4.

Gibb S *et al.* (1998) Assessing strength of preference for abortion method using 'willingness to pay': a useful research technique for measuring values. *Journal of Advanced Nursing*, **27**(1), 30–6.

Gilchrist A C (1995) Abortion: who needs support? *Nursing Standard*, **10**(11), 49.

Gilchrist A C *et al.* (1995) Termination of pregnancy and psychiatric morbidity. *British Journal of Psychiatry*, **167**(2), 243–8.

Gouk E V *et al.* (1999) Medical termination of pregnancy at 63–83 days gestation. *British Journal of Obstetrics and Gynaecology*, **106**(6), 535–9.

Government Statistical Service (2003) *Abortion Statistics, England and Wales: 2002*, Bulletin 2003/23, HMSO, London.

Gregory P (2000) Patient assessment and care planning: sexuality. *Nursing Standard*, **15**(9), 38–41.

Handy P (2002) Nurse-directed services in genitourinary medicine. *Nursing Standard*, **17**(11), 33–8.

Health Protection Agency (2004) *Focus on Prevention – HIV and Other Sexually Transmitted Infections in the United Kingdom in 2003*, HPA, London.

Heard M and Guillebaud J (1992) Medical abortion – safe, effective and legal in Britain. *British Medical Journal*, **304**(6821), 195–6.

Henshaw R C *et al.* (1993) Comparison of medical abortion with a surgical vacuum aspiration: women's preferences and acceptability of treatment. *British Medical Journal*, **307**(6906), 714–7.

HFEA (1990) *Human Fertilisation and Embryology Act*, HMSO, London.

Hollander D (2000) Most abortion patients view their experience favourably, but medical abortion gets a higher rating than surgical. *Family Planning Perspectives*, **32**(5), 264.

Holmgren K (1992) Women's evaluation of three early abortion methods. *Acta Obstet. Gynecol. Scand.*, **71**, 616–23.

Hughes G *et al.* (1998) *New Cases at Genitourinary Medicine Clinics: England 1997*, Communicable Disease Report 8 (supplement), S1–S11.

Hughes S J (2003) The biopsychosocial aspects of unwanted teenage pregnancy. *Nursing Times*, **99**(12), 32–4.

Irwin R (1997) Sexual health promotion and nursing. *Journal of Advanced Nursing*, **25**(1), 170–7.

Johnson A *et al.* (2002) Sexual behaviour in Britain: partnerships, practices and HIV risk behaviours. *Lancet*, **358**(9296), 1835–42.

Jolley S (2001) Promoting teenage sexual health: an investigation into the knowledge, activities and perceptions of gynaecology nurses. *Journal of Advanced Nursing*, **36**(2), 246–55.

Jolley S (2002) Taking a sexual history: the role of the nurse. *Nursing Times*, **98**(18), 39–41.

Jones S *et al.* (1997) Teenage sexual health through the eyes of a teenager: a study using focus groups. *Ambulatory Child Health*, **3**, 3–11.

Kumar U *et al.* (2004) Peri-abortion contraception: a qualitative study of users' experiences. *Journal of Family Planning and Reproductive Health Care*, **30**(1), 55–6.

Leishman J (2004) Childhood and teenage pregnancies. *Nursing Standard*, **18**(33), 33–6.

Marquiegui A, Huish M (1999) ABC of sexual health: a woman's sexual life after an operation. *British Medical Journal*, **318**(7177), 178–81.

Mawer C, McGovern M (2003) *Early Abortions: Promoting Real Choice for Women*, FPA, London.

Medical Protection Society (2005) Consent. *Registrar GP*, Issue 9.

Metcalf T (2004) Sexual health: meeting adolescents' needs. *Nursing Standard*, **18**(46), 40–3.

Moss T R (2001) *International Handbook of Chlamydia*, Euromed Communications Limited, Haslemere.

Mullens A (1998) 7:10 am, Nov. 8, 1994. *Canadian Medical Association Journal*, **158**(4), 528–31.

Murray S and Muse K (1996) Mifepristone and first trimester abortion. *Clinical Obstetrics and Gynaecology*, **39**(2), 474–85.

Nicoll A *et al.* (1999) Sexual health of teenagers in England and Wales: analysis of national data. *British Medical Journal*, **318**(7194), 1321–2.

Norwich Union Healthcare (2002) Adolescents' needs not met. *Nursing Times*, **98**(4), 7.

Nursing and Midwifery Council (2002) *Code of Professional Conduct*, NMC, London.

Office for National Statistics (1999) *Population Trends (Autumn Issue)*, The Stationery Office, London.

Paterson C (1998) Induced abortion, Part 1. *Trends in Urology, Gynaecology and Sexual Health*, March, 33–5.

Poenariu M Z (2003) *Patients' Satisfaction with First Trimester Mifepristone – Misoprostol Medical Abortion Services. A Literature Review.* Review prepared for the 12th Postgraduate Course in reproductive medicine and biology, Geneva, Switzerland, www.gfmer.ch/Endo/Course2003/Mifepristone-misoprostol_medical_abort (accessed June 2005).

Roper N *et al.* (1996) *The Elements of Nursing: A Model for Nursing Based on a Model of Living*, Churchill Livingstone, Edinburgh.

Royal College of Nursing (2000) *Sexuality and Sexual Health in Nursing Practice*, RCN, London.

Royal College of Nursing (2001) *Sexual Health Strategy*, RCN, London.

Royal College of Nursing (2004) *Sexual Health Competencies: An Integrated Career and Competency Framework for Sexual and Reproductive Health Nursing*, RCN, London.

Royal College of Nursing (2005) *Chlamydia – An Educational Initiative for Nurses*, RCN, London.

Royal College of Obstetricians and Gynaecologists, Faculty of Family Planning and Reproductive Healthcare (2003) *Service Standards for Sexual Health Services*, RCOG Press, London.

Royal College of Obstetricians and Gynaecologists (2004) *The Care of Women Requesting Induced Abortion*, Evidence-based Guideline No. 7, RCOG, Press, London.

Rumbold G (1999) *Ethics in Nursing Practice*, 3rd edition, Bailliere Tindall, Edinburgh.

Scott C (1999) Tackling teenage pregnancies. *Nottingham Evening Post*, Nottingham, 11 August.

Shaff E A *et al.* (2000) Vaginal misoprostol administered 1, 2, or 3 days after mifepristone for early medical abortion: a randomized trial. *Journal of American Medical Association*, **284**, 1948–53.

Smith R (1997) Promoting the sexual health of young people: Part 1. *Paediatric Nursing*, **9**(2), 24–7.

Social Exclusion Unit (1999) *Teenage Pregnancy*, The Stationery Office, London.

Society of Sexual Health Advisers (2004) *Sexual Health Adviser*, www.ssha.info/public/jobs/desc_adviserasp (accessed December 2004).

Stirrat G M (1997) *Aids to Obstetrics and Gynaecology*, 4th edition, Churchill Livingstone, London.

Swann C *et al.* (2003) *Teenage Pregnancy and Parenthood: A Review of Reviews*, Health Development Agency, London.

Tang O *et al.* (1993) Further acceptability evaluation of RU486 and ONU802 as abortifacient agents in a Chinese population. *Contraception*, **48**(3), 267–76.

Templeton A E (1996) *The prevention of pelvic infection*, RCOG Press London.

Thistle S (2003) *Secondary Schools and Sexual Health Services: Forging the Links*, National Children's Bureau, London.

Urquhart D R *et al.* (1997) The efficacy and tolerance of mifepristone and prostaglandin in termination of pregnancy of less than 63 days gestation: UK multicentre study – final results. *Contraception*, **55**, 1–5.

Walker S (2000) A nurse-led service for termination of pregnancy. *Professional Nurse*, **15**(8), 506–9.

Warner P H *et al.* (1999) Shedding light on the sexual history. *American Journal of Nursing*, **99**, 38–41.

Waterhouse J (1996) Nursing practice related to sexuality: a review and recommendations. *Nursing Times Research*, **1**(6), 412–8.

Weston A (1998) Warts and all. *Nursing Times*, **94**(3), 26–8.

Weyman A (2002) Let nurses take the lead. *Nursing Times*, **98**(29), 16.

Weyman A (2003) Promoting sexual health to young people: preventing teenage pregnancy and sexually transmitted infections. *Journal of the Royal Society for the Promotion of Health*, **123**(1), 66–9.

White H (2005) Local reported data at QMC, Nottingham (unpublished).

Winikoff B (1995) Acceptability of medical abortion in early pregnancy. *Family Planning Perspectives*, **27**(4), 142–8.

Winikoff B *et al.* (1998) Acceptability and feasibility of early pregnancy termination by mifepristone–misoprostol: results of a large multicenter trial in the United States. *Archive of Family Medicine*, **7**(4), 360–6.
Wright S (1999) Sexually transmitted diseases. *Nursing Standard*, **13**(46), 37–42.
Zapka J G *et al.* (2001) The silent consumer: women's reports and ratings of abortion services. *Medical Care*, **39**(1), 50–60.

USEFUL WEBSITES

www.rcn.org.uk/sexualhealthlearning
www.ffprhc.org.uk
www.ssha.info
www.ruthinking.co.uk
www.playingsafely.co.uk

3 A Vital Role for Nurse Colposcopists

SUE JOLLEY and SALLY WRIGHT

The majority of women never visit a colposcopy department and therefore have little or no understanding of what colposcopy means. Those that are referred for colposcopy quickly appreciate the significance of this examination, but usually experience high levels of anxiety (Gath *et al.* 1995; Peate 1999). Although the Colposcopy Service plays a crucial role in the National Health Service Cervical Screening Programme (NHSCSP), it faces enormous challenges in meeting current levels of demand. This chapter examines these challenges and describes how the service is responding. It focuses on the impact that nurse colposcopists are having on the delivery of care.

Challenges	Service developments
• High numbers of abnormal smears, placing excessive demands on the service • Targets for waiting times following referral to colposcopy • Shortage of trained colposcopists • Debate surrounding the management of mildly abnormal smears • High levels of anxiety following referral	• Training nurse colposcopists • Flexible clinic times and locations • Reducing visits – 'select and treat' • Researching and testing for human papilloma virus • Improving information, support and counselling

CERVICAL SCREENING AND COLPOSCOPY

The UK has a very successful and well-organised cervical screening programme, designed to detect and treat abnormal cells in order to reduce the incidence of cervical cancer. Screening is one of the best defences against

Gynaecology: Changing Services for Changing Needs. Edited by Sue Jolley
© 2006 by John Wiley & Sons, Ltd

cervical cancer and can prevent around 80–90 % of cancer cases in women who attend regularly (Sasieni *et al.* 2003). Each year nearly 4 million women are screened in England (Department of Health 2004a), saving 1300 lives and preventing 3900 cancers throughout the UK (National Health Service Cervical Screening Programme 2000, 2003; Sasieni & Adams 1999). A more recent study by Peto *et al.* (2004) suggests that these figures underestimate the success of the screening programme and that the annual number of lives saved in England is actually 4500. The incidence of cervical cancer fell by 42 % from 1988 to 1997 and has fallen by over 25 % since 1992 (National Health Service Cervical Screening Programme 2003; National Statistics 2000; Sasieni & Adams 1999). This fall is directly related to the cervical screening programme.

Until 2003, guidelines recommended that women between the ages of 20 and 64 years should have cervical screening every three to five years (Department of Health 1998), with most health authorities operating a three-year programme (Smith 2000). Following research by Sasieni *et al.* (2003), these guidelines have changed. Screening is now offered to women from the age of 25. They are recalled for tests every three years until the age of 49, then every five years until the age of 64. Cervical cancer is rare under the age of 25, which is why routine screening under this age has stopped. There is no plan to screen those over 64, who are at low risk, unless they have had a recent abnormality.

Nurses and doctors have traditionally used a spatula to take a sample from the cervix (see Figure 3.1). The sample is then transferred to a slide and sent to a laboratory for examination under a microscope. Following recommendations by the National Institute for Clinical Excellence (NICE), the traditional cervical smear test is slowly being replaced by liquid-based cytology (LBC). The new method uses a cervix brush (see Figure 3.1), and the head of the

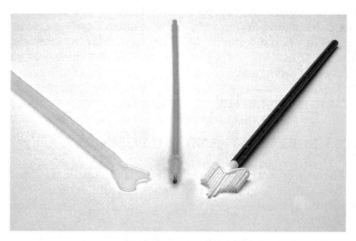

Figure 3.1. Spatula and brushes used for taking cervical samples

device is rinsed or broken off into a vial of preservative fluid so that most or all of the cervical cells are retained. The main advantage is a reduction in inconclusive smears that have to be repeated.

If there is a problem following the initial screening process, women are referred for an outpatient appointment in a colposcopy department. Each year, in England alone, approximately 300000 women have an abnormal smear (Department of Health 2004a). This represents approximately 7 % of adequate smears. Not all abnormal changes need immediate referral, and in 2003–2004 128000 referrals were actually made (Department of Health 2004a). At the appointment a colposcope, which is a low-powered microscope (see Figure 3.2), is used to examine the cervix under magnification. This is performed 'to assess the extent of any problem and to determine appropriate treatment' (National Health Service Cervical Screening Programme 1999a) and therefore plays a central role in the management of pre-malignant disease. If necessary, a biopsy may be taken and sometimes minor treatment is carried out.

The usual reasons for referral, summarised in Table 3.1, are 'borderline nuclear abnormalities', which are minor changes in the cervical cells, or 'dyskariosis', which refers to an abnormality in the nucleus of the cell, suggesting that the cell could have pre-cancerous changes. Dyskariosis is a cytological definition based on examination of the cervical cells. Women are also referred with clinical symptoms such as postcoital bleeding or with persistent inadequate smears (Jolley 2004). In England the rate of inadequate smears has risen steadily and is about 10 % (Department of Health 2004a). This reflects the rise in sexually transmitted infections, which is the main cause of inadequate smears (National Health Service Cervical Screening Programme 2000). Hopefully this will be reduced with the implementation of LBC. There used

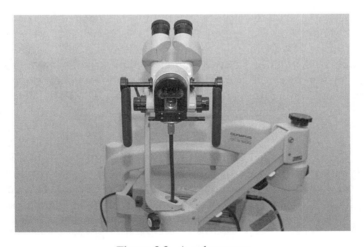

Figure 3.2. A colposcope

Table 3.1. Reasons for referral to colposcopy

Through the cervical screening programme:
  Severe dyskariosis
  Moderate dyskariosis
  Mild dyskariosis
  More than one result showing borderline nuclear abnormalities
  Persistent inadequate smears

From GP for clinical symptoms:
  Postcoital bleeding
  Intermenstrual bleeding
  Vaginal discharge in the absence of any obvious infection
  Any cervix that looks abnormal on examination

References: Jolley (2004); Peate (1999); Smith (2000).

to be wide variations in the way negative, abnormal and inadequate smears were classified, but there are now clear guidelines covering reporting and classification in cervical cytology and recommendations for management (Johnson & Patnick 2000).

Despite clear referral guidelines, there is some controversy surrounding the management of mild dyskariosis because only a small proportion of women are likely to progress to severe dyskariosis. The majority, if left, will revert to normal or persist as mild dyskariosis. Although appropriate management is clearly important, there are many women being investigated unnecessarily. Some argue that continued surveillance might be preferable to immediate referral to colposcopy (Austoker & Davey 1997). Until recently NHSCSP recommendations specified that two results showing mild dyskariosis were required before referral to colposcopy but this was amended in 2003 to suggest referral after one abnormal result (Prendiville & Davies 2005). Therefore colposcopy workloads will continue to be high until more specific screening tests are available to distinguish between significant and insignificant minor abnormalities. Further research is needed into the optimal management of mild dyskariosis, and testing for human papilloma virus (HPV) may help.

HPV is linked with nearly all cervical cancers (Butcher 2001; National Health Service Cervical Screening Programme 2000) and the relationship between the two is now well proven (Cuzick *et al.* 1999; Peate 1999; Shlay *et al.* 2000). 'Research has indicated that women with a mild or borderline smear result, who have no evidence of high risk HPV infection, are very unlikely to develop cervical cancer' (National Health Service Cervical Screening Programme 2005). Therefore the HPV test could be used to indicate those women who are at a higher risk of developing cervical cancer (Kitchener 2003; Prendiville & Davies 2005). This has been piloted at three sites – Norwich, Bristol and Newcastle (National Health Service Cervical Screening Programme 2000). At the time of writing, the final evaluation is not available, but during the pilot there was some modification to the protocol based on the finding that older women with HPV are more likely to need treatment than younger women with HPV (Prendiville & Davies 2005).

Research into the role of HPV testing is continuing (Prendiville & Davies 2005). The TOMBOLA (trial of the management of borderline and other low-grade abnormal smears) is a large seven-year multicentre trial, which was started in 1999. One of the aims is to determine whether colposcopy, repeat cervical smears or HPV testing can best determine which women need further treatment (National Health Service Cervical Screening Programme 2005). HPV testing might also be used to identify any asymptomatic women who are at risk of developing cervical cancer (Cuzick *et al.* 1999). ARTISTIC (a randomised trial of HPV testing in primary cervical screening) is a new trial started in 2001 to investigate HPV as a primary screening test (National Health Service Cervical Screening Programme 2005).

PRESSURES ON THE COLPOSCOPY SERVICE

The increasing number of patients being referred for colposcopy has placed pressure on colposcopy services, with prolonged waiting times (Department of Health 2004a; Todd *et al.* 2002). Once a patient is referred to colposcopy, the waiting time should be as short as possible, partly because prompt treatment may be necessary but also to alleviate patient anxiety. Naturally women become very anxious on hearing that they have an abnormal smear and a significant number of women worry that their condition might become worse while waiting for appointments and become angry at any delay (Doherty *et al.* 1991; Gath *et al.* 1995).

The NHSCSP has set guidelines to ensure that waiting times are kept to a minimum. At least 90 % of all referrals should be seen in less than eight weeks and at least 90 % of women with moderate or severe dyskariosis should be seen within four weeks (National Health Service Cervical Screening Programme 1997). Unfortunately, these targets are not being met (Jolley 2004). In a study at the John Radcliffe Hospital, Oxford, Gath *et al.* (1995) found that women waited between six and 24 weeks for their first appointment. At the time of writing the Queen's Medical Centre, Nottingham, cannot meet these targets and most referrals wait for more than eight weeks for a clinic appointment. In general only 76 % of all referrals and 61 % of those with moderate or severe dyskariosis are seen within the target times (Department of Health 2004a). At regional level the proportion of women offered an appointment within eight weeks ranges from 64 % in London to 91 % in the northeast, demonstrating wide regional variations; 10 % of women wait for 12 weeks (Department of Health 2004a).

It is important to consider why waiting time standards are not being met. Clearly there is excessive demand on the service. This is related to the overall success of the screening programme because more patients are being screened, leading to more referrals for abnormal results (National Health Service Cervical Screening Programme 2000). A steady increase in abnormal smears is directly related to the increasing incidence of HPV (Cuzick *et al.* 1999; Shlay *et al.* 2000). The high levels of inadequate smears have already been mentioned and the service is also receiving more referrals for patients with clinical symptoms, rather than abnormal smear results, because the colposcope is the best way of examining the cervix. Unfortunately, the long waiting times for new referrals seems to be associated with a high rate of patients who do not keep their appointments, and this in turn exacerbates the problem (Lester & Wilson 1999).

The colposcopy service needs to expand but there is a shortage of colposcopists. This is partly because the training takes time and commitment but doctors tend to move around to gain experience. The recent reductions in the hours worked by junior doctors (Department of Health 2004b) also means that there is less cover. Working as a colposcopist, even part time, involves a serious commitment in time, so training would only be an option for those doctors interested in pursuing a career in gynaecological oncology.

TRAINING NURSE COLPOSCOPISTS

Although doctors have traditionally practised colposcopy, in the mid-1990s some centres began to train nurse colposcopists in order to cope with the increased demand. The introduction of a national training programme in colposcopy has meant that nurses can attain the same standards of practice as doctors, leading to the British Society of Colposcopy and Cervical Pathology (BSCCP) accreditation, and therefore become colposcopists in their own right. The first nurse colposcopist was certified in 1996. Other centres quickly appreciated the potential advantages of nurse practitioners who could not only help to reduce waiting times but also deliver a more flexible and responsive service offering continuity of care. By 2002 there were 52 certified nurse colposcopists with 62 in training (Barnes 2002). This has now increased to 121 nurse colposcopists with 91 in training (Lewis 2005).

Before expanding their scope of professional practice all nurses should be aware of the importance of delivering safe, effective and appropriate care (Nursing and Midwifery Council 2002). The Royal College by Nursing (RCN) Colposcopy Nurses' Forum has described the essential qualifications nurses need before undertaking training to be a colposcopist. These include at least 18 months of nursing experience in women's health; a thorough knowledge of the colposcopy service and women's needs; evidence of good organisational and communication skills; and a supportive, sensitive and approachable manner (Smith 2000). Nurse colposcopists may also need to detect and diagnose different abnormalities of the genital tract, such as warts and other infections, so they need to be aware of all potential problems and know where to refer patients for appropriate treatment.

During training, nurses need to attend a theory course and then undertake 50 supervised colposcopies, 20 of which must be on new patients. Following this they undertake another 100 unsupervised colposcopies, of which at least 30 must be on new patients (National Health Service Cervical Screening Programme 1999b). A designated trainer is needed to support the nurses throughout this process so all patients can be reviewed and discussed as necessary. At the end of training the nurse has to present 10 case studies to the national training body (BSCCP) before accreditation is given. Nurses receive the same colposcopy training as doctors but also need additional input in cytology and histopathology because basic nursing programmes, unlike medical courses, do not cover these subjects (Royal College of Obstetricians and Gynaecologists 1999). Counselling and family planning courses are also useful.

Following accreditation nurses can undertake unsupervised work but are encouraged to work in teams (National Health Service Cervical Screening Programme 1999b). All colposcopists need to maintain their standards of competence through continuing professional development in order to renew their accreditation every three years. This means that each colposcopist should maintain a regular caseload of at least 100 patients a year, attend a BSCCP recognised national colposcopy meeting at least once every three years and participate in audit and continuing education (Jolley 2004; National Health Service Cervical Screening Programme 2002; Royal College of Obstetricians and Gynaecologists 1999).

THE WORK OF A NURSE COLPOSCOPIST

Nurse colposcopists are responsible for their own sessions. Firstly, a full history is taken from all patients referred to the colposcopy clinic. This covers medical, obstetric and sexual histories including details of previous smears. It is also important to ask about their menstrual cycle, if they take any medication or smoke. Some patients have attended colposcopy before, so records of any previous abnormalities on smears or treatment to the cervix are needed.

The obstetric history is very relevant when a cancer is found on the cervix and treatment is required. Extensive or repeated treatment to the cervix may affect cervical competence, which could have implications during a future pregnancy. If a younger woman who has not had any children needs a hysterectomy, the impact can be devastating. Knowledge of contraceptive cover is necessary because if a woman has a coil *in situ* it may not be possible to treat her on that visit. If treatment is required, the coil is usually removed so alternative contraceptive cover should be discussed. Medication may also affect decisions about treatment. Especially important are hormone replacement therapy (HRT), which could be linked to any problems and may need discontinuing, and warfarin, which could cause excessive bleeding if a biopsy or any treatment is carried out. Smoking is relevant because there is evidence that it increases the risk of developing cervical cancer (National Health Service Cervical Screening Programme 1999b). The exact mechanism is unclear but it is thought that smoking depresses the immune system, allowing the HPV to take hold. Clearly women should be given advice about the benefits of stopping smoking in this context.

Once the history has been taken, the patient is prepared for her examination. It is important that she understands exactly what will happen. Women are always sent an explanatory leaflet with their appointment, but it is reassuring to explain what will happen and check that they understand. This should be done before the woman undresses. A nurse colposcopist should always have a designated nurse to assist in running the clinic (Royal College of Obstetricians and Gynaecologists 1999) in order to provide help with the practical preparation of the patient. A colposcopy couch is used to ensure that the patient is as relaxed as possible. She needs to be examined in a modified lithotomy position, so knee rests are helpful. It is important that the examination is carried out in a warm room and that dignity and privacy are maintained throughout.

The colposcopy examination allows magnification and illumination of the cervix. 'This technique can be used to assess and identify pre-invasive lesions on the cervix and lower genital tract' (Smith 2000). A suitably sized speculum is inserted into the vagina and the cervix exposed. The cervix and upper vagina can then be examined under magnification. Two types of epithelium, columnar and squamous, cover the cervix and meet at the squamo-columnar junction. Normal squamous epithelium on the cervix is described as smooth and flat while the columnar epithelium, which lines the cervical canal, has a grape-like or villous appearance (Anderson *et al.* 1992; Sellors & Sankaranarayanan 2005). Sometimes the columnar epithelium changes to form squamous metaplasia. This occurs in the 'transformation zone' where cervical intraepithelial neoplasia (CIN) and invasive carcinoma are likely to arise. CIN is a histological definition and refers to changes in the squamous cells of the cervix. The cervical appearance of women with an invasive cervical cancer would be raised, uneven and will usually bleed when touched.

The first essential prerequisite is that the entire cervix must be fully visualised and the transformation zone identified. This means that the full length of the squamo-columnar junction should be visible. If this is not the case, the colposcopic assessment would be considered unsatisfactory because it would not be possible to exclude the presence of CIN or cervical neoplasia in the hidden areas of the transformation zone. If a cervical smear is required, it would be taken at this stage. Some colposcopists will then apply saline to the cervix. This, in conjunction with a green filter on the colposcope, enables detection of any abnormal blood vessels in the cervix. Acetic acid is then applied to the cervix with a cotton wool ball, a gauze swab or a spray. Not only will this help to remove any mucus but it will also highlight any abnormal epithelium, causing this to show up white. This is known as aceto-whitening. There is a sharp line of demarcation between the normal and abnormal epithelium, and the vessels, although less readily visible than with the saline technique, are much more visible than in the normal epithelium. Occasionally, in minor changes, there is no vessel pattern to be seen following the application of acetic acid and the abnormal epithelium simply appears white.

Aceto-white change is the most important of all colposcopic features. Some degree of aceto-white will be visible when a woman has CIN. Unfortunately, epithelial changes other than CIN may also turn white with the application of this fluid. It is important that these physiological and minor changes are recognised by the colposcopist. However, distinction between these changes by colposcopy alone is not always possible and therefore any abnormal area should be biopsied.

The colposcopist has to take into account many features when looking at the cervix. Vascular patterns within the area of aceto-white are extremely important when assessing an area of abnormality. There are three main patterns. 'Mosaic' or 'crazy paving' pattern is when the capillaries appear parallel to the surface, giving a mosaic effect. 'Punctuation' is easily recognised as the stromal capillaries produce a stippled or punctuated appearance. With both these patterns the degree of abnormality increases with the severity of the changes and the size of the affected area (Luesley *et al.* 1996). Thirdly, there are atypical vessels, which are small irregular vessels arranged in a totally haphazard way. The presence of these vessels is an indication of early stromal invasion.

Aceto-white changes on the cervix can also be graded. As a general rule the more severe the degree of whitening the more severe the lesion is likely to be. The colposcopist should also note how quickly the lesion reaches its maximum whiteness and how long this lasts. Not only do severe abnormalities become whiter more quickly but they also stay white for longer than minor abnormalities. If the edges of the lesion are clearly defined, then this is likely to indicate CIN. If the edges are fuzzy, then the lesion is more likely to be associated with viral changes. If mosaic and punctuation are present as well as aceto-white, it is not always easy to determine whether a particular area of punctuation represents a more severe abnormality than an adjacent area of aceto-white and therefore both should be biopsied. Although colposcopic grading is a useful guide, it is not an assessment of the histological grade of the underlying lesion (Anderson *et al.* 1992).

Decisions about treatment are crucial because not all women with CIN will go on to develop cervical cancer. Therefore the colposcopist has to decide whether immediate treatment is necessary or not. This is based on the likelihood of the abnormal cells progressing to cancer. The more severe abnormalities should always be treated but a mild or moderate degree of CIN may either progress to a more severe form or will in time regress. The milder the degree of CIN the more likely it is to regress. However, these differentiations are not clear-cut and some of the lower-grade abnormalities will eventually lead to invasive disease if untreated (Peate 1999). Therefore the optimal treatment of low-grade abnormalities is controversial (Shlay *et al.* 2000). If the nurse colposcopist is at all unsure, she should discuss her decision with a more senior colposcopist before proceeding. When a decision is made to manage women with low-grade abnormalities conservatively, they should be followed up closely. This involves six-monthly appointments until two consecutive smears are reported as normal. During this time if the lesion worsens it will be treated. Abnormalities persisting for longer than two years should also be treated.

No woman with abnormal cytology should be treated without prior colposcopic assessment (Anderson *et al.* 1992). The treatment of CIN should be tailored to meet the needs of each patient and there are several factors to consider. Firstly, the size of the area to be treated is important. If this is very large, then it may be difficult to treat satisfactorily under a local anaesthetic. Some patients find colposcopy extremely difficult and uncomfortable and may prefer to be treated under a general anaesthetic. If colposcopic assessment suggests that the patient may have invasive cancer, she may require an examination under general anaesthetic in order to further assess the lesion. Despite these considerations, the majority of women are treated in the colposcopy clinic under a local anaesthetic.

There are different excisional treatment methods including a laser cone biopsy (shallow cone) and knife cone biopsy (large cone), but the most popular treatment is a large loop excision of the transformation zone, or LLETZ. This method of treatment removes the whole of the transformation zone, which is then sent for histological assessment. Local anaesthetic is used prior to the procedure and a hot-wire loop diathermy is then used to stop any bleeding.

Immediate complications of this treatment may be pain and haemorrhage. However, very few women complain of pain and the bleeding is usually well controlled using diathermy. Suturing may be required in exceptional circumstances. Secondary haemorrhage can occur following treatment, usually within the first 14 days. This is usually as a result of infection within the area treated and will often settle when treated with antibiotics and the woman is advised to rest. All patients treated should be given advice following treatment and informed of the possible complications and what to do in the event of this happening. Written information leaflets should always be available following treatment (Department of Health 1997) and all patients advised not to use tampons and to avoid sexual intercourse for about four to six weeks after treatment in order to reduce the risk of infection. Cervical stenosis affects between 1 and 2 % of women treated, which can make follow-up difficult as the new transformation zone might become inaccessible.

A small proportion of women who are found to have invasive disease need to have a hysterectomy, but it is widely accepted that treatment of CIN should have a success rate of 95 % (Paraskevaidis *et al.* 1991). Strict guidelines for the follow-up of patients are essential in order to identify any residual disease or any new abnormalities and reassure the patient (Peate 1999). Usually the GP follows up any histology showing a complete excision of CIN with a smear at six and 12 months after treatment. If both of these are reported as negative, they are followed by annual smears for five years. If all results are negative after this time, the woman can return to routine recall every three years. However, when the excision of CIN is thought to be incomplete, patients need colposcopic follow-up (Dobbs *et al.* 2000) and are reviewed back in the colposcopy clinic six months following treatment. The distinction between residual and recurrent disease is arbitrary but it is likely that CIN discovered up to 12 months after treatment represents residual disease, and beyond that time it would be considered to be new disease (Anderson *et al.* 1992).

HOW EFFECTIVE ARE NURSE COLPOSCOPISTS?

The introduction of nurse colposcopists has been associated with reduced waiting times (Todd *et al.* 2002). Apart from the overall impact on waiting times, there are many more advantages to training nurse colposcopists. For the nurses themselves, the extended role leads to a greater involvement and increased job satisfaction. Because nurses can concentrate solely on colposcopy, unlike the doctors who have other responsibilities, they can build up their expertise, which in turn benefits the patients. Research on the effect of nurse colposcopists is still limited but evidence so far suggests that nurses compare favourably with doctors (Gifford & Stone 1993; Morris *et al.* 1998; Todd *et al.* 2002). 'For the majority of patients who require colposcopic assessment and treatment, the nurses are as good as, if not better than, many consultants' (National Health Service Cervical Screening Programme 1999b).

The main advantage, in terms of quality for the patient, is increased choice. Many women specifically ask to see a female practitioner, sometimes for religious or ethnic reasons or simply because they find it less embarrassing (Gifford & Stone 1993; Morris *et al.* 1998). Some patients express a preference for the nurse to carry out their diagnosis and treatment (National Health Service Cervical Screening Programme 1999b, 2000). This may be because many women find it easier to talk to a nurse than a doctor. They tend to think of nurses as more approachable and are not so embarrassed about expressing their anxieties or asking 'silly' questions. This is supported by audits carried out at Addenbrooke's Hospital in Cambridge and Royal Oldham Hospital. These showed that the role of the nurse colposcopist has been well accepted by patients. Some requested to see a nurse colposcopist, whereas none specifically requested to see the doctor (Barnes 2002).

The quality of patient contact is extremely important, as a referral to colposcopy is associated with high levels of anxiety (Austoker & Davey 1997; Peate 1999; Smith 2000). Anxiety is related to fear that they may have cancer, concerns about their fertility and sex life and uncertainty about the actual procedure (Austoker & Davey 1997; Doherty *et al.* 1991; Gath *et al.* 1995). Some women feel particularly vulnerable and out of control (Rogstad 2002). If this is not addressed, it may prevent women from attending colposcopy for further investigations and treatment. Publicity linking abnormal smears with sex and HPV can also cause feelings of guilt and shame (Baileff 2000; Butcher 2001).

Nurse colposcopists are able to minimise these adverse effects. Nurses are trained to support and empathise with patients and nurse colposcopists usually have good counselling skills. Clear verbal and written information can reduce anxiety and nurse colposcopists are often able to spend more time with the patient. Patients need to understand what is involved in the examination, even including an understanding that the colposcope is not inserted into the vagina (Patnick 1998). The nurse colposcopist can also provide continuity of care by seeing the patient right through the process from start to finish, including any repeat visits. She can also offer a contact number in case the patient has any queries or concerns. This creates a friendly and supportive approach, which is much less intimidating for the patient. Therefore nurse-led treatment is associated with increased acceptability, reduced anxiety and improved compliance (Cassard *et al.* 1997; National Health Service Cervical Screening Programme 2000).

THE FUTURE

The role of the nurse colposcopist is now well established and has become an essential part of the service. As the numbers of nurse colposcopists continue to increase, it is important that they have access to a professional support network. A Nurse Colposcopy Association now exists covering nurses allied to the discipline. This includes nurses involved in running colposcopy clinics, nurses who have been trained to do diagnostic colposcopy but not treatment and also nurse colposcopists trained in both diagnosis and treatment. Hopefully this will help to maintain high standards of care and also raise the profile of nurses working in the field of colposcopy.

Nurse colposcopists are becoming more and more involved with innovative ways of running clinics and delivering care. Some women do not attend for their colposcopy appointment due to problems with accessibility. Some hospitals do not have the facilities for a colposcopy clinic, so patients need to go to a more specialised hospital. This might require a long journey and some cannot afford the time or money (Peate 1999). There may also be problems with taking time off work or child care facilities. This can be alleviated with more flexible clinic times, and many centres now run evening clinics.

These problems are exacerbated when patients need to have a biopsy taken, wait for the results and possibly return for treatment. This process can take three or four weeks between each visit. One way of improving this situation is the introduction of 'one-stop' colposcopy clinics like the one at the Queen Elizabeth Hospital, Gateshead, where women are given the results of their biopsy in two hours and offered immediate treatment. An audit of the first 300 patients showed that about 25 % of women with low-grade smear changes needed treatment and overall patient satisfaction with the service was increased (National Health Service Cervical Screening Programme 2000). However, this clinic is only possible due to high investment in new technology and it remains to be seen whether such investment will be possible on a more sustained basis.

Future investment and the direction of the colposcopy service will be heavily influenced by the development of two vaccines against HPV (Crum 2002; Davis 2004; Koutsky *et al.* 2002). The new vaccines have been developed to protect women against the strains of HPV that are responsible for the majority of cervical cancers (Types 16 and 18) (Villa *et al.* 2005*)*. Several clinical trials are now examining the efficacy of the vaccine including the FUTURE Study, which is a multicentred trial involving 5700 women worldwide. All participants have been given a course of three injections, either the vaccine or a placebo, and are being followed up over four years. The trial is in its final stages but interim results are already demonstrating 100 % protection against the highest risk strains and the vaccine should be available for general use within five years (Davis 2004). It would probably be offered to younger adolescent girls, hopefully before they become sexually active, although this is controversial (Cohen 2005; MacKenzie 2005). This would not immediately remove the need for a colposcopy service as it would depend on the uptake and there would still be large numbers of older women without protection. In addition, claims that the vaccine will end cervical cancer are slightly exaggerated, as the vaccine would not protect against all strains of HPV. There will always be a variety of different problems and rarer cancers affecting the cervix. However, there will undoubtedly be long-term implications for the development of both the screening and colposcopy services.

CONCLUSION

Following the development of a formalised training programme, nurses are assessing, diagnosing and treating patients in colposcopy clinics all over the UK. There are still high levels of demand and enormous pressure to reduce waiting times, but undoubtedly 'nurse colposcopists have made a major contribution to the provision of colposcopy services in the UK' (National Health Service Cervical Screening Programme 2002).

REFERENCES

Anderson M C et al. (1992) A Text and Atlas of Integrated Colposcopy, Chapman & Hall Medical, London.

Austoker J, Davey C (1997) Cervical Smear Results Explained: A Guide for Primary Care, Cancer Research Campaign, London.

Baileff A (2000) Cervical screening: patients' negative attitudes and experiences. Nursing Standard, 14(44), 35–7.

Barnes G (2002) Nurse Colposcopist: The Patient's Choice? Presented at the 'Spotlight on Gynaecological Care' Conference, 9 May, Aston University, Birmingham (unpublished).

Butcher M (2001) Education for women undergoing HPV testing. Professional Nurse, 16(4), 1044–7.

Cassard S D et al. (1997) Physician gender and women's preventive services. Journal of Women's Health, 6(2), 199–207.

Cohen J (2005) High hopes and dilemmas for a cervical cancer vaccine. Science, 308(5722), 618–21.

Crum C P (2002) The beginning of the end for cervical cancer? New England Journal of Medicine, 347, 1703–5.

Cuzick J et al. (1999) A systematic review of the role of human papillomavirus testing within the cervical screening programme. Health Technology Assessment, 3(14), 1–196.

Davis K (2004) Vaccine may protect against cervical cancer, NewScientist.com news service (12 November).

Department of Health (1997) Improving the Quality of the Written Information Sent to Women about Cervical Screening, HMSO, London.

Department of Health (1998) Cervical Screening Programme, England: 1997–98, The Stationery Office, London.

Department of Health (2004a) Cervical Screening Programme, England: 2003–2004, Bulletin 2004/20, The Stationery Office, London.

Department of Health (2004b) Junior Doctors Contract, www.doh.gov.uk/juniordoctors/(accessed September 2005).

Dobbs S et al. (2000) Does histological incomplete excision of cervical intraepithelial neoplasia following large loop excision of transformation zone increase recurrence rate? A six year follow-up, British Journal of Obstetrics and Gynaecology, 107(10), 1298–301.

Doherty I et al. (1991) The assessment of the psychological effects of an abnormal cervical smear result and subsequent medical procedures. Journal of Psychosomatic Obstetrics and Gynaecology, 12, 319–24.

Gath D et al. (1995) Emotional reactions in women attending a UK colposcopy clinic. Journal of Epidemiology and Community Health, 49(1), 79–83.

Gifford M S, Stone I K (1993) Quality, access and clinical issues in a nurse practitioner colposcopy outreach programme. Nurse Practitioner, 18(10), 25–9, 33–6.

Johnson J, Patnick J (Eds) (2000) *Achievable Standards, Benchmarks for Reporting and Criteria for Evaluating Cervical Cytopathology*, NHSCSP Publications, Sheffield.

Jolley S (2004) Quality in colposcopy. *Nursing Standard*, **18**(23), 39–44.

Kitchener H (2003) The value of human papillomavirus testing. *The Obstetrician and Gynaecologist*, **5**, 10–13.

Koutsky L A *et al.* (2002) A controlled trial of a human papillomavirus type 16 vaccine. *New England Journal of Medicine*, **347**(21), 1645–51.

Lester H, Wilson S (1999) Is default from colposcopy a problem and if so what can we do? *British Journal of General Practitioners*, **49**, 223–9.

Lewis D (2005) Personal communication with Debbie Lewis, PA to Liz Dollery, Co-ordinator for the British Society for Colposcopy and Cervical Pathology, on 8 November 2005.

Luesley D *et al.* (Eds) (1996) *Handbook of Colposcopy*, Chapman & Hall, London.

MacKenzie D (2005) Will cancer vaccine get to all women? *New Scientist*, **2495**, 8.

Morris D *et al.* (1998) Evaluation and treatment by gynecologists and nurses. *Nurse Practitioner*, **23**(4), 113–14.

National Health Service Cervical Screening Programme (1997) *Cervical Screening: A Practical Guide for Health Authorities*, NHSCSP Publications, Sheffield.

National Health Service Cervical Screening Programme (1999a) *Cervical Screening Programme Review*, NHSCSP Publications, Sheffield.

National Health Service Cervical Screening Programme (1999b) *Cervical Screening: A Pocket Guide*, NHSCSP Publications, Sheffield.

National Health Service Cervical Screening Programme (2000) *Reducing the Risk*, NHSCSP Publications, Sheffield.

National Health Service Cervical Screening Programme (2002) *Building on Experience – Annual Review*, NHSCSP Publications, Sheffield.

National Health Service Cervical Screening Programme (2003) *Cervical Cancer Deaths Fall Below 1000 as New Research Suggests Changes to Screening Frequency*, NHSCSP Publications, Sheffield, www.cancerscreening.nhs.uk/cervical/news/008.html (accessed February 2004).

National Health Service Cervical Screening Programme (2005) *Human Papilloma Virus*, www.cancerscreening.nhs.uk/cervical/hpv (accessed October 2005).

National Statistics (2000), *Health Quarterly Statistics 07, Autumn*.

Nursing and Midwifery Council (2002) *Code of Professional Conduct*, NMC, London.

Paraskevaidis E *et al.* (1991) Pattern of treatment failure following laser of cervical intraepithelial neoplasia: implications for follow-up protocol. *Obstetrics and Gynecology*, **78**, 883.

Patnick J (1998) Cervical screening without tears. *Practice Nurse*, **15**(5), 253–6.

Peate I (1999) Cervical Cancer 2: colposcopy, treatment and patient education. *British Journal of Nursing*, **8**(12), 805–9.

Peto J *et al.* (2004) The cervical cancer epidemic that screening has prevented into the UK. *Lancet*, **364**(9430), 249–56.

Prendiville W, Davies P (Eds) (2005) *The Health Professional's HPV Hanbbook 2. Current Evidence-based Applications*, Taylor and Francis, London.

Rogstad K (2002) The psychological impact of abnormal cytology and colposcopy. *BJOG: an International Journal of Obstetrics and Gynaecology*, **109**(4), 364–8.

Royal College of Obstetricians and Gynaecologists (1999) *Standards in Colposcopy*, RCOG Press, London.

Sasieni P, Adams J (1999) Effect of screening on cervical cancer mortality in England and Wales: analysis of trends with an age period cohort model. *British Medical Journal*, **318**(7193), 1244–5.

Sasieni P *et al.* (2003) Benefit of cervical screening at different ages: evidence from the UK audit of screening histories. *British Journal of Cancer*, **89**(1), 88–93.

Sellors J W, Sankaranarayanan R (2005) *Colposcopy and Treatment of Cervical Intra-epithelial Neoplasia: A Beginner's Manual*, IARC, Lyon, France.

Shlay J *et al.* (2000) Prediction of cervical intraepithelial neoplasia grade 2–3 using risk assessment and human papillomavirus testing with atypia on papanicolau smears. *Obstetrics and Gynaecology*, **96**(3), 410–16.

Smith T (2000) Colposcopy. *Nursing Standard*, **15**(4), 47–52.

Todd R W *et al.* (2002) Effect of nurse colposcopists on a hospital-based service. *Hospital Medicine*, **63**(4), 218–23.

Villa L L *et al.* (2005) Prophylactic quadrivalent human papillomavirus (types 6, 11, 16 and 18) L1 virus-like particle vaccine in young women: a randomised double-blind placebo-controlled multicentre phase II efficacy trial. Oncology.thelancet.com. Published online 7 April 2005 (accessed 18 October 2005).

USEFUL CONTACTS

www.cancerscreening.nhs.uk
British Society of Colposcopy and Cervical Pathology, www.bsccp.org.uk

4 Optimising Care for Women with Problems in Early Pregnancy

ANNE WALTON, CINDY WILSON and SIAN SCHMIDT

Exerpt from *Nature's Way, Rotten As It May Be*

Treatment for women who can get pregnant but cannot stay that way is neither standard nor readily available, and the reasons for this split between the wealth of infertility and dearth of miscarriage treatments are complicated.

Between 50 percent and 70 percent of the time the loss is chromosomally abnormal. A treatment that disrupts this built-in purging system could potentially result in more babies with birth defects and that's probably not a treatment worth having.

The clinics succeed by confronting their patients' despondence, fatalism and panic. . . . A lot of women will settle for a knowledgeable hand to hold. Those hands aren't always easy to find. Miscarriage isn't a specialty that pays well – with no big-ticket procedure to offer, the exams and counseling add up to a lot of time spent without much remuneration.

Emily Bazelon (2005)
Reproduced by permission of Emily Bazelon and Slate.

This chapter discusses the causes, presentation and diagnosis of miscarriage and ectopic pregnancy, followed by the management options. Problems in early pregnancy have created many challenges, resulting in the development of early pregnancy assessment units and nurse specialists in early pregnancy. The main aim is to demonstrate how this has completely changed the way care is delivered, with enormous benefits for women facing the trauma of miscarriage.

Gynaecology: Changing Services for Changing Needs. Edited by Sue Jolley
© 2006 by John Wiley & Sons, Ltd

Challenges	Service developments
• Fragmented service provision for patients with problems in early pregnancy • Shortage of trained sonographers • Increasing number of patients with ectopic pregnancies • Pressure on inpatient beds • High levels of anxiety, especially for patients with recurrent miscarriages	• Collaboration between hospitals both locally and nationally • Multiprofessional teams providing 'one-stop clinics' • Nurse specialists who can lead hospital and community services • Trained nurse/midwife sonographers • Fast-track referrals and assessments

MISCARRIAGE – A COMMON BUT SIGNIFICANT EVENT

The medical definition of miscarriage is the spontaneous loss of a pregnancy before 24 weeks gestation (Mackay *et al.* 1992). It is difficult to quantify the exact number of women who suffer pregnancy losses because at present no national statistics are collected for miscarriages. However, it is estimated that 1 in 4 pregnancies under 12 weeks end in miscarriage (The Miscarriage Association 2003). Women with a possible miscarriage commonly present with vaginal bleeding and abdominal pain having confirmed the pregnancy with a pregnancy test. Of those presenting with bleeding 30–50 % go on to have a failed pregnancy (Bryan 2003). There are different types of miscarriage (see Table 4.1) and this classification is important in determining the appropriate management.

It is not always easy to determine the exact cause of a miscarriage and, because it is such a common occurrence, investigations are not normally carried out until a woman has had three consecutive miscarriages with the same partner. The main cause of miscarriage is chromosomal abnormalities. Errors can occur when chromosomes taken from the mother and father can lead to too many or too few chromosomes, so the fetus does not develop normally from the start and is incompatible with life. This is usually a totally random occurrence and does not automatically mean that one of the parents has abnormal chromosomes.

Other causes include hormonal problems, blood clotting disorders, infection and anatomical abnormalities. Research is currently being carried out into the relationship between progesterone levels and miscarriage (Regan 2004). Women with polycystic ovaries (PCOs) often find it difficult to conceive (Kousta *et al.* 2000), because the condition is associated with a hormonal imbalance such as increased level of luteinising hormone (LH) and testosterone. Further research is currently taking place to investigate the connection between PCOs and miscarriage (Amer *et al.* 2003). Women with early

Table 4.1. Classification of miscarriages

Type of miscarriage	Presentation	Scan findings	Management
Threatened	Slight bleeding in early pregnancy with cervix closed. Uterus correct size for dates. Usually no pain (Pearce & Easton 2005)	Viable pregnancy determined by heart pulsation	Reassurance and rest (there is no scientific evidence that rest prevents miscarriage but can prevent subsequent self-blame)
Inevitable	Heavy bleeding in early pregnancy followed by pain. Cervix opens to allow passage of uterine contents (Clayton & Chamberlain 1994)	Non-viable pregnancy	Conservative if gestation < 13 weeks and HCG < 1000. Active if bleeding is heavy
Complete miscarriage	Heavy vaginal bleeding and abdominal pain, which has stopped. Uterus smaller than expected. Cervix closed	No pregnancy sac or retained products of conception	Conservative if uterus empty. Serial HCGs to confirm pregnancy finished.
Incomplete miscarriage	Heavy vaginal bleeding and abdominal pain	Retained products of conception present in the uterus	As inevitable miscarriage

Table 4.1. *Continued*

Type of miscarriage	Presentation	Scan findings	Management
Missed miscarriage	Often present with slight brown vaginal loss. Uterus small for dates. Cervix closed. Often feel 'less pregnant'	Gestation sac often with a yolk sac and a fetal pole > 6 mm crown rump length with no fetal heart movements (Rosevear 2002)	Active, medical or surgical
Anembryonic pregnancy (blighted ovum)	May have some vaginal bleeding and pain. Women often unaware that anything is wrong	Gestation sac > 20 mm but no embryo or yolk sac (Luise *et al.* 2002)	As for missed miscarriage
Hydatidiform mole or molar pregnancy (when the chorionic villi of the placenta degenerate into clusters of cysts like hydatids)	Usual miscarriage symptoms but classically describe vaginal loss as like 'prune juice'. Increased amount of nausea and sickness due to high levels of HCG	'Snowstorm' appearance. Can be indistinguishable from retained products of conception	Surgical removal needed because malignant growth likely to follow if any remnants left in the uterus. Close follow-up at a regional centre until HCG levels have been normal for 6 months
Ectopic pregnancy (outside the uterus, commonly in the uterine tubes)	One-sided abdominal pain with sudden onset of bleeding after pain has stopped. May develop shoulder tip pain	Ectopic pregnancy may be seen or complex cystic adnexal masses. Sometimes free fluid (blood) in abdomen	Usually surgical intervention, often involving a salpingectomy. Medical management using methotrexate is becoming more common

pregnancy loss are often found to have high levels of follicle stimulating hormone (FSH). This hormone drives the ovaries to start growing follicles and high levels can mean that the ovaries have become menopausal.

A pregnant woman's blood tends to thicken but recently it has been shown that this can become a problem affecting the flow of blood to the baby. This decrease of blood supply can lead to miscarriage. Research has detected antiphospholipid antibodies present in women who have suffered from recurrent miscarriages, the two most important ones being lupus anticoagulant and the anticardiolipin antibodies that cause the blood to clot more easily (Rai *et al.* 1995). Women who have tested positive to either of these antibodies are said to have the primary antiphospholipid syndrome (PAPS), also called Hughes syndrome (Holden 2002).

Anatomical abnormalities of the uterus that may increase the risk of miscarriage include fibroids and a bicornate uterus, which is where a septum is found down the whole or part of the uterus. Cervical incompetence is often thought to be a cause of miscarriage in the second trimester, usually after the 14th week. It is usually diagnosed when a woman has a history of spontaneous miscarriages in the second trimester and it is recommended that a cervical suture be inserted at around 14 weeks gestation.

Healthcare professionals often underestimate the psychological impact of bleeding and pain in early pregnancy (O'Connor & Kovacs 2003) and the significance of miscarriage has been recognised only relatively recently within the medical world. The changing roles of women and the greater awareness of women's issues within the healthcare setting have helped raise the profile of pregnancy loss. Until only a few years ago miscarriage was viewed as a 'minor medical event' and the emotional upset and reaction to the grief was not addressed until some qualitative studies were carried out in the 1980s (Moulder 1998). These highlighted the fact that the women often felt alone in their grief and mourning, as they felt nobody else around them understood or acknowledged their loss, be it family, friends or health professionals. Quantitative research has also demonstrated that miscarriage can trigger grief, anxiety and depression (Brier 2004; Maker & Ogden 2003). 'Grief can be profound for both the woman and her partner, and is similar to that experienced with any major loss or bereavement' (Pearce & Easton 2005).

EARLY PREGNANCY ASSESSMENT CENTRES

Changing attitudes towards miscarriage paved the way for the development of Early Pregnancy Assessment Centres (EPACs). Prior to the advent of EPACs, service provision was very fragmented and often inadequate. Patients with problems in the first and second trimester of their pregnancies were admitted to a gynaecology ward, often needlessly, at any time of the day or night. Sometimes they were kept in hospital for up to 3 days while they were assessed. During their stay in hospital, patients saw a succession of different people including nurses, doctors, phlebotomists, porters and radiographers. Following the initial admission and assessment, they often had to wait for an available slot in the ultrasound department for a scan. Then they were not necessarily told the result by the radiographer and so returned to the ward to wait for a doctor. If the scan confirmed a miscarriage, surgical management was the most common option and patients booked for theatre had a further wait, often spending many hours starved in preparation.

This was a difficult time for many patients, separated from their partners or family and feeling alone and isolated at an anxious time. Psychological support following pregnancy loss was virtually non-existent and totally dependent on the patient asking for support via their general practitioner (GP). Partners often felt excluded from any decisions.

The clear need to provide more patient-centred care in this area led to the introduction of EPACs in the early 1990s (Pearce & Easton 2005). At the time this seemed very innovative and a much more efficient way of organising the service (Bigrigg & Read 1991). The main advantage was the potential to speed the diagnosis process and reduce inpatient nights in hospital. It was also an ideal opportunity for nurses with a defined interest in this area to develop specialised roles. The European Directive to reduce junior doctors' hours (British Medical Association 2004) created a climate that was conducive to this general development. EPACs have gradually been established in most large gynaecology departments (Ward 2000), but literature relating to this service is limited (Pearce & Easton 2005).

The development of an EPAC at Queen's Medical Centre (QMC), Nottingham, illustrates the process, difficulties and advantages. A nurse specialist was employed to set up an EPAC in 1993, initially as a pilot scheme to assess need and effectiveness. The unit was a one-stop clinic served by all healthcare professionals, so patients did not need to visit different departments (Royal College of Obstetricians and Gynaecologists 2000). This was initially very challenging as many healthcare professionals felt secure in their own department and found it difficult to leave their 'safe environment' to work alongside staff from different disciplines.

It soon became apparent that the nurse specialist and sonographer were leading the clinic and felt secure in the new working area as they saw the benefits both for the patients and the service providers. This reflects experience in other EPACs (Habayeb & Konje 2004). The nurse specialist took on the phlebotomy work, as this was part of the process of assessment, planning and implementing care. The holding of anti-D immunoglobulin on the unit was essential because isoimmunisation can occur in early pregnancy. Anti-D should be administered to all non-sensitive Rhesus negative women who have any vaginal bleeding after 12 weeks gestation and to all Rhesus-negative women who miscarry before 12 weeks if medical intervention is required (National Institute for Clinical Excellence 2004; Royal College of Obstetricians and Gynaecologists 2000). This prophylaxis will prevent the production of antibodies by the mother against fetal Rhesus positive cells. It was agreed that it would be easy to regulate the situation if the nurse specialist was responsible for storing and administering anti-D. This also enabled a better working partnership between the unit and haematologists (National Institute for Clinical Excellence 2004). Doctors were only called to see patients when diagnosis necessitated admission to a ward, which reduced the workload for junior doctors.

Referrals from primary care trusts were slow at first as many doctors and midwives wanted their patients seen immediately and felt that admission to hospital was a 'safer option'. The nurse specialist contacted all the GPs to highlight the new service and subsequently attended numerous practice meetings to describe how the service would work and explain the protocols for referral. QMC was also keen to introduce a hospital-at-home service for patients so the nurse specialist visited and networked with successful schemes already in operation and was able to promote the benefits of keeping patients in their homes with access to specialists.

Although quicker diagnosis, especially of ectopic pregnancy, was one of the main advantages of an EPAC, it also enabled patients and their families to have better psychological support. This increased dramatically as there had previously been no support from professionals with specialist knowledge in this field (Royal College of Obstetricians and Gynaecologists 2000). The nurse specialist was also able to offer a follow-up counselling service for couples who had suffered a pregnancy loss and the GPs were keen to make referrals to this service.

The service at QMC has developed steadily, with appointments rising from 20 per week to the current rate of 70. There are now two additional nurses working on the unit supported by a full-time receptionist. Sonographers attend for regular sessions and designated doctors are available when required. It has been clear that a successful EPAC needs support and commitment from the hospital trust, the gynaecology consultants and the GPs. Above all staff need to be motivated and dedicated to the work.

THE ROLE OF THE SONOGRAPHER IN AN EPAC

'Over the past 15 years ultrasonography has revolutionized the management of complications in early pregnancy' (Pearce & Easton 2005). Medical ultrasound uses high-frequency sound waves to obtain a real-time moving image. Transvaginal ultrasound uses higher frequencies, resulting in better resolution; thus imaging of the uterus, ovaries, adnexae and fetus is obtained in greater detail.

Ultrasound should only be performed by a trained and qualified health professional. Historically only radiographers and radiologists performed ultrasound. However, the need for ultrasound has dramatically increased and nurses and midwives are also being trained in ultrasound specific to their specialties. All healthcare professionals should hold a postgraduate diploma in medical ultrasound or a postgraduate certificate in obstetric and gynaecology ultrasound. Sonographers should be trained in both transabdominal and transvaginal ultrasound and produce reports using standardised documentation (Royal College of Radiologists/Royal College of Obstetricians and Gynaecologists 1996).

Women generally accept transvaginal ultrasound, even when anxious (Braithwaite & Economides 1997; Proud 1997). However, departmental guidelines must be established and adhered to. Those women not acceptable for a transvaginal scan (TVS) include virgo-intactus, under 16 years unless with parental permission, prolapse with a ring *in situ* or for social reasons.

To establish gestation and viability in a normal intrauterine pregnancy it is necessary to know at what stage each development is visualised on an ultrasound scan and with human chorionic gonadotrophin (HCG) values (see Table 4.2). At 5 weeks from the last menstrual period, an intrauterine pregnancy is characterised by an intrauterine sac (Rosevear 2002). This is usually positioned at the fundus of the uterus. It has an eccentric, asymmetrical ring, which may have a double-ring appearance (Figure 4.1). This represents the amnion and yolk sac. No contents are seen within this sac, which has a mean sac diameter (MSD) of 10 mm. The yolk sac is the first structure demonstrated within the gestation sac and disappears at 10 weeks. It is seen as a bright rounded structure with an internal echo-free area (James *et al.* 1995) (Figure 4.2).

Table 4.2. Determining gestation and viability

Stages of development visualised on ultrasound scan		
Embryonic/fetal structure	Transvaginal scan	Transabdominal scan
Empty intrauterine gestation sac	4 weeks 1–3 days	5 weeks
Yolk sac	5 weeks	6–7 weeks
Fetal heart pulsations	5 weeks 4 days	6 weeks 4–7 days
Fetal movements	7 weeks	8 weeks
Limb buds and head	8 weeks	9 weeks

Values of human chorionic gonadotrophin	
3–4 weeks	9–130 IU[a]
4–5 weeks	75–2600 IU
5–6 weeks	850–20 800 IU
6–7 weeks	4000–100 200 IU
7–12 weeks	11 500–290 000 IU

[a] International unit.

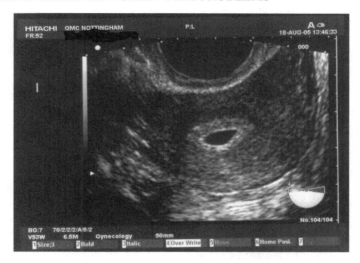

Figure 4.1. Intrauterine gestation sac positioned at the fundus demonstrating a double decidual ring. (Reproduced by kind permission of Queen's Medical Centre Nottingham)

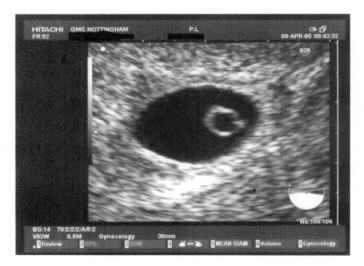

Figure 4.2. Yolk sac within gestation sac. (Reproduced by kind permission of Queen's Medical Centre Nottingham)

The fetal pole is visualised within the gestation sac when the MSD is 16–18 mm. It is seen as a few small echoes (Figure 4.3). Fetal heart pulsations are seen almost as soon as the fetus is detected. This can often be as small as 2 mm. The crown rump length (CRL) is used to measure the fetus and thus determine the gestational age. This is the most accurate way of estimating

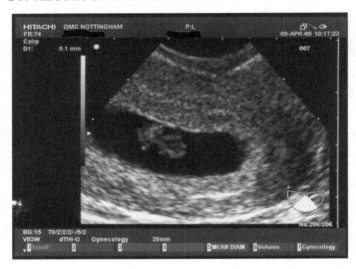

Figure 4.3. Fetal pole lying close to the yolk sac. CRL: 5 mm = 6 weeks and 2 days. Fetal heart pulsations were demonstrated on real-time scanning. (Reproduced by kind permission of Queen's Medical Centre Nottingham)

gestational age as the fetus grows rapidly. From 7 weeks the fetus grows approximately 1 mm per day (Chudleigh & Pearce 1992). Fetal heart pulsations can always be detected at a CRL of 6 mm (Chisolm & Jenkins 2003).

Implantation bleeds are often seen at this stage. Size is not related to pregnancy outcome (Chudleigh & Pearce 1992). It is measured and important to distinguish from an empty second gestation sac (Figure 4.4). A twin pregnancy is diagnosed when two fetal poles are visualised simultaneously. Twin gestation sacs can be seen from approximately $4^{1}/_{2}$ weeks but the amnion cannot be clearly seen until 8 weeks. Therefore chorionicity should only be determined after 8 weeks by the transvaginal approach. The optimal time to determine chorionicity is between 9 and 10 weeks (Smith & Smith 2002).

The ovaries and adnexae are always examined in early pregnancy ultrasound as the cause of any pain may be related to factors not associated with the pregnancy. The most common findings on ultrasound are:

- Corpus luteal cyst. This is part of normal cyclical change within an ovary. The corpus luteum is formed after the rupture of the mature follicle and should then regress. When this does not happen, a corpus luteal cyst develops. This can be visualized in the first trimester and generally measures 20–25 mm. Haemorrhage can present in up to 60 % of cases (Bates 1997). By the 20-week scan the cyst has normally resolved (Figure 4.5).
- Follicular or simple cyst. A simple cyst on ultrasound has a smooth, thin wall and contains fluid (seen as black on ultrasound). Any cyst greater than 3 cm

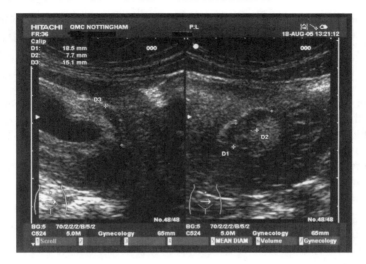

Figure 4.4. Implantation bleed inferior to the gestation sac measuring 18 × 8 × 15 mm. (Reproduced by kind permission of Queen's Medical Centre Nottingham)

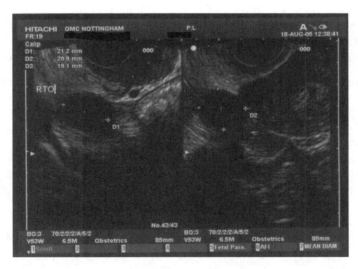

Figure 4.5. Corpus luteal cyst in the right ovary measuring 21 mm. (Reproduced by kind permission of Queen's Medical Centre Nottingham)

in diameter is generally considered pathological as opposed to a corpus luteal cyst. Size can vary although they do not generally exceed 10 cm.
• Dermoid cyst. These can be either cystic or solid with cystic being more common (Bates 1997). Dermoid cysts contain all types of cell types except gonadal tissue. If a solid component is identified, this may contain bone,

teeth or cartilage. They may have a complex appearance on ultrasound due to the variety of elements that may be involved.

Routine fetal anomaly scanning at 18–20 weeks is well established in Europe (Twining *et al.* 1999). Early pregnancy ultrasound is used for viability, dating, diagnosing ectopics and reassurance. The majority are scanned at 6–8 weeks gestation. This is too early to diagnose fetal anomalies, the fetus being only a few small echoes and anatomy often incomplete before 12 weeks. However, it is possible to detect some anomalies in the first trimester while others have a variable onset and may only present at a later gestation. Certain factors may inhibit this such as fetal position, fibroids, limited time caused by the patient's anxiety and contraction of the uterus (Twining *et al.* 1999).

Anomalies that can be detected include:

- exencephaly: absence of the cranium with complete but abnormal development of the brain. Prolonged exposure to amniotic fluid and repeated mechanical trauma leads to anencephaly. Diagnosis cannot be made before 10 weeks (Figures 4.6a and 4.6b).
- conjoined twins. Late division of the zygote will result in conjoined twins.
- cystic hygroma: a congenital malformation of the lymphatic system resulting in large swellings to the back of the fetal neck. There is a high incidence of chromosomal disease, predominantly Turner's syndrome, but also Trisomy 21 and Trisomy 18 (Figure 4.7).
- increased nuchal translucency (NT). As part of a screening programme the NT is measured from a CRL of 45 mm. However, an increased thicken-

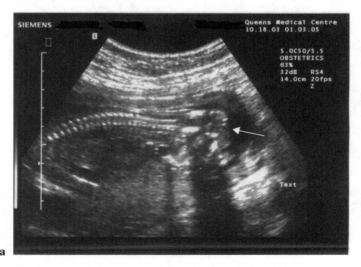

a

Figure 4.6a. Anencephaly. Sagittal section of a 10-week fetus demonstrating underdevelopment of the cranium (arrow). See Figure 4.6b for a normal cranium in comparison. (Reproduced by kind permission of Queen's Medical Centre Nottingham)

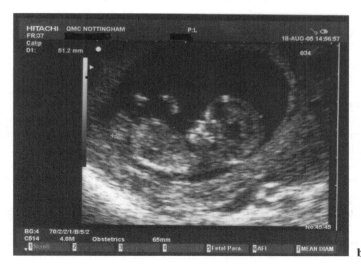

Figure 4.6b. Sagittal section of a normal fetal cranium at 12 weeks. (Reproduced by kind permission of Queen's Medical Centre Nottingham)

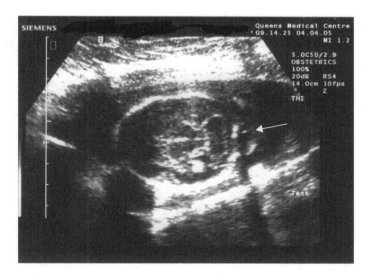

Figure 4.7. Cystic hygroma. Transverse section of fetal head at approximately 20 weeks. Note the multiseptate cystic mass at the back of the neck (arrow). (Reproduced by kind permission of Queen's Medical Centre Nottingham)

ing at the back of the neck may be detectable by an experienced sonographer earlier than this. Increased NT is associated with a high risk of chromosomal disease and also structural anomalies including major cardiac defects.

- anterior abdominal wall defects. Normal mid-gut herniation occurs between the 7th and 11th week of gestation and has usually resolved by the 12th week. This is important to consider before a defect is suspected. These include omphalocoele and gastroschisis (Figures 4.8a and 4.8b).
- renal defects. These include renal agenesis and hydronephrosis.

The role of the sonographer has changed in recent years with report writing leading to a greater autonomy. In an EPAC environment the sonographer works single-handed and makes a diagnosis, taking into consideration the clinical details. A report is then written with the findings clearly described and a diagnosis, if appropriate. Departmental guidelines and protocols need to be followed when reporting to ensure correct care is provided for the patient (e.g. a re-scan is arranged where appropriate) and to protect the sonographer medico-legally. The whole process requires the sonographer to have an open mind, to think of all diagnoses and to make a decision. The final aspect of a sonographer's role is to inform the often anxious patient of the findings. To break bad news is often the most difficult part of the sonographer's work.

The advantage of working closely with specialist nurses in an EPAC is that the nurse and sonographer are both present during the scan and when the sonographer tells the patient of the scan findings the specialist nurse is able to counsel her immediately. This is also advantageous for the sonographer, who will learn more of the role of specialist nurses and for the nurses who will have a greater understanding of ultrasound. The environment in EPAC

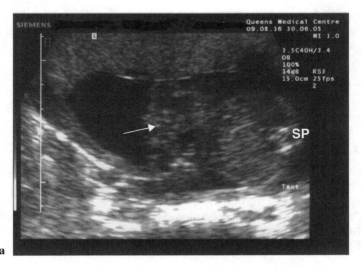

Figure 4.8a. Gastroschisis. Transverse section of the abdomen. Herniation of the bowel into the amniotic cavity (arrow). SP: spine. See Figure 4.8b for a normal abdomen in comparison. (Reproduced by kind permission of Queen's Medical Centre Nottingham)

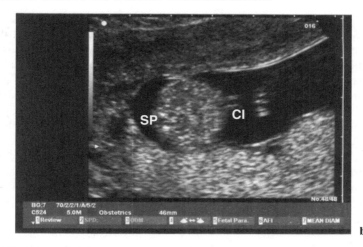

b

Figure 4.8b. Normal abdomen at 12 weeks. SP: spine; CI: cord insertion. (Reproduced by kind permission of Queen's Medical Centre Nottingham)

breeds a multidisciplinary team, which is better for the staff and also for patient care.

MANAGEMENT OF MISCARRIAGE

The majority of patients can be managed in a well-established EPAC where there is access to modern ultrasound scanning, including transvaginal probes and laboratory facilities for HCG assays within two hours and rhesus antibody testing (Bradley & Hamilton-Fairley 1998; Fox *et al.* 2000; Walker & Shillito 1997). The Royal College of Obstetricians and Gynaecologists (RCOG) has produced good-practice guidelines that provide a framework for the delivery of care in EPACs (Royal College of Obstetricians and Gynaecologists 2000).

FIRST TRIMESTER MISCARRIAGE

When managing women with early pregnancy complications, such as miscarriage, it is important to recognise the normal sonographic milestones in the first trimester. Understanding the pattern of serum HCG changes in early normal pregnancy and the spontaneous resolution of a pregnancy is also important. With the increased use of sensitive pregnancy tests that can be used before a woman's period is even due, women can have their pregnancies confirmed much earlier. Therefore they sometimes present with problems when 5 or even 4 weeks pregnant. If the bleeding does occur at this early stage, the HCG levels are often monitored, as a scan may not be clinically indicated. Production of HCG commences at the start of a pregnancy and gives a positive pregnancy test. The HCG levels increase rapidly in early pregnancy, approximately doubling every 48 hours in the 4th to 8th week of pregnancy (Thorstensen 2000). If the pregnancy is more advanced, then an ultrasound scan will be offered in order to reassure the woman and confirm the viability of the pregnancy.

Patients who are referred to an EPAC must have a comprehensive history taken detailing date of last menstrual period, usual menstrual cycle, previous pregnancies and outcomes, history of pelvic infection and treatment, history of pelvic surgery, particularly tubal surgery, and any contraception use. A transvaginal scan (TVS) will be required in approximately 40 % of women referred to an EPAC (Royal College of Obstetricians and Gynaecologists 2000). It is important that the woman is given information about why a TVS is needed and understands that this will aid her in getting a faster diagnosis. A TVS is an acceptable intervention in early pregnancy with 88 % of women accepting a TVS and 95 % stating that they would have one again in the future (Braithwaite & Economides 1997). Ultrasound assessment should be followed up with an HCG assay if there is doubt about the location of the pregnancy. This is because lower levels of HCG are produced with an ectopic pregnancy.

Until recently surgical uterine evacuation has been the standard treatment offered to women who miscarry, and the majority of women (88 %) who miscarry in the first trimester are currently managed surgically (Royal College of Obstetricians and Gynaecologists 2000). This is because retained tissue can increase the risks of infection and haemorrhage. It should always be the treatment of choice where bleeding is excessive, if vital signs are unstable or when infected tissue is present in the uterine cavity. However, studies suggest that less than 10 % of women fall into these categories (Ballagh et al. 1998), so most women who have miscarried can now be offered either medical or conservative management as well as surgical management.

Although women should be given choices about their management, they are often too distressed to take in much information and need time to make decisions (Engelhard 2004). It therefore makes sense that women who are not requiring immediate admission to hospital should be given verbal information, backed up with written information, and allowed home to consider their options. If patients are being offered choices, they must be given a contact number so that when they feel ready they can telephone to discuss their options again and arrange their care pathway. Many women prefer expectant or medical management because they prefer not to have a general anaesthetic and feel more in control. It is important that they have a telephone, transport to the hospital and a responsible adult available, especially at night-time.

Expectant management

Expectant (conservative) management is where a pregnancy has failed and is allowed to spontaneously miscarry without any medical intervention. Most women will expel the products of conception within 2 weeks of the commencement of bleeding (Luise *et al.* 2002). Expectant management is eminently suitable for many women, but they do need a good explanation and understanding of the process. It is essential that women are supported when making this decision and are given a contact number for 24-hour support. They need a follow-up appointment in the EPAC to confirm that the miscarriage is complete and to ensure their psychological well-being. They must be made aware of the need for adequate sanitary protection and be advised that analgesia, usually paracetamol and an anti-inflammatory such as Nurofen, may be required. If patients are made aware of the possibility of fairly heavy vaginal bleeding and the need for analgesia, they tend to be more prepared and therefore cope better. All the women who undergo expectant management express a desire to have a 'natural' experience or wish to avoid surgery and general anaesthesia.

Women who opt for expectant management are often well supported by family and friends, although some do report that, as they have not been admitted to hospital, they are not seen as 'being as ill' and therefore do not receive as much sympathy (Ogden & Maker 2004). Many of the men who support their partners with expectant management report feeling they can share more in the bad experience (*Nursing Standard* 2000).

Success rates for expectant management vary from 100% successful (Chipchase & James 1997) to as low as 25% (Jurkovic *et al.* 1998). These studies do not explain the reasons for such a big discrepancy except to say that the lowest efficacy rates were related to cases with an intact gestational sac and closed cervix. When patients are counselled, it is important they understand that resolution may take several weeks or 20% will request surgical management during the observation period (Hurd *et al.* 1997).

At QMC the women are asked to contact the nurse specialist when they feel they have miscarried, and the nurse may need to rearrange the follow-up ultrasound until the bleeding has settled and ultrasound can confirm an endometrial thickness of less than 15mm. If the women have not miscarried after two weeks and this is confirmed by ultrasound, other management options should be discussed.

Since the appointment of a nurse specialist at QMC there has been an increase in the number of women opting for expectant management, and this is now seen as a normal and accepted way to care for women. All women who have had expectant management will be aware of the support and advice that is available and know they can contact the EPAC and speak to one of the nurses.

Medical management

Medical management of first trimester miscarriage is the combination of the antiprogestogen mifepristone and the prostaglandin analogue misoprostol.

The mifepristone acts as a priming stage and is given 48 hours prior to the misoprostol. Medical management is usually considered successful if the miscarriage is complete 12 hours after the misoprostol is given. If at this time the miscarriage has not occurred, then the patient will be booked for an evacuation of uterus. The overall success rate for medical management is less than 50% with some centres reporting rates as low as 13% (De Jonge *et al.* 1995). Many reports comparing expectant management with medical management suggest that medical management has no benefits over expectant management and has side effects, with up to 48% of patients reporting gastrointestinal problems (De Jonge *et al.* 1995). Studies of this kind are very limited as only small numbers are included, but Bagratee *et al.* (2004) claim in a study of 131 women that there were no differences in side effects, bleeding duration, analgesia use, pain score and satisfaction with treatment. However, it appears that the success rate of medical management was better (88.5% compared with 44.2%) than for expectant management in patients with a missed miscarriage, but there was no significant difference in success rates (100% versus 85.7%) in women treated with an incomplete miscarriage.

The women who opt for medical miscarriage often want to speed up the process but wish to try and avoid a general anaesthetic. When a patient opts for medical management of miscarriage, it is essential that she is given a full and detailed explanation. In order for a patient to be offered medical management she must fulfil certain criteria. She must not be taking steroids, anticoagulants or aspirin and must not have diabetes, high cholesterol or a bleeding disorder.

It is essential to understand that the miscarriage may occur after the initial priming with mifepristone and then the patient must contact the nurse specialist for advice. She will not need to attend for the mifepristone but will need a follow-up appointment to ensure the miscarriage is complete. Approximately one-third of women will miscarry after the mifepristone (Royal College of Obstetricians and Gynaecologists 2000). It is essential when the patient arrives for the misoprostol that they are monitored closely throughout their time on the ward for the signs of miscarriage and that all bleeding and clots are checked. She also needs to be cared for by experienced and sympathetic nurses. On discharge from hospital she must be aware that the bleeding will continue. At QMC patients are telephoned by a nurse to ensure that they are physically recovering and also to check on their mental state and offer support if required. Many patients after miscarriage have a low self-esteem and if medical management of miscarriage fails and they require a surgical evacuation this can exacerbate their negative feelings.

Surgical management

Although expectant and medical methods are effective in managing miscarriage, they have not replaced surgical evacuation. In the UK surgical uterine evacuation is usually sharp/blunt curettage for cases of incomplete miscarriage and suction curettage for delayed miscarriage. A randomised trial comparing the two methods in the management of incomplete miscarriage concluded that suction curettage was safer and easier (Verkuyl & Crowther 1993). Serious complications of surgery include perforation of the uterus, cervical tears, intraabdominal trauma, intrauterine adhesions and haemorrhage. The reported incidence of serious morbidity using a surgical management is 2.1 % with a mortality of 0.5 % per 100000 (Lawson *et al.* 1994; Royal College of Obstetricians and Gynaecologists 2000).

Women who are anxious to have the experience over with and want to return to normal life as soon as possible usually choose surgical treatment. These women very often make the decision immediately and are admitted the following day. It has been reported that some women feel they should have been given more time to make the decision (Ogden & Maker 2004). Ideally these women should only be admitted to hospital for the shortest possible amount of time. Many hospitals admit patients to their day case units and have a separate operating time specifically for these women. Unfortunately, many units are still unable to offer this and women are admitted to the ward having been put on an emergency list with a second-level rating according to the Confidential Enquiry into Perioperative Deaths (CEPOD), indicating that as they must have their operation within 24 hours they often wait for a theatre slot. If it is not possible to perform the procedure on the same day that the patient is admitted, she should be told as soon as possible and given the choice of being allowed home for the night and returning the next day. It is wrong for these patients to be operated on in the middle of the night and equally wrong to keep them starved for many hours, even meaning that they may require intravenous fluids to maintain hydration. The longer patients are kept waiting in hospital for the procedure the more negative the experience becomes.

An hour before transfer to the theatre patients with a missed miscarriage should have cervical priming, usually with misoprostol. On return from theatre patients should be aware that they will have some vaginal bleeding and this may continue for a few days. If the patient has period-type pain, she should be offered simple analgesia such as paracetamol. It is usual to keep patients resting for 2–3 hours and then encourage them to gently mobilise, particularly to the toilet to void, and have fluids and possibly a light diet as they wish. When they are discharged, they should have contact numbers for the nurse specialist and be aware of the need to call if bleeding becomes heavy, they have severe pain or they feel unwell with a raised temperature or offensive discharge.

After miscarriage

Apart from supporting patients through the practical management of their miscarriage, other issues need addressing. Miscarriage 'can be associated with significant psychological sequelae' (Royal College of Obstetricians and Gynaecologists 2000) and women often feel a sense of failure and possibly shame and insecurity (Grudzinskas & O'Brien 1997). Therefore it is essential that women and their partners are offered adequate support after miscarriage. At QMC the nurses phone the couple at home and offer continuing support.

When miscarriage has occurred, patients are keen to know the cause of the loss. Unfortunately, for many couples there is no absolute answer. As The Miscarriage Association support leaflet states, 'it is usually difficult to know the exact cause and it can be hard to accept that no one can say for certain why it happened' (The Miscarriage Association 2003). Although most pregnancy loss is due to chromosomal reasons, it is impossible to know for sure. Most women who miscarry, even three times, will eventually carry a baby to term, but unfortunately this cannot be guaranteed. Women that have had recurrent miscarriage should be offered genetic testing of the tissue as well as genetic testing of their serum. Genetic testing, if successful, will mean the couple will know the sex of their baby and this can help with their grief process.

Many couples fear 'what happens to the baby now?' There should be an honest and direct approach when discussing both histological examination and disposal arrangements. Histological examination would always be the ideal and optimum care for a patient and pathologists would always be keen to examine the tissue from a miscarriage. Heath et al. (2000) suggest that there is no obvious benefit in routine histological investigation of tissue obtained from cases of pregnancy termination and miscarriage. However, in view of the maternal risks associated with both ectopic pregnancy and gestational trophoblastic disease an RCOG study group recommended that all tissue should be sent for histological examination (Royal College of Obstetricians and Gynaecologists 1997).

It is most important for couples to be fully informed about the histological examination. The reporting of public enquiries into high-profile cases such as post-mortem tissue sampling in babies (Kennedy 2001) have added further impetus to provide high-quality information. The nature and results of any tests that are done should be clearly communicated. Often women are aware that some tests have been done but they do know what or why. 'Expectations are raised that tests will bring answers, when only the most basic assessment of the tissue has taken place' (Moulder 2001). If a direct approach is taken and couples are offered choices, some of the control is given back to them and they have more understanding. It is essential that women are not told that histological examination will explain a cause for miscarriage but that it can only help to exclude ectopic or hydatidiform molar pregnancy. This can be difficult for the couple that desperately wants answers.

When the couple is clear about histological examination and has signed a consent form to agree or refuse examination, then disposal arrangements must be discussed. The disposal of tissue is very emotive and Royal College of Nursing (RCN) consultations have raised this sensitive issue for many healthcare professionals. Many women are relieved to know that there is a 'funeral', as many have concerns that it will be incinerated with other clinical waste.

At QMC all miscarried tissue is either cremated at a local crematorium or couples can make their own arrangements for burial. For Muslim women burial is offered on non-consecrated ground or again they can make their own arrangements. Each month in the hospital chapel there is a short service of remembrance that women and their families can attend, light a candle and have time for reflection. There is also a book of remembrance. At QMC a chaplain will conduct the service and a nurse specialist will be present in case couples ask for support other than pastoral care.

SECOND TRIMESTER MISCARRIAGE

Second trimester miscarriage is a lot less common than first trimester loss. Approximately 25 % of miscarriages are in the second trimester (Rosenthal 2003) and are often diagnosed when women attend a routine antenatal appointment and no fetal heartbeat can be detected. All women have an ultrasound in this situation for confirmation of fetal death and to assess the size of the baby. During the second trimester, women are not expecting to go into labour and the warning signs that something is going wrong are often missed (Moulder 2001). If a woman has had a second trimester miscarriage, it is highly likely she has already had an ultrasound scan for either dating purposes or a nuchal translucency measurement. If a subsequent ultrasound then confirms a missed miscarriage, then it may come as a huge shock as she has experienced no symptoms of miscarriage. There have been reports of acute and post-traumatic stress disorder following the immense shock of the diagnosis (Bowles *et al.* 2000).

Some women will begin to have signs of impending miscarriage such as leaking liquor (amniotic fluid), vaginal bleeding or contraction-type pains. These signs of miscarriage can be apparent for a few hours up to a few weeks before the miscarriage happens. Kohn and Moffitt (1992) describe anticipatory grief, in which 'you begin to mourn while the baby is still in the womb'. Many women describe being unable to believe fully that the pregnancy is over until it is physically over.

If a woman has a spontaneous onset of labour in the second trimester, then usually the baby and placenta can be delivered naturally and the need for dilatation and curettage is reduced. It is important that the placenta is closely examined to confirm the presence of all the lobes of placenta.

If a diagnosis of a missed miscarriage is made on ultrasound, then there has to be a discussion about the management of this condition. Couples are likely to need time to begin to come to terms with what is happening to them but require an enormous amount of support while they do this.

If the pregnancy has progressed beyond 13 weeks, then medical management of miscarriage will be required to terminate the pregnancy. There needs to be a full explanation of what this will entail and the facts about how delivery will occur.

In an early pregnancy unit these couples must be allowed time to begin to believe what they have been told. If they need time to go home and decide when they wish to begin induction of their labour, then this should be allowed and they must have contact numbers for the nurse specialist.

The patient will require antiprostogen mifepristone followed 48 hours later by the prostaglandin analogue misoprostol. As with first trimester miscarriage the mifepristone can initiate rapid onset of delivery, and admission to hospital for these women must be quickly available (Royal College of Obstetricians and Gynaecologists 2000). When the patient is admitted to the ward for misoprostol, she should have privacy and the facility for her partner to stay with her.

During her time from diagnosis to delivery, it is important, at an appropriate time, to discuss what will happen when delivery is imminent and following delivery. Anxiety disorders following mid-trimester loss may be increased where thorough explanation has not occurred (Geller *et al.* 2001).

The couple will need to understand the size of the baby when it is delivered and to know they will be able to see, touch and hold the baby. If they wish to bring in a special blanket to wrap the baby, then this should be encouraged. Cameras can be brought in although most hospitals will have photographs taken for the couple and they should be encouraged to discuss any wishes they may have. Some hospitals also offer footprints from the baby for the couple. It is important to thoroughly explain about post-mortem examination and ensure they give consent for any examination and retention of any tissue, blocks and slides (Kennedy 2001).

If the couple wishes to see a chaplain at any time, this should be arranged and they may wish to give their baby a name and have a naming and blessing service performed shortly after delivery. Many couples fear discussing funeral arrangements but this discussion must be encouraged so that they have time to decide what they wish. The chaplain may be the right person for this discussion. It is important that no unrealistic promises be made to the couple. Many couples will ask about having the ashes following the cremation and it is vital to be honest and explain that at this gestation of pregnancy there will be no ashes after cremation. Memory boxes are often helpful to couples, and nurses and sonographers, doctors and chaplains can all help to contribute to this.

At QMC a referral is made to the nurse specialist so that a follow-up visit at home to provide advice, support and counselling can be arranged. At this visit it is essential that all the patient's wishes have been accounted for and organised. Following discharge home a follow-up appointment for the results of the post-mortem should be made. This is usually around 6 weeks after the miscarriage.

ECTOPIC PREGNANCY

Ectopic pregnancy is defined as a pregnancy that occurs outside the uterus, and in the UK approximately 1 in a 100 pregnancies are ectopic (Department of Health 1998). Over 95 % of these pregnancies occur in the uterine (fallopian) tube (Rosevear 2002), the remaining implanting more rarely in an ovary, in the abdominal cavity or in the cervix. Within the uterine tube the majority of ectopics present in the ampulla (Campbell & Monga 2000; Luesley 1997) (see Figure 4.9). Healthy uterine tubes are narrow, but fine hair-like structures on the cells lining the tubes, called cilia, can easily move along a fertilised egg to the uterus. If the tube has been damaged, this can prevent the movement of the egg, resulting in the premature implantation in the tube. Once this has taken place, the pregnancy will start to develop within the tube and if undetected may cause the tube to rupture. This remains a real danger to women, resulting in a total of 80 % of first trimester deaths in the UK (Department of Health 1998).

The current rise in ectopic pregnancies has been closely linked to the increase in the incidence of chlamydial infection and it is now estimated that 60 % of ectopics are caused by tubal damage brought about by infective damage (Gerbaud *et al.* 2004; Hillis *et al.* 1997; Tay *et al.* 2000). It is hoped that by improving the screening programme in the UK we can help reduce the incidence of ectopics as it has done in some of the Scandinavian counties (Egger *et al.* 1998). Other risks include tubal damage caused by adhesions from previous abdominal surgery, the use of intrauterine contraceptive devices, previous sterilisation, endometriosis, termination of pregnancy, *in vitro* fertilisation (IVF) pregnancies and smoking, but often women will have no known risk factors.

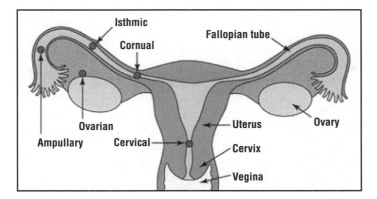

Figure 4.9. Sites of ectopic pregnancies. From J. I. Tay *et al.* (2000), Ectopic pregnancy, *BMJ*, **320**(7239), 916–19. Reproduced with permission from BMJ Publishing Group

Women with an ectopic pregnancy usually present at an EPAC with abdominal pain, often on one side, and abnormal vaginal bleeding following a positive pregnancy test. Ectopic pregnancy is difficult to diagnose in the community by the GP or the midwife, which is why it is so important that women get a prompt referral to a specialised unit (Tay *et al.* 2000).

Women referred to an EPAC will have quick and easy access to an early vaginal ultrasound and a reading of the HCG level. The use of these two investigations together has improved the early diagnosis of ectopics, enabling the treatment to occur before rupture has occurred (Ankum 2000). In the absence of any signs of a pregnancy in the uterus, when there is a positive pregnancy test, an ectopic must always be considered. Ultrasound findings of a suspected ectopic include a pseudo-sac, a tubal echogenic ring, live extrauterine fetus, complex mass or free fluid in the peritoneal cavity. When a pseudo-sac is present, it is located centrally within the uterine cavity, contains endometrial fluid and has a mean sac diameter of 10 mm or less. It may be surrounded by a single echogenic ring as opposed to the double decidual ring seen in a normal intrauterine pregnancy. This finding is not diagnostic of an ectopic but can be an indicator (Figure 4.10).

In some cases free peritoneal fluid may be the only finding to suggest an ectopic and this fluid may well be the result of active bleeding from the fimbriated end of the fallopian tube, tubal rupture or tubal abortion (Botash & Spirt 2000). A true diagnosis of an ectopic pregnancy can only be made when a tubal ring has been visualised containing a yolk sac or a fetal pole with or without a fetal heart pulsation (Figure 4.11).

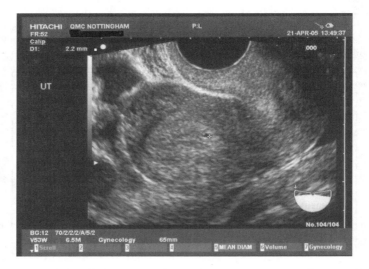

Figure 4.10. Pseudo-sac in a suspected ectopic pregnancy. Note the central location within the uterine cavity and surrounding single echogenic ring. Compare Figure 4.1. (Reproduced by kind permission of Queen's Medical Centre Nottingham)

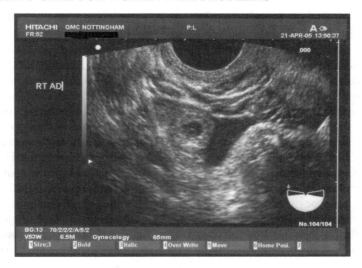

Figure 4.11. Right-sided ectopic pregnancy. A rounded, echogenic mass is seen in the right adnexa separate from the right ovary. Note the yolk sac within the central fluid of the ring. Free fluid is surrounding the mass. (Reproduced by kind permission of Queen's Medical Centre Nottingham)

An empty uterus can be misdiagnosed as a complete miscarriage, which has a devastating outcome for the woman's health and future fertility (Tay *et al.* 2000). Most fatal cases still occur because of delayed or inappropriate treatments. An ectopic pregnancy is not always seen on an early ultrasound scan and it is therefore necessary to use the measurement of the HCG levels to aid the diagnosis. By using this combination of history-taking, scans and same-day HCG levels within an EPAC, the number of women who are stable and have unruptured ectopics has increased. It is therefore of great importance that the EPAC has a dedicated and experienced team of nursing staff to record and interpret the information collected, as they are the ones who will be in frequent touch with the women to keep them informed of results and when to return for further blood samples and scans. This allows for rapid and accurate diagnosis with one person coordinating the path of care within the unit, which improves the continuity of care that women receive.

The most common treatment for a suspected or diagnosed ectopic is surgical removal (Rosevear 2002). Before the introduction of the laparoscope in the late 1960s the only option was a laparotomy. The use of the laparoscope has greatly shortened the hospital stay and convalescence. If the uterine tube is damaged or if there is significant haemorrhage, it may be necessary to remove the tube or part of the tube (salpingectomy). Sometimes the ectopic can be removed and the tube conserved by either milking the ectopic out of the tube or by opening the tube surgically (salpingostomy). If the tube is not removed, then it is important that the HCG levels are monitored until negative, as there is a risk of persistent trophoblasts. The nurse specialist in the EPAC must ensure that the women understand the need for follow-up in order to obtain further blood samples.

Medical treatment is a second option available in some units. This takes a great deal of commitment from both the women and the staff within the unit. This method of treatment should only be recommended for women who are haemodynamically stable. The chosen method is the injection of methotrexate, a chemotherapy agent, either intramuscularly (IM) or directly into the ectopic, but this requires either laparoscopic surgery or ultrasound guidance, which makes it more convenient to use the IM approach. Following this HCG levels, kidney function and full blood count need monitoring. If the HCG level has not dropped by 15 % in 4–7 days, a second dose may be given. It is important that the women fully understand the plan of care before embarking on it. Frequent return visits to the EPAC are needed as there is still always the real threat of a rupture of the tube. Trials have shown that the use of methotrexate can have up to a 76 % success rate (Jimenez-Caraballo & Rodriguez-Donoso 1999) and that it can be a reliable alternative to surgery, but it has been found that this treatment can result in some side effects.

Expectant management of ectopic pregnancies has been researched but is not yet widely used within the UK (Condous *et al.* 2003). It is known that some ectopics will resolve without any surgical or medical intervention, but again women do need to be closely monitored and a high level of commitment is needed from them.

Whichever path of care is taken it must never be overlooked that this woman and her family have lost the pregnancy. It may feel as though a very personal loss has been turned into a medical emergency. However, this loss can have a huge physical and psychological impact on the woman, which has been shown to lead to post-traumatic stress disorder (Abbott 2002). These women may suffer from flashbacks, especially women who have suffered ruptured ectopics, lack of understanding from family and friends about the pregnancy loss and the added worry relating to fertility and future pregnancies, just as a woman would do after a miscarriage (Brier 2004). It is therefore an important part of the role of the nurse specialist to offer follow-up care either in the home or within the unit in order to provide support and advice for the woman and the partner (*Nursing Standard* 2000) so they can talk about the sadness and grief felt.

As well as the psychological support the women need to know about the impact of an ectopic pregnancy on future pregnancies. It is accepted that women with a history of ectopic pregnancy have a higher risk of experiencing a second ectopic and the recurrence rate is 10–15 % (Luesley 1997; Moore 1998). Therefore a woman will be extremely anxious when she next gets a positive pregnancy test. This is where the EPAC staff must support the woman from the start, ensuring she has the contact phone number of the unit so that

HCG levels can be monitored and an early scan arranged in order that an ectopic is ruled out at the earliest opportunity.

MOLAR PREGNANCY

In a normal pregnancy, once fertilisation has taken place, the zygote reaches the uterus and divides into two main groups of cells. One group will form the fetus and the other will form the placenta and membranes, which are called the trophoblasts. The trophoblasts invade the lining of the uterus and anchor the pregnancy. The cause is unknown, but with molar pregnancy trophoblasts grow in a disorganised way and fill the uterus at the expense of the fetus. This type of pregnancy is rare in Caucasians (1 in 3000) but more common within the Asian community (1 in 300) (Chudleigh & Pearce 1992).

Molar pregnancy may be complete or partial (Figure 4.12). Sometimes an egg does not carry any genetic material so when it fuses with the sperm it would normally die and the pregnancy would continue no further, but if it does implant in the uterus only the trophoblasts grow in a disorganised way, giving rise to a complete mole. On ultrasound this looks like a 'Snowstorm' and in the first trimester can be indistinguishable from retained products of conception (Figure 4.13). A partial mole is caused when the egg is fertilised by two sperm. This means there is too much genetic information and the pregnancy does not develop normally, with the placenta growing at a faster rate. If there is a fetus present, it will not survive (Govan 1993).

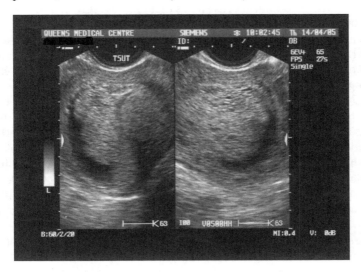

Figure 4.12. A partial molar pregnancy. Irregular echogenic mass with a classic 'snowstorm appearance' within the endometrial cavity. Inferior to this is a fluid-filled structure possibly representing a gestation sac. Molar pregnancy is confirmed by histology. (Reproduced by kind permission of Queen's Medical Centre Nottingham)

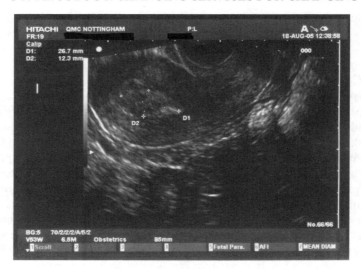

Figure 4.13. Retained products of conception. The endometrial cavity at the fundus is separated by a mixed echo mass measuring 27 × 12mm. (Reproduced by kind permission of Queen's Medical Centre Nottingham)

Women will present with symptoms similar to that of miscarriage but classically describe their vaginal loss as like 'prune juice', but also with an increased amount of nausea and sickness. This is due to the fact that HCG is produced by the trophoblast cells and as these are overgrown massive amounts are produced.

Once a molar pregnancy has been confirmed by histology results following surgical removal, it is important that the women understand the need for close follow-up because trophoblast cells can invade and spread systemically, becoming cancerous (choriocarcinoma). This is a very small risk because it can be detected very early and the cure rate is almost 100%. Follow-up is carried out at a regional centre. There are three in the UK, at London, Sheffield and Dundee. The HCG levels will be monitored with urine samples. Once the HCG levels have been normal for between 6 months and 2 years, the couple can try for another pregnancy. Prior to this it is important that the woman has clear advice about not getting pregnant until she has had the all-clear. Advice on the type of contraception she can use is essential. The use of the contraceptive pill is not advised as it can make the molar tissue proliferate, so it is best to use some other method until the HCG levels return to normal.

Women who have had a molar pregnancy will need a great deal of support as they have not only lost the pregnancy but also have the worry of the consequences of the molar pregnancy. A woman's fertility will not be affected and most couples go on to have a normal pregnancy. The couple should be offered an early scan in any future pregnancy at around 8 weeks gestation to rule out another molar pregnancy.

CONCLUSION

The advent of EPACs has completely changed the way that women are cared for in early pregnancy. The most important influence in this change has been the development of nurse specialists who have taken a strong lead. Early pregnancy assessment is an ideal area for nurses and midwives to undertake advanced practice roles (Pearce & Easton 2005). The nurse specialist needs a dedicated team of nurses who are well motivated and able to provide high-quality care in assessing and diagnosing as well as psychological support and advice. A counselling qualification can be beneficial. It is also essential that nurses always keep up to date with any research that is available, implement updated and robust care guidelines and protocols and become good change managers.

A substantial amount of work has looked at advanced nurse practice, and some have suggested that the role of a nurse specialist is dependent on the attitudes of the medical staff involved. The cooperation of medical staff and the relationship between medical and nursing staff is of great importance for both patients and staff (Woods 1999). With nurses specialising in the care of women with early pregnancy problems, it is important that junior doctors do not become de-skilled in this area. It is quite often the case that the doctor is only called to see women opting for surgical or medical management of miscarriage or if the patient is unwell. This approach can lead to a poor overall learning environment and it is therefore advisable to invite junior doctors to observe the clinic sessions and have regular teaching sessions on early pregnancy (Royal College of Obstetricians and Gynaecologists 2000).

Early pregnancy assessment forms the majority of acute gynaecological workload (Fox *et al.* 2000; Pearce & Easton 2005). Care can be complex and sometimes protracted, so it is a big challenge to the staff. However, when nurses manage a caseload they can support each woman through a very difficult time so that she does not suffer any harm to her physical health and that a bad experience does not leave her with long-term mental health problems.

At QMC nurses visit couples in their own homes and are able to work in both a hospital and community setting and so provide a continuity of care and blurring of the traditional boundaries. The challenge of initiating and running an early pregnancy service has thus provided better patient-centred care for women and their families, has allowed quicker diagnoses, reduced the number of inpatient nights and provided better psychological outcomes.

REFERENCES

Abbott L J (2002) *Ectopic Pregnancy: A Personal Account*, The Association for Improvement in Maternity Services.

Amer S A K *et al.* (2003) Long-term follow-up of patients with polycystic ovarian syndrome after laparoscopic ovarian drilling: clinical outcome. *Obstetrical and Gynecological Survey*, **58**(2), 117–18.

Ankum W M (2000) Diagnosing suspected ectopic pregnancy. *British Medical Journal*, **321**(7271), 1235–6.

Bagratee J S *et al.* (2004) A randomized controlled trial comparing medical and expectant management of first trimester miscarriage. *Human Reproduction*, **19**(2), 266–71.

Ballagh S A *et al.* (1998) Is curettage needed for uncomplicated incomplete spontaneous abortion? *American Journal of Obstetrics and Gynecology*, **179**(5), 1279–82.

Bates J (1997) *Practical Gynaecological Ultrasound*, Greenwich Medical Media Ltd, London.

Bazelon E (2005) *Nature's Way, Rotten As It May Be*, http://slate.msn.com/id/2114147/ (accessed March 2005).

Bigrigg M A, Read M D (1991) Management of women referred to early pregnancy assessment unit: care and cost effectiveness. *British Medical Journal*, **302**(6776), 577–9.

Botash R J, Spirt B A (2000) Ectopic pregnancy: review and update. *Applied Radiology*, **29**(1), 7–13.

Bowles S V *et al.* (2000) Acute and post-traumatic stress disorder after spontaneous abortion. *American Family Physician*, **61**(6), 1689–96.

Bradley E, Hamilton-Fairley D (1998) Managing miscarriage in early pregnancy assessment units. *Hospital Medicine*, **59**(6), 451–6.

Braithwaite J M, Economides D L (1997) Acceptability by patients of transvaginal sonography in the elective assessment of the first trimester fetus. *Ultrasound Obstetrics and Gynecology*, **9**(2), 91–3.

Brier N (2004) Anxiety after miscarriage. *Birth*, **31**(2), 138–42.

British Medical Association (2004) *Hospital Doctors – Junior Doctors' Hours*, www.bma.org.uk/ap.nsf/content/HospitalDoctorsJunHrs (assessed April 2005).

Bryan S (2003) Current challenges in the assessment and management of patients with bleeding in early pregnancy. *Emergency Medicine*, **15**(3), 219–22.

Campbell S, Monga A (2000) *Gynaecology by Ten Teachers*, 17th edition, Hodder Arnold, London.

Chipchase J, James D (1997) Randomised trial of expectant vs. surgical management of spontaneous miscarriage. *British Journal of Obstetrics and Gynaecology*, **104**(7), 840–1.

Chisholm R, Jenkins J P R (2003) Obstetric ultrasound. In Sutton D (Ed.), *Textbook of Radiology and Imaging*, Churchill Livingstone, London.

Chudleigh P, Pearce J M (1992) *Obstetric Ultrasound: How, Why and When?*, Churchill Livingstone, Edinburgh.

Clayton S G, Chamberlain G V P (1994) *Gynaecology by Ten Teachers*, Hodder Arnold, London.

Condous G *et al.* (2003) The conservative management of early pregnancy complications: a review of the literature. *Ultrasound in Obstetrics and Gynaecology*, **22**(4), 420–30.

De Jonge E T *et al.* (1995) Randomised clinical trial of medical evacuation and surgical curettage for incomplete miscarriage. *British Medical Journal*, **311**(7006), 662.

Department of Health (1998) *Why Women Die. Report on Confidential Enquiries into Maternal Death in the UK 1994–1996*. The Stationery Office, London.

Egger M *et al.* (1998) Screening for chlamydial infections and the risk of ectopic pregnancy in a county in Sweden: ecological analysis. *British Medical Journal*, **316**(7147), 1776–80.

Engelhard I (2004) Miscarriage as a traumatic event. *Clinical Obstetrics and Gynecology*, **47**(3), 547–51.

Fox R *et al.* (2000) Early pregnancy assessment. *The Obstetrician and Gynaecologist*, **2**(2), 7–12.

Geller P A *et al.* (2001) Anxiety disorders following miscarriage. Journal of Clinical Psychiatry, **62**(6), 432–8.

Gerbaud L *et al.* (2004) Ectopic pregnancy is again on the increase. Recent trends in the incidence of ectopic pregnancies in France 1992–2002. *Human Reproduction*, **19**(9), 2014–18.

Govan D T (Ed.) (1993) *Gynaecology Illustrated*, 4th edition, Churchill Livingstone, Edinburgh.

Grudzinskas J G, O'Brien P M S (Eds) (1997) *Problems in Early Pregnancy*, RCOG Press, London.

Habayeb O M H, Konje J C (2004) The one-stop recurrent miscarriage clinic: an evaluation of its effectiveness and outcome. *Human Reproduction*, **19**(12), 2952–8.

Heath V *et al.* (2000) Should tissue from pregnancy termination and uterine evacuation routinely be examined histologically? *British Journal of Obstetrics and Gynaecology*, **107**(6), 727–30.

Hillis S D *et al.* (1997) Recurrent chlamydial infections increase the risks of hospitalization for ectopic pregnancy and pelvic inflammatory disease. *American Journal of Obstetrics and Gynecology*, **176**(1), 103–7.

Holden T (2002) *Living with Hughes Syndrome. Your essential guide to 'sticky blood'.* Sheldon Press, London.

Hurd W W *et al.* (1997) Expectant management versus elective curettage for the treatment of spontaneous abortion. *Fertility and Sterility*, **68**(4), 601–6.

James D K *et al.* (1995) *High Risk Pregnancy – Management Options*, W B Saunders, London.

Jimenez-Caraballo A, Rodriguez-Donoso G (1999) A 6-year clinical trial of methotrexate therapy in the treatment of ectopic pregnancy. *European Journal of Obstetric and Gynecological Reproductive Biology*, **82**(2), 233.

Jurkovic D *et al.* (1998) Expectant management of missed miscarriage. *British Journal of Obstetrics and Gynaecology*, **105**(6), 670–1.

Kennedy I (2001) *Learning from Bristol. The Bristol Royal Infirmary Inquiry*, HMSO, London.

Kohn I, Moffitt P (1992) *A Silent Sorrow: Pregnancy Loss – Guidance and Support for You and Your Family*, Dell Publishing, New York.

Kousta E *et al.* (2000) The prevalence of polycystic ovaries in women with infertility. *Obstetrical and Gynaecological Survey*, **55**(5), 299–300.

Lawson H W *et al.* (1994) Abortion mortality, United States, 1972 through 1987. *American Journal of Obstetrics and Gynecology*, **171**(5), 1365–72.

Luesley D M (1997) *Common Conditions in Gynaecology. A Problem-Solving Approach*, Chapman & Hall Medical, London.

Luise C *et al.* (2002) Outcome of expectant management of spontaneous first trimester miscarriage: observational study. *British Medical Journal*, **324**(7342), 873–5.

Mackay E V *et al.* (1992) *Illustrated Textbook of Gynaecology*, 2nd edition, W B Saunders, London.

Maker C, Ogden J (2003) The miscarriage experience: more than just a trigger to psychological morbidity? *Psychology and Health*, **18**(3), 403–15.

Moore L (1998) Ectopic pregnancy. *Nursing Standard*, **12**(38), 48–55.

Moulder C (1998) *Understanding Pregnancy Loss (Perspectives and Issues in Care)*, Macmillan Press, London.

Moulder C (2001) *Miscarriage – Women's Experiences and Needs*, 2nd edition, Harper Collins, London.

National Institute for Clinical Excellence (2004) *Full Guidance on the Use of Routine Antenatal anti-D Prophylaxis for RhD-Negative Women*, Technology Appraisal Guidance No. 41, NICE, London.

Nursing Standard (Editorial) (2000) Big boys do cry. *Nursing Standard*, **14**(27), 24.

O'Connor V, Kovacs G (2003) *Obstetrics, Gynaecology and Women's Health*, Cambridge University Press, Cambridge.

Ogden J, Maker C (2004) Expectant or surgical management of miscarriage: a qualitative study. *Obstetrical and Gynaecological Survey*, **59**(8), 585–7.

Pearce C, Easton K (2005) Management of complications in early pregnancy. *Nursing Standard*, **19**(34), 56–64.

Proud J (1997) *Understanding Obstetric Ultrasound*, 2nd edition, Books for Midwives Press Hale, Cheshire.

Rai R S *et al.* (1995) High prospective fetal loss rate in untreated pregnancies of women with recurrent miscarriage and antiphospholipid antibodies. *Human Reproduction*, **10**(12), 3301–4.

Regan L (2004) *Gynaecology Forum – Overview of Recurrent Miscarriage*, Medical Forum International BV, www.medforum.nl/gynfo/leading6.htm- (accessed 21 July 2005).

Rosenthal M S (2003) *The Gynecological Sourcebook*, McGraw-Hill, New York.

Rosevear S K (2002) *Handbook of Gynaecology Management*, Blackwell Science, Oxford.

Royal College of Obstetricians and Gynaecologists (1997) *Problems in Early Pregnancy: Advances in Diagnosis and Management*, RCOG Press, London.

Royal College of Obstetricians and Gynaecologists (2000) *Clinical Green Top Guidelines. The Management of Early Pregnancy Loss*, RCOG Press, London.

Royal College of Radiologists/Royal College of Obstetricians and Gynaecologists (1996) *Guidelines on Ultrasound Procedures in Early Pregnancy*, RCOG Press, London.

Smith N C, Smith P M (2002) *Obstetric Ultrasound Made Easy*, Churchill Livingstone, London.

Tay J I *et al.* (2000) Ectopic pregnancy. *British Medical Journal*, **320**(7239), 916–19.

The Miscarriage Association (2003) *Acknowledging Pregnancy Loss – We Are Sorry that You Have Had a Miscarriage*, The Miscarriage Association, Wakefield.

Thorstensen K A (2000) Midwifery management of first trimester bleeding and early pregnancy loss. *Journal of Midwifery and Women's Health*, **45**(6), 481–97.

Twining P *et al.* (1999) *Textbook of Fetal Abnormalities*, Churchill Livingstone, London.

Verkuyl D A, Crowther C A (1993) Suction conventional curettage in incomplete abortion: a randomized controlled trial. *South African Medical Journal*, **83**(1), 13–15.

Walker J, Shillito J (1997) Early pregnancy assessment units: service and organizational aspects. In Grudzinskas J G and O'Brien P M S (Eds) *Problems in Early Pregnancy*, RCOG Press, London.

Ward A (2000) Early pregnancy sessions: a formative evaluation. *The Practising Midwife*, **3**(3), 40–2.

Woods L P (1999) The contingent nature of advanced nursing practice. *Journal of Advanced Nursing*, **30**(1), 121–8.

USEFUL ADDRESSES AND WEBSITES

The Ectopic Pregnancy Trust
c/o Maternity Unit
Hillingdon Hospital
Pied Heath Road
Uxbridge, Middlesex UB8 3NN
www.ectopic.org.uk

www.womens-health.co.uk/miscarr.htm

The Miscarriage Association
c/o Clayton Hospital
Northgate
Wakefield
West Yorkshire WF1 3JS
www.miscarriageassociation.org.uk

5 Developing an Effective but Realistic Fertility Service

JILL YATES

According to the Human Rights Act (1998) Article 12: 'Men and Women have the right to marry and found a family.' At first this seems a very reasonable statement and in fact approximately 80–95 % of the population can achieve this goal (National Institute for Clinical Excellence 2004). However, is this still a realistic right for 3–5 % of couples that suffer from infertility and require some form of active treatment to achieve a pregnancy? Can we meet the demands and fulfil the desires of all the couples seeking fertility treatment? Do we as providers of the service allow an open and fair access to reflect fulfilment of this right?

Challenges	Service developments
• Changes in sexual behaviour have increased infertility problems • Media coverage and Internet access have led to high expectations • The NICE guidelines on funding and treatment allocation aim to reduce inequalities • Investigations and treatments can cause high levels of anxiety • Advances in technology create more ethical dilemmas	• Patients receive fast and efficient diagnosis of problems delivered in a non-judgemental way • There has been an expansion of flexible service provision and nurse-led fertility clinics • Fertility nurse specialists can offer continuity of care, psychological support and accurate but realistic information • The HFEA supports and protects the service by setting standards and guidelines

Gynaecology: Changing Services for Changing Needs. Edited by Sue Jolley
© 2006 by John Wiley & Sons, Ltd

INTRODUCTION

This chapter analyses the above challenges, which have acted as a catalyst for changes within the NHS Fertility Service. The service has evolved rapidly over the past three decades in its provision, accessibility and technical expertise. Huge financial implications and complex ethical issues have accompanied the outstanding development of treatments for infertility. The steadily increasing demand for solutions to fertility problems has been caused by changes in both sexual behaviour and career trends. Unfortunately, it has also been fuelled by some of the more sensational reporting of developments in fertility treatment, often leading to unrealistic expectations (Balen & Jacobs 2003).

Fertility nurses have played a crucial role in developing the service because a large proportion of the investigations and treatment instigated in the fertility clinic are now nurse-led (Allan & Barber 2004). This involves a greater participation of nursing skills under the guidance and safeguard of formulated policies and procedures. Therefore fertility nurses have had to constantly review and expand their roles, which have evolved from the once-traditional sympathetic handmaiden approach to become technical and knowledgeable nurse practitioners able not only to carry out investigations, procedures and treatments but also to cope with high patient expectations invariably accompanied by emotion and stress.

INFERTILITY

Infertility is defined as failure to conceive after regular unprotected sexual intercourse for 2 years in the absence of known reproductive pathology (National Institute for Clinical Excellence 2004). One in six couples have problems in conceiving (Monash 2005; Taylor 2003a) and it is predicted that this could rise to one in three couples over the next 10 years (Seal 2005). Approximately half of these will conceive either spontaneously or with relatively simple help. The others will need more complex treatment.

The total fertility rate is slowly falling in the UK. In 2003 it was only 1.71 children per woman (National Statistics 2004), which was a slight increase from the record low of 1.63 between 2000 and 2002. As well as falling fertility rates, over the last 30 years there have been changes in fertility patterns. This has mainly been caused by an increase in the average age at first birth. There are also higher levels of childlessness (Balen & Jacobs 2003). Government statistics show that one in five women currently reach the end of their female lives childless compared to the mid-1940s when one in ten women remained childless (National Statistics 2004). This is not necessarily all due to infertility, because more women are remaining childless through choice.

The causes of infertility are complex and include, for women, poor or absent ovarian function, blocked fallopian tubes and endocrinal dysfunction such as hypothyroidism and fibroids, which may prevent implantation. The man may have a problem with the production of sperm or there could be some obstruction of the seminal ducts. There has been some decline in male fertility mainly caused by a fall in average sperm density (Balen & Jacobs 2003) and male factors are the most commonly recorded causes of infertility (HFEA 2005). Sometimes sexual dysfunction can prevent effective intercourse. Much emphasis today has been placed on a woman's age in relationship to her fertility. Age is a crucial factor in fertility so if women choose to start a family when they are older this is an important factor in increasing fertility problems. Taylor (2003a) re-enforces this fact, stating, 'the reduction in fertility is greatest in women in their late 30s and early 40s'.

Changes in sexual behaviour have led to a reported rise in sexually transmitted diseases. Sexually transmitted infections among teenagers have doubled in the past 10 years and more than 1.3 million people under 20 were diagnosed with sexually transmitted infections (STIs) in 2001 (National Statistics 2004; *The Independent* 2004). Chlamydia trachomatis, the most common sexually transmitted infection in the UK, causes particular concern because there are often no symptoms associated with the infection, but there can be reproductive problems if it is not treated (Khalaf 2003). Chlamydia is the main cause of pelvic inflammatory disease (PID), which affects 10–30 % of untreated infected women (Health Protection Agency 2005). There is a high incidence of PID among 15- to 25-year-old women (Public Health Laboratory Service 2003). PID affects fertility because it can cause tubal damage, resulting in ectopic pregnancy or tubal infertility. Gonorrhoea can cause similar problems. Infective tubal damage can also occur after miscarriage, termination of pregnancy, puerperal sepsis or insertion of an intrauterine device (Khalaf 2003). It been estimated that tubal damage causes 14 % of subfertility in women (National Institute for Clinical Excellence 2004) and that 12–33 % of infertile women have fallopian tube obstruction (Khalaf 2003).

Women undertaking consultation in the fertility clinic may be unaware of the proven connection with past sexual behaviour in fertility problems. Education in schools and colleges concentrates on safe sex, unwanted pregnancies and sexually transmitted diseases, but there is much less emphasis on successful reproduction and an individual's future fertility status. Teenagers can receive very mixed messages. There is always peer group pressure to engage in sexual activity and sometimes the media portrays risky sexual activity as the norm. At the other extreme sex can still cause embarrassment and is not discussed openly, especially with parents! The main emphasis is still on the short-term prevention of teenage pregnancies, and future reproduction is often taken for granted.

Table 5.1. Factors influencing early investigation or referral

- Age is more than 35 years
- Previous ectopic pregnancy or tubal surgery
- History of pelvic inflammatory disease or sexually transmitted disease
- Amenorrhoea or oligomenorrhoea
- Fibroids
- Prior treatment for cancer

References: Taylor (2003b); National Institute for Clinical Excellence (2004).

INVESTIGATIONS

When a woman cannot conceive, the first line of contact is the general practitioner (GP). GPs play a vital role in collating a full health and sexual history, instigating the appropriate investigations and pre-conceptual advice, and finally referring to a fertility clinic. Usually investigations are not started until after, at least, a year of unprotected regular sexual intercourse, but some factors, especially age, may warrant earlier investigation and referral (see Table 5.1).

In recent years a higher profile has been given to the importance of pre-conceptual advice to couples seeking fertility advice. Gone are the days of the classic clichés: 'relax', 'it will happen in time' or 'book a holiday'. Marathon intercourse sessions and the planning of intercourse around the foreplay of a thermometer are not advised. Indeed, the National Institute for Clinical Excellence (NICE) Fertility Guidelines (2004) recommend, 'Timing intercourse to coincide with ovulation causes stress and is not recommended.'

The NICE Fertility Guidelines (2004) recommend which investigations should be performed in the primary care sector. Both partners need investigating 'because an appropriate plan of management cannot be formulated without considering both male and female factors that may occur concurrently' (Taylor 2003b). Investigations should follow a systematic protocol. The main aim is to identify tubal or uterine abnormalities, anovulation or impaired spermatogenesis (Taylor 2003b).

Apart from general health screening including weight and blood pressure, the main initial investigation for women is a hormone profile. Hormone levels are measured by taking a sample of blood. Concentrations of follicle stimulating hormone (FSH) and luteinising hormone (LH) should be measured in the early follicular phase (day 2 to day 6) and provide information on the ovarian function. The FSH concentration is considerably raised in women with ovulation failure. The LH concentration tends to be elevated and higher than the FSH level in women with polycystic ovarian syndrome – the FSH concentration in these women usually presents at a normal level. Women with considerable weight loss or increased induced ovulation dysfunction will present with low FSH and LH levels. A serum progesterone level should be performed in the mid-luteal phase (day 21 or 7 days before an expected period). This is the best test for confirming ovulation. Other blood tests such as prolactin level, thyroid function tests and oestrodial concentration are no longer recommended as an initial screening test unless the female's history, e.g. irregular menstrual cycle, would indicate this.

In addition the GP needs to ensure the woman is rubella immune and that her cervical smears have been performed and reveal no abnormalities. The GP should also screen for chlamydia, which should always be treated before any treatments are started (National Institute for Clinical Excellence 2004). Prompt treatment of chlamydia can reduce the incidence of pelvic inflammatory disease, ectopic pregnancy and tubal infertility (MacMillans *et al.* 2000).

One of the first investigations in the fertility clinic would be an ultrasound scan of the pelvis. This is used to assess the pelvic organs and especially to identify polycystic ovaries (PCO), which can be related to ovulatory disorders. A woman who has PCO does not necessarily have polycystic ovarian syndrome (PCOS), which includes menstrual disturbances, hyperandrogenism and obesity. With 20 % of the female population having PCO and 10 % having PCOS (Seal 2005), it is essential that the nurse is able to recognise these conditions and offer appropriate advice. PCOS is the major reason for not ovulating (HFEA 2005). However, an assessment of PCO is important in fertility treatment because there can be risks and complications during ovarian stimulation (Balen & Jacobs 2003).

The GP can also refer the woman for a test of tubal patency. This would probably be carried out under the auspices of the fertility clinic and would not be pursued until an assessment of ovulation has been completed and also not before her male partner's semen analysis has been performed, as these results will indicate the next step of the fertility treatment pathway. The two main tests recommended for tubal patency would be hysterosalpingo-contrast sonography (Hycosy) or a laparoscopy and dye test. The Hycosy is an outpatient procedure using ultrasonography and echo-contrast fluid. It is the recommended tubal patency test for females with no history of previous pelvic surgery or pelvic infections. Laparoscopy and the dye test performed under general anaesthetic gives a more detailed assessment for females with possible tubal occlusion, and also enables other pelvic pathology, such as endometriosis, to be assessed.

It is also helpful to assess the uterus. Endometrial changes can be seen using pelvic ultrasound, but hysteroscopic evaluation is not usually carried out on its own unless clinically indicated. However, if the patient needs a laparoscopy a hysteroscopy is often performed at the same time. It is unusual to discover significant problems but any intrauterine adhesions should be divided and polyps are usually removed (Balen & Jacobs 2003).

The initial investigation for men is a semen analysis. This is a difficult test for most men and some can be quite anxious and reluctant to contribute because they view this as a very intrusive test where their manhood is placed under close scrutiny. World Health Organisation (2000) reference values are used to analyse and grade the semen. Two semen analyses should be performed 3 months apart (National Institute for Clinical Excellence 2004) as this provides greater specificity in identifying sperm abnormalities. However, if the first semen analysis reveals gross deficiency or abnormality, the semen analysis should be repeated as soon as possible. Hormone levels (gonadotrophin) may also be measured.

REFERRAL TO A HOSPITAL FERTILITY CLINIC

Rising competition from the private sector and government waiting list targets have increased the pressure on hospital fertility clinics to provide a swift and efficient service, so once a referral is made patients should be seen fairly quickly. At Queen's Medical Centre, Nottingham, patients are seen within 4 weeks, well under the government target of 11 weeks. However, a recent survey by the All Party Parliamentary Group on Infertility found that more than half the trusts have waiting lists of a year or more (Hope 2005).

The results collated from the primary investigations on both partners will accompany a referral letter to the fertility clinic. This initial synopsis of the couple's fertility status will give the consultant information that can assist in:

(a) priority of consultation/appropriateness of referral
(b) evidence for a preliminary diagnosis
(c) guidance in planning further investigations or establishing a provisional pathway of treatment

The main aim is to 'minimize the time taken to reach diagnosis and direct a couple to appropriate treatment' (Balen & Jacobs 2003).

SELECTING THE RIGHT TREATMENT

Lockwood (2005) states that 'modern infertility treatments are highly effective and current fertility practice can achieve successful pregnancies for about two-thirds of all couples referred for specialist treatment where the woman is less than 40 years of age'. When couples embark on a treatment cycle, the following principles should be considered (Balen & Jacobs 2003):

1. The interests of the unborn child always take priority.
2. The treatment is relevant for the infertility factors diagnosed.
3. The treatment success rate and relevant implications are fully understood by the couple so they can give a realistic appraisal.

4. The financial implications for treatment have been addressed and are able to be met.
5. The commitment required for the treatment cycle, e.g. the need to attend for frequent scanning or injection regimes, has been prioritised and agreed upon.
6. All possible side effects and complications of treatments have been explained to and understood by the couple. These include ovarian hyper-stimulation, multiple pregnancy and possible long-term risks such as ovarian cancer.
7. The couple have been made aware of the potential stress and rollercoaster of emotions that occur during a treatment cycle and that counselling is available to give them assistance and support.

Treatments can vary from the administration of 'fertility drugs' to tubal surgery, artificial intrauterine insemination or more complex *in vitro* fertilisation (IVF) techniques. Ovulatory disorders are estimated to cause 21% of female fertility problems (National Institute for Clinical Excellence 2004). There are three main groups of problems: hypothalamic pituitary failure, hypothalamic pituitary dysfunction (predominately polycystic ovarian syndrome) and ovarian failure. The so-called fertility drugs stimulate ovulation, and hormone levels then need monitoring carefully to avoid hyperstimulation and multiple pregnancies.

Artificial insemination may involve the use of the husband's semen or that of a donor. The NICE Guidelines (2004) provide the clinical practice algorithm for guidance in the assessment and treatment of people with fertility problems (see Table 5.2). Key recommendations in the Guidelines include:

- Screening all women for chlamydia before they undergo procedures to check if their fallopian tubes are blocked.
- Offering women who do not have any history of problems with their fallopian tubes an X-ray to see if their tubes are blocked, rather than an invasive procedure.
- Offering six cycles of intrauterine insemination (IUI) to couples with unexplained fertility problems or slightly abnormal sperm count or mild endometriosis.
- Offering three cycles of stimulated IVF to couples, where the woman is aged 23–39, who have an identified cause of their fertility problems or unexplained fertility of at least 3 years.

THE HUMAN FERTILISATION AND EMBRYOLOGY AUTHORITY

From the first test tube baby born over 20 years plus ago, fertility has moved on rapidly and, as with any fast-moving technology involving human cells and reproduction, ethical dilemmas are bound to arise. The fine line between scientific research and progress and value of life has caused numerous press

Table 5.2. Assessment and treatment for people with fertility problems – algorithm

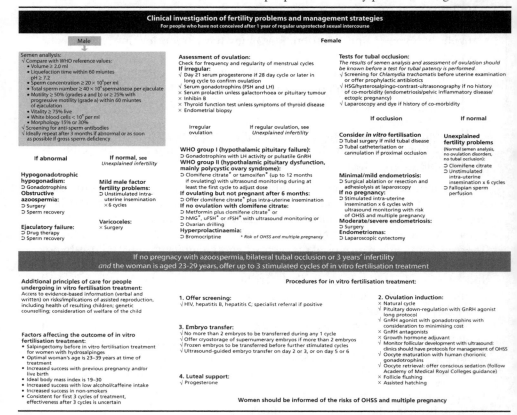

Clinical investigation of fertility problems and management strategies
For people who have not conceived after 1 year of regular unprotected sexual intercourse

Male

Semen anallysis:
√ Compare with WHO reference values:
 • Volume ≥ 2.0 ml
 • Liquefaction time within 60 miuntes
 • pH ≥ 7.2
 • Sperm concentration ≥ 20 × 10⁶ per ml
 • Total sperm number ≥ 40 × 10⁶ spermatozoa per ejaculate
 • Motility ≥ 50% (grades a and b) or ≥ 25% with progressive motility (grade a) within 60 miuntes of ejaculation
 • Vitality ≥ 75% live
 • White blood cells < 10⁶ per ml
 • Morphology 15% or 30%
√ Screening for anti-sperm antibodies
√ Ideally repeat after 3 months if abnormal or as soon as possible if gross sperm deficiency

If abnormal

Hypogonadotrophic hypogonadism:
⊃ Gonadotrophins
Obstructive azoospermia:
⊃ Surgery
⊃ Sperm recovery

Ejaculatory failure:
⊃ Drug therapy
⊃ Sperm recovery

If normal, see
Unexplained infertility

Mild male factor fertility problems:
⊃ Unstimulated intra-uterine insemination × 6 cycles

Varicoceles:
× Surgery

Female

Assessment of ovulation:
Check for frequency and regularity of menstrual cycles
If irregular:
√ Day 21 serum progesterone if 28 day cycle or later in long cycle to confirm ovulation
√ Serum gonadotrophins (FSH and LH)
√ Serum prolactin unless galactorrhoea or pituitary tumour
× Inhibin B
× Thyroid function test unless symptoms of thyroid disease
× Endometrial biopsy

| Irregular ovulation | If regular ovulation, see *Unexplained infertility* |

WHO group I (hypothalamic pituitary failure):
⊃ Gonadotrophins with LH activity or pulsatile GnRH
WHO group II (hypothalamic pituitary dysfunction, mainly polycystic ovary syndrome):
⊃ Clomifene citrate* or tamoxifen* (up to 12 months if ovulating) with ultrasound monitoring during at least the first cycle to adjust dose
If ovulating but not pregnant after 6 months:
⊃ Offer clomifene citrate* plus intra-uterine insemination
If no ovulation with clomifene citrate:
⊃ Metformin plus clomifene citrate* or
⊃ hMG*, uFSH* or rFSH* with ultrasound monitoring or
⊃ Ovarian drilling
Hyperprolactinaemia:
⊃ Bromocriptine   * Risk of OHSS and multiple pregnancy

Tests for tubal occlusion:
The results of semen analysis and assessment of ovulation should be known before a test for tubal patency is performed.
√ Screening for *Chlamydia trachomatis* before uterine examination or offer prophylactic antibiotics
√ HSG/hysterosalpingo-contrast-ultrasonography if no history of co-morbidity (endometriosis/pelvic inflammatory disease/ectopic pregnancy)
√ Laparoscopy and dye if history of co-morbidity

If occlusion

Consider *in vitro* fertilisation
⊃ Tubal surgery if mild tubal disease
⊃ Tubal catheterisation or cannulation if proximal occlusion

Minimal/mild endometriosis:
⊃ Surgical ablation or resection and adhesiolysis at laparoscopy
If no pregnancy:
⊃ Stimulated intra-uterine insemination × 6 cycles with ultrasound monitoring with risk of OHSS and multiple pregnancy
Moderate/severe endometriosis:
⊃ Surgery
Endometriomas:
⊃ Laparoscopic cystectomy

If normal

Unexplained fertility problems
(Normal semen analysis, no ovulation disorders, no tubal occlusion):
⊃ Clomifene citrate
⊃ Unstimulated intra-uterine insemination × 6 cycles
⊃ Fallopian sperm perfusion

If no pregnacy with azoospermia, bilateral tubal occlusion or 3 years' infertility
and the woman is aged 23–29 years, offer up to 3 stimulated cycles of in vitro fertilisation treatment

Additional principles of care for people undergoing in vitro fertilisation treatment:
Access to evidence-based information (verbal and written) on risks/implications of assisted reproduction, including health of resulting children; genetic counselling; consideration of welfare of the child

Factors affecting the outcome of in vitro fertilisation treatment:
• Salpingectomy before in vitro fertilisation treatment for women with hydrosalpinges
• Optimal woman's age is 23–39 years at time of treatment
• Increased success with previous pregnancy and/or live birth
• Ideal body mass index is 19–30
• Increased success with low alcohol/caffeine intake
• Increased success in non-smokers
• Consistent for first 3 cycles of treatment, effectiveness after 3 cycles is uncertain

Procedures for in vitro fertilisation treatment:

1. Offer screening:
√ HIV, hepatitis B, hepatitis C; specialist referral if positive

3. Embryo transfer:
√ No more than 2 embryos to be transferred during any 1 cycle
√ Offer cryostorage of supernumerary embryos if more than 2 embryos
√ Frozen embryos to be transferred before further stimulated cycles
√ Ultrasound-guided embryo transfer on day 2 or 3, or on day 5 or 6

4. Luteal support:
√ Progesterone

2. Ovulation induction:
× Natural cycle
⊃ Pituitary down-regulation with GnRH agonist long protocol
√ GnRH agonist with gonadotrophins with consideration to minimising cost
× GnRH antagonists
× Growth hormone adjuvant
√ Monitor follicular development with ultrasound: clinics should have protocols for management of OHSS
⊃ Oocyte maturation with human chorionic gonadotrophins
⊃ Oocyte retrieval: offer conscious sedation (follow Academy of Medical Royal Colleges guidance)
× Follicle flushing
× Assisted hatching

Women should be informed of the risks of OHSS and multiple pregnancy

Key: FSH, follicle-stimulating hormone; gnRH, gonadotrophin-releasing hormone; HIV, human immunodeficiency virus; hMG, human menopausal gonadotrophin; HSG, hysterosalpinography; LH, luteinising hormone; OHSS, ovarian hyper-stimulation syndrome; rFSH, recombinant FSH; uFSH, urinary FSH; WHO, World Health Organisation.

Section of Algorithm in National Institute for Clinical Excellence (2004) *Fertility: Assessment and Treatment for People with Fertility Problems*, NICE Clinical Guideline 11, NICE, London. Available from www.nice.org.uk. Reproduced with permission.

headlines and debates, both negative and positive. The Human Fertilisation and Embryology Authority (HFEA) was set up in August 1991, following the Warnock Report (1985), to monitor and protect the interests of patients, doctors, nurses, scientists and children; and also to consider the wider implications of the general public and future generations. The HFEA's statutory functions include (HFEA 2003):

• producing an HFEA code of practice which give guidelines to clients about the proper conduct of HFEA licensed activities

- maintaining a formal register of information about donors' treatments and children born from these treatments
- providing relevant advice and information to patients, donors and clinics
- regularly reviewing information about human embryos and any subsequent development of such embryos.

Fertility clinics that provide assisted conception treatments require an HFEA licence, which may include a treatment licence, a storage licence or a research licence (Braude & Muhammed 2003). To practise legally, the centre will undergo an annual inspection involving the centre and its facilities, interviewing staff and reviewing patient notes and records. If the centre has acceptable practice, a licence will be granted to the named individual who is responsible for the centre. The HFEA supports and protects the service and the public by setting guidelines and protocols, which must be followed.

THE ROLE OF THE FERTILITY NURSE

The fertility nurse is governed by the regulations of the HFEA and her role when working in a licensed centre would be to (HFEA 2003):

1. complete relevant legal documentation
2. maintain confidentiality – ensure patients' records are securely locked away and do not leave the clinic
3. ensure patients receive accurate information, both written and verbal
4. ensure helpers are offered counselling support
5. ensure the welfare of the child is considered in all aspects of treatment and report to the person in charge any areas of concern when involved with a couple
6. ensure protocol is followed and that witnessing of samples is carried out as recommended by the HFEA
7. ensure that all relative forms are available for consultation and that all relevant consent forms are completed.

Although the HFEA regulates the fertility nurse's work, this list does not really give a proper insight into this specialised role. A much fuller description and discussion, explaining different aspects of the work, are therefore needed.

RUNNING CLINICS

The fertility nurse plays a vital part in running a clinic where appointments run to time yet sufficient time is allocated for delicate and intimate discussion. She is also responsible for ensuring that the couple's notes and results are collated and present for the consultation. If results are abnormal during the referral stage, tests should be repeated before the appointment. This not only ensures clarity of results and comparison when the couple come for consultation but also avoids delays in diagnosis and wasting time in initiating repeated investigations, which become tiresome and frustrating for the couple and do not instil confidence in the clinic.

The fertility nurse is required to work flexible hours so the clinic can offer varied appointments that are accessible for working couples, to enable them to attend outside working hours. It also means that there is no need to divulge their private life and intentions to their employers. Flexibility includes being available on bank holidays and weekends. The female menstrual cycle and the response to ovulation induction and stimulation is no respecter of bank holidays and weekends.

CONSULTATIONS

A couple's initial reaction to the fertility clinic can determine the quality of the whole experience so the approach of the fertility nurse at the first visit is vital. From the outset people need to be reassured that all information obtained will be completely confidential. Most people have difficulty in discussing the most intimate details of their sexual behaviour with complete strangers. Sometimes couples can become very emotional and may fluctuate between tears and aggression during a consultation. There is great skill in guiding clients through a difficult pathway of embarrassing yet essential history taking and eventually agreeing on a proposed outcome and plan of treatment. The fertility nurse can support the couple and also act as a diplomat for the clinic.

Couples undergoing investigations often receive results that reflect past sexual behaviour. A history of termination of pregnancy, recurrent miscarriages, sexually transmitted infections or sterilisation can all cause a huge amount of emotional fall-out, self-inflicted guilt and a possible sense of failure (Bagshawe & Taylor 2003). These couples firstly want to receive reassurance that there is some hope of recovery and a chance of achieving a pregnancy. Couples will cling onto the remotest of chances, so care must be taken to clearly define outcomes when discussing potential treatments. The fertility nurse very often has to set a fine balance between positive encouragement and reassurance and support to a couple undergoing treatment mixed with continued re-enforcement of realistic outcomes. For example, the average success rate for IVF treatment for women under 35, using fresh eggs, is 28 % and this falls to 10 % for women over 40 (Seal 2005).

WELFARE OF THE CHILD

The fertility nurse must liaise with couples in a non-judgemental manner, and keep personal prejudices and moral stances outside their delivery of care. The

Human Fertilisation and Embryology Act (1990) states that the welfare of the child must be considered in all aspects of fertility treatment: 'When considering the treatment of any women, treatment centres must take into account the welfare of the child that may be born as a result of treatment . . . Treatment centre staff are expected to be aware of the need to show both care and sensitivity in this decision making process.'

Couples undergoing the emotional demands of committing to a treatment cycle, both financially and practically, not only have to face up to the need for treatment to achieve a pregnancy but also have to be aware that their ability as prospective parents will be under scrutiny. Sometimes changes in lifestyle and diet, especially giving up smoking and losing weight, are recommended to increase the success of fertility treatments. Occasionally the risks to the unborn child, e.g. from the use of crack cocaine, mean that treatment cannot be advised. All of this could be viewed as quite offensive and insulting if handled clumsily. Once again the role of the fertility nurse is crucial in this aspect of the relationship between staff and clients.

ASSISTING IN TREATMENT CYCLES

The fertility nurse plays an active role in the interpretation of scan results, the instigation of treatment cycles and the administration of hormonal preparation in ovulation induction. This involves planning and making decisions regarding the exact timing of treatment, release of hormones for ovulation, insemination or egg collection and embryo transfer.

The fertility nurse must be confident and comfortable in discussing treatment and investigations with the clients. This involves assessing the couple's knowledge of infertility and using terminology that they are comfortable with and ultimately understand. The fertility nurse must come over not as a patronising, condescending, superior person but as an understanding, sympathetic yet efficient and confidential source.

KNOWLEDGE

A thorough knowledge and understanding of all aspects of infertility and the available treatments are essential because couples arriving at the fertility clinic are often very well informed. Fertility issues now receive a much higher profile than the days when infertility was perceived as a silent stigma. Much publicity through soap operas, journalism, chat shows, documentaries and campaigning by fertility support groups has contributed to a more widespread acknowledgement of fertility being both a physical and emotional condition that requires specialised investigations and treatment, like any other illness suffered by an individual or couple.

Another major factor that has contributed to more informed and astute couples presenting to the GP or clinic armed with up-to-date knowledge has been the introduction of computer technology. Most households and public amenities are now equipped with computers allowing couples to freely network and receive open access to a world of up-to-date websites. Information can be obtained on infertility, investigations and treatments to anyone seeking that expert knowledge. Many couples now present to clinics for a consultation with files of information printed off websites. This at first can appear quite daunting and threatening to staff, especially if couples become dogmatic about demanding treatment, which in their opinion will be the ultimate cure for their problem. However, a knowledgeable couple is not necessarily a negative aspect of the consultation. It becomes quite challenging to all clinic staff when couples find it hard to equate statistics and convert result tables into a realistic prospective, pinning their personal hopes and convincing themselves that they will be part of the percentage that succeed in having a baby.

Greater emphasis should be placed on advising couples who are searching for information to use a reliable and professionally recognised website. There is a large number of misrepresented facts and cures that entice couples to part with their finances to get a result. The Internet has been a useful tool to promote fertility centres. Most centres have a website with detailed information of investigations and treatment programmes available, accompanied by published results tables, price lists and details of information evenings available for public attendance. In addition, all assisted conception units are obliged to have written information leaflets available (Braude and Muhammed 2003).

The fertility nurses based at National Health Service clinics that do not perform IVF are not ethically encouraged to recommend specific centres for couples to attend for treatment. Fertility nurses will give directive advice and reliable information to empower couples to make an informed choice. It is quite daunting to think that some couples would take the nurse's word for a personal recommendation of a centre of preference, even when great sums of money are involved. It is imperative that all the staff are continually updated in the latest technology and progress in current treatment techniques. The introduction of these information websites, directories of fertility clinics and educational leaflets available from the HFEA will empower the couple in their decision making concerning venues for treatment (HFEA 2005).

COUNSELLING

Reproduction is an area where we all assume we will achieve an offspring if we choose to and we do not expect to have any difficulties. Discovering a problem can have devastating effects, especially if endless efforts, commitment and financial input do not produce a result. Questioning, examining, discussing and ultimately medicalising sexual activity can lead to a very tense couple, and the thought of making love for pleasure can be a thing of the past, replaced by LH surges, ovulation mucus and human chorionic gonadotrophin (HCG) injections.

The couple undergoing fertility treatment can, very often, become isolated from family and relatives due to the painful reminder of childlessness when attending family weddings and especially christenings. They may not want to divulge their private failings to relatives and, if they did discuss this with close friends, they would come under pressure to update them with outcomes after every cycle of treatment. The psychological toll of infertility may include loss of self-esteem, anger, mutual resentment, guilt, depression and disappointment (Bagshawe & Taylor 2003; Greil 1997; Lockwood 2005; Slade *et al.* 1997). Some studies have suggested that infertility is 'one of the most distressing medical conditions treated in the health service' (Monash 2005).

Different cultural groups have specific views on infertility, which need to be recognised. Some cultures, particularly in Africa, associate infertility with impotence. Often women are blamed for infertility even though the problem may be associated with the sperm. The beliefs associated with some of the major religions can create stress for a couple who are infertile. For example, the Roman Catholic Church considers that infertility is predestined and should be accepted; contraception is banned in the Jewish faith so a couple without children feel immense pressure; and Islamic law prohibits the use of donated gametes. There are still large numbers of Muslim and Hindu women in this country who are under pressure to produce a family, but have a poor grasp of English, are relatively isolated and unsure of what help is available. When they do become involved in the fertility service, they need special support.

The recognition of the level of distress for infertile people, together with the emotional and ethical dilemmas, has meant that infertility counselling is a statutory requirement for clinics providing assisted reproduction services, with patients facing challenging decisions, intense treatment cycles and the pressure of high expectations for a result (Human Fertility and Embryology Act 1990). The HFEA (2003) states that counselling is recognised as beneficial in relation to all licensed treatments. Counselling should be offered before, during and after investigation and treatment (National Institute for Clinical Excellence 2004). No one is obliged to accept it, but centres are expected to take into account refusal of the offer of counselling, prior to either donation or treatment with donated gametes or embryos, in the centre's decision to proceed with that donation or treatment. Although nurses have traditionally fulfilled the role of counsellor, it is now recognised that patients should be able to talk in confidence with someone who is not involved with the treatment. This could still be a nurse, depending on how the work is organised in each clinic (Balen & Jacobs 2003).

In addition to helping patients cope emotionally with the medicalisation of their sexuality and the feelings of loss of control (Earle & Letherby 2002), counselling can also contribute to the success of the treatment programme because high levels of psychological distress will make conception less likely (Monash 2005). Ningel and Strauss (2002) suggest that counselling and psychological support can have an impact on wasteful uncompleted programmes of treatment and there is some evidence that patient support groups run by skilled counsellors and nurses are effective in raising the live birth rate (Domar *et al.* 2000).

There are several types of counselling offered in the fertility clinic can be (Bagshawe & Taylor 2003; Balen & Jacobs 2003; HFEA 2003; Monash 2005).

1. Implications counselling, enabling the individual being counselled to reflect and consider the action or decision being taken and explore the wider implications for themselves, family and future siblings.
2. Support counselling, giving support to individuals and couples in times of stress. This can be at any stage of their treatment.
3. Therapeutic counselling, assisting people to adopt coping strategies for the duration of a treatment cycle. This involves a discussion about what to expect in relation to personal circumstances, and the consequences of investigations, diagnosis, treatment and outcomes.

Whatever stage of the infertility journey, there is strong evidence of a need for not only structured counselling but also informal emotional support, which still involves counselling skills. The fertility nurse is in an excellent position to offer this help. She becomes a part of the lives of the infertile couple who attend the clinic for treatment on a frequent basis and so will go through the emotions that they face and can offer empathy, reassurance, encouragement and a lifeline on the end of a telephone should they need it. A fertility nurse can help to maintain humour, normality and reality in a couple's experience. When a couple has completed their cycles of treatment and still remain childless, there is a need to accept the finality of this and for support in adapting and coming to terms with life without a family.

TRAINING NEEDS FOR A DEVELOPING ROLE

As the fertility nurse's role has developed and become more specialised, one might expect a training programme or dedicated course to be available in order to support and equip the nurse in this field. The HFEA Code of Practice (2003) states that:

> All nursing staff are expected to be appropriately qualified and registered by the nursing and midwifery council, to be experienced in women's reproductive health and be working towards:
>
> (1) National and/or locally set competences to ensure appropriate standards of clinical competences.
> (2) A higher level award with a focus on women's reproductive health.
> (3) An accredited ultrasound course/qualification, if involved in that procedure.

McTavish (2003), for the RCN Fertility Nurses Group, responds to this Code of Practice by saying: 'This does not truly reflect the roles nurses are undertaking in centres, nor the extent of professional development that many undertake to ensure patients receive high standards of care from appropriately trained nurses.' The Royal College of Nursing Fertility Nurses Group are addressing this and have requested comments and feedback from fertility nurses.

Enquiring at various centres about what training is available for fertility nurses to equip them with specific skills to fulfil their role, it is soon discovered that there are various limited specialist training courses. These range from a nurses' sonography course to an accredited 1-year course composed of 3 weeks of taught modules requiring the nurse to submit various assignments on psychological aspects, anatomy and physiology, holistic approaches to care and discussions of shared practice. In addition there are general training programmes that are useful, such as counselling and nurse prescribing.

There does not appear to be any specialised training for the procedural aspects of fertility, although nurses are recommended to keep a log book on their procedural practice. Most nurses learn their practice skills on the job; some centres offer a comprehensive induction package, but most personal updates and fertility information is gleaned from nationally organised study days and conferences with the added support from the Fertility Nurses Group.

There seems to be a need for a standardised training programme, but this is very difficult while the role of fertility nurses is still developing. The skills and responsibilities can also vary considerably from giving basic tuition on injection techniques to embryo retrieval and transfer. It has been suggested that fertility nurses want to expand their roles in order to offer better support to women because they strongly empathise with their need to have a baby (Allan & Barber 2004). This means that they are not prepared to limit their role to organising clinics and delivering fragmented care (Allan 1999), but prefer to give total holistic care (Allan & Barber 2004). There is therefore more continuity in their relationship with the patients and a much more personalised approach than a doctor would usually have time to provide.

While consolidating these new roles, fertility nurses need to consider whether existing frameworks can guide training and competency requirements or whether a more radical approach is needed. Spencer (2004) suggests that the NICE guidelines algorithm can contribute to the development of a specialised fertility nursing role: 'The algorithm lends itself very well to mapping frameworks or pathways, which could very easily be nurse-led.' Therefore Spencer seems to suggest that role development should be limited by existing recommendations and practice guidelines. A more radical approach is to create a new role, and Woods (2000) describes the need to *deconstruct and reconstruct*. This method of transition gives the nurse the confidence to justify her rationale of practice, combined with a stronger influence on her role, and not just view herself as a nurse simply helping out the doctors with their workloads (Woods 2000).

PERSONAL QUALITIES

Although knowledge, experience and training are crucial, a good fertility nurse also needs to have the right personal qualities. As for all specialist nurses, it is important to be able to work independently, take responsibility for a caseload of patients and make decisions based on the available information. In this field of work it is particularly important to be sympathetic, caring and supportive, but also realistic. It is sometimes necessary to break bad news, e.g. when a scan shows that there is no fetal heartbeat. This can be very distressing, but honesty is essential. The fertility nurse needs to cope with desperate couples with a whole range of reactions from joy and celebration to disappointment, grief and mourning. Therefore it is important to have a stable personality and also to sort out coping mechanisms and possible support networks. Staff should be able to meet and discuss any difficult consultations in order to defuse tensions (Balen & Jacobs 2003).

INEQUALITIES

In the twenty-first century there seems to be general public sympathy for those that cannot conceive. The principle of variable eligibility according to rigid criteria can be viewed as a violation of human rights and equal opportunities. Unfortunately, there is still evidence of inequality in the provision of treatment and allocation of funding. Many couples still pay for their treatment and more than 70 % of IVF cycles in the UK are funded privately (Lockwood 2005; Seal 2005). This puts poorer couples at an obvious disadvantage.

Therefore there is more impetus to streamline treatment protocols and recommendations for appropriate treatments for infertility. The publication of the NICE Guidelines (2004), based on clinical research, will make a significant difference. The guidelines recommend that eligible women should get up to three full cycles of IVF treatment paid for. The Royal College of Obstetricians and Gynaecologists (RCOG) fully supports the implementation of the guidelines and has urged the government to support equal and fair access to NHS infertility treatment across the country (Royal College of Obstetricians and Gynaecologists 2005). The government has accepted this and has widened the right to state-funded fertility treatment from April 2005, pledging that all women in clinical need should have at least one cycle of IVF on the NHS (Seal 2005).

Although the guidelines represent a huge step forward, they will not bring instant access to IVF treatment for everyone demanding it. The HFEA directory of clinics for 2005–2006 demonstrates obvious geographical variations in clinic availability (HFEA 2005). An assessment of the infertile population, together with availability of services and treatments, will be required to monitor the level of demand. These guidelines provide excellent recommendations, but financial restraints may still require a system of prioritising and criteria to gain access. A survey by the All Party Parliamentary Group on Infertility and the National Infertility Awareness Campaign has found that some trusts are not ready to provide free treatment (Hope 2005). A total of 214 of 302 trusts in England were questioned and results showed that only 22 % of trusts are meeting the requirement, 58 % have taken steps to achieve it and 16 % are still assessing the action needed or did not comment. Spencer (2004) argues that fertility nurses are in a good position to manage 'a criteria-led waiting list in the most equitable and just manner, certainly within financial constraints and perhaps within time constraints'. This is supported by the work of the fertility nurses at Queen's Medical Centre, Nottingham.

CONCLUSION

There are still some inequalities in service provision but the overall situation is improving. The implementation of the NICE Guidelines (2004) and the work of the HFEA have made a significant impact on the NHS Fertility Service. This chapter has examined the role of the fertility nurse specialist in developing the fertility service. This role has many dimensions and is still evolving. Speaking on behalf of the RCN Fertility Nurses Group, Spencer emphasises the importance of nurses in service provision because in many centres 'fertility patients spend most of their time with nurses' (Spencer 2004).

Fertility nursing is both challenging and demanding not just in terms of skills and intellect but also in relating to each individual's emotions, ethics and beliefs. It is important to be well informed and knowledgeable about complex scientific developments, but also realistic about likely outcomes. There is a delicate balance between offering hope and support but not false promises.

REFERENCES

Allan H T (1999) 'Sister will see you now': an ethnographic study of fertility nursing. Manchester University, PhD thesis. In Allan H, Barber D, Nothing out of the ordinary: advanced fertility nursing practice. *Human Fertility*, **7**(4), 277–84.

Allan H, Barber D (2004) Nothing out of the ordinary: advanced fertility nursing practice. *Human Fertility*, **7**(4), 277–84.

Bagshawe A, Taylor A (2003) Clinical review: ABC of sub-fertility – counselling. *British Medical Journal*, **327**(7422), 1038–40.

Balen A H, Jacobs H S (2003) *Infertility in Practice*, Churchill Livingstone, London.

Braude P, Muhammed S (2003) Clinical review: ABC of sub-fertility – assisted conception and the law in the United Kingdom. *British Medical Journal*, **327**(7421), 978–81.

Domar A D et al (2000) Impact of group psychological interventions on pregnancy rates in infertile women. *Fertility and Sterility*, **73**(4), 805–11.

Earle S, Letherby G (2002) Whose choice is it anyway? Decision making, control and conception. *Human Fertility*, **5**(2), 39–41.

Greil A L (1997) Infertility and psychological distress: a critical review of the litera-ture. *Social Science and Medicine*, **45**(11), 1679–704.

Health Protection Agency (HPA) (2005) *Chlamydia*, http://www.hpa.org.uk/infections/topics (accessed 12 May 2005).

HFEA (2003) *Human Fertilisation and Embryology Authority Code of Practice*, HFEA, London.

HFEA (2005) *The HFEA Guide to Infertility and Directory of Clinics*, HFEA, London.

Hope J (2005) Survey by the All Party Parliamentary Group on Infertility and the National Infertility Awareness Campaign. *Daily Mail*, April.

Human Fertilisation and Embryology Act (1990) Section 13, parts 5 and 6. HMSO, London.

Human Rights Act (1998) Article 12, Marriage 3.103. In *Study Guide – Human Rights Act 1998*, HRG2 10/2000, Home Office, London.

Khalaf Y (2003) Clinical review: ABC of sub-fertility – tubal sub-fertility. *British Medical Journal*, **327**(7415), 610–13.

Lockwood G (2005) Infertility, Chapter 9, pp. 150–73. In Rees M, Hope S, *Specialist Training in Gynaecology*, Elsevier Mosby, London.

MacMillans S *et al.* (2000) Which women should be tested for *Chlamydia trachomatis*? *British Journal of Obstetrics and Gynaecology*, **107**, 1088–93.

McTavish A (2003) *HFEA Code of Practice*, 6th edition, update 3 June 2003, http://www.r.c.n.org.uk/members/yourspeciality/newsletter-plus/forum/news (accessed 15 February 2005).

Monash J (2005) *Psychosocial Aspects of Infertility*, British Fertility Society Factsheet, www.fertility.org.uk (accessed 15 February 2005).

National Institute for Clinical Excellence (2004) *Fertility: Assessment and Treatment for People with Fertility Problems*, Clinical Guideline 11, February, NICE, London.

National Statistics (2004) *Fertility*, http://www.statistics.gov.uk (assessed 14 February 2005).

Ningel K, Strauss B (2002) *Psychological Diagnosis, Counselling, and Psychotherapy*. In Strauss B (Ed.), *Involuntary Childlessness: Psychological Assessment, Counselling, and Psychotherapy*, pp. 19–34, Hogrefe & Huber, Kirkland.

Public Health Laboratory Service (PHLS) (2003) Pelvic inflammatory disease. *Communicable Disease Report Weekly*, **13**(5), 9.

Royal College of Obstetricians and Gynaecologists (RCOG) (2005) http://www.rcog.org.uk/pressreleases (accessed 21 February 2005).

Seal R (2005) Young, childless, anxious. *The Observer*, 26 June, 18.

Slade P *et al.* (1997) A prospective, longitudinal study of emotions and relationships in *in-vitro* fertisation treatment. *Human Reproduction*, **12**(7), 183–90.

Spencer L (2004) *NICE Guidelines: Implications for Nurses*, http://www.rcn.org.uk/members/yourspeciality/newsletter-plus/forum/news (assessed 15 February 2005).

Taylor A (2003a) Clinical review: ABC of sub-fertility – extent of the problem. *British Medical Journal*, **327**(7412), 434–6.

Taylor A (2003b) Clinical review: ABC of sub-fertility – making a diagnosis. *British Medical Journal*, **327**(7413), 494–7.

The Independent (2004) Sexually transmitted diseases in young people double in 10 years, Wednesday 31 March, www.independent.co.uk.

Warnock M (1985) *A Question of Life: The Warnock Report on Human Fertilization and Embryology*, Blackwell, London.

Woods L P (2000) *The Enigma of Advanced Nursing Practice*, Mark Allan Publishing Ltd, Wiltshire.
World Health Organisation (2000) *WHO Laboratory Manual for the Examination of Human Semen and Sperm – Cervical Mucus Interaction*. Cambridge University Press, Cambridge.

USEFUL WEBSITES

British Fertility Society (BFS): www.britishfertilitysociety.org.uk
Donor Conception Network: www.dcnetwork.org
Fertility UK, an Educational Service: www.fertility.org
Human Fertilisation and Embryology Authority (HFEA): www.hfea.gov.uk
National Institute for Clinical Excellence (NICE): www.nice.org.uk
NHS Direct: www.nhsdirect.nhs.uk
Royal College of Obstetricians and Gynaecologists (RCOG): www.rcog.org.uk

6 The Role of the Urogynaecology Nurse

LIZ TOWELL

Urinary incontinence, or loss of bladder control, is a very common and distressing health problem that can have a profound impact on quality of life. Approximately 6 million people in the UK have bladder problems, and urinary incontinence is about twice as common in women as it is in men (Royal College of Physicians 1995). Unfortunately, many women are reluctant to seek medical help, either through embarrassment or because they assume that the condition cannot be treated (Borrie *et al.* 2002; National Institute for Clinical Excellence 2003). Not only do they suffer in silence, but also they often limit social, physical and sexual activity in order to cope with their problems. This can lead to relationship problems, social isolation and loss of self-esteem (Rekers *et al.* 1992; Sandvik *et al.* 1993).

Challenges	Service developments
• More women being identified with urinary continence problems • Some women move from primary to secondary care without proper assessment • Poor management of incontinence problems in hospitals often due to inadequate medical education • The Department of Health recommends that all women are properly assessed and managed • Women have high expectations of treatment	• Integrated continence services are being set up involving primary and secondary care • Specialist urogynaecology services ensure that appropriate treatment is given • Trained urogynaecology nurses are experts in investigation techniques and management, can teach medical staff, ensure continuity of care and give necessary support

Gynaecology: Changing Services for Changing Needs. Edited by Sue Jolley
© 2006 by John Wiley & Sons, Ltd

BACKGROUND

Over the last 20 years there has been a huge shift in the way in which women with lower urinary tract symptoms are managed. As a consequence, the sub-specialty of urogynaecology has evolved and the Royal College of Obstetricians and Gynaecology (RCOG) has accredited a training programme specifically for gynaecologists who wish to become expert in this field.

The development of continence adviser roles, mainly based within primary care, has paved the way for the development of nursing roles within urogynaecology. In 1983 the King's Fund published *Action on Incontinence: A Multidisciplinary Approach to Continence Promotion*. This paper advocates change and promotes good practice across district continence services. Further work by Norton (1995), Roe *et al.* (1996) and Button *et al.* (1998) advocates multidisciplinary education of healthcare professionals in order to increase knowledge and awareness of continence promotion. New training programmes meant that many nurses from secondary care realised that they could play a major role in improving care provision to their patients by applying their newly acquired knowledge.

Prior to the development of urogynaecological expertise, many women who had urinary incontinence were offered surgery, often with very little investigation or assessment of their symptoms. The subsequent results of surgery were often variable. This is illustrated by the fact that hundreds of different types of continence procedures have been tried over the last century (Culligan 2004; O'Shaughnessy 2005).

Within gynaecology units, urodynamics or bladder pressure studies began to gain popularity as a diagnostic tool in the mid-1980s. As with many new services, some units started performing urodynamics as an aid to research. Spending more time on investigation, prior to embarking on treatment, began to produce benefits in terms of better patient selection prior to surgery and therefore better outcomes and higher satisfaction rates among patients. There was also a direct impact on waiting times for surgery, which were reduced, although targets for waiting lists were not as exacting as at present. The result was that many gynaecology units decided that urodynamics should become part of their service. Often multidisciplinary teams of doctors, nurses and physiotherapists, who had complementary skills, developed the new service. This enhanced the patient experience. The role of the nurse in these services developed and, in addition to providing continence advice, began to encompass performing urodynamic assessments and writing reports. Many units are now completely nurse-led and the nursing role has expanded to include training new urodynamics practitioners (medical and nursing) and also teaching medical, nursing and other professional colleagues (professionals allied to medicine, or PAMs), from both primary and secondary care.

When extending nursing roles, it is imperative that the practitioner should be both safe and credible. The urogynaecology nurse should have an extensive knowledge of gynaecological care. This should be supplemented by a working knowledge of continence advice and further training. If the nurse is to perform urodynamics studies, then both theoretical and practical training must be undertaken. This should be followed by a period of mentorship by an experienced urogynaecology practitioner in order to develop the knowledge and physical skills needed to perform this role.

The urogynaecology nurse has a key role in working with colleagues from all care settings to influence the development of Integrated Continence Services as described in *Good Practice in Continence Services* (Department of Health 2000). This document advocates equitable, coordinated and research-based care for those suffering from continence problems. Many areas are well ahead in the development of care pathways for both primary and secondary care patients with continence problems. The urogynaecology nurse is able to contribute to improving care at each stage of the patient journey through the care pathway.

ASSESSMENT

Urinary incontinence occurs when the pressure in the bladder is greater than the pressure in the urethra. It is a symptom rather than a disease. There are several possible causes including birth defects, injury to the pelvic region or spinal cord, neurological diseases, multiple sclerosis, polio infection, pelvic surgery, degenerative changes associated with ageing, pregnancy and childbirth. Women are particularly affected because it is common in pregnancy, after childbirth, after some gynaecological surgery such as hysterectomy and after the menopause. Around 80 % of urinary incontinence can be cured or improved providing the exact nature of the problem is diagnosed (National Association for Continence 2005; netdoctor.co.uk 2005).

There are different types of incontinence including stress, urge, overflow and neurogenic incontinence, and the symptoms can be confusing. Therefore all patients with a continence problem should have a comprehensive assessment. This should ideally be carried out in primary care. However, this is sometimes not the case as women often under-report continence problems (Borrie *et al.* 2002; Department of Health 2000) and will only reveal their problem after direct questioning, e.g. in a gynaecology clinic. In this scenario a nurse-led urogynaecology clinic may be the best place for the patient to have a history and assessment of her problem. History taking and assessment should include:

- age
- onset of the problem
- frequency of voiding/leaking
- precipitating events such as coughing, sneezing, physical activity
- bladder symptoms like urgency, frequency, nocturia

- medical/surgical/obstetric history
- bowel function
- fluid intake – type and amount
- medications
- mobility/cognitive issues
- desire for treatment.

It is worth checking whether basic investigations have been done rather than assuming that they were performed at an earlier appointment. Although very basic, they nevertheless provide very valuable information in assessing the patient.

- urinalysis and/or mid-stream urine to laboratory to exclude urinary tract infection
- post-void residual to exclude urinary retention (ideally using a bladder scanner as it is less invasive than a catheter)
- fluid intake/voiding diary to give a baseline assessment of the problem
- abdominal/rectal/vaginal examination to exclude physical cause for problem.

An assessment of all these factors is needed to help build a picture of the nature of the problem being faced.

MAINTAINING A HEALTHY BLADDER

Where necessary, advice about lifestyle and maintaining a healthy bladder can be given in order to help address any issues identified by the assessment.

- Adequate fluid intake is important because many women cut down on fluids to try to avoid leaking urine or having to void. Concentrated urine is a bladder irritant and can cause frequent voiding. Insufficient fluid intake can lead to urinary tract infections. Equally, excessive oral fluids can lead to excessive voiding. The nurse should assess fluid intake with the patient and a more appropriate intake should be agreed with her. A daily intake of no fewer than 6–8 cups (approximately 1000–2000 ml) should be encouraged.
- Caffeine intake should be considered, particularly where urgency is an issue. The diuretic properties of caffeine are well known. It has also been urodynamically demonstrated to be a bladder irritant (Creighton & Stanton 1990). Most people are aware that coffee contains caffeine but are sometimes less aware that it is also found in tea, cola drinks and chocolate.
- Avoiding constipation can help to reduce the pressure on the pelvic floor and therefore reduce episodes of incontinence. Some medications, e.g. analgesics, can cause constipation. Advice about increasing fluid intake and dietary fibre can help with this.
- When frequent urinary tract infections are a problem, the patient can be advised to drink cranberry juice in order to protect against infections

(Avorn *et al.* 1994). This is thought to work by preventing pathogens from adhering to the bladder wall. The usual advice is to consume 2–3 glasses daily.

• Some women develop coping strategies in order to try to avoid leaking. One of these is to void very frequently, which can then lead to an inability to delay voiding. Women should be advised to try to void at 3- to 4-hourly intervals and may need help in developing techniques to achieve this in the form of bladder retraining.

• Women should be advised that alcohol and the artificial sweetener aspartame are bladder irritants and that intake therefore may need to be reduced.

• An objective assessment of pelvic floor function and teaching pelvic floor exercises can be beneficial, as discussed in Chapter 7.

Many of these steps are simple lifestyle changes that can have a positive effect on bladder symptoms. By suggesting that women adopt these steps the urogynaecology nurse can empower women to take some control and ownership of their problem. Some may still, however, need further investigation in order to reach a satisfactory level of cure.

URODYNAMICS

Urodynamics is the investigation of the function and dysfunction of the lower urinary tract and refers to 'studies of pressure and flow of urine within the urinary tract' (National Institute for Clinical Excellence 2003). It has been carried out in various forms for over 100 years. Urodynamics is not necessarily indicated where the history and examination are indicative of either stress incontinence or an overactive bladder. The RCOG recommends urodynamic testing prior to pelvic floor surgery (Royal College of Obstetricians and Gynaecologists 2003). Other indications are where previous surgery has been performed with a poor result and also where there is failure to respond to treatment for an overactive bladder.

The terminology used in urodynamics has been standardised by the International Continence Society, initially in 1973 and then in 1988. The latest revision was in 2002 and was radical in that it removed the numerical values (Abrams *et al.* 2002). Urodynamics is a diagnostic tool that should be used in conjunction with a proper history, assessment and examination. Different techniques may be used to aid diagnosis. These range from pad testing and simple flow studies to videocystourethrography, where a contrast medium is introduced into the bladder during urodynamics and the bladder is then visualised on X-ray imaging.

Before a urodynamics test, a urinary tract infection should always be excluded. The patient should be asked to complete a diary recording fluid intake, voids and leaks, ideally for a week prior to testing, and should be asked

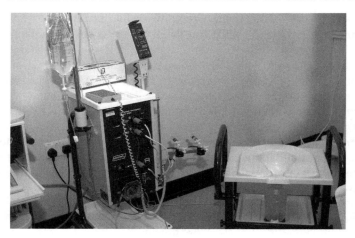

Figure 6.1. Urodynamics machine

to arrive with a full bladder. She should also be given an information leaflet about the test, including contact numbers. The equipment needed for the examination includes the urodynamics machine (see Figure 6.1), a bladder scanner, filling and pressure catheters, fluid sets and some normal saline for bladder irrigation. The procedure should always take place in a private room.

The urodynamics test procedure varies slightly between clinics and the clinicians who are performing them, but the basic aim is to measure the way the bladder fills and empties, particularly the changes of pressure inside the bladder and in the abdomen generally. The practitioner should take time to explain the process to the patient in order to gain their cooperation. If a patient is very tense, the quality of the recording can be adversely affected. The voiding diary should be consulted to see whether there is any pattern to the problem. Every effort should be made to maintain privacy and dignity, and careful thought should be given to whether observers should be present. This should only be after patient consent has been sought.

The urodynamics machine commode incorporates a voiding recorder and the patient is asked to void into the commode. The speed and volume of the void can be measured. This is why it is helpful if patients arrive with a full bladder. Following the voiding study the patient will have their residual urine checked with a bladder scanner to ascertain whether the bladder empties correctly. Using an aseptic technique and anaesthetic gel, two fine catheters will be placed in the bladder, one to fill the bladder and the other to record the pressure. Another catheter will be placed in the rectum or posterior fornix of the vagina. This is to record the abdominal pressure so that it can be subtracted from the bladder pressure and give a more accurate indication of the detrusor pressure. The pressure catheters will be attached to the urodynamics machine and the transducers and pressure lines flushed with fluid. The machine will be zeroed prior to testing. The patient will be asked to cough to ensure that the machine is recording accurately. When the operator is happy that the machine is working correctly, the test can commence.

During the test the patient may be supine or sitting on the commode; this practice varies between clinics. The bladder is filled with saline. Medium fill cystometry is performed at a rate of 60 ml per minute. Slower or faster speeds are used in some clinics. The patient is asked to cough at various intervals. This is to see whether stress incontinence can be demonstrated. The patient may be asked to stand and cough or heel bounce to try to provoke either a leak or a detrusor contraction. The patient is asked to inform the operator of their first desire to void. The urodynamics monitor records activity within the bladder during the test.

The patient is asked to inform the operator when the bladder feels full. When bladder capacity is reached, the filling pump is stopped. The patient will be asked to cough with a full bladder. The filling catheter is removed and the patient is asked to void into the commode. If the pressure catheters have been retained, they will record the pressure during voiding. When the void is completed, if the bladder has emptied fully, the catheters will be removed and the patient will be able to get dressed. If there is any doubt about whether the bladder has emptied, the residual should be checked and the bladder catheterised to empty it if needed.

Once dressed, the patient should be advised that she might feel some slight discomfort once the local anaesthetic has worn off, but that this should not last longer than 24 hours. She should also be advised to consume one cup or glass of fluid each hour for at least 6 hours after the test. Before going home she should be told who to contact in the event of any problems after the test.

Ideally the test results should be discussed with the patient before she leaves the department. An explanation of the results can be used as an aid to gaining cooperation with any proposed treatment regimes. This is particularly useful if changes in patient behaviour, like reducing caffeine intake, are to be advised to help control an overactive bladder. A written record of the test, to accompany the printout from the urodynamics machine, should be made. A record of any advice given to the patient, both written and verbal, should be made. The nurse should ensure that the patient knows what is to happen next and that any appointments needed are organised. A back-up record of the test should be made. Urodynamics can be used to help diagnose a large number of bladder problems. However, a urodynamics observation does not represent a definitive diagnosis and should always be interpreted in conjunction with the history, assessment, examination and information from the voiding diary (Abrams *et al.* 2002). This will give a more robust picture of the problem than just using the urodynamics graph.

Pad testing is used to quantify the involuntary loss of urine in stress incontinence. The International Continence Society suggests standardising pad testing, although the regime may need to be modified to allow for patient mobility and can be adapted for use over longer periods by the patient at home.

PAD TESTING

- The pad should be waterproof backed and weighed prior to testing.
- The initial test should be planned to last for one hour but may be extended by further one-hour periods if the first assessment is not considered to be representative of the usual patient symptoms.
- The patient does not void immediately prior to or during the test.
- The patient is asked to drink 500 ml of low sodium fluid over a 15-minute period and then rests for 15 minutes.
- The patient then walks for 30 minutes and is also asked to climb up and down a flight of stairs.
- A range of activities is performed: standing up from sitting 10 times, coughing vigorously 10 times, bending to pick up an object from the floor 5 times, running on the spot for a minute and hand washing under running water for a minute.
- The pad is removed and weighed at the end of an hour. If leakage has occurred, it can be quantified.

URODYNAMIC STRESS INCONTINENCE

Urinary stress incontinence is described as involuntary leakage of urine during increased abdominal pressure, in the absence of a detrusor contraction (Abrams et al. 2002; National Institute for Clinical Excellence 2003). This may be experienced during coughing, sneezing or on exertion. The symptoms occur because either the pelvic floor muscles have been damaged or the urethral sphincter muscle becomes weakened. As a result, the base of the bladder may either move from its normal position or the urethral sphincter may no longer close sufficiently, causing accidental loss of urine. In women it is the commonest form of incontinence and when the condition has been confirmed by urodynamic investigations it is termed *urodynamic stress incontinence* (Abrams et al. 2002; National Institute for Clinical Excellence 2003).

The voiding diary may contain a record of leakage. On testing, the residual urine is usually low. There are no detrusor contractions demonstrated on filling the bladder. Asking the patient to cough or heel bounce can provoke a leak. The bladder capacity is usually normal (around 400–500 ml). The voiding study is usually normal although if the flow is slow it may be because the patient is inhibiting the flow due to embarrassment. This should be discussed with the patient to explore whether this is a reflection of their normal voiding pattern.

The RCOG (2003) and the NICE (2003) both recommend that surgery should only be offered following a trial of conservative management. The role of physiotherapy is discussed in the following chapter. In those clinics that are not fortunate enough to have access to a women's health physiotherapist, the urogynaecology nurse may undergo further training in order to provide some aspects of conservative management. A key role for the urogynaecology nurse is to encourage the patient to persevere with conservative treatments. She can also influence medical colleagues to ensure that conservative management is offered prior to planning surgery.

Conservative management involves education and exercises to strengthen the pelvic floor muscles. Recently drug therapy has also been considered, and in 2004 a new drug called Duloxetine was launched. It is a dual serotonin and noradrenaline reuptake inhibitor (SNRI). Serotonin and noradrenaline are believed to have a role in normal urethral sphincter closure. Duloxetine is thought to increase the tone and contraction of the urethral sphincter and therefore reduce stress urinary incontinence. Four trials involving over 1900 women demonstrated a significant decrease in weekly incontinence episodes in the Duloxetine group (52 % from 17 to 8 episodes) versus the placebo group (33 % from 17 to 11 episodes) (Trent Medicines Information Service 2004). The most common side effect was nausea, which was experienced by 23 % of women compared with 3.7 % in the placebo group. It is important that when discontinuing treatment the dose is gradually reduced before stopping.

As it is a new treatment the indication for using Duloxetine will probably become clearer as clinicians become more familiar with it. It could be used to postpone surgery. The urogynaecology nurse should remain up to date with current usage and efficacy of the medication. She can therefore provide patient support and also act as a resource for other healthcare staff by ensuring that she possesses up-to-date knowledge to share with them.

Sometimes surgery does become necessary. The role of the urogynaecology nurse in relation to surgery is one of ensuring that the patient is adequately prepared beforehand. She can also influence nursing and medical colleagues to give appropriate, evidence-based post-operative care. Health professionals have a duty to ensure that patients are given verbal and written information about the risks, benefits and alternatives to surgery, in addition to likely success rates, before consent is sought (Department of Health 2001). The urogynae-cology nurse can ensure that appropriate information is provided about the various operative procedures and that the patient has a realistic view of what surgery can achieve.

The aim of surgery is to achieve continence by elevating the bladder neck, supporting the urethra or increasing urethral resistance. The most common procedures are:

- colposuspension. In this procedure the bladder neck is surgically elevated. This can be performed abdominally or laparoscopically. It has long-term follow-up data from over 15 years and a cure rate of 80–95 % (National Institute for Clinical Excellence 2003). The main complications are blood

loss at operation, damage to other organs, urinary tract infection, voiding difficulties, *de novo* urge symptoms and *de novo* detrusor overactivity.
- anterior repair. Anterior repair was once used extensively in the treatment of stress incontinence. It is still a valid option in the treatment of prolapse but has been superceded by other, more effective, procedures for the correction of stress urinary incontinence, which tend to have better outcomes (Department of Health 2000).
- slings. These can be made from either fascial or synthetic materials and anchored to pelvic or abdominal structures and have been shown to be effective with short-term rates similar to those for colposuspension (National Institute for Clinical Excellence 2003). The main complications of slings are haemorrhage, voiding difficulties, urinary tract infection and *de novo* detrusor overactivity.
- tension-free vaginal tape (TVT). TVT is a minimal-access technique that can be performed under local or regional anaesthesia and can therefore be used for patients who would not be suitable for general anaesthesia. The tape is inserted to form a U-shaped sling around the middle third of the urethra. There is no bladder neck elevation and the procedure is associated with a quick recovery time and has cure rates comparable with colposuspension (National Institute for Clinical Excellence 2003). The complications include bladder injury at operation, which occurs more frequently than with other surgical procedures for stress incontinence, haemorrhage, urinary tract infection, voiding difficulties and *de novo* detrusor overactivity.

Information about surgery should start in the pre-operative period. When a decision is made to offer surgery, a knowledgeable healthcare practitioner should immediately give the patient appropriate advice and information. If the urogynaecology nurse is able to attend clinics, she could provide this service. If not, then she should ensure that the information, both verbal and written, is an accurate reflection of the care pathway. In order to do this, she may need to educate her colleagues. Ideally pre-operative physiotherapy advice should also be arranged.

Post-operative advice should include information about the likely length of stay in hospital and the recovery period. The patient should be given information about when she should return to normal activities including work, driving, lifting and sexual activity. Information about risks, benefits and alternatives to surgery should be given. She should also be advised about who to contact in the event of any problems and where to obtain further advice or information should she require it.

Some women suffering from uterine prolapse and stress urinary incontinence may not be fit enough to have surgery owing to the risks of anaesthesia. For this group of women the insertion of a vaginal pessary can bring relief from their symptoms. While a doctor would usually perform initial fitting, a nurse who has been trained in their use can perform subsequent renewals.

Where this is a nurse-led service local protocols should be drawn up to ensure that safe care is provided. Pessaries are changed every 4–6 months. The vagina should be inspected before inserting a new pessary to ensure that there are no signs of ulceration. Following insertion of a pessary the patient should be asked to remain in the clinic until she has voided, as urinary retention can occasionally occur.

URGE URINARY INCONTINENCE

Urge urinary incontinence is defined as the complaint of involuntary leakage of urine accompanied by, or preceded by, urgency (Abrams *et al.* 2002; Hampel *et al.* 1997; Ouslander 2004). It occurs when the nerve pathway from the bladder to the brain is not functioning correctly, causing bladder contractions that cannot be consciously inhibited. It can be caused by stroke, dementia or multiple sclerosis, but often there is no obvious explanation. In urge urinary incontinence the bladder is overactive and contracts irregularly during filling, creating a strong desire to pass urine. Therefore the patient often suffers from frequency of micturition, urgency and nocturia accompanied by urge incontinence. Laboratory testing does not reveal any infection in the urine.

The overactive bladder sufferer may have developed various mechanisms in order to try to cope with the problem (Kelleher 2002). These may include an in-depth knowledge of the location of public toilets and avoiding oral fluids in an attempt to reduce the number of voids. Social activities can be severely affected by the fear of leaking or not being able to find a toilet. This can alter other people's perception of the patient, e.g. someone being thought a 'killjoy' because she dare not participate in social activities out of fear of leaking, but not feeling able to share this information. This can lead to feelings of isolation.

On investigation, a voiding diary will usually record many voids and may also document leaks. At urodynamic testing, despite being asked to attend with a full bladder, there is sometimes a smaller than average voided volume due to the bladder being emptied frequently. The voiding pressure may be high. The residual volume of urine is usually small and if the patient is avoiding oral fluids in an attempt to reduce the number of voids the urine may be concentrated. During the test detrusor contractions may be noted. The first desire to void is sometimes very early in the test and the bladder capacity may be reduced. Following testing, the urodynamics trace can be used to describe the overactive bladder to the patient in order to seek her cooperation with proposed treatment.

Treatment of urinary urge incontinence or overactive bladder is conservative and a lot of the onus is on the patient to change behaviour (Ouslander 2004). This requires the support of healthcare professionals, and the urogynaecology nurse in particular. Patients are often relieved to find that there is an explanation for their symptoms. They are usually receptive to advice that will help them to deal with their problem. By consulting the voiding diary a picture of the frequency of voiding can be obtained to use as a baseline before starting treatment. One of the treatments is bladder retraining, which will focus on actively inhibiting voids in order to increase gradually the time interval between them. Most people are able to cope socially with voiding every 3 or 4 hours and this is the endpoint that most women would be happy to aim for.

The urogynaecology nurse should also work with the patient to explore lifestyle changes that will help to achieve control. These will include ensuring an adequate oral fluid intake and avoiding caffeine. Where there is access to a women's health physiotherapist the nurse could refer the patient for input about pelvic floor education and exercises in order to strengthen the pelvic floor. This will help with bladder retraining by increasing the patient's confidence to increase the interval between voids. In the absence of a physiotherapist the nurse should consider undertaking further training in order to be able to assess the pelvic floor and advise about exercises.

Often behavioural interventions alone can effectively treat this problem. They work best when a healthcare professional reinforces them (Borrie et al. 2002). The nurse can provide a follow-up clinic to provide support to women who are undergoing these regimes. At this time goals to increase voiding intervals can be agreed. The main advantage is that the patient receives consistent advice and support rather than getting varying advice from different people, who may not necessarily be skilled in continence advice.

Some women also need to take medication in combination with behavioural changes. Recent pharmacological innovations mean that there are now many medications available for the treatment of the overactive bladder and urge urinary incontinence. They are antimuscarinic or anticholinergic and work by inhibiting bladder contractions, increasing bladder compliance and decreasing sensory input to increase bladder capacity and reduce symptoms. These include the most commonly used, tolterodine, and the recently launched solifenacin (Abrams et al. 1998; Chancellor et al. 2000). The advantage to having several medications is that if a patient is unable to tolerate the effects of a medication, they may be better suited to one of the other preparations. The main side effects tend to be dryness of the mouth and dizziness, but effects vary between medications and patients. The urogynaecology nurse should have a working knowledge of the commonly used medications in order to be able to advise patients.

THE WAY FORWARD

The urogynaecology nurse will find that, as the role develops, the amount of teaching she is asked to provide will expand. The diversity of groups may increase to include patients and medical staff from both primary and secondary care in addition to nursing and PAM colleagues. Continence is an area that is often not well covered in medical education and colleagues are often grateful for some input about basic continence advice. This applies to both hospital- and community-based colleagues of all grades, from medical students to consultants. Staff from the gynaecology unit where the nurse works should be included in teaching in order to increase nursing knowledge and enhance patient care.

More specialised teaching, e.g. about urodynamics, is an area where the urogynaecology nurse may be asked to provide input. Continence advisers and women's health physiotherapists require information about urodynamics and gynaecology care in order to equip them to perform their roles. The trade-off for this can be that these two colleagues can provide teaching for the urogynaecology nurse or her staff.

A urogynaecology nurse with experience of urodynamics may become a mentor for practitioners who are learning urodynamics, as this can be very challenging. Initially, one-to-one support will be needed, but as the learner becomes more proficient the mentor may be able to be more distant. It is useful to have another person to discuss findings with, which can be beneficial for both the mentor and mentee as sometimes the specialist role can be isolating.

Multidisciplinary teaching is often a useful way to communicate with the primary care team and to provide education in the ways of being more proactive in terms of managing continence. Many district nurses have undergone continence training but their medical colleagues may not be aware of this. A facilitated meeting can help a primary care team to develop a strategy for managing continence and looking at where they link in with the local Integrated Continence Service. The starting point for this could be an educational session to raise awareness within the team. These sessions usually receive very positive evaluations from nursing and medical colleagues and help to foster links between primary and secondary care staff.

There is endless scope for the urogynaecology nurse to expand her role and the form that this takes will be dictated by the service in which she works. Health promotion, both for the public and colleagues, is another area of potential involvement for the urogynaecology nurse. At hospital open days there is an opportunity for women to seek advice about who to go to in order to get help with continence and other problems. A display of women's health literature can often prompt women to ask for advice. Similarly, many employers are seeking Improving Working Lives initiatives and would welcome the offer of either group educational sessions or, alternatively, individual appointments for staff, perhaps facilitated by the occupational health department.

Another area for role expansion is to develop skill as a surgical assistant and work alongside the urogynaecologist in theatre. This would have major benefits in terms of continuity and quality of care. Role expansion should always be to benefit patients and enhance their care. At the same time this can give opportunities for the urogynaecology nurse to really make a difference in patient care and will therefore be a satisfying career path to choose.

REFERENCES

Abrams P *et al.* (1998) Tolterodine, a new antimuscarinic agent: as effective but better tolerated than oxybutinin in patients with an overactive bladder. *British Journal of Urology*, **81**(6), 801–10.

Abrams P *et al.* (2002) The standardization of terminology of lower urinary tract function: Report from the Standardisation Sub-committee of the International Continence Society. *Neurourology and Urodynamics*, **21**(2), 167–78.

Avorn J *et al.* (1994) Reduction of bacteriuria and pyuria after ingestion of cranberry juice. *Journal of the American Medical Association*, **271**(10), 751–4.

Borrie M J *et al.* (2002) Interventions led by nurse continence advisers in the management of urinary incontinence: a randomized controlled trial. *Canadian Medical Association Journal*, **166**(10), 1267–73.

Button D *et al.* (1998) *Continence: Promotion and Management by the Primary Health Care Team: Consensus Guidelines*, Whurr, London.

Chancellor M *et al.* (2000) Tolterodine, an effective and well tolerated treatment for urge incontinence and other overactive bladder symptoms. *Clinical Drug Investigations*, **19**, 83–91.

Creighton S, Stanton S (1990) Caffeine: does it affect your bladder? *British Journal of Urology*, **66**(6), 613–14.

Culligan P, for Atlantic Health System (2004) *Urogynecology*, www.mybladdermd. com/faq (accessed 21 November 2005).

Department of Health (2000) *Good Practice in Continence Services*, DoH, London.

Department of Health (2001) *Good Practice in Consent*, DoH, London.

Hampel C C *et al.* (1997) Definition of overactive bladder and epidemiology of urinary incontinence. *Urology*, **50**(Supplemet 6A), 4–14.

Kelleher C (2002) Economic and social impact of OAB. *European Urology Supplements*, **1**, 11–16.

King's Fund (1983) *Action on Incontinence*, Report of a Working Group, King's Fund Project Paper 43, King Edward's Hospital Fund, London.

National Association for Continence (2005) *Continence Fact Sheet*, www.nafc.org/ index.asp (accessed 22 November 2005).

National Institute for Clinical Excellence (2003) *Guidance on the Use of Tension-Free Vaginal Tape (Gynecare TVT) for Stress Incontinence. Technology Appraisal Guidance No. 56*, NICE, London.

netdoctor.co.uk (2005) *What is Urinary Incontinence?*. www.netdoctor.co.uk (accessed 19 November 2005).

Norton C (1995) *Commissioning Comprehensive Continence Services: Guidelines for Purchasers*. The Continence Foundation, London.

O'Shaughnessy M (2005) *Incontinence, Urinary: Comprehensive Review of Medical and Surgical Aspects*, www.emedicine.com/med/topic2781 (accessed 21 November 2005).

Ouslander J O (2004) Management of overactive bladder. *Journal of the American Medical Association*, **350**(8), 786–99.

Rekers H *et al.* (1992) Urinary-incontinence in women from 35 to 79 years of age – prevalence and consequences. *European Journal of Obstetrics, Gynecology and Reproductive Biology*, **43**(3), 229–34.

Roe B *et al.* (1996) *An Evaluation of Health Interventions by Primary Health Care Teams and Continence Advisory Services on Patient Outcomes Related to Incontinence*. Health Services Research Unit at Oxford University, Oxford.

Royal College of Obstetricians and Gynaecologists (2003) *Surgery for Urodynamic Stress Incontinence*, RCOG, London.

Royal College of Physicians (1995) *Incontinence: Causes, Management and Provision of Services*, Royal College of Physicians, London.

Sandvik H *et al.* (1993) Female urinary incontinence: psychosocial impact, self care, and consultations. *Scandinavian Journal of Caring in Science*, **7**(1), 53–6.

Trent Medicines Information Service (2004) *New Product Evaluation – Duloxetine*. Trent Medicines Information Service, Leicester.

USEFUL CONTACTS

Association for Continence Advice
102a Astra House
Arklow Road
London SE14 6EB

Continence Foundation
307 Hatton Square
16 Baldwin Gardens
London EC1N 7RJ
Tel. 0845 3450165
www.continence-foundation.org.uk
Advice and information provided by specialist nurses for the public and health professionals

Incontact
United House
North Road
London N7 9DP
Tel. 0870 7703246
www.incontact.org
Information and support for people affected by bladder and bowel problems

Royal College of Nursing Continence Care Forum
c/o RCN20 Cavendish Square
London W1M OAB

UK Continence Society, formerly ICS UK: www.ukcs.uk.net

7 The Role of the Women's Health Physiotherapist in Gynaecological Care

JUDITH LEE

The women's health physiotherapist (WHP) plays an important role in the prevention of pelvic floor disorders and the overall delivery of gynaecological care. The aim of this chapter is to describe and explain some of this work, discuss the challenges in the context of clinical effectiveness and explore the opportunities for service development.

Challenges	Service developments
• All pregnant women should receive appropriate antenatal advice and information about childbirth and pelvic floor exercise • Women with a third-degree tear should be referred to the WHP because of the increased risk of developing faecal incontinence • Incontinence and prolapse symptoms require early assessment and appropriate referral to the WHP • Major gynaecological surgery can cause potential pelvic floor dysfunction	• WHPs are working closely with other health professionals to ensure an equitable, quality parent craft education service in primary and secondary care • Identification of risk factors and development of care pathways ensure referral to women's health physiotherapy services • WHPs cooperate with other professionals in delivering an integrated continence service. • The WHP provides pre- and post-operative support and advice to minimise risks

Physiotherapy is a health care profession concerned with human function and movement and maximising potential. It uses physical approaches to promote, maintain and restore physical, psychological and social well-being, taking account of variations in health status. It is science-based, committed to extending, apply-

Gynaecology: Changing Services for Changing Needs. Edited by Sue Jolley
© 2006 by John Wiley & Sons, Ltd

ing, evaluating and reviewing the evidence that underpins and informs its practice and delivery. The exercise of clinical judgement and informed interpretation is at its core (Chartered Society of Physiotherapy 2002).

Physiotherapists working in the speciality of women's health embrace these values to deliver health care to women. By involvement in antenatal education physiotherapists are well placed to provide information, advice and instruction to women to maximise their well-being. The priority is the prevention and early alleviation of the physical stresses of pregnancy and childbirth. Common consequences of pregnancy and childbirth are either the physical problems of pelvic girdle and low back pain or incontinence. The aim in the postnatal period is to address healthcare needs to enable each woman to recover and return to pain-free and symptom-free normal function. There is strong evidence to support health education in the perinatal period to reduce the risk of future pelvic floor dysfunction and urinary symptoms. The WHP's skills are also utilised in the conservative management of pelvic floor disorders that develop in the postnatal period or later in women's lives. In addition, the WHP can contribute to the care of women undergoing gynaecological surgery.

Clinical effectiveness is the provision of high-quality health care in a way that allows the recipient to achieve maximum health gain. It relies on the healthcare provider being the right person to do:

• the right thing (based on current evidence based practice)
• in the right way (having the skills and competence)
• at the right time (providing treatment/services when the patient needs them)
• in the right place (the appropriate location of treatment/services with patient choice)
• with the right result (clinical effectiveness/maximising health gain measured by the evaluation of practice through clinical audit, outcome measures and achievement of individual goals).

ANTENATAL EDUCATION AND ADVICE FOR PREGNANT WOMEN

The provision of high-quality and accessible antenatal education and advice for all pregnant women is important in order to prevent pelvic floor disorders. The most common of these is urinary incontinence, which is defined as the involuntary leakage of urine. This is a major clinical problem that can have a profound impact on quality of life (Laycock *et al.* 2001). It affects about 10–30 % of women aged 15–64 years, with a much higher incidence among pregnant women, estimated at between 20 and 67 % (Hannestad *et al.* 2000; Morkved *et al.* 2003). Lower urinary tract symptoms are so common in early pregnancy that they are often considered to be normal (Cutner & Cardozo 1990). Norwegian studies have reported an incidence of 42 % during pregnancy and symptoms persisting at 8 weeks for 38 % of all women (Morkved & Bo 1999). These figures highlight the need for a prevention and treatment strategy for these women in the perinatal period.

An integrated system of muscles, fascia, ligaments and neural control is needed to maintain urinary continence during raised intra-abdominal pressure. Active contraction of the pelvic floor muscles elevates and supports the anterior vaginal wall (Laycock *et al.* 2001). In addition, a competent urethral sphincter is necessary. Pregnancy and vaginal delivery are main risk factors of urinary incontinence because they can involve damage to the nerves, muscles or ligaments involved in this continence mechanism.

Antenatal instruction in pelvic floor exercises can reduce the likelihood of incontinence for women during and after their pregnancy. In a Norwegian study women had individual instruction in pelvic floor anatomy and how to properly contract the pelvic floor muscle. Then they attended a 12-week intensive pelvic floor exercise programme supervised by a physiotherapist and were given a home exercise programme. The pelvic floor muscle strength improved significantly after the intensive training programme. These results were also measured postnatally at 3 months (Morkved *et al.* 2003). However, further research is needed to determine whether this type of training can prevent incontinence in later life.

It is unrealistic to provide this type of WHP-led intensive programme for all pregnant women in the UK, but it is possible that the multidisciplinary obstetric team could facilitate a satisfactory level of input to teach the pelvic floor exercises and promote compliance. During their pregnancy women are regularly seen by their GP, hospital or community midwife and obstetrician. All women should have access to and the opportunity to attend antenatal classes and have written information about antenatal care (National Institute for Clinical Excellence 2003).

Therefore there are many opportunities to encourage pelvic floor exercises. If each woman had the necessary instruction during a visit to any of these health professionals and a reminder to continue with her home exercise programme at each subsequent visit, then information could be made available to the majority of women using the current NHS resources. The WHP may be involved in some parenthood education, or in education to midwives, health visitors and doctors to ensure consistency of input. It is essential that the guidance given to women is as up to date as possible, and any written information is clear, concise, in a format that she can understand and is evidence based. Also, all health professionals involved in the woman's care should utilise the same written information.

The correct exercise regime to 'prescribe' for pregnant asymptomatic women to maintain optimal pelvic floor muscle function and primary prevention is not yet fully understood. However, the Association of Chartered

Physiotherapists in Women's Health (ACPWH) has produced 'Fit for Pregnancy' information leaflets containing evidence-based information and well-explained exercises. The exercises are explained in such a way that each woman can exercise at her own level. Studies have shown that women who had learned and been self-compliant with a home exercise programme in pregnancy have a reduced risk of postnatal incontinence (Mason *et al.* 2001).

It is especially important to target pregnant women who already have symptoms. The Royal College of Obstetricians and Gynaecologists (RCOG) recommends that every booked antenatal patient should be asked about urinary and faecal incontinence (Royal College of Obstetricians and Gynaecologists 2002). There are several opportunities to ask trigger questions relating to urinary symptoms.

- NICE (2003) recommends seven antenatal appointments for uncomplicated pregnancy where women will see their GP, midwife of obstetric consultant team.
- Women frequently attend antenatal classes, antenatal exercise classes, aquanatal, yoga or pilates for pregnancy with the WHP, midwife or fitness instructor.
- Women may also be having treatment for other problems in their pregnancy. Of special importance is low back and pelvic girdle pain when urinary incontinence may develop or already coexist.

Although there is strong evidence to support antenatal education, there are some problems to overcome. The main one for WHPs is the enormous task of empowering midwives, health visitors and doctors with the knowledge and skills to be competent to teach effective pelvic floor exercises. Ensuring that trigger questions are asked at every opportunity is also difficult. The provision of easily accessible and conveniently timed antenatal classes is still not adequate (Sing & Newburn 2000). There are some groups that are especially difficult to target, such as teenagers and ethnic minorities. Therefore classes need to be community based and ideally held not only during week days but also in the evenings and at weekends. However, this also raises issues for staff who may be working alone.

Patient compliance can never be assumed. Studies continually show that supervised pelvic floor exercise programmes gain better compliance and outcome than just an exercise leaflet. Women also need to be given relevant evidence. Some women query the effect on labour of pelvic floor muscle training during pregnancy, often thinking that a tight pelvic floor muscle will not 'give' to facilitate vaginal delivery. The contrary has in fact been shown to be true. In a randomised controlled trial of pelvic floor muscle training during labour there were fewer cases of active pushing in the second stage of labour lasting longer than 60 minutes and fewer episiotomies in the training group. The improved muscle control, strength and flexibility seemingly facilitates rather than obstructs labour (Salvesen & Morkved 2004).

There is also good evidence that postnatal pelvic floor exercises are effective in reducing urinary incontinence. Studies have shown that women who had instruction by the physiotherapist and had been compliant with the exercises had less incidence of stress incontinence up to one year postnatally (Morkved & Bo 2000). Episiotomy does not appear to protect the pelvic floor, and caesarean section is not completely protective against urinary and faecal incontinence (Royal College of Obstetricians and Gynaecologists 2002; Rortveit *et al.* 2003). Ideally this information should be given to women in the antenatal period to empower them with the information so that they can make an informed choice about embarking on the postnatal exercise regime.

Exercise is not usually a high priority in the mind of the new mother in the immediate postnatal period. Many women have not attended antenatal classes, and all women are at some risk of developing future problems, so they should all be reminded of the importance of pelvic floor exercises and supervised while doing them. The ward-based health professionals have a duty of care to promote this health education and support it with quality written information.

In many units, WHPs are not routinely able to see all postnatal women. This is influenced by early discharges of postnatal women, the volume of patients who are at risk or symptomatic and the fact that physiotherapists in most units work a Monday to Friday service. Therefore women who are asymptomatic and have had uncomplicated deliveries are often neglected. More evidence is required to establish the effectiveness of pelvic floor exercises for this group, but, until found otherwise, all women should be considered to be at some risk and given the best possible advice. Clearly if funding was made available to provide a 7-day physiotherapy service, a more equitable service could be provided. Until the multidisciplinary team is better funded, the WHP needs to prioritise care to high-risk postnatal women.

THE RISK ASSESSMENT AND MANAGEMENT OF WOMEN WITH CONTINENCE PROBLEMS AND PERINEAL PAIN FOLLOWING CHILDBIRTH

Epidemiological studies have not only linked incontinence with pregnancy and childbirth but also suggest that assisted deliveries and high birth weight babies are particularly high-risk factors. This means that women who are more at risk can be identified after delivery and there is an opportunity to promote continence (Persson *et al.* 2000). In Chiarelli's study (2002) physiotherapy was targeted at women who had delivered by forceps or ventouse or whose babies had a birth weight of more than 4000 g. These women were visited on the postnatal ward, instructed in pelvic floor exercises and bladder advice, given a detailed home exercise programme and given an outpatient physiotherapy appointment at 8 weeks postnatally and treated as necessary. Data were collated at 3 months postnatally. The incidence and severity of incontinence at this time was much improved in the intervention group and proved that a high level of intervention for the patient group most at risk was effective (Chiarelli 2002).

Childbirth is also a major factor in faecal incontinence, which can affect up to 10 % of female adults (Abramowitz *et al.* 2000). Incontinence of stool and flatus are frequent complications of childbirth and associated with anal sphincter laceration and forceps delivery. Sphincter damage may occur as a result of a spontaneous perineal tear or a tear as an episiotomy extends (Samuelsson *et al.* 2000). Following third- or fourth-degree tears 13 % of primiparae and 23 % of multiparae have symptoms of urgency and/or faecal incontinence 3 months after delivery (Sultan *et al.* 1993), but sphincter defects account for only 45 % of incidence of postnatal faecal incontinence (Abramowitz *et al.* 2000). Damage to the pelvic and pudendal nerves during vaginal delivery may lead to partial denervation and subsequent weakness of the pelvic floor and anal sphincter. In a few cases this damage is severe and is associated with faecal incontinence (Allen *et al.* 1990).

Faecal incontinence is a distressing and disabling condition, especially for new mothers, and is often under-reported (Clarkson *et al.* 2001). MacArthur *et al.* (1997) found that only 14 % of women with new faecal incontinence after childbirth had consulted a doctor and those doing so were unlikely to voluntarily report incontinence as one of their symptoms. This supports the recommendation for health professionals to ask postnatal women about symptoms. A risk assessment tool in regular use on the postnatal wards (see Table 7.1) can help to identify women who are at risk, and a care pathway gives the opportunity to discuss symptoms by asking direct questions relating to faecal incontinence. There are many opportunities in the postnatal period to assess women:

Table 7.1. Risk assessment tool for use on a postnatal ward

Postnatal factors to be completed before discharge		
Precipitate delivery	4	
Prolonged active pushing > 1.5 hours	4	Score 0–6 Low risk
Instrumental delivery	4	WHP or midwife give instruction in pelvic
Failed ventouse or forceps	5	floor exercises
Large baby > 3.63 kg	4	
Episiotomy/second-degree tear	3	Score 7 and above
Third-/fourth-degree tear/ urethral tear	10	Moderate risk Refer to WHP
Episode of postnatal urinary incontinence	5	Offer open appointment with WHP at 6 weeks if symptomatic at 6 weeks postnatal
Episode of postnatal faecal incontinence	6	Score 10 and above High risk Refer to WHP Give appointment with WHP for 6 weeks postnatal

- on the postnatal ward – midwife, nurse auxiliary, WHP, obstetric medical team
- postnatal home visits up to 10 days postnatal – community midwife/GP
- Postnatal 6-week check – GP/obstetrician
- Postnatal exercise class – WHP/fitness instructor
- Postnatal parentcraft class reunion
- Baby check clinics – health visitor/GP.

Questions regarding urinary and bowel symptoms may also be asked by offering the patient a self-completion questionnaire. This may result in a more accurate assessment of their symptoms and may be used as an outcome measure to assess efficacy of intervention. For example, Bugg *et al.* (2001) have produced the Manchester Health Questionnaire, which is a valid and reliable health-related, quality-of-life questionnaire for the assessment of women with anal incontinence.

A third-degree tear is defined as a partial or complete laceration of the external anal sphincter and a fourth-degree tear as a complete rupture of the external anal sphincter including the anorectal mucosa (Royal College of Obstetricians and Gynaecologists 2001, 2004). These degrees of tear are easily recognised at the time of delivery and should be sutured in theatre (Royal College of Obstetricians and Gynaecologists 2001). An overall care pathway should be in place-for-women with a third- or fourth-degree tear beginning immediately postnatally, which should include prophylactic antibiotics, laxatives, perineal hygiene and referral to the obstetric ward WHP.

The WHP should advise an inpatient not to attempt pelvic floor exercises for 10 days but explain how to do them, beginning gently, building up to ten 10-second contractions five times a day from day 10 to allow healing of the sphincter. The patient then needs a 6-week outpatient appointment, following the routine appointment with the obstetrician. At that appointment the WHP would:

Take a subjective assessment of:
- healing problems – discharge, prickly stitches
- bladder or bowel problems – urgency, frequency, incontinence, pain on defaecation/micturition (consider using a questionnaire)
- pain – where, when; dyspareunia.

Take an objective assessment involving:
- vaginal and rectal examination
- contraindications to vaginal assessment – failure to consent, vaginal discharge, evidence of poor healing
- observation – scarring, pelvic floor contraction vaginally and anally
- palpation – vaginally for tenderness, scarring, pelvic floor muscle resting tone, strength and endurance.

Follow the third-degree tear physiotherapy care pathway (see Table 7.2).

Table 7.2. Third-degree tear postnatal physiotherapy care pathway from 6 weeks

Assessment findings	Action
No symptoms	
Pelvic floor muscle and anal sphincter strength grade 3 or more Oxford scale	Check technique of pelvic floor contraction Advise continued exercises, up to 10 × 10-second contractions 5 times a day in standing if comfortable until 5 months postnatally Discharge from physiotherapy
Pelvic floor or anal sphincter muscle strength grade 2	Check technique of pelvic floor contraction Give home exercise programme, hold time to patient's ability up to 10 seconds, repetitions up to 10 in position of comfort Reassess in 4 weeks
	No progress – check compliance and technique of exercise programme Consider course of electromyogram (EMG) biofeedback or muscle stimulation up to 12 treatments, 2× weekly course and continued exercise programme. Reassess by digital examination every 2 weeks
	When grade 3 or more achieved advise continued exercises, up to 10 × 10-second contractions 5 times a day in standing if comfortable until 5 months postnatally Discharge from physiotherapy
Pelvic floor or anal sphincter muscle strength grade 0–1	Use EMG to assess and facilitate active pelvic floor contraction
	Active contraction facilitated – give home exercise programme, hold time to patient's ability up to 10 seconds, repetitions up to 10 in position of comfort Reassess in 4 weeks
	No active contraction – muscle stimulation up to 12 treatments, 2× weekly course and continued exercise programme. Reassess by digital examination every 2 weeks
	When grade 3 or more achieved advise continued exercises, up to 10 × 10-second contractions 5 times a day in standing if comfortable until 5 months postnatally Discharge from physiotherapy
Symptoms	
Pain	Assess scarring Consider: ultrasound therapy 　Self-massage 　EMG to reduce resting tone 　Pelvic floor exercise programme
Urinary symptoms	Urinalysis Consider bladder drill Pelvic floor exercise programme ± vaginal EMG/muscle stimulation

Table 7.2. *Continued*

Assessment findings	Action
Bowel symptoms	Discuss positions of defaecation
	Pelvic floor exercise programme ± anal EMG/muscle stimulation
	Assess regularly and treat for up to 3 months
	When symptoms are improving and muscle strength grade 3 or more – discharge
	If no improvement in symptoms after 3 months refer to obstetric/gynaecology/urology/colorectal consultant teams

A system of clear referral criteria should be established so those women who require additional care are managed and treated by the WHP when problems are identified. Sometimes no sphincter damage is noted at the time of delivery but women subsequently develop symptoms that are picked up when they are seen by the GP or obstetrician after 6 weeks. Problems may include:

- superficial dyspareunia
- faecal incontinence, faecal urgency or poor control of flatus
- urinary incontinence, urinary urgency
- history of symptoms of prolapse in pregnancy or since delivery – heaviness, dragging sensation.

Physiotherapy intervention will be as the third-/fourth-degree care pathway (Table 7.2).

There are still some problems to overcome in optimising the care for women with these problems following childbirth. A big problem is the under-reporting of third-degree tears (Royal College of Obstetricians and Gynae-cologists 2001), which means that appropriate care may be delayed. Often women are not given the opportunity to divulge symptoms and, when they do, services may not be adequate, especially as access to a specialist WHP is not always available. This highlights the need for not only more resources but also continuing clinical evidence to support the value of interventions by the WHP.

THE ROLE OF THE WHP IN AN INTEGRATED CONTINENCE SERVICE

A truly integrated continence service, which can deliver a first-class service, relies on the team efforts of all health professionals involved in continence care (Department of Health 2000). These include continence nurses (in hospitals, nursing homes and the community), GPs, urologists, obstetricians, gynaecologists and WHPs. Conservative management of urinary stress incontinence is the recommended first choice of treatment. In order for this management to be effective it is essential that health professionals have a clear understanding of the continence control mechanism and the factors that may affect it, the assessment skills to identify specific defects and the treatment skills to optimise rehabilitation outcomes.

Continence relies on the optimal function of the urethral support system and the sphincteric closure system. During a cough the urethral closure pressure is known to rise simultaneously with abdominal pressure and despite a rise in intravesical pressure the urethra remains closed. When this fails, stress incontinence can result (Ashton-Miller *et al.* 2001). The pelvic floor provides support for the urethra and is a musculoskeletal unit that has passive, neural and active subsystems of control. Panjabi's model of stability (Panjabi 1992) refers specifically to spinal stability but Lee and Lee (2004) suggest that this model can be applied to load transfer through the pelvis and urethral support.

The passive system involves the endopelvic fascia, which attaches to the pelvic sidewalls and to the thick fascial band of the arcus tendineus fascia. The fascial layers allow a degree of movement and the extensibility varies with age and past obstetric history. Regular straining to open the bowel may compound the situation. There may also be genetic factors, which ultimately determine the inherent strength of collagen, fascia, elastin and connective tissue. It may be possible, in the future, to screen for inherently weak fascia and advise those women at risk by education or treat with medication to strengthen these tissues.

The neural system includes the pudendal nerve, which innervates the levator ani, the central control of reflex function between the detrusor muscle and the pelvic floor and the sensory feedback from the muscle spindles within the pelvic floor muscle. Slow or rapid stretch of these spindles will generate slow sustained or rapid brief muscle activation.

In the active system the levator ani muscle, commonly named the pelvic floor muscle, contains primarily type I muscle fibres and maintains constant tone to provide urethral support against gravity. This muscle exhibits an increase in activity in response to slow, rapid and unpredictable loading, and when the central nervous system can predict the timing of increased intra-abdominal pressure the muscle has the ability to activate prior to that increase. Type I muscle fibres respond to pain and pathology by inhibition and delayed timing of recruitment, which may result in incontinence and prolapse. Type II muscle fibres respond to pain by overactivity and, in order to compensate for a dysfunctional passive support system, become overactive and fail to release. This may result in voiding dysfunction, hesitancy and incomplete emptying, dyspareunia, vaginismus, obstructive defaecation and perineal pain, which tends to be worse when sitting.

As well as a sound knowledge of the functional anatomy of the structures responsible for controlling urinary incontinence, the WHP has access to women during pregnancy and postnatally in order to give preventative care and to identify at-risk and early symptomatic women. She also has the relevant assessment and treatment skills. Recognising the skills of the WHP should help to ensure appropriate referrals. Ideally the referral criteria to the WHP for patients with urinary incontinence are:

- pelvic floor grade 0–1 Oxford scale for patients with potential for compliance with an exercise programme
- poor technique of the pelvic floor exercise – breath holding, bearing down, abdominal doming
- asymmetry of pelvic floor, right versus left
- overactivity/high resting tone
- pelvic pain – after exclusion of gynaecological problems by medical teams
- coexisting low back and/or pelvic girdle pain
- coexisting neurological disease
- antenatal or in a 1-year postnatal period
- in a 1-year post major gynaecological surgery period
- patients with grade 2 or more pelvic floor who have not responded to continence nurse intervention – but not end-of-line patients.

Once a patient has been referred to the WHP, both subjective and objective assessments are needed (see Table 7.3). The aim of the subjective assessment is to determine whether the pathology is due to a problem with the connective tissue, the nerves or the muscles. The objective assessment includes a musculoskeletal assessment of muscle analysis and posture and movement, as faulty movement can induce pathology, not just be a result of it (Sahrmann 1993).

The physiotherapy treatment involves a holistic approach tailored to the individual, which may include:

- pelvic floor facilitation and individualised home exercise programme with regular supervision; the recommendation is that the pelvic floor muscle training programme should be for 15–20 weeks after achieving a good technique of the exercise
- trigger point therapy
- posture correction
- movement pattern correction
- electromyogram biofeedback
- electrical muscle stimulation
- general fitness advice.

There is a relationship between pelvic floor activity, pelvic floor disorders and low back and pelvic pain. Physiotherapists working in the speciality of women's health have in the past focused on pelvic floor function and

Table 7.3. Assessment of incontinence problems by WHP

Subjective assessment
Clues relating to connective tissue dysfunction – the passive system

- Menopausal, cyclical symptom pattern
- Coexisting prolapse
- Obstetric history
- Drug history – steroids
- Collagen status – stretch marks/varicose veins/haemorrhoids
- Respiratory problems
- History of constipation
- Obesity
- Heavy lifting

Clues relating to neural system dysfunction – the neural system

- Obstetric history
- Neurological disease
- Radiotherapy
- Altered sensation

Clues relating to problems with the muscles – active system

- Pregnancy
- Perineal tears/episiotomy
- Respiratory problems
- Abdominal surgery
- Exercise/activities – under- or over-activity
- Chronic fatigue
- Pain
- History of pain

Objective assessment
The musculoskeletal assessment

- Control of the local stability system – the co-contraction of the pelvic floor with transversus abdominis, the diaphragm and multifidus
- Posture analysis and movement patterns
- Pelvic floor assessment by digital vaginal examination
  Pain
  Prolapse/fascial defect
  Resting tone – hyper-/hypotonicity
  Timing of recruitment
  Control
  Endurance
  Strength
  Repetitions
  Symmetry/dominance
  Maintenance of urethrovesical angle with cough, strain, voluntary contraction

---

rehabilitation when treating incontinence and discouraged the use of the abdominal muscles. Musculoskeletal physiotherapists would not have considered the pelvic floor when treating low back or pelvic girdle pain. However, if asked, women often report that they suffer both urinary incontinence and low back and pelvic girdle pain, and physiotherapists commonly note that the management of one problem often improves the other. This has not been a coincidence. Lee and Lee consider that the two therapy groups have been treating the same condition, which is a failed load transfer through the lumbopelvic region. This manifests itself as either dysfunction of the joints and subsequent pain or ineffective support to the urethra and subsequent incontinence (Lee & Lee 2004).

Research has led to a greater understanding of the synergy of the pelvic floor and abdominal muscles, and physiotherapists in both women's health and musculoskeletal specialities are finding common ground and changing to a more integrated approach, addressing stability and normal function of the whole lumbopelvic region. Sapsford has designed a rehabilitation programme for the management of stress incontinence. It specifically utilises the abdominal muscles to initiate low-level pelvic floor activity, and then progresses to strengthening work through expiratory actions and eventually to impact training (Sapsford 2004).

Therefore it is now generally recognised that the pelvic floor muscle should not be considered in isolation but as an integral part of the local stability system. In 1989 Bergmark first described the classification of muscles into two systems (Lee 2004). A global system is responsible for regional stabilisation during movement of the thorax and pelvis or the pelvis and legs. There is also a local system of muscles, which are essential for stabilising the joints of the spine and pelvic girdle in preparation for or in response to external loading. The pelvic floor muscle works synergically with the local stabilising muscles of the transversus abdominis, the diaphragm, and the deep fibres of multifidus contributing to intra-abdominal pressure, increasing tension on the thoracodorsal fascia and increasing intra-articular stiffness, thus preventing excessive shearing during loading (see Figure 7.1).

In order to utilise the unique contribution the WHP can make within the integrated continence service, clear referral criteria, pathways of care and treatment protocols need to be established and distributed to all concerned. Early interventions and appropriate referrals to the WHP are essential. There are many opportunities for developing the service, which include more involvement by WHPs in urogynaecology clinics such as WHP/nurse-led clinics and drop-in sessions. It is essential that there is consistency of terminology, assessment forms and written patient information. Adequate funding is needed to support an integrated service, encourage interdisciplinary approaches and ensure that health professionals continue their professional development.

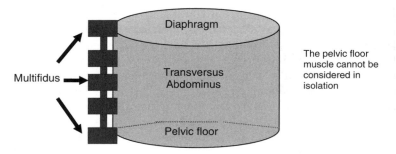

Figure 7.1. The local stability system

THE PROVISION OF APPROPRIATE CARE FOR WOMEN UNDERGOING GYNAECOLOGICAL SURGERY

All surgery is associated with the risk of post-operative complications (see Table 7.4). The WHP is well placed to work with the nursing and medical staff to prevent, identify and treat post-operative problems, especially following major gynaecological surgery. Ideally this begins at the pre-operative assessment, the WHP particularly wishing to identify any pre-existing respiratory and mobility issues. High-risk patients can be identified and action taken to ensure the appropriate level of post-operative intervention, and all patients are given information to empower them to reduce their own risk. The process continues on the post-operative wards with monitoring, pain management, bed exercises and promotion of early ambulation and education to patients to support their recovery when home.

Haemorrhage, shock and myocardial infarction, wound infection and paralytic ileus are complications that are not within the scope of the WHP to prevent, but an awareness of the clinical signs of these problems and the action to be taken if suspected are essential skills. Other general complications relating to respiratory, circulatory or mobility problems are within the remit of the WHP to address, as are more specific problems relating to pelvic floor dysfunction and lymphoedema.

Many preventative measures can be discussed pre-operatively. For respiratory problems these include:

- teaching an active cycle breathing technique and supported cough pre-operatively
- advice to stop smoking – ideally a minimum of 6 weeks pre-operatively but just 24 hours will be beneficial
- promotion of upright positions in bed
- promotion of early ambulation.

Table 7.4. General post-operative complications

Complication	Description	Clinical signs
Haemorrhage	Primary haemorrhage – occurs during surgery and continues Reactionary haemorrhage – occurs within 24 hours (commonly 4–6 hours) and may be caused by a slipping ligature or movement of a primary clot with cough or sudden rise in blood pressure Secondary haemorrhage – occurs 7–14 days post-operatively secondary to infection	Restless, cold, clammy, pallor Tachycardia Air hunger – sighing, gasping, reduced respiratory rate Hypotension – may be delayed Increased blood in drainage bottle
Shock	A complex syndrome caused by the effects of anaesthetic, trauma of surgery or blood loss	Tachycardia Hypotension Peripheral shutdown – pallor, sweaty, clammy Reduced urine output Restlessness Coma
Myocardial infarction	At-risk patients include those with pre-operative hypertension, congestive cardiac failure, intraoperative hypotension or when the operation lasts > 3 hours	Chest pain Distressed, cold, clammy Dyspnoea, cyanosed Sudden change in pulse rate and/or blood pressure
Wound infection	An infection that develops at the wound site and prevents healing	Pyrexia Redness around wound Pain
Paralytic ileus	Intestinal ileus and/or gastric dilation	Absent bowel sounds Abdominal distension Vomiting Abdominal pain
Respiratory problems	The anaesthetic, reduced mobility and reluctance to cough reduces the efficacy of clearing secretions and increases the risk of respiratory morbidity. At greater risk are smokers and patients with pre-existing respiratory pathology. Post-operative analgesia, especially opiates, will reduce the cough reflex and depress respiratory function	Pyrexia Shortness of breath Confusion Cough Hypoxia
Mobility problems	General morbidity reduces muscle strength, confidence and motivation. Pain and attachments may limit ability to move in bed and mobilise independently	Joint stiffness Low back pain Increased dependency

In order to prevent a deep vein thrombosis (DVT) or pulmonary embolism (PE), mechanical measures to prevent venous stasis and increase venous return should be promoted for all patients undergoing major gynaecological surgery. These are:

- advice relating to foot and leg circulatory exercises – ideally 1 minute hourly until fully mobile
- encouragement of early post-operative and continued mobility
- anti-thromboembolic stockings.

There are also more specific risks associated with gynaecological surgery including the prevalence of urinary symptoms after hysterectomy and lymphoedema. Some women report incontinence, prolapse and abnormal bladder emptying problems after their hysterectomy. This may be due to the resultant falling oestrogen levels, nerve damage, damage to the pelvic support structures or lifestyle changes. The incidence of urinary incontinence after hysterectomy has been investigated by a systematic review of evidence, which showed mixed results (Brown *et al.* 2000). Generally the risk of developing incontinence was 40 % higher than for women who had not undergone hysterectomy. Some studies have reported no rise in incontinence in the first 6–12 months, suggesting that the cause is damage to connective tissue rather than nerve damage. The odds of developing incontinence problems increased to 60 % among women who were 60 years or older, again supporting the connective tissue theory as this loses strength and elasticity with age. Brown *et al.* (2000) suggest that when women are counselled about the effects of hysterectomy, incontinence should be discussed as a possible long-term adverse effect. However, this recommendation is disputed by Roovers *et al.* (2000), who recommend that doctors should not counsel their patients until randomised controlled trials can prove that hysterectomy is a risk factor for urinary incontinence.

Taking into account these opinions, enough is known about the mechanism of continence and possible disruption of this mechanism by surgical intervention and that pain can result in muscle inhibition to merit some action. It is also well known that patients undergoing hysterectomy may already have pre-existing incontinence problems. Therefore the recommendation is that all women undergoing major gynaecological surgery are taught pelvic floor exercises by the WHP post-operatively on the ward. Women who are experiencing symptoms at 6 weeks post-operatively should be referred to the WHP for assessment and treatment as indicated.

Women who undergo radical surgery for gynaecological cancer where lymph nodes are surgically removed, or who require radiotherapy to the nodes, are at risk of developing lymphoedema at any time in the future. Lymphoedema is a chronic swelling due to a failure of the lymph drainage system. If it develops, it is essentially incurable, but the main problems associated with swelling of the lower limb, cellulitis, pain and joint stiffness can be improved and controlled with specialist care (British Lymphology Society 2005). Prevention, however, is much better than cure and with the appropriate input the risk can be reduced. The recommendation is that post-operative and post-radiotherapy education and the teaching of exercises and instruction in simple lymphatic massage are available for all women in the immediate post-operative or post-radiotherapy period, and follow-up is available for them. It is the role of the WHP to provide this support, usually in liaison with the oncology nurse specialist. The operations that are likely to create problems are a radical, or Wertheim's, hysterectomy (for cervical cancer) and a vulvectomy (for vulval cancer). Therefore specific care pathways have been developed (see Table 7.5) and written information on abdominal massage should be available.

Table 7.5. Physiotherapy care pathway for a Wertheim's or vulvectomy

Pre-operative advice

- Respiratory and mobility assessment
- Teach breathing exercises
- Teach circulatory exercises
- Explain lymphoedema risk and preventative management
- Teach abdominal massage

Day 1 post-operative

- Breathing exercises
- Foot exercises – 2 minutes every hour, supervised when possible
- No crossing of legs
- Gentle pelvic rocking
- Static gluteal and quadriceps contractions

Day 2

- Out of bed if observations are stable
- Pelvic floor and transversus abdominis exercises

Days 3–5

- Exercises as above
- Mobilise as able
- Upper quadrant abdominal massage only if drains still *in situ*
- Measure legs at mid-thigh, mid-calf and ankle and record

Before discharge

- Advise to include lower quadrant abdominal massage
- Advise to measure legs weekly
- Give lymphoedema prevention advice leaflet
- Make a 6-week outpatient physiotherapy appointment

6-week out patient appointment

- Check for understanding of advice given on ward and in advice leaflet
- Check wound
- Measure legs
- Check skin care
- Check massage technique

Because women are not usually admitted until the day of their surgery, it is not always easy for the WHP to see them pre-operatively. However, the ideal opportunity is during the pre-operative assessment process. At Queen's Medical Centre, Nottingham, the WHP attends each pre-assessment session to talk to any relevant patients. Usually this involves an informal session with all of the women who are having a major operation, so the WHP discusses breathing techniques, exercises and advice on mobility. She is able to identify any potential problems on an individual basis and give appropriate advice. She usually meets the oncology patients separately as they often need special support. This works very well, and having met the women pre-operatively it becomes easier to follow them up post-operatively, offering greater continuity of care.

CONCLUSION

Members of ACPWH promote the special role that physiotherapists can play in women's health. This role is very varied and may include involvement in continence or urotherapy, anorectal problems, pelvic pain, antenatal and postnatal services, inpatient gynaecology and research/audit work (Brook & Laycock 2005). Education during pregnancy can provide women with the knowledge and skills to reduce their own risks of incontinence and back pain as a consequence of pregnancy and childbirth, but also to enable them to make lifestyle changes that can impact on their own health and that of their families. The challenge is to preserve this role and build on it in order to keep health promotion high on the agenda for the woman's health. WHPs are well placed to be greatly involved in this.

Increasingly healthcare providers are recognising the important role specialist physiotherapists are able to contribute to women's gynaecological health, especially as the benefit of physiotherapy is often highlighted in government guidelines (Department of Health 2000). Increasing the number of physiotherapists with specialist skills in women's health has therefore become a long-term challenge. There is also scope to expand the role of the WHP in areas such as menopause and osteoporosis. Although there is research to support physiotherapy for urogenital dysfunctions and anorectal problems, 'there is a dearth in many other areas of the women's health service' (Brook & Laycock 2005). Therefore more research is needed to provide the evidence that will secure the ongoing funding of physiotherapy services in this field.

Experienced clinicians in the workplace cannot always find the time to be involved with research, and may not have the necessary skills to do so. Historically, physiotherapists have not been good at collecting outcome data. However, this is improving and validated outcome measure tools are now in widespread use. In order to maximise the overall benefit of this routine data, and to ensure that quality research is carried out, funding must be secured for more specific research posts. However, in the interim clinicians must trust their sound clinical reasoning and experience to find new ways of collating evidence.

If the WHP role in women's gynaecological care is to flourish in the future, the physiotherapy profession itself has to recognise the need to equip students and newly qualified physiotherapists with the relevant specialist skills. To do this it should include obstetrics and gynaecology as a core module in the undergraduate training and provide more student placements. Experienced WHPs who are in clinical practice should try to be involved in this under-graduate training and welcome students. It is usual for newly qualified phys-iotherapists to rotate through several specialities during their first 2 years of clinical practice. Women's health is often not considered a core rotation and in many hospitals the women's health service is very small, or non-existent, so newly qualified physiotherapists do not have the opportunity to work in that team. Sharing of skills within the workplace is essential, and indeed physio-therapists who work with musculoskeletal problems, especially those who are specialists in back care, are increasingly interested in women's health. Physio-therapists who were traditionally obstetrics and gynaecological specialists are also learning new skills from their work colleagues.

Women's health physiotherapy offers clinicians an exciting career. There is still much need for research and many unanswered questions, but there is no doubt that the WHP has a valuable role to play in gynaecological care.

REFERENCES

Abramowitz L et al. (2000) Are sphincter defects the cause of anal incontinence after vaginal delivery? Results of a prospective study. Dis Colon Rectum, 43(5), 590–6.

Allen R E et al. (1990) Pelvic floor damage and childbirth; a neurophysiological study. British Journal of Obstetrics and Gynaecology, 97(9), 770–9.

Ashton-Miller J A et al. (2001) The functional anatomy of the female pelvic floor and stress incontinence control system. Scandinavian Journal of Urology and Nephrology (Supplement 207).

British Lymphology Society (BLS) (2005) What is Lymphoedema?, www.lymphoedema.org/bls/ (accessed 16 November 2005).

Brook G, Laycock J (2005) Setting up a Women's Health Physiotherapy Service, www.acpwh.org.uk/docs/WH_physiotherapy_service.pdf (accessed 17 November 2005).

Brown J S et al. (2000) Hysterectomy and urinary incontinence: a systematic review. The Lancet, 356(9229), 535–9.

Bugg G J et al. (2001) A new condition-specific health-related quality of life question-naire for the assessment of women with anal incontinence. British Journal of Obstetrics and Gynaecology, 108(10), 1057–67.

Chartered Society of Physiotherapy (CSP) (2002) Curriculum Framework for Quali-fying Programmes in Physiotherapy, CSP, London.

Chiarelli P (2002) Promoting urinary incontinence in women after delivery: randomised controlled trial. *British Medical Journal*, **324**(7348), 1241.

Clarkson J *et al.* (2001) Achieving sustainable quality in maternity services – using audit of incontinence and dyspareunia to identify shortfalls in meeting standards. *BMC Pregnancy and Childbirth*, **1**, 4.

Cutner A, Cardozo L (1990) Urinary incontinence: clinical features. *Practitioner*, **234**(1497), 1018–24.

Department of Health (2000) *Good Practice in Continence Services*, HMSO, London.

Hannestad Y S *et al.* (2000) A community-based epidemiological survey of female urinary incontinence. *Journal of Clinical Epidemiology*, **53**(11), 1150–7.

Laycock J *et al.* (2001) *Clinical Guidelines for the Physiotherapy Management of Females Aged 16–65 with Stress Urinary Incontinence*, Chartered Society of Physiotherapy, London.

Lee D (2004) *The Pelvic Girdle: An Approach to Examination and Treatment of the Lumbo–Pelvic–Hip Region*, 3rd edition, Churchill Livingstone, Edinburgh.

Lee D, Lee L J (2004) *Stress Urinary Incontinence – A Consequence of Failed Load Transfer through the Pelvis.* Presented at the 5th World Interdisciplinary Congress on 'Low Back and Pelvic Pain', Melbourne, 2004.

MacArthur C *et al.* (1997) Faecal incontinence after childbirth. *British Journal of Obstetrics and Gynaecology*, **104**(1), 46–50.

Mason I *et al.* (2001) The relationship between antenatal pelvic floor muscle exercises and post partum stress incontinence. *Physiotherapy*, **87**(12), 651–61.

Morkved S, Bo K (1999) Prevalence of urinary incontinence during pregnancy and postpartum. *International Urogynecology Journal of Pelvic Floor Dysfunction*, **10**(6), 394–8.

Morkved S, Bo K (2000) Effect of postpartum pelvic floor muscle training in prevention and treatment of urinary incontinence: a one-year follow up. *British Journal of Obstetrics and Gynaecology*, **107**(8), 1022–8.

Morkved S *et al.* (2003) Pelvic floor muscle training during pregnancy to prevent urinary incontinence: a single-blind randomized controlled trial. *Obstetrics and Gynecology*, **101**(2), 313–9.

National Institute for Clinical Excellence (2003) *Antenatal Care: Routine Care for the Healthy Pregnant Woman*, NICE Clinical Guideline 6, NICE, London.

Panjabi M M (1992) The stabilizing system of the spine. Part 1. Function, dysfunction, adaptation and enhancement. *Journal of Spinal Disorders*, **5**(4), 383–9.

Persson J *et al.* (2000) Obstetric risk factors for stress urinary incontinence: a population-based study. *Obstetrics and Gynecology*, **96**(3), 440–5.

Roovers J P W R *et al.* (2000) Correspondence in reaction to: urinary incontinence after hysterectomy. *Lancet*, **356**, 2012.

Rortveit G *et al.* (2003) Urinary incontinence after vaginal delivery or caesarean section. *The New England Journal of Medicine*, **348**(10), 900–7.

Royal College of Obstetricians and Gynaecologists (2001) *Guideline No. 29: Management of Third- and Fourth-Degree Perineal Tears Following Vaginal Delivery*, RCOG, London.

Royal College of Obstetricians and Gynaecologists (2002) *Setting Standards to Improve Women's Health*, RCOG, London.

Royal College of Obstetricians and Gynaecologists (2004) *Guideline No. 23: Methods and Materials Used in Perineal Repair*, RCOG, London.

Sahrmann S A (1993) *Movement as a Cause of Musculoskeletal Pain.* In Proceedings of the 8th Biennial Conference of the Manipulative Physiotherapists Association of Australia, Perth.

Salvesen K A, Morkved S (2004) Randomised controlled trial of pelvic floor muscle training during pregnancy. *British Medical Journal*, **329**(7462), 378–80.

Samuelsson E *et al.* (2000) Anal sphincter tears: prospective study of obstetric risk factors. *British Journal of Obstetrics and Gynaecology*, **107**(7), 926–31.

Sapsford R (2004) Rehabilitation of pelvic floor muscles utilising trunk stabilisation. *Manual Therapy*, **9**(1), 3–12.

Sing D, Newburn M (Eds) (2000) *Access to Maternity Information and Support: The Experiences and Needs of Women Before or After Giving Birth*, National Childbirth Trust, London.

Sultan A H *et al.* (1993) Anal sphincter disruption during vaginal delivery. *The New England Journal of Medicine*, **329**(26), 1905–11.

USEFUL WEBSITES

The Association of Chartered Physiotherapists in Women's Health: www.acpwh.or.uk
The Association for Continence Advice (ACA): www.aca.uk.com
The British Lymphology Society (BLS): www.lymphoedema.org/bls/

8 The Menopause and Beyond: A Positive Approach

JOAN MEYEROWITZ and SARAH KORDULA

One hundred years ago the life expectancy for women was 52–54 years. As a result postmenopausal health and well-being was not an issue that needed to be addressed. Today British women can expect more than 30 years of post-menopausal life and, because more and more will live until the age of 100 years, the menopause is increasingly a mid-life event, with many women spending over a third of their lives postmenopause (Eurohealth 2005; Rees & Purdie 2002).

This chapter describes the menopause and its effects on the future lives of women. The importance of managing menopausal symptoms to prevent long-term health problems is also discussed. The last few years have been a difficult time for menopausal women, with results of trials and the interpretation of the results giving very mixed views. Many women are now looking at alternative treatments. Therefore specialist nurses have a vital role to play in providing up-to-date information about the menopause and the prevention of osteoporosis.

Challenges	Service developments
• Increasing numbers of postmenopausal women • Expectations around quality of life – 'eternal youth' • Conflicting messages and media scares about HRT • Improved knowledge about the causes, effects and treatment of osteoporosis • Importance of early detection of osteoporosis	• Designated menopause clinics • Nurse specialists – menopause and osteoporosis • Extended roles for nurses – hormone implants and bone density scanning • New services – bone densitometry and psychosexual counselling • Interdisciplinary and interdepartmental approach – cooperation with orthopaedics

Gynaecology: Changing Services for Changing Needs. Edited by Sue Jolley
© 2006 by John Wiley & Sons, Ltd

THE MENOPAUSE

The menopause is an inevitable, individual lifetime event in women and can occur naturally from 45 to 55 years, with the average age being 51 years. Menopause occurs with the final period and refers to the permanent cessation of menstruation, resulting from loss of ovarian follicular activity (Rees & Purdie 2002; World Health Organisation 1996). Natural menopause is recognised to have occurred after 12 months of amenorrhoea for which there is no other cause. The perimenopause, or climacteric, refers to the period preceding menopause from when clinical, biological and endocrinological features of the approaching menopause start and the 12-month period after the last bleed. The postmenopause is the phase dating from the final menstrual period.

The menopause is the result of ovarian failure due to the ovaries being depleted of follicles, or germ cells. At mid-gestation the ovaries contain several million germ cells. These decline rapidly until the menarche, when there are approximately 300000. During the reproductive years the number steadily declines until the mid/late forties when there are very few left. As a result there is a fall of oestrogen production and an increase in gonadotrophin levels. Gradually the ovary becomes less responsive to the gonadotrophins. This may be several years before the periods stop. Serum blood levels show an increase of follicle stimulating hormone (FSH) and luteinising hormone (LH), and a decrease in the oestradiol level. An FSH and LH above the levels of 30 p/mol are suggestive of ovarian failure (Rees & Purdie 2002).

The menopause is not affected by:

- number of pregnancies
- use or non-use of oral contraceptives
- age at menarche
- race
- socioeconomic factors.

However, women who smoke can expect to have a menopause 1–2 years earlier than average (Midgette & Baron 1990; Sharara et al. 1994).

PREMATURE MENOPAUSE

A menopause before the age of 45 years is classed as premature, with approximately 1 % of women experiencing ovarian failure before the age of 40 years (Banerd 2004; Betterhealth 2003). Primary, premature ovarian failure can occur at any age as either primary or secondary amenorrhoea. This can be caused by:

- chromosome abnormalities including Turner's syndrome, Down's syndrome and women suffering from fragile X permutations

- metabolic disorders such as galactosaemia
- autoimmune diseases such as Addison's disease, diabetes and hypothyroidism.

Women who experience premature ovarian failure are usually totally unprepared. Frequently it is of sudden onset when they are young and in what they expected to be their normal reproductive years. It can be devastating and very difficult to come to terms with, especially if the cause is unknown. This group of women have very different needs from older menopausal women. Their main fears and worries are usually associated with fertility, premature ageing and the need to take hormone replacement therapy (HRT) on a long-term basis. For these reasons they require extra support for emotional and psychological problems and for their physical needs.

This has prompted some gynaecology units to consider how support can best be provided. At the Queen's Medical Centre (QMC), Nottingham, the gynaecology team has initiated a Premature Menopause Clinic, which runs every 2–3 months, depending on need. A fertility expert is also available to offer advice. Specific patient literature is limited for this group of women but there is a charity support group, 'The Daisy Network', which provides excellent information.

Secondary premature ovarian failure happens when normal functioning ovaries are removed or damaged. This can be caused by surgery (bilateral oophorectomy with or without hysterectomy). In this group of women symptoms of ovarian failure occur very soon after surgery and are frequently very severe. Nowadays survival of childhood cancers and malignancies are on the increase but the treatment for these conditions can also lead to secondary ovarian failure. Ovarian damage from radiation treatment tends to be dependent upon the age at treatment and the dose used. Ovarian damage from chemotherapy treatments is related to the length of treatment time and the cumulative dose given.

Before secondary ovarian failure occurs, there is usually time to talk to the young women and advise them on future treatments and medications and the prevention of osteoporosis. Patient literature is very helpful. CDs and videos have been produced in the past for patients but the uptake is not as good as for printed literature.

The need for HRT in the premature menopause patient is advised and should be encouraged up to the age of 50 years in order to replace the hormones lost. At QMC the menopause nurse talks to patients well before their surgery to give them literature and information about the menopause and HRT. She also visits the gynaecology ward twice-weekly to see women following their surgery. All women are given a contact number but it may be necessary to see patients again for additional support should they require this. Time spent helping women who experience a premature menopause is usually of great benefit to them and a very worthwhile use of the menopause nurse's time.

Case study 8.1

As a teenager Judith was diagnosed with primary premature ovarian failure of unknown aetiology and commenced on the combined oral contraceptive pill and ethinyloestradiol in the pill-free week. She had no symptoms with this treatment and was advised to find information about premature menopause on the Internet.

When she started university in Nottingham, she registered with a new GP on campus. On a routine visit to the GP for a prescription renewal, the GP mentioned her early menopause. Judith dissolved into tears and became very distressed. The GP was concerned that she had not come to terms with the diagnosis and needed some guidance and help, so he contacted the menopause nurse at QMC to arrange a consultation.

Judith attended the Menopause Clinic a few weeks later. She was really enjoying her four-year university course but was still devastated by the diagnosis and had no idea what to do about it. After a long chat she was given some literature and the website address for The Daisy Network. Counselling was offered at QMC rather than the university, which she preferred as she would rather her friends did not know about her diagnosis. She had not discussed this with anyone other than her family. She felt well on her treatment, and no different from all her friends who were also on the pill, so her management was not changed in any way.

Time was devoted to talking about the here and now and the importance of being a normal student, enjoying herself and having boy friends. The question of fertility seemed years away for Judith, and hopefully there would be many changes and advances before becoming an issue for her. Her case was discussed with the consultant, who agreed that she had lots of information and support for the present. Counselling was arranged through the social work department with a counsellor who has a special interest in women's health and Judith was given an open appointment for 1 year and the nurse's contact details.

During the consultation Judith cried on four separate occasions and was clearly devastated to be diagnosed with premature ovarian failure. Clearly all the time and effort we can give to help support women in this position is very worthwhile.

SYMPTOMS OF THE MENOPAUSE

Symptoms of the menopause are a result of declining levels of oestrogen circulating in the bloodstream. Women experience these symptoms very differently, with no two women being exactly the same. There can be variations in both the length of time the symptoms last and also in the severity of individual symptoms, neither of which appear to be linked to blood oestrogen levels.

Some women experience symptoms while having regular periods and others after the last period.

The variation in time of onset, with or without symptoms, often results in confusion for women, who are unsure about what is happening to them and as a result seek advice from the practice nurse or menopause nurse at the hospital, rather than the general practitioner (GP). Between two and six women a week seek advice from the menopause nurse specialist at QMC. They have either referred themselves or are seen at the request of a practice nurse or other health professional. Women's knowledge and understanding of the menopause is very variable. It helps if women can be given basic literature about the menopause when they see the practice nurse for routine smear tests in their 40s. This helps prepare them for changes that will be taking place in the future.

The menopause causes very mixed feelings among women. The end of periods marks the end of fertility and any chance of pregnancy, which for women who have been unable to conceive can be a very distressing time. Equally for others the end to heavy, painful, prolonged periods and no further need for contraception can be a welcome relief. The menopause marks a lifetime change into the later phase of life, which can be equally positively or negatively received. Frequently women may be influenced by other major events at this time. These include general ill health; employment changes involving loss of job or redundancy, for either the woman or her partner; problems with adolescent offspring; 'empty nest' syndrome; separation or divorce; and ageing parents, making the menopause a difficult time for large numbers of women. A positive non-biased approach by health professionals offering advice and information about the menopause is helpful to many.

Symptoms can be categorised as short, intermediate or long term, as illustrated in Table 8.1, and for clarity will be discussed in this order.

SHORT-TERM SYMPTOMS

Short-term symptoms can present in the perimenopause or following the final period. Up to 80 % of women will experience symptoms at some time and of varying degrees of severity (Avis *et al.* 1993). The vasomotor symptoms are the most common and are experienced in approximately 75 % of women. Over 50 % will describe these as causing acute physical distress and up to 25 % say they last for 5 years or more (Avis *et al.* 1993). The exact cause of hot flushes during the day and sweats at night is unknown, but thought to be due to fluctuating FSH levels. The duration of a hot flush can be anything from 20 seconds long to 20 minutes, with either several an hour or as few as five or six per week. Night sweats can vary from waking up hot in the night to waking up with bed clothes and sheets wet through and needing to be changed. Over a period of time this can be very disruptive to both the woman and her partner. Clearly the severity and intensity of the flushes and sweats has a big effect on the man-

Table 8.1. Symptoms associated with the menopause

Short term	Vasomotor	■ Hot flushes/night sweats ■ Headaches ■ Giddiness ■ Insomnia ■ Faintness
	Psychological	■ Depression ■ Irritability/mood swings ■ Loss of confidence ■ Poor memory ■ Difficulty in concentrating ■ Panic attacks ■ Tiredness ■ Loss of libido
Intermediate	Vaginal	■ Dryness/burning ■ Pruritus ■ Dyspareunia ■ Prolapse
	Bladder	■ Urgency ■ Frequency ■ Dysuria ■ Urinary tract infections ■ Incontinence ■ Voiding difficulties
	Sexual	■ Desire ■ Arousal ■ Orgasm ■ Pain
Long term	Osteoporosis Cardiovascular disease Alzheimer's disease	

agement of the symptoms and whether women will seek advice and help or not. Not all women will seek medication for vasomotor symptoms, but advice to limit caffeine and alcohol intake, hot drinks, hot rooms/offices, smoking and hot spicy foods may help to limit the flushes and sweats.

Randomised controlled trials have produced good evidence to support the use of HRT for vasomotor symptoms. Relief from symptoms is usually within 4 weeks (MacLennan *et al.* 2001). When prescribing HRT, women who have a uterus should be prescribed oestrogen on a daily basis and progestogen either daily or for between 10 and 14 days of the month, in order to protect the endometrium. Women who have had a hysterectomy need only to be prescribed oestrogen. The lowest effective dose should be used for the shortest possible period, with treatment being reviewed every year. Short-term use should be considered as up to 5 years and is usually given to women in their early 50s for the relief of symptoms. If menopause symptoms return after stopping, women may wish to re-start their HRT and, provided they are fully informed of the risks, it should not be withheld (Royal College of Obstetricians and Gynaecologists 2004). The prescribing of HRT for women without symptoms is not recommended.

Up to 85 % of women will complain of some psychological symptoms at the time of the menopause (Barlow 2004). The belief that menopause and clinical depression are linked is complex and has yet to be totally proven. There is a higher incidence of depression in women than in men, especially between the ages of puberty and 55 years, and most studies have found that hormone levels are no different in depressed menopausal women as opposed to non-depressed menopausal women (Gebbie & Glasier 2004). HRT is not recommended and is not licensed as a primary treatment for clinically significant depression.

Depressed mood, mood swings, poor memory and concentration are all symptoms of the menopause. Whether these symptoms are definite menopause symptoms or as a consequence of the 'domino effect' remain unclear (Gebbie & Glasier 2004). Examples of the domino theory are:

1. Night sweats → insomnia → tiredness → irritability → poor concentration → poor memory
2. Dry vagina → dyspareunia → loss of libido

With the domino effect in mind, if HRT is taken for vasomotor symptom control, then there may be improvement in the psychological symptoms that were as a result of many nights of broken sleep and disturbances due to night sweats. It is also important to remember the other events, described earlier, that could influence sleep pattern and therefore tiredness, irritability and mood swings. Further research is required before it can be established whether or not HRT is of benefit for these psychological symptoms alone.

INTERMEDIATE SYMPTOMS OF THE MENOPAUSE

Symptoms of the lower urogenital tract usually present themselves up to 5–10 years after the menopause. Treatment for lower urogenital tract and vaginal symptoms respond well to oestrogen therapy. This can be given either systemically or topically via the vagina. Local oestrogen appears to be more effective than systemic HRT, but treatment is often required to be long term in order to reverse the symptoms of urogenital atrophy. Sexuality may be improved with oestrogen alone or may require the addition of testosterone (British Menopause Society 2004). Urinary symptoms such as urgency, urge incontinence, frequency and nocturia may be improved with vaginal oestrogen, but stress incontinence cannot be successfully treated with oestrogen alone.

Many women feel that the menopause is a time to address problems of a sexual nature, some of which have been present for several years, occasionally since young adulthood, and some of which have developed at the time of the menopause as a result of other symptoms (domino effect). There are regular referrals to menopause clinics for sexual problems, mostly lack of libido. Women may also present with menopause problems when the main underlying problem is sexual. At QMC a clinician who has completed the Diploma in Psychosexual Medicine works as part of the multidisciplinary team. Psychosexual counselling is offered and women start with a 1-hour appointment, followed by shorter follow-up sessions as required. The work has demonstrated that the menopause clinic appears to be a good environment for identifying women with psychosexual problems. These findings were presented by a poster, 'Great sex, no sweat', at the British Menopause Meeting in 2003 (Hobson *et al.* 2003).

LONG-TERM SYMPTOMS OF THE MENOPAUSE

Osteoporosis

'Osteoporosis is defined as a skeletal disorder characterised by compromised bone strength predisposing to an increased risk of fracture' (National Institute of Health 2000). Osteoporosis affects one in two women and one in five men over the age of 50, costing the government and National Health Service (NHS) £1.7 billion annually, which is equal to £5 million per day (National Osteoporosis Society 2005).

Osteoporosis is considered to be a disease associated mainly with postmenopausal women and equivalent-aged men. Osteoporotic-related fractures are associated with excess mortality, substantial morbidity and major health and social expenditure (Ross 1996). It is more common among white women than black, and 1 in 2 white women will sustain a fragility fracture in their lifetime (Ross *et al.* 1993). Many have described it as a 'silent epidemic' as there are generally no associated symptoms or warning signs until it is too late and a low trauma fracture has occurred. It can be associated with height loss or back pain, but so can other conditions (Gunter *et al.* 2003). The most common fractures occurring are the wrist, hip and vertebrae. Hip fractures in particular are related to excessive mortality. Postmenopausal women who have already sustained a distal radius fracture have nearly twice the risk of a hip fracture (Freedman *et al.* 2000), and it is predicted that the number of hip fractures occurring worldwide will rise dramatically over the next 50 years due to the increasing age of the population (Compston & Rosen 2004).

A decision to treat patients or initiate preventative options must be based on an individual assessment of risk for that person. Three of the most useful are bone mineral density (BMD), a personal history of fracture and age. However, occurrence of fractures is multifactorial, including the propensity

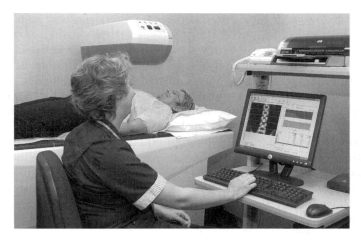

Figure 8.1. DXA Machine, used to measure bone mineral density

to fall and chance (Department of Health 2001; Royal College of Physicians 2000).

Since 1987 when dual X-ray absorptiometry (DXA) was first introduced, it has become widely recognised as the 'gold standard' for the evaluation of BMD (Blake *et al.* 1999; Genant *et al.* 1996, Grampp *et al.* 1997). The machines (see Figure 8.1) were designed to measure hip and spine BMD, which are the main fracture sites, although they can also measure practically any site of interest, including the total body. They are precise in their measurement, have low radiation exposure, highly reproducible measurements and short scanning times. Provided that the manufacturer's instructions on quality assurance and control scans are carefully followed, they are also used to monitor long-term changes to BMD, assessing the rate of response and effectiveness of treatment (Eastell 1998).

There are other methods used to measure bone mineral density including single-energy X-ray absorptiometry, which measures forearm and calcaneus; quantative computed tomography, which can be used to measure spine, femur and radius; and quantatative ultrasound, which measures calcaneus, forearm and patella but does not measure bone density directly.

In 1994 the World Health Organisation (WHO) task group published a format expressing measurements of BMD as a T score, calculated by taking the difference between an individual's BMD and the mean value for a normal young adult female (World Health Organisation 1994):

- T score above −1 would be considered in the normal range.
- T score between −1 and −2.5 represents osteopenia.
- T score below −2.5 represents osteoporosis, and a greatly increased risk of fracture.

- T score below −2.5 plus one or more fragility fractures is established osteoporosis.

Clinicians have used T scores as a basis from which treatment options are taken but the original intention was to provide a definition for epidemiological studies rather than a guide to treatment. Osteopenia and osteoporosis can be present at more than one site where other areas are in the normal range. The clinical significance of osteopenia is less well defined.

It is helpful to understand the pathophysiology of postmenopausal osteoporosis. Bone is a highly specialised tissue consisting of an extracellular matrix where mineral is deposited. Instead of replacing our skeletons every few years, vertebrates rely on three types of bone cells: osteoclasts, osteoblasts and osteocytes, which can detect damage, dissolve this damaged bone and replace it. In adulthood the process of each cycle is balanced and lasts between 90 and 130 days and is called 'remodelling'.

There are two types of bone: cortical bone makes up 80 % of the skeleton and is found in the long bones and outer surfaces of flat bones and trabecular bone is found mainly at the ends of the long bones and inner parts of flat bones. Cortical bone is arranged in concentric circles around the Haversian systems that contain blood, lymph nerve and connective tissue. Trabecular bone is made up of interconnecting plates making a honeycomb effect.

One of the major predisposing factors for osteoporotic fractures is low bone mineral density or bone mass. Bone mass is affected by peak bone mass and the degree of subsequent bone loss. Formation of bone is prominent at 12–15 years, reaching a peak by 20–30. Several factors regulate optimum peak, and one of the most important are genetic determinants. Others include dietary intake of calcium, physical activity, hormonal status, general nutrition and medications. This is illustrated in Figure 8.2.

Persistent bone loss is a feature of osteoporosis, and impaired acquisition of peak bone mass can cause as much as 80 % variance of bone mass at any age; hormonal and environmental factors remain strong determinants for rate of loss after the age of 40. Osteoporosis is the result of an increase in the remodelling cycles and/or an imbalance occurring within the remodelling unit, resulting in an overall loss of bone (see Figure 8.3). The risk factors for osteoporosis, listed in Table 8.2, are well known.

During the menopause oestrogen deficiency increases the rate of absorption of bone and, although bone formation is accelerated in an attempt to match loss, the time required for the process results in a net loss of bone (Bland 2000). There is an accelerated period of loss for 6–10 years, which then slows but continues. There is some evidence that density in women can begin to decrease even in the perimenopausal phase of life (Riggs et al. 1996). The rate of loss can be as little as 1 % or more than 5 % per year. The rate is faster in trabecular bone of the spine (Recker et al. 2000).

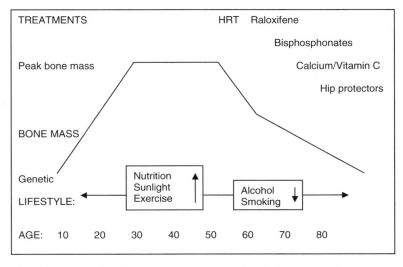

Figure 8.2. The rise and fall of bone mass: regulating factors and relevant treatments

There is also an age-associated loss resulting from calcium and vitamin D deficiency. Older people eat less foods containing calcium, but also ageing causes reduced production of vitamin D, so less calcium is absorbed. This leads to increased secretion of the parathyroid hormone (PTH) enhancing bone resorption as the body struggles to maintain calcium in the system by stripping calcium from its resident source, the skeleton. Vitamin D is also associated with muscle weakness, which in turn increases the likelihood of falls (Holick 1998).

Physical activity can be a marker for general health, and there are some studies suggesting a relationship which is U-shaped, where there is an increase risk in falls either by the frail or sedentary and the very active, with a decrease in risk of falls among those engaging in moderate physical activity.

There are both non-pharmacological and pharmacological treatment options for osteoporosis. Exercise regimes that include resistance stresses and load bearing can provide minor gains in skeletal mass but major gains in mobility, body strength and balance, and could even reduce some pain and increase self-confidence. There has been some evidence that balance and muscle strengthening exercises such as those found in T'ai Chi can reduce the risk of falls (Tinetti 1994). Hip protectors are basically stretchy, cotton-rich pants that have a shell of polypropylene fitted into the pants on either side over the hip area. The shield is thought to disperse the impact of a fall from the hip to the surrounding soft tissue. Initial studies appeared to show some benefit with a reduction in the number of hip fractures (Lauritzen *et al.* 1993).

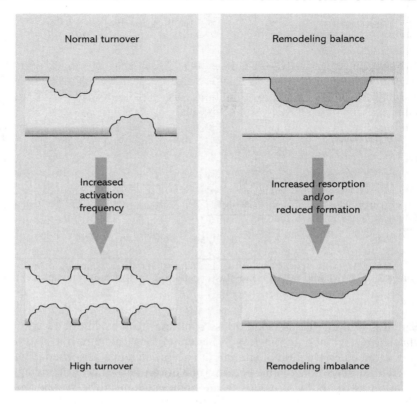

Figure 8.3. Comparison of turnover and remodelling of bone. Reproduced with the permission of Health Press Limited from J. E. Compston and C. J. Rosen, *Fast Facts – Osteoporosis,* 4th edition, Health Press, Oxford, 2004

Table 8.2. Risk factors for osteoporosis

Maternal history of hip fracture (Soroko *et al.* 1994)
Hypogonadism (primary or secondary)
Premature menopause (before 45)
Prolonged secondary amenorrhoea
Secondary causes such as glucocorticoid therapy, hyperthyroidism, anticonvulsant
    therapy, myeloma, skeletal metastasis (Caplan *et al.* 1994)
Previous fracture (Klotzbuecher *et al.* 2000)
Low body mass index (Cummings *et al.* 1995)
Smoking (Law & Hacksaw 1997)
Excessive alcohol (Hernandez-Avila *et al.* 1991)
Low dietary calcium intake (COMA 1998)
Vitamin D deficiency (COMA 1998)
Physical inactivity (Cummings *et al.* 1995)

Subsequently, more recent studies have found no measurable benefit and showed problems with compliance as a consequence of poor comfort and fit (Parker *et al.* 2004).

Vertebroplasty is a developing procedure, which involves injection of bone cement into cervical, thoracic or lumbar vertebrae. It is extremely effective for the relief of pain from fracture that has not responded to the usual treatments and appears to provide permanent relief in 80–90% of appropriately selected patients (Pfeifer *et al.* 2004). There can be significant complications with this procedure, with cement leakage and damage to the spinal cord.

There is a range of pharmacological treatments available and these are summarised in Table 8.3. In 2005 the National Institute for Clinical Excellence (NICE) published a technology appraisal of treatments for women with osteoporosis in order to address who should be targeted and to reduce the number of fractures in postmenopausal women. This work on secondary prevention relates to how treatments should be used to prevent further fractures in postmenopausal women who have already broken a bone. Bisphosphonates are recommended for women who have had a fracture:

- if they are over 75 years, without the need for a DXA bone density scan
- if they are 65–75 years, as long as osteoporosis is confirmed on a DXA scan
- if they are younger than 65 years and have a very low bone mineral density (BMD) or a low BMD plus one or more risk factors.

HRT has been relegated to second-line therapy for osteoporosis because it is only considered to be effective for a short time while being taken. However, new research is suggesting that HRT given for 2 or 3 years in the early postmenopausal period does indeed provide long-term benefits in terms of bone loss and osteoporotic fractures (Bagger *et al.* 2004). Osteoporosis treatments need to be taken for a number of years, and patients can move through the spectrum of options as they get older and their needs change (see Figure 8.2), but compliance is essential and they need support and encouragement from family and professionals associated with their care to continue protecting their bones from fracture by all means necessary.

It is vital to monitor treatment, which involves identifying non-responders and investigating and improving adherence to treatment if possible. Non-responders could be as a result of secondary causes like malabsorption, secondary to coeliac disease, conditions like thyrotoxicosis or simply taking the medication at the wrong time or with food. Repeat DXA scans help in monitoring treatment. Most areas rescan 18 months to 2 years after baseline/starting treatment, as it can take up to this length of time to have more than the least significant change. The lumbar spine region is the best site as it has the greatest response and the best precision, but of course is a region where there can be degenerative change in patients, particularly over the age of 60. In some places bone turnover markers are used. These tend to be only available at

Table 8.3. Pharmacological treatments for osteoporosis

Treatment	Action	Effectiveness	Disadvantages
Bisphosphonates Etidronate (cyclical) Alendronate (daily or once weekly) Risedronate (daily or once weekly)	Powerful preparations that inhibit bone resorption by affecting osteoclastic activity	All can reduce incidence of further vertebral fracture by 40–60 % and can improve bone density. Alendronate and risedronate can increase bone density of hip by 2.8–5.9 % (Harris *et al.* 1999; Watts *et al.* 1990)	Poorly absorbed so timing of medication is critical. This can affect compliance. Can cause gastrointestinal disturbances
Raloxifene	Selective oestrogen receptor modulator. Interacts with oestrogen receptors with both agonist and antagonist responses	Licensed for treatment and prevention of vertebral osteoarthritis in postmenopausal women (Ettinger *et al.* 1999)	Gives some women hot flushes and leg cramps. Slight increase in risk of thromboembolism
HRT	Replaces oestrogen	Treats established disease and reduces risk of hip and vertebral fracture (Women's Health Initiative Study 2002)	Continuous and lifelong use required to be totally effective (Royal College of Physicians 2002). Concern over possible risks of breast cancer, heart attack and stroke (Women's Health Initiative Study 2002)
Calcitonin	Natural thyroid hormone that helps regulate the level of calcium in the blood	Can reduce vertebral fractures by up to 30 %. Has an analgesic effect, helpful in the acute phase	Localised irritation and flu-like symptoms. Sometimes associated with hot flushes
Calcium and vitamin D	Supplements may decrease parathyroid hormone and increase bone density (Chapuy *et al.* 1992)	Beneficial to frail elderly who are at risk of vitamin D deficiency (Beaufrere *et al.* 2000)	Conflicting evidence. New studies found no benefits (Grant *et al.* 2005; Porthouse *et al.* 2005)
PTH	Anabolic effect on bone turnover	Improves bone volume and strength. Enhances trabecular structure	High cost, but NICE says should be available for those needing it
Strontium ranelate	New class of drugs with dual action: stimulating bone formation and decreasing bone resorption	Reduces fractures by 41 % in spine and 36 % in hips of women over 74 years after 3 years of treatment (Meunier *et al.* 2004)	Mild transient side effects such as nausea and diarrhoea

specialist centres, but they are able to measure response to treatment much sooner than DXA.

Cardiovascular disease

Cardiovascular disease rarely affects women before the menopause yet it is the commonest cause of death in postmenopausal women, with oestrogen deficiency being strongly implicated in the disease (Rymer et al. 2003). Early observational studies have shown that postmenopausal oestrogen reduces the incidence of cardiovascular disease by approximately 40 % but that the addition of progestogen, which is needed to give protection to the endometrium for women who still have a uterus, may reduce that benefit (Grodstein and Stampfer 1995).

The Women's Health Initiative Study (2002) and the Heart and Estrogen/ Progestin Replacement Study (1998) found a small but significant increase in cardiovascular events. To date the recommendation from the British Menopause Society (BMS) (2004) states that the role of HRT either in primary or secondary prevention remains uncertain and currently HRT should not be used primarily for the prevention of cardiovascular disease.

Alzheimer's disease

Alzheimer's disease (AD) is the most common form of dementia, with a higher incidence in women than men. The number of sufferers increases with age and due to the general population now living longer it has become a major health issue worldwide. The role of oestrogen has been demonstrated to have an effect on different brain regions, other than reproduction or gonadal regulation. It has been shown to impact on the development, maturation and function of brain regions involved in cognition (Norbury et al. 2004).

Studies have shown that oestrogen may delay or reduce the risk of AD but will not significantly improve established disease (Kesslak 2002). The Women's Health Initiative Study (2002) found a two-fold increase in dementia in women over 75 years taking HRT. Clearly there are conflicting reports and to date it is unclear if there is a specific age, or a duration of exposure to oestrogen, necessary in order to prevent AD. The BMS recommends that HRT should not currently be prescribed for the use of AD prevention (British Menopause Society 2004).

MANAGEMENT OF THE PATIENT IN THE MENOPAUSE CLINIC

Women will seek help and advice at the time of the menopause, and a major part of the menopause nurse's role is helping women understand the different treatments that are available. Accurate and unbiased advice and literature is essential and is usually very well received. It is important to recognise that the lack of, or severity of, symptoms will seriously affect choice of treatment. Even women who experience few symptoms should receive health information and literature in order to be fully informed. The quality of information about the menopause can vary greatly and is available from the usual sources, including the media, magazines, books, telephone help lines and the Internet. Women who want to carry out their own search should be given some of the more reputable Internet sites and associations (listed at the end of the chapter).

The menopause nurse should be able to take a detailed history from her patient, gathering information about previous illnesses, operations, family and personal history of breast cancer and other cancers, and venous thromboembolism (VTE), as well as presenting problems associated with the menopause and details of any treatments tried, both HRT and alternatives. After gathering information it needs to be clearly documented. A specially designed menopause history sheet is helpful. This enables information to be both clearly documented and recalled when necessary. A history sheet should include: weight and BMI, smoking and alcohol intake, diet and exercise and a brief sexual history. Following this, treatment and advice should be personalised to the woman, with the risks and benefits explained and documented, and any relevant leaflets or literature to support the choice given to her. Clinic consultations should not be rushed as there is a large amount of information to share, and it is often necessary to have more than one appointment. This also allows the woman time to think and be involved in deciding whether or not to accept treatment with HRT or alternatives.

The menopause nurse should be familiar with the different types of HRT available, the different delivery methods and information about alternative treatments for different menopause symptoms. The most up-to-date information about the different types of HRT is in the *Monthly Index of Medical Specialities* (MIMS), which is updated each month. An enlarged photocopy of the page with all the products listed is a very valuable tool when discussing this with the patient. This is usually sufficient information when selecting a product. It is also important to understand the different oestrogens and progestogens in HRT preparations, their actions and side effects, which are usually short lasting, being most severe in the first 2 months, less in the next 2 months and settled thereafter. The patient also needs information on possible side effects because many prescriptions have been stopped due to side effects and the lack of support when first starting a new preparation. A realistic expectation from the chosen product is also very important.

To date there are six different delivery methods of HRT. These are tablets, patches, gels, implants, vaginal rings and nasal spray. The hormonal intrauterine system (IUS) has recently been licensed for use as the progestogen component in HRT. It is important that the menopause nurse is familiar with the types of HRT, those that are available for peri- and postmenopausal women and the preparations for women who have had a hysterectomy. It is useful to have samples of the different HRT products to show women, especially with patches and gels, as it helps them make a choice. Choice is important as 'the one they choose is usually the one they use'. Most women will have a preference out of the six options, but not all of them may be suitable and often the choice is between only two or three methods of delivery. However, there is a huge choice of HRT preparations available (58 in MIMS 4/2005), so with patience and tolerance it should be possible to help most women find a product to suit them.

The menopause nurse should explain the delivery methods and how the hormones are absorbed and work. Advice about the application and use of patches, gel and nasal spray is vitally important. If the product is not applied correctly, in the correct place and worn for the correct length of time, then the efficacy of the product will be compromised. Most preparations have literature available and it is helpful if this can be given when prescribing new methods of delivery/preparations. When evaluating the use of the product, compliance should always be checked. Follow-up and support are very important, so a follow-up appointment with the menopause nurse and a contact number are helpful.

HRT IMPLANTS AND A NURSE-LED SERVICE

Estradiol implants are crystalline pellets of estradiol, which are inserted into the adipose tissue of the buttock or abdomen and release estradiol slowly over several months. This is a minor procedure using local anaesthetic and can be prescribed for women after hysterectomy. Implants have been available for over 20 years but now, with many other different products available for the posthysterectomised women, implants have become less popular as a first choice. There are, however, many women who are very happy with this method of delivery and feel it is unnecessary to change to another product.

At the QMC there are approximately 200 women who attend either 6-monthly or annually for their implants. In the past (before 1999) the junior doctors provided this service in the Gynaecology Out Patient Department on a rotational basis. Owing to doctors frequently changing jobs, the patients saw different doctors every visit, with little continuity, ownership of the patient group or ongoing support. Following a review of services the clinic became nurse-led, with the completion of a Scope of Professional Practice package approved by the Trust.

The underlying reason for change has to be to improve the provision of service to the patient. A named person performs the insertion of implants and coordinates the implant service. Patients are provided with a contact phone number for any worries or problems and can use this same number for blood results prior to re-implantation. Patients telephone for their oestradiol/testosterone levels before an appointment is made for re-implantation. This reduces the number of wasted appointments. Blood level tests for oestradiol/testosterone levels are very important for the management of the patient. A level of <1000 p/mol for oestradiol and <1.8 p/mol for testosterone is used at the QMC, although many units use lower levels than this. Levels chosen are the consultant's choice and the BMS offer guidance on this (Rees & Purdie 2002).

Six clinics are held per month, with patients attending for blood tests when they feel their symptoms have returned, telephoning for the results within 7 days and receiving an appointment for implantation usually within 2 weeks. Weight and blood pressure are checked at each visit. The patient is able to build up a relationship with the nurse, making it easier to talk about problems and worries. Advice is available following trial results such as the Women's Health Initiative Study (2002) and the Million Women Study (2003) and encouragement given to comply with the breast screening programme.

Audit of this clinic at 3 years showed an efficient service, with satisfied patients in over 95 % of those asked. Women felt they were well informed and were satisfied with the efficiency of the service. Many of the women who attend this clinic had a hysterectomy at a young age, some in their 20s, have been attending for 20 years or more and are still under 50 years. These women do not attend their GP for smear tests and are often overlooked as a group in the practice. The implant clinic therefore helps provide them with up-to-date health information and advice and they have a named person and contact number to use. This is a very satisfying role for menopause nurses. Not all women want to change to new, different preparations, especially if they are happy with implants and the service by which they receive the implant works well. Many hospitals do not offer implants as a form of HRT but, when given a choice, many women will choose this method, especially if other preparations have failed. Implants are still a good method of HRT and a large number of women are very satisfied with them, so an efficient, nurse-led service is beneficial to these women.

MEDIA EFFECT ON HRT PRESCRIBING

Following recent trial results from the Women's Health Initiative Study (WHIS) (2002) and the Million Women Study (MWS) (2003), there has been widespread confusion, both for women already taking HRT or about to consider it and for health professionals who prescribe HRT both in hospitals and general practice. Subsequent media coverage was misjudged and ill-informed (Cubie 2004), with the press publishing the results in a sensational rather than an educational way, which left many women totally confused and very worried.

As a result many stopped their HRT immediately and others went to their GPs, who advised them to discontinue their HRT, despite the preparations used in the WHIS only being available in the USA. There is at present no right or wrong way to stop HRT that has been proven by controlled trials, but many menopause nurses and doctors would advise stopping slowly over a period of several weeks or months. Two years after the publication of the WHIS and MWS results, the menopause nurse at QMC carried out a survey on the effect of this on the attitudes of GPs in Nottinghamshire and their prescribing habits. The results showed that 'the WHI and MWS have had a profound effect on the attitudes and prescribing habits of the GPs in Nottinghamshire. Only half of the GPs had actually read the studies, leaving us to surmise that the other half gained their information from the media and press' (Meyerowitz *et al.* 2004).

Three years on from the WHIS many women are now returning to their GP or being referred to menopause clinics to ask for HRT again. They have tried without and many have tried alternative medicines, but prefer HRT. Slowly the trial results are being unravelled and the flaws of these are being shown, very much less publicly (Naftolin *et al.* 2004). There are consensus statements issued by the BMS (2004) and RCOG (2004) available as a guide to medical professionals working in the area of menopause. Many areas, including Nottingham, issued a consensus from the members of the menopause team to all the GPs in the area as a resource at this time of confusion. However, there has been an increase in GP referrals resulting from the recent trial publications and the confusion it has caused to both the patient and the doctor.

RISK FACTORS TO CONSIDER WITH HRT

As with all medications, there are some risks associated with taking HRT and alternatives to HRT. The menopause nurse must be aware of this and have information available for the patient. It is a very important part of the advice that should be available to women and should not be overlooked or rushed.

Without doubt breast cancer appears to be the biggest risk factor when taking HRT, in the eyes of the woman, the health professionals and experts in the field of menopause. It is an exception in a consultation for the woman not to be concerned about this fact and to ask how this will affect her. In 1997 trial results showed an increase in breast cancer cases in women who used HRT for more than 5 years (Collaborative Group on Hormonal Factors in Breast Cancer 1997), and the WHIS and MWS have added to this theory. It is important that the menopause nurse is fully aware of current research and data on the issue of breast cancer, that she can personalise information to the individual and inform her of the facts that are available to date. Information from the BMS consensus statement in March 2004 has reported that 'the life time risk of developing breast cancer is significantly increased with current long-term use when started in the 50+ age group. Such an effect is not seen in women who start their HRT early for a premature menopause, indicating that it is the duration of lifetime oestrogen exposure that is important' (British Menopause Society 2004). There is a greater risk for women using a combined oestrogen and progestogen preparation than oestrogen alone or tibolone. Studies have also shown that after 5 years of discontinuation of HRT, the risk returns to that of never users. When HRT is taken short term for symptom control, often for 5 years or less, from the age of 50, there is no increased risk of breast cancer.

Current figures for breast cancer cases per 1000 women in the 50–65 years of age group are:

- estimated cases of breast cancer per 1000 women not on HRT = 32 cases
- estimated cases of breast cancer per 1000 women using oestrogen-only HRT for 5 years = 33/34 cases
- estimated cases of breast cancer per 1000 women using oestrogen + progestogen HRT for 5 years = 38 cases
- estimated number of breast cancer cases per 1000 women using tibolone for 5 years = 33/34 cases.

(Beral 2003)

Unopposed oestrogen therapy in the non-hysterectomised woman is associated with a significantly increased risk of endometrial hyperplasia and, with continued use, endometrial cancer. The use of unopposed HRT should be limited to the posthysterectomised woman. The addition of progestogen for a minimum of 10 days in the cycle, as in sequential HRT, reduces this risk, but studies have shown that the risk is not totally eliminated if treatment lasts longer than 5 years (Weiderpass et al. 1999). There is no increased risk of endometrial cancer with the continuous combined group of HRT, and women should be encouraged to change to one of these preparations after 5 years of sequential HRT use.

All women who start HRT should be counselled about the risk of venous thromboembolism (VTE), and prior to starting, a detailed history is important to eliminate additional risks. The history should be extended to include details of family history of VTE in a first- or second-degree relative. HRT increases the risk of VTE, with the greatest risk being in the first year of use. The baseline risk of VTE in menopausal women is in the order of 1 in 10 000 per year. Advancing age and obesity are also important factors and increase the risk significantly (British Menopause Society 2004). It is recommended that women who develop a VTE while on HRT should discontinue it unless long-term anti-coagulant therapy is commenced. Non-oral oestrogen therapy is associated with a lower risk than oral oestrogen therapy (Royal College of Obstetricians and Gynaecologists 2004).

ALTERNATIVE TREATMENTS AT THE TIME
OF THE MENOPAUSE

Women have looked for alternative treatments for symptom control at the time of the menopause for many years, but recent highly publicised findings from the WHIS and MWS have further increased the demand for health professionals to provide women with safe and reliable alternative treatments. In the 45- to 60-year age group 80 % of women have used over-the-counter preparations for the relief of menopausal symptoms (Albertazzi 2003). Many women perceive alternative treatments to be safer than HRT and, as they can be purchased over the counter rather than by prescription, they are not harmful, and frequently as a result they do not inform their GP when taking these additional medicines. Alternative treatments include vitamins and minerals, herbal medicines, traditional Chinese medicines, homeopathy, chiropractic, reflexology, massage and acupuncture.

HRT has the potential to reverse symptoms of the menopause in a single preparation but it may be necessary to take several different alternative medicines to control symptoms. Finding a suitable treatment or preparation can be both expensive and time consuming; women should be encouraged to use reputable products from reliable shops and always to inform their GP what they are taking. Finding a reliable practitioner for chiropractic, reflexology or massage with appropriate experience and knowledge of the menopause and its symptoms can be very difficult, and there is little evidence to support the effectiveness of the treatments. However, studies have demonstrated a reduction in vasomotor symptoms using acupuncture (Dong et al. 2001; Tukmachi 2000).

Many of the different complementary medicines available have not been submitted to clinical trials. Of those that have, the results are mixed. Much more research is required with randomised/placebo-controlled trials. The health professional should be honest with the woman and inform her that to date HRT has the most data to support its use for symptom control (Ernst 2004). No complementary therapy has been shown to rival the efficacy of HRT to control menopause vasomotor symptoms.

In the area of dietary supplements, there are three products for which trials have demonstrated beneficial effects on hot flushes: black cohosh, soy products and red clover. Black cohosh is an indigenous plant from North America and has been used for gynaecological conditions by the Native Americans since before the arrival of European settlers (Albertazzi 2003). In 1989 the German government approved the use of black cohosh for climacteric ailments. Four randomised controlled trials have shown good evidence to support the efficacy of black cohosh, which displays oestrogen effects (Ernst 2004). Soy extracts are rich in phytoestrogens, which are plant derivatives with weak oestrogenic properties. They are found in legumes, wholegrain products, fruit and vegetables. The most common source ingested is from soy protein and another source is red clover. Several randomised controlled trials have tested the effect of supplementing the diet with phytoestrogens and have shown a moderate reduction in the number of hot flushes daily. Eleven randomised controlled trials have shown red clover to produce a small reduction in the frequency of hot flushes.

Sadly many of the trial results show a mixed picture, with little compelling evidence to support the use of these three products, the effects of which are mild at best. To date, however, they appear to be the most commonly used over-the-counter preparations for menopausal symptoms, which are mainly vasomotor symptoms. There is a need for more research and regulatory attention as food supplements are a fast-growing industry. The menopause nurse needs to be aware of all these facts and have a reasonable knowledge and understanding of the different types of complementary medicines available. In the past consultations were mainly to advise HRT for treatment of symptoms but today there are more women who are interested in alternatives. Nurses are registered with the Nursing and Midwifery Council (NMC), and should not recommend named, specific, alternative medicines which are not in the British National Formulary (BNF).

Advice should also be given about weight and control of obesity, if applicable, and diet, including calcium intake for long-term bone health and exercise, both for general cardiovascular and bone health. Advice and encouragement should be given to women to stop smoking as this has been shown to have antioestrogenic effects (Baron *et al.* 1990).

MANAGEMENT OF THE PATIENT IN THE OSTEOPOROSIS CLINIC

In the last 10 years there has been an increase in the number of nurses operating bone scanning services both in primary and secondary care. This has resulted from service development, extension of nursing roles and as part of a drive towards more collaboration across traditional boundaries between specialities and providers of care (National Osteoporosis Society 2002). Ten years ago there was no specific training for operating equipment like the DXA scanners and nurses needed to sort out their own training from relevant experts. Gradually appropriate training has developed, including the Foundation Course of Bone Densitometry and the National Osteoporosis (NOS) Training Course on Radiation Protection in Bone Densitometry. The Ionising Radiation (Medical Exposure) Regulations (IR(ME)R) lay down a legal requirement that practitioners and operators involved in bone densitometry have a basic knowledge of the hazards of radiation, the statutory requirements governing its use and the principles of radiation protection. In addition physiotherapists, radiographers and nurses are now able to complete a Postgraduate

Certificate in Osteoporosis and Falls Management, with the possibility of extending it to Master's level. This is an important qualification to have when working in the field.

At the Tenth National Osteoporosis Conference held in Harrogate the Bone Density Forum of the NOS displayed the results of a study surveying the provision of bone densitometry in the UK. It found that lack of funding for the provision of DXA is a significant obstacle to the implementation of the integrated falls and osteoporosis services. Recently the government has announced a £3 million initial funding with a further £17 million in the next 3 years to Primary Care to invest in the provision of bone densitometry services. This must be due to persistent lobbying of government by the NOS and they can only be commended for their efforts.

The QMC is fortunate to have a number of scanners with one based in the Women's Centre, Department of Gynaecology, which is believed to be the only scanner in the UK based in this setting. It allows in-house provision of DXA scans for women attending many different gynaecology services including oncology, fertility, menopause and family planning. Unfortunately, owing to financial and staffing issues, the equipment is only operated 2 days a week and currently scans up to 25 patients during this time, but this is a great progression as initially it was only 2 half days and six patients. In the osteoporosis clinic, nurses who are also trained in many aspects of women's health are able to answer many questions in a safe, private environment. With the support of other skilled practitioners a multidisciplinary service is provided.

The clinic accepts NHS referrals from GPs and other specialist areas such as neurology. Often these are women suffering from multiple sclerosis who have an increased risk of osteoporosis due to treatment with high doses of steroids and are also more likely to fall. The gynaecology nurse specialist for osteoporosis has also developed very close links in the last 3 years with the trauma and orthopaedic osteoporosis nurse specialist operating the Fracture Liaison Service within the hospital. Joint Bone/Menopause Clinics are also run in association with a consultant physician specialising in osteoporosis.

In 2000 an Open Access Service for women was commenced at QMC. The service started because women were becoming more aware of osteoporosis, mainly through the media, and wanted to know if they were at risk. After completion of a comprehensive questionnaire women are sent an appointment for a DXA scan if appropriate (in accordance with IR(ME)R 2000). There is a small charge for this service. This is because there is not enough funding to expand this service and women attending the Open Access Service would not fulfil the criteria for an NHS scan. Once the service was established, an audit demonstrated that 3 % of women who attended were found to have osteoporosis and 42 % had osteopenia (Kordula *et al.* 2003). This demonstrated the value of the service. In addition all of the women were receiving useful health advice.

Waiting times, currently 5–6 weeks, are closely monitored. In 2002 and 2003 as a result of the WHI and the MWS the requests for questionnaires increased

Table 8.4. Assessment form used in the Osteoporosis Clinic

Assessment for Bone Densitometry	
Name:	Date of Birth:
Indication:	Referral: NHS or OPEN ACCESS
Operator:	
GYNAECOLOGY HISTORY	**FAMILY HISTORY**
Menarche:	Episodes of amenorrhoea:
Contraception:	Gravida ...... Para ......
Premenopausal/Perimenopausal/Postmenopausal	
Age of menopause (if applicable):	
Hysterectomy/BSO/RSO/LSO	
MEDICAL HISTORY	
Illnesses:	Operations:
Fractures:	Any periods of bedrest:
Medication: Past	
Present	
DIET	
Eating disorders/allergies/malabsorption	
How often per week you consume – Milk: ...... Cheese: ...... Yoghurt:	
Assessment of calcium/vitamin D intake:	
LIFESTYLE	
Smoking:	Alcohol intake:
Exercise:	

(Kordula *et al.* 2004). As clinics are nurse-led, they are can be adjusted according to need. There are plans to increase the availability but this is dependent on how the local strategic planning of services unfolds.

All women attending the osteoporosis clinic have a DXA scan of the lumbar spine and hip and an assessment of risk using a questionnaire (Table 8.4). Results are analysed and then discussed in a language that the clients are able to understand. If necessary, information is given relating to treatment options, using written information provided by the NOS. Copies of the results are given to the client and a copy is usually sent to the GP.

A case study of a client attending the Open Access Service demonstrates the value of providing an individual risk assessment.

Case study 8.2

Linda, a 58-year-old woman, completed an Open Access questionnaire stating, 'I am concerned about my bones and my future after seeing how my Mum has suffered.' There was a family history of her mother having vertebral fractures with associated height loss, pain and mobility impact.

Her personal history revealed:

- menopause at 50
- no known personal history of fracture
- no use of steroid
- never taken HRT
- daily calcium intake approximately 700 mg
- exercise once weekly, but active lifestyle
- non-smoker, 2 units of alcohol weekly.

On the basis of her family history a scan was appropriate. Results of densitometry showed normal range in the left neck of the femur and −1.9 in the lumbar spine (L2–L4), which is moderately osteopenic.

These results show that there is an increased risk of fracture, although it is not high at present. Dietary advice was given and the importance of exercise discussed. If she were to sustain a low trauma fracture, treatment options could be reviewed, with a possible re-scan to assess change from the baseline.

Osteoporosis and its associated fractures will become more of a problem as the population ages, continuing to cause disability, pain and death. Changes are needed nationally and globally to try to prevent and treat patients with this disease. Collaboration on a much larger scale, between primary and secondary care, is needed. Nurses with a sound knowledge base and recognised qualifications should play a major role in a multidisciplinary approach to make the prevention of osteoporosis a subject on a par with cardiovascular disease.

CONCLUSION

There have been many changes in the field of menopause and its management over the last 10 years. Recent research trials have led to confusion for both women and health professionals, and accurate advice is vital. Women need, and should be able to access, professional advice that will enable them to make a decision about treatments and their long-term health. Nurses who work in this area are asked for advice and guidance on treatments available in an ever-changing situation. Unfortunately, there is no recognised training for nurses working in this area. Therefore it is essential that they keep abreast of new developments and join appropriate professional bodies.

Any nurse working in the area of menopause would benefit from becoming a member of the British Menopause Society (BMS). The aim of the BMS is to increase awareness about the menopause and the consequences for both immediate and long-term health. To achieve this aim it publishes a quarterly journal, disseminates information and has an annual scientific meeting. Similarly the NOS offers invaluable support to professionals involved in preventing and treating this condition. There is also a Royal College of Nursing Menopause Group for nurses working in this field.

Supporting women through the menopause offers challenging and rewarding work for nurses, who have to continually adapt to the changing needs of women and new approaches to treatment. It is a field that will continue to expand as demand increases.

REFERENCES

Albertazzi P (2003) Alternative medicines and the menopause: do they work? *British Journal of Sexual Medicine*, **27**(4), 12–16.

Avis N E *et al.* (1993) The evolution of menopausal symptoms. In Burger H (Ed.), *The Menopause*, Bailliere Tindall, London.

Bagger Y Z *et al.* (2004) Two to three years of hormone replacement treatment in healthy women have long-term preventive effects on bone mass and osteoporotic fractures: the PERF study. *Bone,* **34**(4), 728–35.

Banerd K (2004) *Menopause before 40: Coping with Premature Ovarian Failure.* Trafford Publishing, London.

Barlow D (2004) Short-duration use of hormone replacement therapy. In Critchley H *et al.*, *Menopause and Hormone Replacement*, pp. 227–40, RCOG Press, London.

Baron J A *et al.* (1990) The antiestrogenic effect of cigarette smoking in women. *American Journal of Obstetrics and Gynecology*, **162**(2), 503–4.

Beaufrere B *et al.* (2000) Report of the IDECG Working Group on energy and macronutrient metabolism and requirements of the elderly. *European Journal of Clinical Nutrition*, **54**(Supplement 3), S162–3.

Beral V (2003) Breast cancer and HRT in the Million Women Study. *Lancet*, **362**(9382), 419–27.

Betterhealth (2003) *Menopause – Premature (Early) Menopause,* www.betterhealth.vic. gov.au/bhcv2/bhcarticles.nsf/pages/Menopause (accessed August 2005).

Blake G M *et al.* (1999) *The Evaluation of Osteoporosis: Dual Energy X-ray Absorptiometry and Ultrasound in Clinical Practice*, MartinDunitz Ltd, London.

Bland R (2000) Steroid hormone receptor expression and action in bone. *Clinical Science*, **98**(2), 217–40.

British Menopause Society (2004) Managing the menopause – consensus statement on HRT. *Journal of British Menopause Society*, **10**(1), 33–6.

Caplan G A *et al.* (1994) Pathogenesis of vertebral crush fractures in women. *Journal of Royal Society of Medicine*, **87**(4), 200–2.

Chapuy M C *et al.* (1992) Vitamin D3 and calcium to prevent hip fractures in elderly women. *New England Journal of Medicine*, **327**(23), 1637–42.

Collaborative Group on Hormonal Factors in Breast Cancer (1997) Breast Cancer and HRT: collaborative reanalysis of data from 51 epidemiological studies of 52,705 women with breast cancer and 108,411 women without breast cancer. *Lancet,* **350**(10), 1047–59.

COMA (1998) *Nutrition and Bone Health with Particular Reference to Calcium and Vitamin D,* HMSO, London.

Compston J E, Rosen C (2004) *Fast Facts – Osteoporosis,* 4th edition, Health Press, Oxford.

Cubie H (2004) Hormone replacement therapy – communication with the public. In Critchley H *et al., Menopause and Hormone Replacement,* pp. 318–24, RCOG, London.

Cummings S R *et al.* (1995) Risk factors for hip fracture in white women. Study of Osteoporotic Fractures Research Group. *New England Journal of Medicine,* **332**(12), 767–73.

Department of Health (2001) *National Service Framework for Older People – Section 6 – Falls,* HMSO, London.

Dong H *et al.* (2001) An exploratory pilot study of acupuncture on the quality of life and reproductive hormone secretion in menopausal women. *Journal of Alternative Complementary Medicine,* **7**(6), 651–8.

Eastell R (1998) Treatment of post menopausal osteoporosis. *New England Journal of Medicine,* **33**(8), 736–46.

Ernst E (2004) Evidence for complementary therapies to replace HRT. *Pulse,* March, **22**, 62–3.

Ettinger B *et al.* (1999) Reduction of vertebral fracture risk in postmenopausal women with osteoporosis treated with raloscifene: results from a 3-year randomized clinical trial. *Journal of American Medical Association,* **282**(7), 637–45.

Eurohealth (2005) *Trends in Female Mortality,* www.eurohealth.ie/newrep/trends.htm (accessed August 2005).

Freedman K V *et al.* (2000) Treatment of osteoporosis: are physicians missing an opportunity? *Journal of Bone and Joint Surgery of America,* **82-A**, 1063–70.

Gebbie A, Glasier A (2004) Effect of hormone replacement therapy on symptoms. In Critchley H *et al., Menopause and Hormone Replacement,* pp. 33–41, RCOG Press, London.

Genant H K *et al* (1996) Noninvasive assessment of bone mineral and structure: state of the art. *Journal of Bone and Mineral Research,* **11**(6), 707–30.

Grampp S *et al.* (1997) Radiological diagnosis of osteoporosis. *European Radiology,* **7**(10), 11–19.

Grant A M *et al.* (2005) Oral vitamin D3 and calcium for secondary prevention of low-trauma fractures in elderly people (Randomized Evaluation of Calcium or vitamin D, RECORD): a randomized placebo-controlled trial. *Lancet,* **365**(9471), 1621–8.

Grodstein F, Stampfer M (1995) The epidemiology of coronary heart disease and oestrogen replacement in postmenopausal women. *Progress of Cardiovascular Disease,* **38**(3), 199–210.

Gunter M J *et al.* (2003) Management of osteoporosis in women aged 50 and over with osteoporosis-related fractures in managed care population. *Disease Management,* **6**(2), 83–91.

Harris, S T *et al.* (1999) Effects of risedronate treatment on vertebral and nonvertebral fractures in women with postmenopausal osteoporosis: a randomized controlled trial. *Journal of the American Medical Association,* **282**(14), 1344–52.

Heart and Estrogen/Progestin Replacement Study (HERS) reported by Hulley S *et al.* (1998) Randomized trial of estrogen plus progestin for secondary prevention of coronary heart disease in postmenopausal women. HERS Research Group. *Journal of American Medical Association*, **280**(7), 605–13.

Hernandez-Avilam *et al.* (1991) Caffeine, moderate alcohol intake, and risk factors of the hip and forearm in middle aged women. *American Journal of Clinical Nutrition*, **54**(1), 157–63.

Hobson J *et al.* (2003) Poster: 'Great sex, no sweat.' Presented at the BMS Meeting in Manchester, July 2003. In *The Journal of the British Menopause Society – Annual Meeting, Proceedings Supplement*, BMS.

Holick M F (1998) Vitamin D requirements for humans of all ages: new increased requirements for women and men 50 years and older. *Osteoporosis International*, **8**(Supplement 2), S24–9.

Kesslak J P (2002) Can estrogen play a significant role in the prevention of Alzheimer's disease? *Journal of Neural Transmission Supplement*, **62**, 227–39.

Klotzbuecher C M *et al.* (2000) Patients with prior fractures have an increased risk of future fractures: a summary of the literature and statistical synthesis. *Journal of Bone and Mineral Research*, **15**(4), 721–39.

Kordula S *et al.* (2003) Poster: 'A random assessment of 100 women attending an open access bone densitometry service. Were they right to be concerned?' Presented at the BMS meeting in Manchester, July 2003. In *The Journal of the British Menopause Society – Annual Meeting, Proceedings Supplement*, BMS.

Kordula S *et al.* (2004) Poster: 'How did the media reporting of the WHI affect the women attending the Open Access Bone Densitometry Service?' Presented at the BMS Meeting in Harrogate, July 2004. In *The Journal of the British Menopause Society – Annual Meeting, Proceedings Supplement*, BMS.

Lauritzen J B *et al.* (1993) Effect of external hip protectors on hip fractures. *Lancet*, **341**, 11–13.

Law M R, Hacksaw A K (1997) A meta-analysis of cigarette smoking, bone mineral density and risk of hip fracture: recognition of a major effect. *British Medical Journal*, **315**, 841–6.

MacLennan A *et al.* (2001) Oral oestrogen replacement therapy versus placebo for hot flushes. *Cochrane Database System Review*, **2001**(1), CD002978.

Meunier P *et al.* (2004) The effects of strontium ranelate on the risk of vertebral fracture in women with postmenopausal osteoporosis. *New England Journal of Medicine*, **350**(5), 459–68.

Meyerowitz J *et al.* (2004) Poster: 'The effect of the WHI and MWS on the Nottinghamshire GPs' attitudes to HRT and their prescribing habits.' Presented at the BMS Meeting in Harrogate, July 2004. In *Journal of the British Menopause Society – Annual Meeting, Proceedings Supplement*, BMS.

Midgette A S, Baron J A (1990) Cigarette smoking and the risk of natural menopause. *Epidemiology*, **1**(6), 474–80.

Million Women Study (MWS) reported by Beral V (2003) Breast cancer and hormone-replacement therapy in the Million Women Study. *Lancet*, **362**(9382), 419–27.

Naftolin F *et al.* (2004) Early initiation of hormone therapy and clinical cardioprotection: the WHI could not have detected cardioprotective effects of starting hormone therapy during the menopausal transition. *Fertility and Sterility*, **81**(6), 1498–501.

National Institute for Clinical Excellence (2005) *Osteoporosis – Secondary Prevention (No. 87)*, NICE, London.

National Institute of Health (NIH) (2000) Consensus Development Conference Statement *Osteoporosis Prevention, Diagnosis, and Therapy*, **17**(1), 1–36.

National Osteoporosis Society (2002) *Guidelines for the Provision of a Clinical Bone Densitometry Service*, NOS, Bath.

National Osteoporosis Society (2005) *What is Osteoporosis? Facts and Figures*, www.nos.org.uk/osteo.asp (accessed August 2005).

Norbury R *et al.* (2004) Oestrogen: brain ageing, cognition and neuropsychiatric disorder. In Critchley H *et al.*, *Menopause and Hormone Replacement*, pp. 151–9, RCOG, London.

Parker M J *et al.* (2004) Hip protectors for preventing hip fractures in the elderly (Cochrane Review). In *The Cochrane Library*, Issue 2, John Wiley & Sons, Ltd, Chichester.

Pfeifer M *et al.* (2004) Effects of a new spinal orthosis on posture, trunk strength and quality of life in women with postmenopausal osteoporosis: a randomised trial. *American Journal of Physical and Medical Rehabilitation*, **83**(3), 177–86.

Porthouse J *et al.* (2005) Randomized controlled trial of calcium and supplementation with cholecalciferol (vitamin D) for prevention of fractures in primary case. *British Medical Journal*, **330**(7498), 1003.

Recker R R *et al.* (2000) Characterization of perimenopausal loss: a prospective study. *Journal of Bone and Mineral Research*, **15**(10), 1965–73.

Rees M, Purdie D (Eds) (2002) *Management of the Menopause*, BMS Publications Ltd, Marlow.

Riggs B L *et al.* (1996) Drug therapy for vertebral fractures in osteoporosis: evidence that decreases in bone turnover and increases in bone mass determine antifracture efficacy. *Bone*, **18**(Supplement 3), 197S–201S.

Ross P D (1996) Osteoporosis: frequency, consequences and risk factors. *Archive of International Medicine*, **156**, 1399–411.

Ross P D *et al.* (1993) Predicting vertebral fracture incidence from prevalent fractures and bone density among non black, osteoporotic women. *Osteoporosis International*, **3**, 120–6.

Royal College of Obstetricians and Gynaecologists (2004) Consensus views arising from the 47th Study Group. In Critchley H *et al.*, *Menopause and Hormone Replacement*, pp. 345–50, RCOG, London.

Royal College of Physicians (2000) *Osteoporosis: Clinical Guidelines for Prevention and Treatment. Update on Pharmacological Interventions and Algorithm for Management*, RCP, London.

Rymer J *et al.* (2003) Making decisions about hormone replacement therapy. *British Medical Journal*, **326**(7384), 322–6.

Sharara F I *et al.* (1994) Cigarette smoking accelerates the development of diminished ovarian reserve as evidenced by the clomiphene citrate challenge test. *Fertility and Sterility*, **62**(2), 257–62.

Soroko S *et al.* (1994) Family history of osteoporosis and bone mineral density at the axial skeleton: the Rancho Bernardo Study. *Journal of Bone and Mineral Research*, **9**(6), 739–43.

Tinetti M E (1994) A multifactorial intervention to reduce the risk of falling among elderly people living in the community. *New England Journal of Medicine*, **331**(13), 821–7.

Tukmachi E (2000) Treatment of hot flashes in breast cancer patients with acupuncture. *Acupuncture Medicine*, **18**(1), 22–7.
Watts N B *et al.* (1990) Intermittent cyclical etidronate treatment of postmenopausal osteoporosis. *New England Journal of Medicine*, **323**(2), 73–9.
Weiderpass E *et al.* (1999) Risk of endometrial cancer following estrogen replacement with and without progestins. *Journal of the National Cancer Institute*, **91**(13), 1131–7.
Women's Health Initiative Study as reported by Rossouw J E *et al.* (2002) Risks and benefits of estrogen plus progestin in healthy postmenopausal women: principal results from the Women's Health Initiative randomized controlled trial. *Journal of American Medical Association,* **288**(3), 321–33.
World Health Organisation (1994) *Assessment of Fracture Risk and Its Application to Screening for Postmenopausal Osteoporosis.* WHO Technical Study Group Report, Series 843, WHO, Geneva, Switzerland.
World Health Organisation (1996) *Research on Menopause in the 1990s: Report of a WHO Scientific Group*, WHO Technical Report, Series 866, WHO, Geneva, Switzerland.

USEFUL ASSOCIATIONS AND WEBSITES

Amarant Trust: www.amarantmenopausetrust.org.uk

British Menopause Society
36 West Street
Marlow
Buckinghamshire SL7 2NB
www.the-bms.org

Daisy Network: www.daisynetwork.org.uk

Menopause Matters: www.menopausematters.co.uk

National Osteoporosis Society
PO Box 10
Radstock
Bath BA3 3YB
www.nos.org.uk

Women's Health Concern: www.womens-health-concern.org

9 Delivering Patient-centred Cancer Care in Gynaecology

JULIE GOLDING and SALLY WRIGHT

Progress in understanding both the aetiology of cancer and the associated risk factors, such as smoking, diet, lifestyle and genetic predisposition (Cancer Research UK 2004), has been accompanied by developments in screening, diagnosis and a range of successful treatments. Although overall mortality rates from cancer are falling, the incidence has continued to rise (Department of Health 1995, 2000a). One in three people will develop some form of cancer during their lifetime and one in four will die of the disease (Department of Health 1995). This means that every year over 200 000 people are diagnosed with cancer, resulting in 120 000 deaths (Department of Health 2000a).

The high incidence of cancer, together with complexities in managing the disease, has presented a challenge to the National Health Service (NHS), resulting in a major reform of cancer services in the UK. Following *The Calman–Hine Report* (Department of Health 1995), cancer services have been reorganised into Cancer Centres and satellite Cancer Units. All patients diagnosed with cancer should now be assessed and treated in a designated Cancer Centre. Specialisation at the Cancer Centres means that clinicians see enough cases to develop expertise in managing patients with rarer or more challenging cancers. Team working facilitates coordinated care. Patients managed in this way are more likely to be offered appropriate treatments and receive continuity of care through all stages of the disease (NHS Executive 1999a).

Efforts are still being made to reduce variations in the quality of care and treatment across the country, the so-called 'postcode lottery'. *The NHS Cancer Plan* (Department of Health 2000a) has drawn up 'a major programme of action linking prevention, diagnosis, treatment, care and research' and describes the actions and investment needed to improve cancer services up to 2010. This includes targets to reduce waiting times for diagnosis and treatment.

Challenges	Service developments
• Increasing numbers of oncology cases in gynaecology • Discrepancies in service provision ('postcode lottery'): *The Calman–Hine Report* • Delays between referral and first appointment • Poor communication channels leading to fragmented care • Emotional needs of patients following a diagnosis of cancer	• Collaboration between hospitals, forming Cancer Centres • 'Target' clinics to speed referrals • Multiprofessional gynaecological oncology teams • Development of the oncology nurse specialist role within the gynaecology team • Psychosocial support and psychosexual counselling

INTRODUCTION

This chapter describes how the government strategy has affected the provision of cancer services for gynaecology. An overview of gynaecological cancers is followed by a discussion of the oncology nurse specialist role and how this impacts on all stages of the patient's journey.

GYNAECOLOGICAL CANCERS

Gynaecological cancers are a diverse group of diseases with different natural histories and responses to treatments. They cause 24 deaths per 100 000 women (NHS Executive 1999a). The most common gynaecological cancers are ovarian, endometrial and cervical, while cancers of the vulva and vagina are relatively rare.

In order to manage a patient with cancer, both the extent of the disease and knowledge of its biology are essential. The extent of the disease is generally expressed in terms of its stage. There is a simple 1–4 staging system called the FIGO system after its authors – the International Federation of Gynaecology and Obstetrics (see Table 9.1). Stage 1 disease is generally referred to as 'early-stage disease', where the tumour would appear to be confined to the organ of origin. Stage 2 is where the tumour has extended locally beyond the site of origin to involve adjacent organs or structures. Stage 3 then represents more extensive involvement, and stage 4 is metastatic disease. The stage of the disease determines whether further treatment is needed following surgery.

Table 9.1. FIGO (International Federation of Gynaecology and Obstetrics) staging of gynaecological cancers

Type of cancer	Stage 1	Stage 2	Stage 3	Stage 4
Ovarian	Cancer only affects the ovaries	Cancer has grown outside the ovary but is still inside the pelvis	Cancer has spread outside the pelvis into the abdominal cavity	Cancer has spread into other organs such as the liver, lungs or distant lymph nodes
Endometrial	Cancer is confined to the uterus	Cancer also involves the cervix, but not extended outside the uterus	Cancer is outside the uterus in tissues such as the vagina or nearby lymph nodes, but confined to the pelvis	Cancer has spread beyond the uterus and may involve the bladder or bowel or has metastasised to distant sites
Cervical	The cancer cells are only within the cervix	Cancer has spread into surrounding areas such as the upper part of the vagina or tissues next to the cervix	Cancer has spread to surrounding structures such as the lower part of the vagina, nearby lymph nodes or tissues at the side of the pelvic area	There is spread to the bladder or bowel or outside the pelvic area. This stage includes spread to the lungs, liver or bone, but these are uncommon
Vulval	Cancer is confined to the vulva	Cancer is confined to the vulva, is < 2 cm in diameter and no groin nodes are palpable	Cancer is confined to the vulva with suspicious nodes, or beyond the vulva to tissues such as the urethra, vagina or anus with no suspicious nodes	Groin nodes are obviously affected or the cancer involves the rectum, bladder, urethra, bone or pelvis. There may be distant metastases

References: Benedet et al. (2000); CancerBACUP (2004); Smith et al. (1999).

OVARIAN CANCER

Ovarian cancer is the most common gynaecological cancer in the UK and represents approximately 4 % of all female cancers (NHS Modernisation Agency 2001). Nearly 7000 cases are registered each year (Cancer Research UK 2005a). Most ovarian cancers occur in postmenopausal women. Ovarian cancer is often described as the 'silent killer' because in the majority of cases the disease has progressed to a late stage by the time it is diagnosed and prognosis is poorer than for other gynaecological cancers (McCorkle et al. 2003; NHS Modernisation Agency 2001). Often women present with advanced disease and are faced with major surgery followed by chemotherapy treatment, which may last for several months (McCorkle et al. 2003). It is therefore associated with anxiety, depression and uncertainty.

Diagnosis of ovarian cancer is difficult because it has a relatively low frequency in relation to some cancers. For example, one new case is diagnosed for every six cases of breast cancer so a GP may only see one new patient with ovarian cancer every five years. In addition the symptoms are often very vague such as altered bowel habit, frequency of micturition, increased abdominal girth and weight loss and can be easily confused with other conditions such as irritable bowel syndrome.

If the GP suspects an ovarian tumour, the patient should be referred to a gynaecologist urgently. For diagnostic purposes an ultrasound scan is always performed and a blood sample taken to measure the Ca125 level. Ca125 is a protein that is often secreted into the blood by ovarian cells. A Ca125 level up to 60 is considered normal. Approximately 80 % of women who have ovarian cancer will have an elevated Ca125 level at the time of diagnosis (NHS Executive 1999b). Occasionally an elevated Ca125 test indicates conditions not associated with cancer such as pregnancy or endometriosis.

The pelvic ultrasound scan will give an indication of the exact size and location of the tumour. The gynaecologist will also carry out a bimanual pelvic examination to verify this and assess whether it is fixed or mobile. The presence of ascitic fluid, another indication of ovarian cancer, will also be seen on the scan. There may be many litres of ascitic fluid in the abdomen by the time that a patient reaches a gynaecologist. It is constantly surprising how much discomfort people will endure before seeking the help of professionals to determine the cause of the problem. Many women attribute the weight gain to the menopause or a sign of their age and have often purchased new clothes several sizes larger than their norm to accommodate their ever-expanding waistlines.

When ascites is present, a sample can be obtained and sent for cytological examination. Malignant cells are often present in this fluid where there is an ovarian cancer, and this is a good diagnostic tool. The bulk of the ascitic fluid may be drained off by abdominal paracentesis. This will give the patient relief from some of the symptoms associated with this condition, as it is often

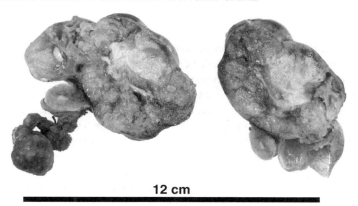

12 cm

Figure 9.1. Stage 1 ovarian cancer: serous carcinoma with a nodular necrotic yellow-ish cut surface. The surface of a healthy cervix would appear smooth and pink. (Reproduced by kind permission of Queen's Medical Centre Nottingham)

extremely difficult to eat properly and breathe freely with an abdomen full of fluid.

If the patient is medically fit and the disease is felt to be respectable, as in a stage 1 carcinoma (see Figure 9.1), and has not metastasised to other organs such as the liver, surgery would be the treatment of choice. All patients should be operated on in Cancer Centres by designated surgical oncologists, as this improves the quality of care and increases overall survival rates (Munstedt *et al.* 2003; Munstedt & Franke 2004; NHS Executive 1999b). A hysterectomy, bilateral salpingo-oophorectomy and omentectomy along with peritoneal washings would be performed whenever possible. If there is a possibility that the tumour might be fixed to other structures, then the bowel may need preparing prior to surgery. A preparation such as Picolax should be administered the day before to clean out the bowel in case a bowel resection is required.

The aim of surgery should be to remove as much of the cancer as possible (optimum debulking) and accurately stage the disease (Munstedt & Franke 2004). It is important to reduce the residual tumour burden to a point at which adjuvant therapy (chemotherapy) will be most effective and optimal debulking has been achieved when nodules of less than 1 cm are remaining (DiSaia & Creasman 2002). Unfortunately it is not always possible to remove a more advanced tumour. These patients will benefit to a limited extent from adjuvant chemotherapy but will eventually die of their disease. New approaches to managing advanced cancers may improve survival rates but more conclusive research evidence is needed (Gallo & Frigerio 2003; Munstedt & Franke 2004). Sometimes primary chemotherapy is given before surgery. This can reduce tumour masses to an extent that allows for 'successful' surgical debulking during interval laparotomy. However, this approach relies on the careful selection of patients and is still largely experimental (Gallo & Frigerio 2003).

Case study 9.1

A 62-year-old teacher was referred to the Cancer Centre in Nottingham with an unpleasant vaginal discharge. A pelvic ultrasound scan showed a solid and cystic mass suspicious of an ovarian cancer. The CA125 tumour marker was raised at 1730. Jane was seen again in clinic with her husband and the results were explained. She was scheduled for a total abdominal hysterectomy, bilateral oopherectomy and omentectomy two weeks later. The nurse specialist was present at both appointments and subsequently spent time with Jane and her husband discussing any concerns. Jane was given written information on ovarian cancer, the surgical procedure and details of her pre-operative assessment appointment. She also had a contact number in case she had any further queries or concerns.

The day before her pre-assessment Jane phoned to say she had been recalled following a routine mammogram. She was obviously very concerned and asked if it was possible that the mass on her ovary could have spread to her breast. The following day Jane had already returned to the breast clinic and had a biopsy under ultrasound. The lump was not palpable on examination and she had been told it was unlikely to be malignant. Her pre-assessment was uneventful, but it was obvious that the concerns about her breast diagnosis had increased her anxiety level.

Before Jane was admitted for surgery, the consultant breast surgeon contacted the gynaecology team to say that the breast biopsy showed invasive carcinoma, which was probably a primary. On the day of her operation Jane was very tearful, finding it hard to cope with the diagnosis of two cancers within eight days and the possibility that they may be connected, which would be a worse outcome than two primary tumours. The nurse specialist accompanied Jane to theatre and stayed until she was asleep.

Jane had her operation as planned. There was an obvious ovarian cancer, which had spread and stuck to the pelvic wall. This meant that she would definitely require chemotherapy. Over the next few days the nurse specialist supported both Jane and her husband, and also liaised with the breast care nurse who would support her through treatment for her breast cancer.

The histology showed that the ovarian cancer was also likely to be a primary. Jane's post-operative recovery was not without problems. Her wound broke down and she needed daily visits from the district nurse. Two weeks later she was admitted for a lumpectomy. Fortunately the breast lump showed a very early cancer, which would not require further surgery. This was the first good news she had received in several weeks and was obviously a great relief during all the uncertainty. The following week she saw the clinical oncologist to discuss the treatment she would require for her ovarian cancer. Jane had chemotherapy for ovarian cancer as an outpatient every three weeks for six treatments. Fortunately her tumour marker came down from 1730 to 22 and she was obviously delighted.

While having her chemotherapy, the nurse specialist kept in touch. Jane needs continuing support, as there is still uncertainty about her future prognosis. She also has to decide whether to accept genetic counselling. A referral was made because she had developed two primary cancers. This could have implications not only for her but also the health of her daughter who would be at risk of carrying the gene.

Jane's case was unusually complex but it gives an insight into the role of the nurse specialist in supporting the patient not only during their hospital stay but also during an unpredictable recovery period.

ENDOMETRIAL CANCER

Endometrial cancer originates in the endometrial lining of the uterus. It is the fifth most common cancer for women in the UK and each year there are about 6000 new cases (Cancer Research UK 2005b). Endometrial cancer is most common in postmenopausal women. Women under 40 years of age are rarely affected, but the incidence rises rapidly between the ages of 40 and 55 years. After the menopause there are about 44 cases per 100000 women (NHS Executive 1999a).

The main risk factor, apart from age, is a high level of oestrogen. Oestrogen is secreted by the ovaries and plays an important role in the development of the female reproductive system and is responsible for changes during menstruation and pregnancy. Progesterone is another hormone secreted by the ovaries and usually balances the effects of oestrogen. High levels of oestrogen are associated with obesity because surplus fat produces oestrogen, with hormone replacement therapy that does not contain progesterone, with tamoxifen therapy for breast cancer and with polycystic ovarian syndrome. Other risk factors include a family history of endometrial cancer, never having been pregnant and a late menopause.

The most common symptom is unusual vaginal bleeding, including menorrhagia or irregular intermenstrual bleeding in premenopausal women and bleeding following the menopause. These types of bleeding should always be investigated. Since most women report any abnormal bleeding, endometrial cancer is usually diagnosed at an early stage. Of women with postmenopausal vaginal bleeding, 8–10 % will have cancer (NHS Executive 1999a).

Investigations may include an ultrasound scan (LUSS), computerised tomography (CT) or magnetic resonance imaging (MRI) scans, hysteroscopy and biopsy or dilatation and curettage (D&C). All women with postmenopausal bleeding should have a transvaginal ultrasound to assess the thickness of the endometrium. This is a highly reliable method for detecting endometrial cancer and its accuracy can be up to 100 % (NHS Executive 1999a). If the endometrium is found to be 5 mm or more, then a biopsy should be carried out. If possible, a biopsy can be taken in an outpatient department using a pipelle aspirator. If this is unsuccessful, then a D&C under general anaesthetic would be performed. Samples would then be sent for histological examination

If endometrial cancer is diagnosed, surgery involving total abdominal hysterectomy and bilateral salpingo-oopherectomy is often sufficient to treat the disease, but radiotherapy is sometimes needed when the cancer is more advanced (Creutzberg *et al.* 2000). The pattern of spread is partially dependent on the degree of cellular differentiation. Well-differentiated tumours tend to limit their spread to the surface of the endometrium and invasion into the myometrium is less common. In patients with poorly differentiated tumours, myometrial invasion occurs more frequently.

Endometrial cancer can progress through five stages. A precancerous condition called endometrial hyperplasia may cause irregular uterine bleeding. Hyperplasia may be only mild but severe hyperplasia with atypia is the earliest detectable stage of endometrial cancer. Treating precancerous hyperplasia with hormones (progestins) or a hysterectomy can prevent abnormal, precancer cells from developing into cancer. About 10–30 % of all hyperplasia cases eventually develop into cancer (Oncologychannel.com 2005). There are then four distinct stages ending with metastatic cancer that has spread to the myometrium (see Figure 9.2), the cervix and vagina, the nearby lymph nodes, the bladder, the bowel, the abdominal cavity and even more distant organs and lymph nodes. Early detection is the best prevention from developing invasive endometrial cancer. Survival rates decrease as the disease progresses.

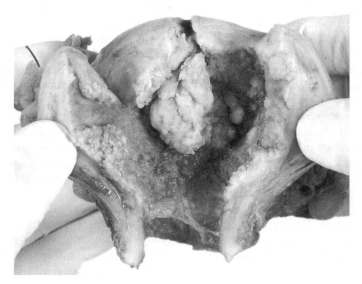

Figure 9.2. Stage 1 endometrial cancer: adenocarcinoma of the endometrium invading into more than 50 % of the myometrium. The tumour is seen centrally and on the inside surface of the womb. (Reproduced by kind permission of Queen's Medical Centre Nottingham)

Average five-year survival rates for endometrial cancer are 90 % for stage 1, 73 % for stage 2, 52 % for stage 3 and 27 % for stage 4 (Irvin & Rice 2002).

Treatment depends on the stage of the cancer (see Table 9.1). When the cancer has progressed beyond stage 1, further treatment will be required after the surgery. This treatment is radiotherapy, which was first used to treat uterine cancer around the turn of the century. For many decades, radiation therapy was used as a standard pre-surgical treatment, but it is no longer done pre-operatively because it prevents accurate surgical staging and may have lasting side effects. It is standard to reserve the use of radiotherapy until an initial hysterectomy, at least, has been performed. Even following a hysterectomy and bilateral salpingo-oophorectomy, the effectiveness of adjuvant radiation therapy is controversial. Although regional pelvic radiation can decrease pelvic recurrences, it does not necessarily improve the survival rate (NHS Executive 1999b). It is most beneficial for patients with tumours that are confined to the pelvis and that have features that increase the likelihood of recurrence (stages 2 and 3). The potential benefits of radiation should be weighed against the risks. There can be permanent adverse effects including damage to the vagina, bowel and urinary tract.

In addition to pelvic radiation, post-operative vaginal irradiation is often used to prevent vaginal cuff recurrences, which are common for certain types of tumours. This involves inserting small metal cylinders, or some other type of applicator, through the vagina, where it releases a radioactive substance over the course of 24 hours.

All patients are followed up at three-monthly intervals for signs of recurrence of the disease. Recurrence is more likely in women with advanced disease and in those whose tumour had certain high-risk features. Usually recurrence happens within three years of the original diagnosis. Hormone therapy can be used to treat recurrent disease, although its effectiveness is unclear. The efficacy of different hormones is currently being evaluated. The use of chemotherapy to treat recurrent disease is also currently being studied. If a woman was originally treated only with surgery and no radiation and the cancer recurs, radiation can be used as therapy. In the case of radiation, the prognosis depends on many features such as the size and extent of the tumour and the time to recurrence (Oncologychannel.com 2005).

CERVICAL CANCER

Nearly 3000 new cases of cervical cancer are diagnosed in the UK each year and the disease causes approximately a thousand deaths each year (Cancer-BACUP 2004; Cancer Research UK 2005c). The relatively low number of cases compared with ovarian or endometrial cancer reflects the success of the cervical screening programme (Elkas & Farias-Eisner 1998). In parts of the developing world, where screening does not take place, cervical cancer is the most common female cancer, whereas in the UK it is only the eleventh most common (Cancer Research UK 2005).

Cervical intraepithelial neoplasia (CIN) is a pre-malignant condition, which can usually be detected by obtaining a sample of cells (the 'smear' test) from the cervix. The assumption is that a significant proportion of women with CIN would eventually develop invasive cervical cancer, so early treatment can prevent this. There is little information on the rate of progression from pre-cancer to invasive carcinoma, mainly because of the moral and ethical impossibility of observing women with a known pre-malignant disease without intervention. However, it is generally accepted that the mean time interval for progression through CIN to invasive carcinoma is 10–15 years with a small number of women progressing very quickly from a normal cervix to cervical carcinoma (Elkas & Farias-Eisner 1998; Sellors & Sankaranarayanan 2004).

Although cervical screening is designed to prevent cancer, it can also detect cancers that have already developed. There are two types of cervical cancer. The most common, squamous cell carcinoma, accounts for approximately 85%. The remaining 10–15% are adenocarcinomas (see Figure 9.3) and screening was not designed to detect this smaller group of cancers (DiSaia & Creasman 2002).

The main risk factor for cervical cancer is infection with the sexually transmitted disease human papilloma virus (HPV). There are many different types of HPV, which is a very common virus. Only a few of these are associated with cell changes on the cervix (Elkas & Farias-Eisner 1998). Usually the immune system can clear the virus but sometimes the virus remains for a number of

7cm

Figure 9.3. Stage 1 cervical cancer: cervical adenocarcinoma. The smooth area at the top is normal, contrasting with the cancerous cells in the lower half. (Reproduced by kind permission of Queen's Medical Centre Nottingham)

years and CIN is more likely to develop into cancer when this happens. Other risk factors include multiple sexual partners, early onset of sexual activity and smoking. Cervical cancer is not linked to genetic changes.

Any woman with an abnormal smear result, postcoital bleeding or inter-menstrual bleeding, persistent vaginal discharge or whose cervix looks or feels abnormal should be investigated. This involves referral to a Colposcopy Clinic where the cervix can be examined under magnification. If the cervix has the appearance of superficial invasion, a loop or a cone biopsy should be carried out. This may be sufficient for both diagnosis and treatment when there is no evidence of tumour at the margins of the sample, but if the biopsy results suggest a higher stage tumour or if there are poor prognostic factors then further treatment would be required.

The standard treatment for early cervical cancer is a radical hysterectomy and lymph node dissection. This includes removal of the uterus, cervix, para-metrium and cuff of vagina plus lymph nodes. If the tumour is completely excised and the lymph nodes are clear, no further treatment is needed. If this is not the case, referral for a course of combined chemotherapy and radio-therapy is usually recommended. Patients diagnosed with more advanced cer-vical cancer would be treated with radiotherapy and chemotherapy rather than surgery. The importance of accurately staging patients with cancer of the cervix cannot be overstated. Ideally combining radical surgery and radiation treatment is avoided in order to minimise the long-term side effects (Elkas & Farias-Eisner 1998; Grigsby 1998).

Unfortunately the standard treatments for cervical cancer make women infertile. As many women are waiting until they are older to start a family and cervical cancer is also affecting younger women, fertility is a big issue. It is esti-mated that 10–15 % of cervical cancers are diagnosed in childbearing years, so there is increasing pressure to investigate fertility-preserving treatments (Plante & Michel 2001; Tongaonkar 2004). In 1992 Dargent, a French gynae-cologist, pioneered a new technique called radical trachelectomy (Plante 2000). Initial reactions were sceptical but the technique has since been accepted and copied worldwide. It involves removing the cervix up to the isthmus of the uterus together with some parametrial tissue and laparoscopic node dissection. So far there have been over 300 recorded cases with a 95 % five-year survival (Plante *et al.* 2004). As this is a relatively new technique, data are still limited because not all patients are five years post-surgery. Follow-up for these patients is very difficult as cytological interpretation of subsequent smears is extremely problematic.

Although there have been reports of successful pregnancies following tra-chelectomy, there are still some recognised problems associated with obstet-ric outcome (Covens *et al.* 1999; Roy & Plante 1999). The chance of conception is reduced and, once pregnant, there is a high probability of developing cer-vical incompetence, where a pregnancy cannot be carried to full term and there is an increased risk of premature labour. Usually a caesarean section is necessary. Therefore women who are offered a radical trachelectomy must have a full understanding of the risks as well as the benefits.

Case study 9.2

Marie, a 29-year-old woman, was referred to the Colposcopy Clinic at Queen's Medical Centre (QMC) following a smear showing moderate dyskariosis. At the initial consultation Maria was very distressed, as she had recently suffered her third miscarriage and also the loss of her mother through cancer. Colposcopic examination showed an area of abnormality confirmed on biopsy as precancer. A large loop excision of the transformation zone (LLETZ) was subsequently performed. This unfortunately showed that Maria had an early stage 1 cervical cancer, which would require further treatment.

Her case was discussed at the weekly multidisciplinary team meeting. The histology showed that this was an adenosquamous carcinoma, which would be suitable for either a trachelectomy or radical hysterectomy. Maria was called in to discuss her results. She came with her husband, who was very supportive but obviously as devastated as she about the results. The consultant who saw Maria and her husband explained the histology results to them and the treatment options. He talked to them about trachelecotmy and radical hysterectomy, explaining both procedures and how they are performed. The advantages, disadvantages and possible complications of both operations were also discussed.

In the following weeks the nurse specialist spent a long time with both Maria and her husband, giving them information and answering their questions. They had to make a very difficult decision: should Maria have fertility-sparing treatment, which carried a greater risk of recurrence, or a radical hysterectomy, which would end any chances of having a family? Added to this Maria was still trying to come to terms with her recent miscarriage. Patients facing such dilemmas must be given time to make a decision. The role of the nurse specialist is to give them relevant information and emotional support.

Maria eventually decided that she would have a radical hysterectomy and conservation of her ovaries. The surgery and recovery following this were uneventful and the final histology showed that she would not require any further treatment. After these traumatic events, Maria has now returned to work and seems to be coping both physically and emotionally. She is seen for regular follow-up visits and still contacts the nurse specialist for a chat. In these situations strong bonds are formed. Although powerless to alter the prognosis, the nurse specialist's role is to support women like Maria during their cancer journey.

VULVAL CANCER

Carcinoma of the vulva is relatively rare and mainly affects postmenopausal women, the incidence increasing with age. It may be asymptomatic, but most

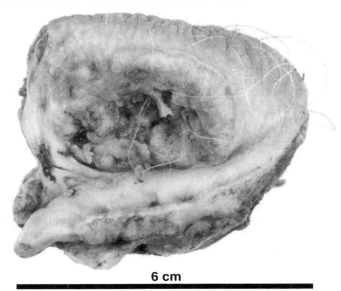

6 cm

Figure 9.4. Ulcerated vulval squamous cell carcinoma, seen in the centre. (Reproduced by kind permission of Queen's Medical Centre Nottingham)

patients present with a vulval lump or ulcer. There is often a longstanding history of pruritus, occasionally bleeding or discharge (Ghurani & Penalver 2001). The most common type of vulval cancer is squamous cell carcinoma. Other types are malignant melanoma, adenocarcinoma underlying Pagets disease of the vulva, verrucous carcinoma, Bartholins gland carcinoma and basal cell carcinoma.

Squamous cell carcinoma of the vulva (see Figure 9.4) progresses through similar stages to squamous cell carcinoma of the cervix and vagina. Vulval intraepithelial neoplasia (VIN) refers to the earliest stage of the disease and is usually seen as a raised area on the skin. Squamous cell carcinomas have been divided into a superficially invasive type and an invasive type. Superficial types may present with an ulcer, a macule or papule. Clinically it is not possible to separate the precursor lesion of VIN from superficial invasion. Deeply invasive tumors are usually solitary and often present as a large ulcer on the labia majora or minora. Occasionally these tumours may produce a parathyroid hormone substance resulting in hypercalcemia. VIN is found adjacent to 60–80 % of superficially invasive squamous cell carcinomas and 25 % of deeply invasive carcinomas (DiSaia & Creasman 2002).

Local spread occurs to the vagina, perineum, clitoris, urethra and pubic bone. Lymphatic spread is to the superficial inguinal, deep inguinal and iliac nodes. Unless the tumour is central, only the nodes on the affected side are involved. A biopsy is performed and at the time of biopsy the vagina and cervix are thoroughly inspected for signs of involvement. Positive nodes can be detected by computerised tomography (CT) or magnetic resonance imaging (MRI) scans.

Surgery is usually necessary to treat vulval cancer. This is not only very mutilating but usually removes the capacity for sexual enjoyment. The aim of surgery is to remove the cancer and minimise the risk of recurrence, but preserve as much function as possible. A wide local incision of the area is usually performed first, because the depth of tumour invasion is an important factor. If the initial biopsy shows the depth of invasion is more than 1 mm, the nodes are dissected. This is because research has shown that cancer spread is unlikely if the invasion is less than 1 mm (NHS Executive 1999b).

Large tumours are treated by radical vulvectomy and bilateral node dissection. If the nodes are positive, follow-up treatment with radiotherapy is needed. Survival figures are excellent but complication rates are high. Complications include wound breakdown, loss of sexual function and groin or lower-limb problems associated with lymph drainage. Since up to 70 % of patients at all stages of the disease have no node involvement, many patients have undergone unnecessary surgery (Sohaib & Moskovic 2003). Therefore surgery is now becoming more individualised to decrease complications in patients with limited disease (Ansink *et al.* 2005; Plante 2000). New diagnostic imaging methods for detecting and assessing groin lymph nodes will hopefully reduce the overall need for groin node surgery (Ghurani & Penalver 2001; Sohaib & Moskovic 2003).

GYNAECOLOGICAL CANCER SERVICES

'The optimum management of gynaecological cancers requires co-ordinated teamwork between three levels of service: primary care, Cancer Units and Cancer Centres' (NHS Executive 1999a) (see Figure 9.5). Women with possible gynaecological cancers should be assessed at the nearest Cancer Unit or Centre. Cancer Units can provide assessment for all types of gynaecological cancers, but treatment only for the first stages of cervical disease and for early cancers of the endometrium. Women with cancers that are less common or more difficult to treat should be referred to a Cancer Centre for management and treatment. This would include ovarian cancer, later-stage endometrial cancer and cancers of the cervix, vulva or vagina.

Good communication and coordination between all levels of the service are important in managing the patient smoothly and quickly. Government targets to reduce waiting times mean that patients must be seen within two weeks from referral by a GP. All patients with cancer should then wait no longer than one month from diagnosis to treatment. The goal is that by 2008 no patient should wait longer than one month from urgent referral to the start of treatment.

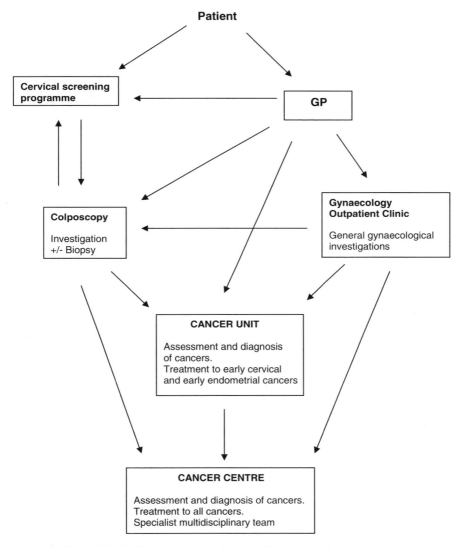

Figure 9.5. Referral pathways for possible gynaecological cancers

These targets put tremendous pressure on the cancer services because diagnosis must be accurate and can take time. Patients may require MRI or CT scans in order to confirm diagnosis or suitability for surgery. They may require an examination under anaesthetic in order to stage a cervical cancer accurately. If surgery is needed, should this be radical hysterectomy or fertility-sparing trachelectomy? If the tumour is too advanced for surgery, the patient would need to see a clinical oncologist to discuss chemotherapy and radiotherapy. Sometimes it is difficult to obtain an endometrial biopsy in the out-patient clinic so this needs to be done under general anaesthetic. Women may also have other medical conditions such as hypertension, diabetes or obesity, which could complicate plans for treatment.

Although women with cancer should not be kept waiting longer than nec-essary, it is important that they have a sound diagnosis and are given time to make an informed decision which they will not later regret. This illustrates the need to have different specialists available apart from the gynaecological oncologists. 'In gynaecological cancer, treatment by specialist teams is likely to improve survival and quality of life' (NHS Executive 1999a). Members of the Cancer Centre team also include a clinical oncologist, chemotherapy spe-cialist, radiologist, histopathologist and cytopathologist. The government has also recommended that a Clinical Nurse Specialist should be a part of the core team (NHS Executive 1999a).

THE ONCOLOGY NURSE SPECIALIST ROLE

This role developed as a direct result of *The Calman–Hine Report* (Depart-ment of Health 1995). Prior to this there were very few specialist nurses in post. The role was made more explicit when *Improving Outcomes in Gynae-cological Cancers* was published: 'From the time of diagnosis, each patient should have access to a named nurse who has been trained in counselling patients, has the specialist knowledge of cancer and can offer continuity of care' (NHS Executive 1999a). Nurses are also governed by the *Code of Pro-fessional Conduct* (United Kingdom Central Council 1992), which states that all nurses have a duty of care to promote and safeguard the well-being and interests of the patient. Therefore the nurse specialist should understand the benefits and risks of all cancer treatments and ensure holistic care is given to the patients.

A clinical nurse specialist is a nurse who, in addition to completing basic training, has gone on to specialise in a particular area. The process of special-isation involves acquiring in-depth experience and training in the specialist area and often the acquisition of specialist qualifications. The oncology nurse specialist for gynaecology will have worked in gynaecology for many years, gaining experience as a junior staff nurse, rising through the grades to senior staff nurse and then ward manager, ensuring that she has a sound knowledge base and years of experience. In addition she needs the knowledge and skills to deal with people affected by cancer. It is especially important to be able to tackle some of the misconceptions about the disease (Department of Health 2000b).

Specific training relating to the role of an oncology nurse specialist con-centrates on providing holistic care for the cancer patient. The Oncology Nursing Course (formally the ENB 237) addresses every aspect of caring for the patient with cancer from diagnosis to management and end-of-life support. It is extremely comprehensive in its content and lasts approximately 30 weeks. At the end of the course the nurse would be competent in taking responsibility for, and making informed judgements about, the management of a cancer patient, ensuring the delivery of quality evidence-based practice in their care. Courses designed specifically around counselling and interpersonal skills are also useful as these usually cover delivering bad news and supporting the patient thereafter. Training in psychosexual medicine is particularly helpful as treatment for gynaecological cancers can result in both emotional and sexual problems (Maughan & Clarke 2001). Some gynaecological oncology nurse specialists have further developed their role to incorporate the skills of colposcopy and hysteroscopy to aid in the diagnosis of their patients.

THE PATIENT JOURNEY

'Nurses have a significant contribution to make in ensuring a coherent service, working with other colleagues and across professional and organisational boundaries' (Department of Health 2000b). In order to ensure continuity of care, the nurse needs to be involved throughout the patient journey. The first time the nurse specialist meets the patient is usually in the clinic, where she has been referred to the consultant gynaecologist by her GP. Some women may suspect the possibility that they may have a serious condition but are often unaware of the severity of the potential problem. Usually women present with symptoms such as postcoital or postmenopausal bleeding and need further investigations before returning for the results. This helps prepare them for a possible diagnosis of cancer.

All patients with a definite or possible cancer are discussed at a multidisciplinary team (MDT) meeting. This is the best way of ensuring that all relevant disciplines and professional groups contribute to decisions on the clinical management of patients (Department of Health 2004). Weekly MDT meetings have been held in the Nottingham Cancer Centre for the last four years. Core members of the cancer team attend, including the nurse specialists. There are three nurse specialists in Nottingham, covering two hospital sites, and they take responsibility for organising the lists of patients to be discussed and ensuring that the relevant notes and results are available. All patients with a definite or possible cancer are discussed and a plan of care and suitable treatment options are documented.

The consultant will see patients back in clinic, preferably with a relative or friend. He or she can then discuss their test results, give them information about their disease and treatment options, and, as far as possible, a realistic assessment of anticipated outcome. The *Patients' Charter* states that each patient has the right to a clear explanation of any treatment proposed, including any risks and alternatives, before any treatment is decided.

Afterwards the nurse specialist's role is to give patients the opportunity to ask any questions they may have. Often patients will perceive doctors as very busy and therefore will not ask many questions, but they perceive nurses as having more time to talk to them (Epstein *et al.* 2004). A diagnosis of cancer is an emotional shock, and it is well known that patients only take in a fraction of what they are told. Therefore they need written information to take home and also contact numbers so that they can phone with any queries. Women should be given sufficient information, adequate time to reflect and the opportunity to discuss treatment options before making decisions (NHS Executive 1999a). While most women will want to be kept fully informed, the amount and timing of information should be consistent with each individual patient's desire for information.

Once treatment has been agreed, the nurse specialist continues to support the patient. Waiting for surgery is very stressful, especially if the outcome is uncertain. Some women continue to phone with questions or simply for reassurance. The nurse specialist can meet the patient again at the pre-assessment appointment and should ideally be available when she is admitted. Post-operatively patients need information about the operation and support as they recover.

The immediate post-operative period can be an anxious time as patients wait for histology results, and the nurse specialist can help by sitting and talking to them. Some women find this period of uncertainty, not knowing if the diagnosis is definitely cancer or whether further treatment is needed, more harrowing than the surgery. Hopefully histology results are available prior to discharge, but if this is not possible the nurse specialist needs to ascertain whether the patient wants to come back to the clinic or is happy to be phoned at home. The nurse specialist needs to talk through these issues so that the patient is fully prepared when the results are available. The nurse specialist is often the person who gives the patient her results. Patients who may need follow-up treatment are usually discussed at the MDT meeting within two weeks of surgery. Patients need further support during the recovery period if further treatment is needed or, sadly, if the cancer is not curable and the patient eventually requires palliative care.

EMOTIONAL AND SEXUAL NEEDS

As well as the obvious distress caused by the diagnosis, gynaecological cancers can precipitate a range of emotional and relationship problems. Unfortunately women usually have a very short time to work through their feelings of shock and grief before beginning treatment.

Sexually active patients and their partners should be offered information about any possible effects on their relationship (Andersen 1994; Jefferies 2002). This is especially relevant as there are more young women now facing major pelvic surgery. Sexuality and sexual function are an important part of our quality of life. Although these terms are often used in the same context, they are separate concepts but both can be affected by a diagnosis of cancer and the subsequent treatment. The physical side effects of treatments for gynaecological cancers can greatly change a woman's sexuality and quality of life. The main difficulties are related to altered fertility, changes in body image and sexual dysfunction (Maughan & Clarke 2001). If she is not warned about the possible destructive effects of the cancer treatment, the result can be devastating for both the woman and her partner (Andersen 1994).

Women of all ages may view the removal of female organs as a loss of femininity, and one Australian study found that 52 % of the study participants reported persistent physical difficulties after cancer treatment (Steninga & Dunn 1997). Psychological aspects of care are particularly important as treatments for these cancers may leave women infertile, damage pelvic organs and precipitate menopause. Patients who have a radical hysterectomy have a shortened vagina that can lead to discomfort during intercourse. Radiotherapy can cause vaginal stenosis in up to 20 % of patients (Denton *et al.* 2000). Following a bilateral oophorectomy, the loss of oestrogen can lead to vaginal dryness and for many women removal of their ovaries might also equate with diminished femininity and sexual attractiveness (Shell 1990). It has been suggested that patients with cervical cancer might also feel upset with 'society's misconceptions that their illness is linked with promiscuity and is sometimes described as a sexually transmitted disease' (Jefferies 2002).

The psychosexual needs of women following treatment for gynaecological cancers were neglected until relatively recently. Maughan and Clarke (2001) argue that this situation should be addressed and that 'psychological, social and sexual rehabilitation following gynaecological cancer demands a proactive approach by professionals who are skilled in the provision of holistic care'. Research has shown that the amount of teaching, counselling and practical support makes a difference in the quality of life of cancer survivors (Maughan & Clarke 2001; Steninga & Dunn 1997). Nurse specialists are in a key position to give support. This can involve both patient education and also management of the side effects of surgery, chemotherapy and radiotherapy. Following assessment the nurse specialist can also refer patients to other health professionals as appropriate. These may include psychosexual counsellors, menopause specialists, physiotherapists and fertility experts.

PROFESSIONAL SUPPORT AND DEVELOPMENT

The nurse specialist's role involves supporting not only the patients and their relatives but also the staff on the ward, who look after patients with a range of gynaecological problems. Ward nurses may not always have a thorough understanding of the treatment and care for women with specific gynaecological cancers. The nurse specialist can support and educate the ward nurses. This includes organising regular study days and also encouraging interested nurses to spend some time working with the nurse specialist. In addition, the nurse specialist can offer practical advice on the post-operative care, such as wound care and analgesia, and also emotional support with the particularly difficult cases. It is not unheard of for young patients to become terminally ill with a previously undetected cancer, and the nursing staff involved in the daily care can become very distressed. At a practical level the nurse specialist often has more time to sit with the patients whereas staff on the ward are often too busy.

The nurse specialists themselves also need emotional support because helping patients cope with a poor diagnosis or unpleasant treatment can be very stressful (Deeny & McGuigan 1999; Morton 1996). The majority of patients are very appreciative of all the help, but people's reaction to bad news is always unpredictable and can frequently include rudeness, anger, hysterics or making unreasonable demands. This demonstrates the importance of good support networks. The MDT can help as can networking with other nurses working in a similar field.

National and regional forums have evolved over the years following the development of nurse specialist roles. These help not only with psychological support but also with professional updating and development. Currently there is a National Forum of Gynaecological Oncology Nurses, which meets annually, usually around the time of the British Gynaecological Cancer Society Meeting. At these forums, specialist nurses from all over the country share their experiences, research and best practice to ensure a consistency in the care given to patients nationwide. In addition to the national forum, there are local groups. The Trent Regional Gynaecology Oncology Nurses Forum consists of the nurses from the Trent regional cancer network who meet two or three times a year. Experiences of patients' journeys, research carried out and ideas for best practice are shared and discussions take place about the best information to give out to patients ensuring a consistency throughout the Trent region. Subspecialist trainee doctors often conduct a teaching session. They are usually involved in research programmes and are up to date with their professional development.

CONCLUSION

Quality of life has become an important issue for patients diagnosed with cancer. Cure is undoubtedly the most important consideration when treating patients, but for some the price of this is very costly. Recent studies relating to the impact of gynaecological cancers suggest that survival without significant morbidity has become an important outcome criterion (Anderson & Lutgendorf 1997; Maughan & Clarke 2001; Plante 2000). Therefore surgery for cancer is becoming less aggressive in order to preserve quality of life. Despite the effects of cancer treatments on fertility, new developments in artificial reproductive technologies may also allow many women to have children in the future. Patients themselves are beginning to question established treatments and challenge doctors. However, it is important that more conservative treatment does not jeopardise patients' long-term survival.

Patients' general experiences of cancer services in the UK have improved since 2000, when research showed that there were not enough nurses who had undertaken cancer specialist training (Department of Health 2000b). Since then at least 10000 nurses have been trained in cancer care but 40 % of patients are still not being allocated a named nurse (National Audit Office 2005a, 2005b). There are no specific figures for gynaecology but it is reasonable to assume that the situation is similar and that great improvements have been made, but there is still some room for improvement. Now that the basic framework for delivering gynaecological cancer care is in place the number of nurse specialists should increase.

It is an exciting time to be a cancer nurse specialist in gynaecology because there are huge opportunities to improve patient care. There is scope for professional development and learning new skills such as colposcopy or hysteroscopy. The role is also becoming more complex as nurses are discussing results, organising treatment and running follow-up clinics as part of the aftercare of cancer patients. Although there is limited research data on the effects of nurse specialists in gynaecological cancers, they are now considered to be essential members of the MDT and therefore play an important role in the delivery of cancer care (NHS Executive 1999b).

Above all, nurse specialists meet patients during a traumatic time in their lives and are able to make a real difference. They can reduce patients' distress, increase satisfaction and improve information flow to patients (NHS Executive 1999b). Anecdotal feedback from patients suggests that they value the nurse specialist's support and research evidence shows that the nurse specialist can improve the quality of life for women facing gynaecological cancer (Maughan & Clarke 2001).

REFERENCES

Andersen B L (1994) Yes there are sexual problems, now what do we do about them? *Gynaecology Oncology*, **52**(1), 10–13.

Anderson B, Lutgendorf S (1997) Quality of life in gynaecologic cancer survivors. *CA: A Cancer Journal for Clinicians*, **47**, 218–25.

Ansink A *et al.* (2005) Surgical interventions for early squamous cell carcinoma of the vulva. In *The Cochrane Library*, Issue 2, John Wiley & Sons, Ltd, Chichester.

Benedet J L *et al.* (2000) FIGO staging classification and clinical practice guidelines of gynecologic cancers. *International Journal of Gynaecology and Obstetrics*, **70**(2), 207–312.

CancerBACUP (2004) *Understanding Cancer of the Cervix*, CancerBACUP, London.

Cancer Research UK (2004) *CancerStats Monograph*, Cancer Research UK, London.

Cancer Research UK (2005a) *Ovarian Cancer*, http://info.cancerresearchuk.org (accessed 7 April 2005).

Cancer Research UK (2005b) *Endometrial Cancer*, http://info.cancerresearchuk.org (accessed 7 April 2005).

Cancer Research UK (2005c) *Cervical Cancer*, http://info.cancerresearchuk.org (accessed 7 April 2005).

Covens A *et al.* (1999) Is radical trachelectomy a safe alternative to a radical hysterectomy for patients with stage 1A-B carcinoma of the cervix? *Cancer*, **86**, 2273–79.

Creutzberg C L *et al.* (2000) Surgery and postoperative radiotherapy versus surgery alone for patients with stage 1 endometrial carcinoma: multicentre randomised trial. *Lancet*, **355**(9213), 1404–11.

Deeny K, McGuigan M (1999) The value of the nurse–patient relationship in the care of cancer patients. *Nursing Standard*, **13**(33), 45–7.

Denton A *et al.* (2000) National audit of the management and outcome of carcinoma of the cervix treated with radiotherapy in 1993. *Clinical Oncology*, **12**(1), 347–53.

Department of Health (1995) *The Calman–Hine Report: A Policy Framework for Commissioning Cancer Services*, HMSO, London.

Department of Health (2000a) *The NHS Cancer Plan: A Plan for Investment A Plan for Reform*, HMSO, London.

Department of Health (2000b) *The Nursing Contribution to Cancer Care*, HMSO, London.

Department of Health (2004) *Cancer Services Collaborative: Improving Services in Cancer Care*, HMSO, London.

DiSaia P, Creasman W (Eds) (2002) *Clinical Gynaecologic Oncology*, Mosby, St Louis.

Elkas J, Farias-Eisner R (1998) Cancer of the uterine cervix. *Current Opinion in Obstetrics and Gynecology*, **10**(1), 41–5.

Epstein R M *et al.* (2004) Communicating evidence for participatory decision making. *Journal of the American Medical Association*, **291**(19), 2359–66.

Gallo A, Frigerio L (2003) Neoadjuvant chemotherapy and surgical considerations in ovarian cancer. *Current Opinion in Obstetrics and Gynecology*, **15**(1), 25–31.

Ghurani G, Penalver M (2001) An update on vulvar cancer. *American Journal of Obstetrics and Gynecology*, **185**(2), 294–99.

Grigsby P W (1998) Should women with carcinoma of the uterine cervix be treated surgically? *Gynaecological Endoscopy*, **7**(4), 177–81.

Irvin W P, Rice L W (2002) Advances in the management of endometrial adenocarcinoma. *Journal of Reproductive Medicine*, **47**(3), 173–90.

Jefferies H (2002) The psychosocial care of a patient with cervical cancer. *Cancer Nursing Practice*, **1**(5), 19–25.

McCorkle R *et al.* (2003) The silent killer: psychological issues in ovarian cancer. *Holistic Nursing Practice*, **17**(6), 300–8.

Maughan K, Clarke C (2001) The effect of a clinical nurse specialist in gynaecological oncology on quality of life and sexuality. *Journal of Clinical Nursing*, **10**(2), 221–9.

Morton R (1996) Breaking bad news to patients with cancer. *Cancer Nursing*, **11**(10), 669–71.

Munstedt K, Franke F E (2004) Role of primary surgery in advanced ovarian cancer. *World Journal of Surgical Oncology*, **2**, 32, www.wjso.com/content/2/1/32 (accessed 30 August 2005).

Munstedt K *et al.* (2003) Centralizing surgery for gynaecologic oncology – a strategy assuring better quality treatment? *Gynecologic Oncology*, **89**(1), 1–3.

National Audit Office (2005a) *The NHS Cancer Plan: A Progress Report*, HMSO, London.

National Audit Office (2005b) *Tackling Cancer: Improving the Patient Journey*, HMSO, London.

NHS Executive (1999a) *Improving Outcomes in Gynaecological Cancers. The Manual*, DoH, London.

NHS Executive (1999b) *Improving Outcomes in Gynaecological Cancers. The Research Evidence*, DoH, London.

NHS Modernisation Agency (2001) *Ovarian Cancer Service Improvement Guide*, Hayward Medical Communications, London.

Oncologychannel.com (2005) http://www.oncologychannel.com/endometrical cancer (accessed 8 April 2005).

Plante M (2000) Fertility preservatioin in the management of gynaecologic cancers. *Current Opinion in Oncology*, **12**(5), 497–507.

Plante M, Michel R (2001) New approaches in the surgical management of early stage cervical cancer. *Current Opinion in Obstetrics and Gynecology*, **13**(1), 41–6.

Plante M *et al.* (2004) Vaginal radical trachelectomy: an oncologically safe fertility-preserving surgery. An updated series of 72 cases and review of the literature. *Gynaecological Oncology*, **94**(3), 614–23.

Roy M, Plante M (1999) Pregnancy after radical vaginal trachelectomy: reply. *American Journal of Obstetrics and Gynecology*, **181**(1), 230.

Sellors J W, Sankaranarayanan R (Eds) (2004) *Colposcopy and Treatment of Cervical Intraepithelial Neoplasia: A Beginner's Manual*, International Agency for Research on Cancer Press, Lyon, France.

Shell J (1990) Sexuality for patients with gynaecologic cancer. *Clinical Issues for Perineal Women's Health Nurses*, **1**(4), 479–514.

Smith J *et al.* (1999) *Gynaecological Oncology: Fast Facts*, Health Press, Oxford.

Sohaib S A, Moskovic E C (2003) Imaging in vulval cancer. *Best Practice Research in Clinical Obstetrics and Gynaecology*, **17**(4), 543–56.

Steninga S K, Dunn J (1997) Women's experiences following treatment for gynecologic cancer. *Oncology Nursing Forum*, **24**(8), 1403–8.

Tongaonkar H B (2004) Changing practice of gynaecologic oncology based on current evidence. *Medical Journal Armed Forces of India*, **60**, 102–6.

United Kingdom Central Council for Nursing, Midwifery and Health Visiting (1992) *Code of Professional Conduct for the Nurse, Midwife and Health Visitor*, UKCC, London.

USEFUL ADDRESSES AND WEBSITES

CancerBACUP
3 Bath Place
Rivington Street
London EC2A 3JR
www.cancerbacup.org.uk

Cancer Counselling Trust
Caspari House
1 Noel Road
London N1 8HQ
www.cctrust.org.uk

Cancer Research UK
www.cancerhelp.org.uk

Carers UK
Ruth Pitter House
20–25 Glasshouse Yard
London EC1A 4JT
www.carersonline.org.uk

Gynae C is a support organisation for women with gynaecological cancers
1 Bolingbroke Road
Swindon
Wiltshire SN2 2LB
www.communigate.co.uk/wilts/gynaec

Macmillan Cancer Relief
89 Albert Embankment
London SE1 7UQ
www.macmillan.org.uk

Marie Curie Cancer Care
89 Albert Embankment
London SE1 7TP
www.mariecurie.org.uk

NHS screening programme
www.cancerscreening.nhs.uk

Ovacome is a UK-wide support group for all those concerned with ovarian cancer.
Elizabeth Garrett Anderson Hospital
Huntley Street
London WC2E 6DH
www.ovacome.org.uk

10 Risk Management in Gynaecology

JULIE GOLDING and SUE JOLLEY

Challenges	Service developments
• An increase in adverse incidents and medical errors in hospitals • Obstetrics and gynaecology – a speciality with greater risk of adverse effects and poor outcomes • High and costly litigation levels • Hospital standards monitored closely (CHI and CNST) • Staff often unwilling to report incidents • Patients need to make informed choices	• Hospital risk management strategies • Gynaecology risk management groups • Role of gynaecology risk management coordinator • Staff education – 'no blame' culture • More comprehensive consent policies • Improved patient information relating to recognised risks

INTRODUCTION

Although risk management is a relatively new concept in healthcare, the importance of minimising risk is not. Florence Nightingale, famous for stating that hospitals should not harm patients, promoted cleanliness in hospitals in order to improve patient outcomes. Unfortunately there will always be some risks for patients but media headlines such as 'NHS blunders help kill 72 000 patients a year' (Hope 2004) and '1m patients suffer harm in NHS hospitals' (Boseley 2002) make alarming reading.

It is hard to establish exact figures for risk, due to problems with data collection and a tendency to under-report adverse events (Barach & Small 2000; Gray 2003). Even 'official' figures for deaths from preventable incidents vary widely from an estimated 25 000 deaths (Department of Health 2001a) to 40 000 deaths (Aylin *et al.* 2004; Carvel 2004). There are between 850 000 and 900 000 adverse events in NHS hospitals each year (Aylin *et al.* 2004; Department of Health 2000; Hope 2004; Lipley 2000), but fortunately a large

Gynaecology: Changing Services for Changing Needs. Edited by Sue Jolley
© 2006 by John Wiley & Sons, Ltd

proportion refers to minor events. These figures are supported by the work of Neale *et al.* (2001), who reported that 10.8 % of patients admitted to two large hospitals in London experienced an adverse event and about half were preventable. It is generally accepted that one in ten patients admitted to an acute hospital in the UK experiences a safety incident of some sort (Vincent *et al.* 2001).

The scale of the problem clearly demonstrates that reducing risk in the NHS needs to be systematic and structured. Therefore risk management now plays an essential role in the organisation of NHS trusts, health authorities and general practices. Central to risk management is 'the reality that while risk is not avoidable, it can often be reduced' (Young 2001). Risk management involves not only identifying risks but also providing methods for improving risk situations and preventing further adverse incidents. It has therefore been described simply as 'a tool for improving the quality of care' (Edozien & Penney 2005).

Risk management originated in the USA in response to high levels of litigation for medical malpractice. Although the avoidance of litigation is still an important factor (Bowden 1996; Sehati & Inkster 1995; Walshe & Dineen 1998), there are other concerns such as health and safety issues and providing a quality service. Therefore both clinical and non-clinical incidents should be considered (Woodward 1998), as risk management includes 'all types of risk to everyone within the healthcare environment, including the staff' (Young 2001). It may range from slippery floors to poor clinical guidelines, from dirty toilets to inadequately trained staff and from illegible writing to errors in drug administration.

Recent government reports have shaped and directed risk management activity. An NHS Confederation Report, based on a survey of 169 trusts, revealed both strengths and weaknesses in the way risk management was organised (Walshe & Dineen 1998). In almost 75 % of trusts the appointment of risk managers, often nurses, and the setting up of strategies had prompted changes in clinical practice. This had resulted in a more open culture so that 'clinical staff felt it was safe to discuss clinical risk areas without fear of recrimination' (Lipley 1998). However, the survey also showed huge variations in how risks were assessed, which clinical incidents were reported and who was responsible for risk management. Before 2000 the National Health Service (NHS) had no standardised method for investigating incidents and it was estimated that there was an 'epidemic of underreported preventable injuries' (Barach & Small 2000a).

An Organisation with a Memory (Department of Health 2000) and *Building a Safer NHS for Patients* (Department of Health 2001b) emphasised the need to learn from clinical error and identified the opportunities that exist to reduce unintended harm to patients. Clearly, reckless or malicious behaviour should be punished, but the government has also tried to change attitudes within the NHS by accepting that some errors are bound to occur in a large and complex organisation and 'mistakes are not the preserve of careless, negligent or lazy practitioners' (Allen 2000). Therefore the emphasis should be on support rather than blame, so that staff can learn and improve on the standards of care (Department of Health 2001c). The reporting of public enquiries into high-profile cases, such as post-mortem tissue sampling in babies (Kennedy *et al.* 2000) and children's heart surgery at Bristol (Department of Health 2001a), added further impetus to the drive to improve the safety and quality of care.

These reports led directly to the infrastructures now in place to manage risk. The National Patient Safety Agency (NPSA) was created in 2001 to improve the safety of patients in NHS care. It does this by collecting and analysing information on patient safety incidents to ensure lessons are learned and shared widely, by considering other safety-related information available and by ensuring that, where risks are identified, work is undertaken to identify solutions and goals are set to ensure action and progress (Department of Health 2001b). The NPSA also issues guidance on patient safety and has developed training and educational material for staff. In 2004 the NPSA launched the National Reporting and Learning System (NRLS), which has started collecting incident reports around certain areas of patient safety. The NRLS will analyse these data and provide feedback and statistics to trusts so that lessons can be learned from any safety incidents. It will also use the data to inform future work and initiate preventative measures.

The Commission for Health Improvement (CHI) began operating in 2000 and has made trusts more aware of their responsibility for risk management (Patterson & Lilburne 2003). It was set up by the government to improve the quality of patient care in the NHS across England and Wales and, in 2004, was taken over by the Commission for Healthcare Audit and Inspection (CHAI). Clinical governance reviews have been carried out in hospital trusts every four years. If a hospital does not meet the standards required, it has to produce an action plan for approval by CHAI and the Department of Health. One of the seven areas of clinical governance reviewed is risk management. In general the reviews have demonstrated that there is 'a reactive, rather than proactive culture' within risk management (Patterson & Lilburne 2003), but they have also encouraged trusts to strengthen their risk management arrangements.

Another impetus for clinicians and managers to implement risk management more rigorously has been the establishment of the Clinical Negligence Scheme for Trusts (CNST). The scheme, run by the NHS Litigation Authority, handles all clinical negligence claims against its members. Negligence claims resulting from clinical errors are not only extremely costly, but rising each year (Department of Health 2000; O'Rourke 2003; Sehati & Inkster 1995), so it is not surprising that all NHS Trusts and Primary Care Trusts in England currently belong to the scheme. The costs of the scheme are met by membership contributions but discounts are available to trusts that achieve good risk management standards. 'The creation of CNST risk management standards represents the first tangible monetary incentive for trusts to develop a structured approach to clinical risk management' (Secker-Walker & Merrett 1997). The standards cover an organisation's approach to risks including factors such as consent procedures, management of health records, infection control and staff training. Standards are divided into three levels and trusts are usually assessed every two years. This has encouraged a much more organised approach to risk management and led to the development of risk management departments and risk management coordinating roles in most trusts and departments.

There are three stages to a successful risk management process. Firstly, there has to be a clear system in place for staff to report not only adverse incidents but also 'near miss' events (Milligan 2004). 'If trusts identify trends and "hot spots" from incidents, and even "near misses" on a routine basis, there will be much that can be done to highlight organisational and communication problems and prevent recurrence' (Secker-Walker & Merrett 1997). The second stage is to establish the underlying cause of any incidents. This can be done by 'root cause analysis'. This involves a thorough investigation to gain a better understanding of the whole situation surrounding the incident (National Patient Safety Agency 2004). Often the root cause is a failure in the management and organisational systems that support the delivery of care, such as poor staffing levels, inadequate training, poor communication or a lack of clear guidelines. In all of these situations the individual involved should not be blamed.

Finally, action is needed and any changes should be monitored to ensure that the system has improved. Simple data collection can help. Florence Nightingale collected data on wounded soldiers who eventually either died or recovered and demonstrated that mortality rates were reduced from 32 % to 2 % as a result of adequate care (Sehati & Inkster 1995). Audit is a more useful tool because it can be used not only to establish whether an incident is part of a general pattern, e.g. when staff are not following a particular guideline, but also to measure the effectiveness of any changes that are introduced.

RISKS IN GYNAECOLOGY

Hospital-wide strategies are imperative, but risk management also needs to be organised within each speciality (Edozien & Penney 2005). The Royal College of Obstetricians and Gynaecologists (RCOG) first issued guidance specifically on clinical risk management in 1999 (Royal College of Obstetricians and Gynaecologists 1999) and further suggested that a risk management coordinator should take day-to-day responsibility for the clinical incident reporting system and subsequent data collection at speciality level (Royal College of Obstetricians and Gynaecologists 2001). A nurse specialist has this role in the Gynaecology Department at Queen's Medical Centre (QMC), a large teaching hospital in Nottingham. It is very relevant for a nurse to hold this position because many adverse events are associated with ward care (Neale *et al.* 2001).

At QMC the risk management process is clear and folders explaining the process are available on wards throughout the trust. There is also guidance on the types of incidents that should be reported, because this has been identified as a potential problem (Walshe & Dineen 1998). When an individual recognises that an incident has occurred in gynaecology, an incident form is completed and forwarded to the risk management coordinator. He or she then assesses the severity of the incident and decides on the appropriate course of action. Only a minority of incidents needs to be analysed in detail, but it is often necessary to interview staff. This is to establish what happened, how it happened and why it happened (Vincent *et al.* 2000).

Sometimes the coordinator can deal directly with the incident so action is always taken locally first and if unresolved moves to the directorate level and then occasionally on to the corporate level. An example of a smaller incident, which can be dealt with by the gynaecology risk coordinator, would be an isolated and minor nursing drug error that has not resulted in any harm to the patient. A local investigation would determine all of the circumstances surrounding the incident. Influencing factors might be staffing levels and the experience of the nurse involved. Action could include more training or a programme of individual supervision.

Incidents of a more serious nature are taken to a monthly gynaecology risk management meeting. This involves other relevant staff including consultants, a registrar, the head nurse/matron and the trust litigation officer. At the departmental meetings incidents such as the failure of diagnostic testing or patients having to return to theatre after surgery would be discussed. The team has to consider several key areas including evidence of system failings, failure in communication, failure of equipment, environmental factors, failings in role design, failure to adhere to health and safety regulations and human error (Bird & Milligan 2003a). The directorate also identifies the top five risks each quarter. For each of these risks an action plan is developed to eliminate or minimise the risk.

A very small minority of incidents are classified as 'serious untoward incidents'. An example of this would be a patient who is given the wrong cross-matched blood, had the wrong operation or died as the result of an error. These cases require a fuller inquiry and would be passed on to the Trust Risk Management Committee. The NPSA would also be informed.

Some risks are common to all areas, such as general infection, drug errors and drug reactions, patient falls, post-operative haemorrhage, anaesthetic risks and equipment failure. However, there are some risks that are very specific to gynaecology (see Table 10.1). Some relate to problems with diagnosis, some are associated with gynaecological treatments or procedures, some are known risks of gynaecological surgical procedures and sometimes the relevant gynaecology guidelines and protocols have not been followed. Gynaecology is known as one of the specialities that carry greater risks of adverse effects and poor outcomes (O'Rourke 2003). Gynaecological complaints provide

Table 10.1. Table of risks in gynaecology

Risk situation	Example of potential incidents
Inadequate diagnosis	• Delayed or missed diagnosis of an ectopic pregnancy resulting in a collapsed patient at risk of dying • Failure to diagnose a gynaecological cancer resulting in terminal illness • Failure to diagnose a sexually transmitted infection, e.g. chlamydia, which if untreated could result in infertility • Incorrect diagnosis of miscarriage based on the scan result
Problem with treatment or procedure	• Incorrect insertion of IUCD, perforating the uterus • Conceiving with IUCD *in situ* • Hyperstimulation of the ovaries during treatment for infertility • Damage or pain resulting from the lithotomy position required for some gynaecological procedures • Cervical shock or extensive bleeding during colposcopic examination and biopsy
Surgical risks	• Failed sterilisation resulting in unwanted pregnancy • Damage to other structures during surgery, e.g. damage to ureters or bowel at hysterectomy • Failed termination of pregnancy • Injury to bowel at laparoscopy • Development of adhesions following repeated pelvic surgery • Wrong fallopian tube removed for an ectopic pregnancy • Perforation of uterus in dilatation and curettage operations or terminations of pregnancy
Not following correct guidelines	• Unconsented procedure, e.g. removing ovaries at the time of hysterectomy • Not obtaining consent for examination and disposal of products of conception • Failure to check blood group on miscarriage or termination, which could result in 'blue baby syndrome' • Not following care pathways for emergency gynaecology, e.g. ultrasound scan or pregnancy test, leading to delayed treatment or unnecessary admission

about 20% of medicolegal problems (Chamberlain & Bowen-Simpkins 2000).

The NPSA has developed a programme to improve patient safety in gynaecology, which includes a number of initiatives to address specific issues, as well as more generic work that will also have an impact (Johnson 2005). The main

project in gynaecology aims to identify factors that lead to operative complications during surgery so that potential solutions can be developed. This is
because 'the incidence of major complications of gynaecological surgery is
poorly documented. Historical figures are often used as a benchmark and
these complications are described as unavoidable and expected risks of
operation' (Johnson 2005). More general initiatives include projects on
improving team working, wristband compliance, ensuring patients receive the
right interventions and efforts to improve hand hygiene.

The nature of risk management work within gynaecology is best illustrated
by some examples described in the following case studies.

RISK MANAGEMENT CASE STUDIES

Case study 10.1

A patient attended the gynaecology pre-operative assessment clinic prior to a
routine hysterectomy. The nurse gave her information about her operation and
a pre-registration house officer ordered relevant investigations and prescribed
medication for the peri-operative period.

On the day of her operation she returned from theatre at around 3 pm in
the afternoon and her recovery was normal until around midnight, when she
started to complain of chest pain and pain on inspiration. On examining the
patient's drug chart, the night sister noticed that she had not been prescribed
any anticoagulation or antibiotics, which is the usual drug regime following a
hysterectomy. The pain became increasingly worse and by 3 am in the morning
the on-call doctor made a tentative diagnosis of pulmonary embolism, so a
therapeutic dose of anticoagulation was given. The next morning she under-
went investigations for a pulmonary embolism. The results were negative and
the treatment was subsequently changed to intravenous antibiotics for a
severe chest infection.

Although the junior doctor had stated that she understood the relevant
drug protocols at the commencement of her placement, an interview with her
demonstrated that this was not the case. She had recently done a general surgical rotation and was under the impression that the gynaecology unit used
the same regime. Nobody had noticed that she was not prescribing the correct
drugs. The patient had gone through several pre-operative checks where this
might have been noticed and corrected. The nurse preparing her for theatre
had actually noticed the missing drugs and had put a note and the required
drugs on the front of the notes, but these became separated. The nurse who
took her down to theatre was only in the second week of her post and assumed
that as no drugs were prescribed none were needed. The anaesthetist was not
used to anaesthetising gynaecology cases and was also unaware of the peri-
operative drug regime.

After obtaining statements from all staff involved, the case was discussed at the next risk management meeting. It was decided that the root cause of this problem was communication about the required protocol for peri-operative medication. At the time no formal induction period was programmed for these very junior medical staff, so they learned 'on the job'. Therefore it was recommended that there should be a proper induction programme. The sister in charge of the pre-admissions unit revised her guidelines for the doctors to include a comprehensive list of drug protocols. All nursing staff were made aware of the importance of checking that correct drugs are prescribed before taking a patient to theatre.

The gynaecology consultants decided to review the whole protocol and then produce pre-printed labels to go on the front of drug charts so that this would only require a signature from the doctor in pre-assessment.

The patient recovered well from her chest infection and was discharged five days after surgery.

Case study 10.2

A young girl attended the accident and emergency (A&E) department with abdominal pain and vaginal bleeding at approximately 10 weeks of pregnancy. She was seen by a doctor and allowed to go to the toilet to collect a mid-stream specimen of urine. While in the toilet, she began to bleed heavily and passed a 'clot' in the toilet pan. The nurse removed this clot and put her back on the trolley. The doctor came back in to see her and the nurse told the doctor that she had passed 'an intact sac' in the toilet and had miscarried. The patient became very distressed as she had only recently lost another pregnancy. She asked if she could take the fetus home to arrange a funeral and the nurse said that she would need to phone the next day to make the relevant arrangements. The doctor agreed and the patient was allowed home from A&E.

The next day the patient contacted the histopathology department. The liaison nurse in pathology had not been informed of this patient by A&E but attempted to sort out the request. She informed the patient that she would ring her back. On inspection of the sample sent to the laboratory it became clear that there was no pregnancy in the tissue, which was in fact a blood clot. She then contacted the nurse in the early pregnancy clinic to ask for advice. They decided to contact the patient and invite her in for an ultrasound scan.

On attending the early pregnancy clinic that same day it became clear that the patient was in fact still pregnant. The patient, who had gone through much pain and distress since thinking that she had lost another baby, was understandably both happy and furious at the same time. She wanted answers as to why this had happened to her and she had not had the correct investigations and assessments.

An investigation began. No attempt had been made by the A&E staff to contact a gynaecology doctor on call to assess the patient after her supposed miscarriage, and appropriate consent had not been obtained for the disposal of the pregnancy tissue. It became clear that the A&E staff were not aware of the correct protocol for the management of problems in early pregnancy. These problems should be referred to a doctor on call for gynaecology and an examination of the cervical os and an ultrasound scan are the minimum investigations that should have been carried out to ascertain the viability of the pregnancy.

After careful discussion at the next risk management meeting, the following strategy was agreed. The nurse specialist from the early pregnancy clinic would formulate a care pathway for the A&E department to use on the management of patients with problems in early pregnancy during both the first and second trimester. She had meetings with the clinical director and senior nursing staff from A&E to ratify these pathways and also gave talks to the junior medical and nursing staff to talk through the pathways, making sure everyone was clear about what was required.

The patient received a formal apology from the trust after meeting with staff from A&E to talk through her experience. At the time of writing she was still pregnant.

Case study 10.3

A young Asian girl was admitted as an emergency with generalised abdominal pain and a positive pregnancy test after 8 weeks' amenorrhoea. A urinary tract infection was suspected which was causing hyperemesis (excessive vomiting in pregnancy). She was prescribed IV fluids and antibiotics. The following day the vomiting had eased and she was allowed home with medication. The doctor who discharged her filled in her discharge documentation and specified that no follow-up was required. The nurse who discharged her gave her this documentation to forward to her GP and she left the ward.

Three months later she was readmitted to the ward at 20 weeks pregnant feeling generally unwell with vaginal bleeding and abdominal pain. She subsequently suffered a spontaneous miscarriage with intrauterine sepsis and was very unwell for the next few days. On reviewing the notes it became apparent that she had received no antenatal care since her last admission three months previously, no appointments had been arranged for the antenatal clinic and she had not been referred by her GP to be booked under an obstetrician for delivery of the baby. She had not queried this as she had no understanding of the antenatal system in this country.

After investigation and discussion at the next risk management meeting several points were highlighted.

- The doctor who discharged her after the admission at 8 weeks pregnant had not requested any follow-up appointment to be made.

- The nurse who discharged her was a relatively new staff nurse who did not realise that she had to check that pregnant patients should have antenatal care arranged before allowing them home.
- The GP with whom she claimed to have registered had never heard of her and she actually had never been registered with any GP since coming to this country.

It was decided that an extra member of staff would be appointed to the early pregnancy clinic whose specific responsibility would be to coordinate the follow-up care of all pregnant patients who come through the gynaecology ward. This would also include liaising with staff and ensuring that they are familiar with the antenatal process.

Each morning this nurse visits the ward for an update of any patients who have miscarried, who may need counselling or people who are still pregnant who need antenatal clinic appointments or follow-up scans. She can also ensure that every pregnant woman is registered with a GP. To date this system seems to be working well and no further incidents of this nature have been reported.

Case study 10.4

A young girl was admitted to the gynaecology ward with an ectopic pregnancy confirmed on an ultrasound scan. She was booked on the emergency theatre list.

The senior registrar on call for obstetrics and gynaecology was scheduled to perform the emergency surgery but several patients were in labour that particular night on the labour suite and he was also in overall charge of the unit. When the call came to go to theatre, he was busy on the labour suite but left the senior house officer in charge while he went to the emergency theatre.

The patient was already anaesthetised and ready when he arrived in theatre. He examined her on the operating table, felt the ectopic pregnancy on bimanual examination and proceeded to perform a laparoscopic *left* salpingectomy. On writing up his operation notes he noticed that the ultrasound scan report showed the ectopic pregnancy was on the *right* side. The patient was re-laparoscoped and the right fallopian tube removed. This meant that the patient would no longer be able to conceive naturally.

The surgeon was very distressed and saw the patient as soon as she was awake and able to take in the information. He explained that he had felt a definite swelling of the left tube that he mistook for the ectopic pregnancy. It even looked convincing with the laparoscope but it was in fact a condition known as hydrosalpinx, a blocked, dilated, fluid-filled tube usually caused by a previous pelvic infection. He had failed to review the patient's notes sufficiently before commencing surgery and admitted that the mistake was entirely his.

The root cause of this incident was the excessive hours worked by doctors. Since this occurrence there has been a major review of the hours that doctors on call work in hospitals (Department of Health 2005). They are now working 'shift patterns' and no longer do a night on call after being on duty all through the day as well. This doctor admits that his workload was extremely difficult on the night in question and his mind was on a difficult delivery that he would have to perform later in the labour suite. He has changed the speciality that he works in within obstetrics and gynaecology and no longer performs laparoscopic surgery.

The patient went on to sue the hospital for the enforced infertility and liability was admitted. As the hospital had a leading infertility unit within the building it offered to fund IVF treatment for the patient and negotiate compensation.

QUALITIES AND SKILLS NEEDED BY A GYNAECOLOGY RISK MANAGEMENT COORDINATOR

The knowledge requirements for this post are twofold and include a good understanding of both risk management and also gynaecological problems and procedures. Although investigations into adverse incidents should be undertaken by individuals who have had 'appropriate training' (Bird & Milligan 2003a), this is not clearly defined and the development of education programmes in risk management has been slow. Evidence from 1998 suggested that only 11 % of trust risk managers had any formal qualifications in risk management and a third had had no training at all (Walshe & Dineen 1998). Fortunately this is now changing as the roles in risk management are developing and there are several excellent courses including an MSc programme in risk management run by University College London.

Knowledge of gynaecology needs to be based on extensive experience in order to understand recognised and acceptable risks of a particular procedure or operation, what can actually go wrong as well as the implications of this. For example, the failure rate for sterilisation using Filshie clips is very low, approximately 2 per 1000 cases (Kovacs & Krins 2002), so a pregnancy would not be expected, could easily be missed and therefore not managed appropriately (O'Rourke 2003). Another example is the risk of adhesions because between 60 and 90 % of women suffer with post-operative adhesions following major gynaecological surgery or laparoscopic procedures (Trew 2004). In some cases this can lead to serious complications including dyspareunia, fertility problems and chronic pelvic pain. In 2003 a panel of gynaecologists decided that this has become a risk management issue and recommended methods to prevent and treat adhesions (Trew 2004). Patients should also be warned of the risk of adhesions.

Familiarity with gynaecological procedures is also helpful when investigating any adverse incidents, because this involves reading the medical notes and operation sheets. These invariably contain both specialised terminology and the inevitable abbreviations such as PID (pelvic inflammatory disease), BSO (bilateral salpingo-oophorectomy), TVT (transvaginal tape), IUD (intrauterine device) and STOP (suction termination of pregnancy).

Good communication skills are crucial, especially when investigating an incident, because 'although a considerable amount of information can be gleaned from written records, interviews with the people involved are the most important method of identifying contributory factors' (Vincent 2003). Therefore the risk management coordinator needs to communicate with both patients and staff at all levels. This can be difficult because anyone involved in an incident is usually anxious and upset (Vincent 2003).

Gynaecological problems can be particularly sensitive and emotive, especially when associated with body image, sexuality or fertility, so patients are often in a vulnerable state even when treatment goes according to plan. If things go wrong, or even if patients perceive that things have not gone well, they can become extremely frightened, distressed or angry. They therefore need a calm and professional reaction to their concerns with full information about what has happened and what is being done. Vincent (2003) argued that the patient's perspective has been neglected and that patients are not always as fully involved as they should be in any investigations.

There can be profound consequences for staff members who are involved in risk situations. If a mistake has been made, the individual can experience shame, guilt and depression. Even if a mistake has not been made, simply being involved in an incident and having to formally report what happened is enough to cause anxiety and stress. Therefore the risk management coordinator needs to be very skilled in gaining the necessary information as well as supporting the staff involved. He or she needs the respect of all staff, including medical staff. The way such investigations are handled is very important in fostering trust. It has been estimated that 50–96 % of adverse incidents remain unreported and lack of trust has been cited as one of the main reasons for this (Barach & Small 2000b). 'Only when staff are not frightened to report incidents will there be a true incident reporting system' (Woodward 1998).

Feedback after an incident is also an important part of the communication process (Woodward 1998) because 'the key to effective clinical risk management is learning from these events and disseminating the information across the NHS' (Bird & Milligan 2003a). As well as specific feedback to the staff involved in a particular incident, more general feedback for all staff about the pattern of incidents and root causes of relevant problems is also important. This helps to encourage openness and honesty about risk management and helps to promote a 'no-blame culture' (Bowden 1996). At QMC a page is devoted to risk management news in a monthly gynaecology magazine.

More formal written feedback is also required. This may include letters to patients and written reports to both the departmental risk management meeting and the trust. Sometimes further written material is required in order to implement necessary changes, and this may include new guidelines for staff based on the best available evidence. Comprehensive patient information leaflets are needed so that patients receive information about the risks and benefits of their clinical treatment and can make informed choices including consent (Woodward 1998). The risk management coordinator does not necessarily have to write these but should be involved in explaining what is required and reviewing anything that is produced.

A risk management coordinator needs to develop good detective skills. Information can be gleaned from a variety of sources including medical records, drug cards, nursing documentation and interviews. It is important to gather as much information as possible to gain a full picture, especially if some of the information is inconsistent. There are many potential problems including illegible notes, missing documentation, poor memory of the sequence of events and, unfortunately, a few staff who are liberal with the truth.

Huge amounts of data about incidents and risk management need to be collected and stored, so good organisation is necessary. Records of adverse incidents and near misses help in identifying trends and planning preventative measures. An example of this may be drug errors. Nurses spend about 40 % of their time administering medications, so it is important to learn from any commonly recurring errors (Bird & Milligan 2003b; Sehati & Inkster 1995). Finally, a risk management coordinator needs to be able to work autonomously, make decisions and implement any changes that are needed.

CONCLUSION

It is evident that risk management is developing rapidly. The rigorous inspections required by the Department of Health are becoming more comprehensive and frequent, so firm policies and processes are needed to manage the inevitable risks that occur.

Most adverse incidents are not caused by individual clinical error, but as a result of systems failure or a combination of several small mistakes occurring at the same time (Bowden 1996). The challenge is to find a way forward that supports people involved but also ensures that lessons are learned (Vincent 2003). Sometimes health professionals need to take some risks in developing more effective methods of treatment and care for patients. However, these should only be taken when the possible consequences and likely outcome of the treatment are fully understood and with the knowledge and consent of the patients involved.

Risk management in gynaecology is always varied and challenging. Sometimes it is frustrating when errors might have been avoided, and sometimes incidents are unusual and completely unexpected. It is very satisfying to implement changes that reduce risks and ultimately improve the healthcare that women receive.

REFERENCES

Allen D (2000) Counting the cost. *Nursing Standard*, **15**(2), 20–1.

Aylin P *et al.* (2004) Dr Foster's case notes – how often are adverse events reported in English hospital statistics? *British Medical Journal*, **329**(7462), 369.

Barach P, Small S (2000a) How the NHS can improve safety and learning. *British Medical Journal*, **320**(7251), 1683–4.

Barach P, Small S (2000b) Reporting and preventing medical mishaps: lessons from non-medical near miss reporting systems. *British Medical Journal*, **320**(7237), 759–63.

Bird D, Milligan F (2003a) Adverse health-care events: Part 2. Incident reporting systems. *Professional Nurse*, **18**(10), 572–5.

Bird D, Milligan F (2003b) Adverse health-care events: Part 3. Learning the lessons. *Professional Nurse*, **18**(11), 621–5.

Boseley S (2002) 1m patients suffer harm in NHS hospitals. *Guardian*, 19 June.

Bowden D (1996) Calculate the risk. *Nursing Management*, **3**(4), 10–11.

Carvel J (2004) Healthcare errors kill 40 000 a year, says charity. *Guardian*, 29 September.

Chamberlain G, Bowen-Simpkins P (2000) *A Practice of Obstetrics and Gynaecology*, 3rd edition, Churchill Livingstone, London.

Department of Health (2000) *An Organisation with a Memory. Report of an Expert Group on Learning from Adverse Events in the NHS Chaired by the Chief Medical Officer*, HMSO, London.

Department of Health (2001a) *Learning from Bristol. The Report of the Public Inquiry into Children's Heart Surgery at the Bristol Royal Infirmary*, HMSO, London.

Department of Health (2001b) *Building a Safer NHS for Patients – Implementing an Organisation with a Memory*, HMSO, London.

Department of Health (2001c) *A Commitment to Quality, A Quest for Excellence*, HMSO, London.

Department of Health (2005) *European Working Time Directive FAQ*, http://www.dh.gov.uk/PolicyAndGuidance/HumanResourcesAndTraining (accessed April 2005).

Edozien L C, Penney G C (2005) *Risk Management for Maternity and Gynaecology. Clinical Governance Advice No. 3.* Royal College of Obstetricians and Gynaecologists, London.

Gray A (2003) *Adverse Events and the National Health Service: An Economic Perspective. A Report to the National Patient Safety Agency.* Health Economics Research Centre, Department of Public Health, University of Oxford, Oxford.

Hope J (2004) NHS blunders help kill 72 000 patients a year. *Daily Mail*, 13 August.

Johnson S (2005) Improving patient safety for women in gynaecology – the role of the NPSA. *RCN Gynaecology Bulletin*, Spring Issue, 4.

Kennedy I *et al.* (2000) *The Inquiry into the Management of Care of Children Receiving Complex Heart Surgery at the Bristol Royal Infirmary. Interim Report*, HMSO, London.

Kovacs G T, Krins A J (2002) Female sterilisations with Filshie clips: what is the risk failure? A retrospective survey of 30 000 applications. *Journal of Family Planning and Reproductive Health Care*, **28**(1), 34–5.

Lipley N (1998) Risky business. *Nursing Standard*, **12**(42), 14.

Lipley N (2000) NHSE bid to cut costs of adverse clinical incidents. *Nursing Standard*, **15**(12), 8.

Milligan F, Dennis S (2004) Improving patient safety and incident reporting. *Nursing Standard*, **19**(7), 33–6.

National Patient Safety Agency (2004) *Documenting Progress – Annual Report 2003–2004*, NPSA, London.

Neale G *et al.* (2001) Exploring the causes of adverse events in NHS hospital practice. *Journal of the Royal Society of Medicine*, **94**(7), 322–30.

O'Rourke A (2003) *Clinical Risk Management*, The Wisdom Centre, Sheffield University, Sheffield.

Patterson L J, Lilburne C (2003) What is the Commission for Health Improvement? *Postgraduate Medical Journal*, **79**(932), 303–5.

Royal College of Obstetricians and Gynaecologists (1999) *Clinical Governance*, RCOG Press, London.

Royal College of Obstetricians and Gynaecologists (2001) *Clinical Risk Management for Obstetricians and Gynaecologists. Clinical Governance Advice No 2*, RCOG Press, London.

Secker-Walker J, Merrett H (1997) Risk in clinical care. *Nursing Management*, **3**(9), 22–3.

Sehati S, Inkster H (1995) Drug error detectives. *Nursing Management*, **2**(5), 22–3.

Trew G (2004) Consensus in adhesion reduction management. *The Obstetrician and Gynaecologist (Supplement)*, **6**(2), 1–16.

Vincent C (2003) Patient safety: understanding and responding to adverse events. *New England Journal of Medicine*, **348**(11), 1051–6.

Vincent C *et al.* (2000) How to investigate and analyse clinical incidents: Clinical Risk Unit and Association of Litigation and Risk Management Protocol. *British Medical Journal*, **320**, 777–81.

Vincent C *et al.* (2001) Adverse events in British hospitals; preliminary retrospective record review. *British Medical Journal*, **322**(7311), 517–19.

Walshe K, Dineen M (1998) *Clinical Risk Management: Making a Difference?*, National Health Service Confederation, Birmingham.

Woodward S (1998) The rocking horse risk. *Nursing Management*, **5**(1), 10–13.

Young AE (2001) Risk management. *British Journal of Surgery*, **88**(8), 1027–8.

USEFUL WEBSITE

www.npsa.nhs.uk.

Glossary

Adhesiolysis Removal of scar tissue called adhesions, which are caused by infection or previous surgery, in patients with chronic pelvic pain or infertility.

Adjuvant treatment Used in addition to main treatment, usually radiotherapy or chemotherapy, given after surgery.

Amenorrhoea Absence of menstruation.

Amnion The innermost membrane enveloping the fetus in the uterus.

Anencephaly Having no brain.

Anovulation The absence of ovulation.

Anticholinergic Anticholinergic medications inhibit the transmission of parasympathetic nerve impulses by blocking the physiological action of acetylcholine and therefore reduce spasms of smooth muscle in the bladder.

Anti D Women whose blood group is Rhesus-negative sometimes form Rhesus antibodies when carrying a Rhesus-positive baby. This can cause anaemia and sometimes death for a Rhesus-positive baby in a subsequent pregnancy. Routine anti-D prophylaxis is offered to all non-sensitised pregnant women who are Rhesus-negative.

Antimuscarinic Antimuscarinic agents reduce spasms of smooth muscle in the bladder by operating on the muscarinic acetylcholine receptors.

Antiprogestogen Progestogen refers to any steroid hormone similar to the female sex hormone progesterone. Antiprogestogen blocks the action of progestogens.

Arcus tendineus The fibrous tissue that separates the bladder and vagina is attached on each side to tough connective tissue called the arcus tendineus.

Ascitic fluid An accumulation of fluid in the abdominal (peritoneal) cavity.

Atrophic vaginitis Inflammation of the vagina caused by degenerative changes in the mucous lining and insufficient oestrogen secretion.

Atypia Slight changes in cells of the cervix.

Auscultation   Using a stethoscope to listen to heart and breath sounds.

Bacterial vaginosis   A condition where the normal balance of bacteria in the vagina is disrupted and replaced by an overgrowth of certain bacteria. It is sometimes accompanied by discharge, odour, pain, itching or burning.

Bartholin's abscess   The Bartholin's glands lie at the entrance to the vagina and secrete mucus. The duct to a gland can become blocked causing a cyst. This cyst may become infected forming an abscess.

Bicornate uterus   A uterus with two sections, or 'horns'. There is a dip in the top of the body of the uterus. The problem often remains undetected until pregnancy, when it can cause abortion, pre-term labour or breech presentation.

Bilateral salpingo-oophorectomy (BSO)   Removal of both uterine (fallopian) tubes and ovaries.

Cellulitis   Inflammation of connective tissue.

Cervical ectropian   Occurs when the inside of the cervical cells come out on to the surface of the cervix. This looks like a red roughened area.

Cervical incompetence   A condition where the cervix is not strong enough to remain closed during pregnancy, leading to miscarriage.

Cervical os   The opening of the cervix into the vagina.

Cervical shock   This is a vagal reaction caused when the cervix is trying to stretch and the vagus nerve is stimulated. This can happen when there is a large tissue mass or clot behind the cervix, e.g. during a miscarriage. Symptoms include intense pain, vomiting and hypotension resulting in fainting.

Cervicitis   Inflammation of the cervix or neck of the uterus.

Chlamydia   A very common sexually transmitted infection caused by the *Chlamydia trachomatis* bacterium.

Choriocarcinoma   A rare cancer in women of childbearing age in which cancer cells grow in the tissues that are formed in the uterus after conception.

Chorion   The outer membrane enveloping the fetus. The placenta is formed from the chorion.

Climacteric   The transition period of time before menopause.

Colposuspension   The bladder neck and anterior vaginal wall are lifted in this surgical technique and sutured into position to correct stress incontinence.

Corpus luteum   A yellow body left on the surface of the ovary and formed from the remains of the follicle after an ovum is released. If pregnancy occurs, it supports the developing embryo until the placenta takes over.

Cystectomy Surgical removal of cyst.

Cystoscopy Visual examination of the lining of the bladder.

Cytology The microscopic study of cells.

Dermoid cyst A non-malignant tumour containing a cyst lined by epidermal cells with a cavity containing other material.

Detrusor muscle A muscle that pushes down or expels.

Dilatation and curettage (D & C) The cervix is dilated and the endometrium is scraped or aspirated. This may be therapeutic or diagnostic.

Dyskariosis Abnormal cells detected by cytology.

Dysmenorrhoea Pain during menstruation.

Dyspareunia Pain during sexual intercourse.

Ectopic pregnancy Implantation of a fertilised ovum anywhere outside the uterus, usually in the uterine (fallopian) tube.

Electromyogram A test to determine nerve function by recording the electrical activity of a muscle.

Endometriosis Location of endometrial tissue outside the uterine cavity.

Endometrium Lining of the uterus.

Episiotomy An incision made during childbirth to the perineum, the muscle between the vagina and rectum, to widen the vaginal opening for delivery.

Epithelium The surface layer of cells, either of the skin or of the lining tissues.

Fascia A sheath of connective tissue enclosing the muscles or other organs.

Fetal pole The fetal pole is a thickening on the margin of the yolk sac of a fetus during pregnancy.

Fibroid or myoma Benign tumour of the uterus composed of myometrium and fibrous tissue.

Follicle stimulating hormone (FSH) A hormone produced by the anterior pituitary gland. It stimulates the maturation of ovarian follicles.

Galactosaemia An inborn error of metabolism in which there is inability to convert galactose to glucose.

Gonadotrophin Any hormone that stimulates either the ovaries or the testes.

Haematocolpos An accumulation of blood in the vagina, often associated with an imperforate hymen.

Haematoma   A swelling containing clotted blood.

Histopathology   This is the science concerned with the study of microscopic changes in diseased tissues by examination of tissue samples.

Hydrosalpinx   Distension of the uterine tubes by fluid.

Hyperandrogenism   An excessive production of male hormones.

Hypercalcaemia   An excess of calcium in the blood.

Hyperemesis   Persistent nausea and vomiting in early pregnancy.

Hyperplasia   Enlargement of an organ, or tissue within it, due to an increase in the number of cells.

Hypothyroidism   An insufficiency of thyroid secretion.

Hysterectomy   Surgical removal of the uterus. This may be done via the abdomen or the vagina.

Hysteroscopy   Visual examination of the uterine cavity, usually to investigate pelvic pain, infertility or abdominal uterine bleeding.

Induced abortion   A deliberate termination of pregnancy.

Intrauterine contraceptive device (IUCD)   A contraceptive device introduced into the uterine cavity.

In vitro **fertilisation (IVF)**   Patient's eggs and her partner's sperm are collected and mixed together in a laboratory to achieve fertilisation outside the body. The embryos produced may then be transferred into the female patient.

Laparoscopy   Endoscopic examination of the female pelvic organs via the abdominal wall.

Laparotomy   Incision of the abdominal wall.

Levator ani   The Levator ani is a broad, thin muscle situated on the side of the pelvis. It forms the greater part of the floor of the pelvic cavity.

Lithotomy position   A position where the patient lies on her back with knees bent and thighs apart for a vaginal examination.

Luteinising hormone (LH)   LH is produced by the anterior pituitary gland and controls the activity of the gonads. It induces the ovulation of mature follicles on the ovary and also supports the continued development and function of the corpus luteum when a pregnancy occurs.

Lymphoedema   Condition where the intercellular spaces contain an abnormal amount of lymph due to obstruction of the lymph drainage.

Menorrhagia   Excessive flow of blood during menstruation.

Metaplasia   Transformation of cells from a normal to an abnormal state.

Metastases   Spread of cancer away from the primary site.

Micturition   Urination.

Mirena coil   A small T-shaped intrauterine device which after insertion releases the hormone levonorgestrel into the uterus. Therefore it not only acts as a contraceptive but can also reduce heavy periods.

Miscarriage   The expulsion of the fetus before the 28th week of pregnancy.

Multifidus   The multifidus is a deep lumbar spine muscle that stabilises the lumbar spine.

Myomectomy   Surgical removal of a fibroid (myoma) from the uterus.

Neo-adjuvant treatment   Treatment given before the main treatment, usually chemotherapy or radiotherapy given before surgery.

Nuchal translucency   A technique for using ultrasound to measure fluid behind the neck of the fetus, usually at 10 to 14 weeks of pregnancy, which can contribute to a diagnosis of Down's syndrome.

Oestradiol   The major type of oestrogen hormone produced by the body.

Omentectomy   Surgery to remove part or all of the omentum.

Oophorectomy   Surgical excision of the ovary.

Osteopenia   Low bone density. If not treated, it may result in osteoporosis.

Ovarian follicle   Fluid-filled sac, located just beneath the ovary's surface, in which an egg grows and develops.

Ovarian hyperstimulation syndrome   An excessive stimulation of the ovaries, caused by fertility drugs. Symptoms include bloating, weight gain, pain, nausea, vomiting, diarrhoea and breathlessness.

Pelvic floor repair   Stitching the bladder and urethra, or the rectum, back into their normal positions and repairing the vagina.

Pelvic girdle   The bony and muscular structure inside a woman's body that supports her internal sex and reproductive organs.

Pelvic inflammatory disease (PID)   Any ascending pelvic infection beyond the cervix. This may occur following childbirth, termination of pregnancy, surgical procedures or contact with sexually transmitted infections.

Polycystic ovarian syndrome (PCOS)   A genetically linked hormonal imbalance that prevents ovulation. PCOS also may cause overproduction of oestrogen, abnormal thickening of the uterine lining, very heavy and/or irregular periods, as well as acne and facial hair. The latter are caused by an overproduction of male hormones, including testosterone.

Polycystic ovaries (PCO)   A seemingly hormonal disorder that frequently causes infertility. One of the most common symptoms is small cysts formed on the ovaries. It is a very common condition and can be part of the polycystic ovary syndrome.

Polyp   Common benign growths occurring mainly in the endometrium and cervix.

Postcoital   Following sexual intercourse.

Primipara   A woman who has given birth to only one child.

Procidentia   Complete prolapse of the uterus so that it comes down through the vagina.

Progesterone   A female steroid hormone secreted by the ovary. It is produced by the placenta in large quantities during pregnancy.

Prolactin   A hormone produced by the pituitary gland that stimulates breast development and milk production.

Prostaglandin   The prostaglandins are a group of fatty acid compounds that have many effects throughout the body, including activity in inflammation, smooth muscle contraction, regulating body temperature, and effects on certain hormones.

Pruritus   Irritation of the skin, especially involving the vulva or anus.

Pseudo sac   Not a genuine sac.

Pudendal nerve   The main nerve supplying the pelvic floor, bladder and urethra. Damage to this nerve can cause incontinence.

Puerperal sepsis   An infection of the female genital tract following childbirth, abortion or miscarriage.

Pulmonary embolism   Blocking of the pulmonary artery or one of its branches by a detached clot, usually due to a thrombosis in the femoral or iliac veins.

Radical hysterectomy   Surgical removal of uterus, uterine tubes, cervix, upper vagina and pelvic lymph glands, used to treat cancer of the cervix.

Radical vulvectomy   A surgical procedure to remove the entire vulva, which usually includes the lymph nodes in the groin.

Salpingectomy   The surgical excision of a uterine (fallopian) tube.

Salpingostomy   A surgical procedure where the wall of the fallopian tube is opened. This may be done to remove an ectopic pregnancy or to unblock the tube.

Seminal duct The tube which carries semen from the testis.

Sepsis Infection of the body by bacteria that create pus.

Speculum Instrument used to open the vagina and allow examination of the vaginal vault and cervix.

Spermatogenesis The production of sperm.

Sphincter The sphincter is a ring of muscle that opens and closes.

Sterilisation Making someone incapable of reproduction.

Tension-free vaginal tape (TVT) A mesh-like tape which can be placed under the urethra like a sling to keep it in the normal position. It is inserted during a minor surgical procedure for the relief of stress incontinence.

Thromboembolism The formation of a clot (thrombus) that breaks loose and is carried by the bloodstream to plug another vessel.

Transversus abdominus The transversus abdominus is the deepest of the abdominal muscles and is very important in the development of intra-abdominal pressure.

Trimester This refers to each three-month period during the nine months of pregnancy.

Vaginal cuff The top of the vagina.

Vaginal mucosa Mucous membrane in the vagina.

Vaginal pessary A vaginal pessary is a device inserted into the vagina to help support the vaginal walls and pelvic organs when there are areas of prolapse. There are a variety of pessaries available, made of rubber, plastic or silicone-based material.

Vaginisimus Vaginisimus is when the muscles of the entrance to the vagina spasm, making sexual intercourse difficult or impossible.

Vulvectomy Surgical removal of part or all of the vulva.

Vulvitis Inflammation of the vulva.

Zygote A single fertilised cell formed from a male and female gamete.

Index

abortion, induced, *see* termination of
  pregnancy
abortion law, 32–3
aceto-whitening, 55
adhesions, 219
adhesiolysis, 15
admissions, emergency gynaecology,
  4–9
  symptoms for, 5–7
Alzheimer's disease, 169
amenorrhoea, 100, 156, 217
anencephaly, 74
Anti D immunoglobulin, 68–9
antibodies, antiphospholipid, 67
  primary antiphospholipid syndrome
    (PAPS), 67
anxiety, patient, 13, 47, 51, 58, 67, 88
ascites, 188
assessment, 1, 3
  gynaecology, 4–18
  incontinence, 143, 144 (Table 7.3)
  nurse-led assessment, 1, 9, 14–18
  preoperative, 12–18
    advantages, 12–13, 18
    history of, 12
    process, 16–17
    purpose of, 13
    role of physiotherapist in, 150
  training needs, 3–4
audit, 11–12, 57, 172, 177, 212
auscultation, 5 (Table1.1), 15

Bartholins abscess, 7, 8 (Table 1.3)
bladder pressure studies, *see*
  urodynamics

bleeding,
  during medical termination of
    pregnancy, 38–9
  dysfunctional uterine, 6 (Table 1.2)
  in pregnancy, 6, 64, 86, 216, 217
  intermenstrual, 6, 50, (Table 3.1), 191,
    195
  post coital, 6, 49, 195
  post menopausal, 6, 191
  vaginal, 5, 6 (Table1.2)
bone densitometry, *see* x-ray
  absorbtiometry (DXA)
bone mineral density, *see* osteoporosis

Ca, 125, 188
Calman–Hine Report, 185
cancer, 185
  centres, 185, 198
  cervical, 47, 50, 193–196, 194 (Figure 9.3)
  endometrial, 191–3, 192 (Figure 9.2)
  gynaecological, 16, 186
  ovarian, 188–191, 189 (Figure 9.1)
  units, 185, 198
  vulval, 196–8, 197 (Figure 9.4)
cardiovascular disease, 169
care pathways, 37, 139, 145 149, 217
cervix,
  cervical cancer, *see* cancer
  cervical intraepithelial neoplasia
    (CIN), 54–7, 194
  cervical screening programme, 47–51,
    193–4
  cervicitis, 6 (Table 1.2)
  competence of, 53, 67
  stenosis of, 56

Gynaecology: Changing Services for Changing Needs. Edited by Sue Jolley
© 2006 by John Wiley & Sons, Ltd